African American
Females

COURAGEOUS CONVERSATIONS SERIES

African American Females

ADDRESSING CHALLENGES AND NURTURING THE FUTURE

Edited by
EBONI M. ZAMANI-GALLAHER
and VERNON C. POLITE

MICHIGAN STATE UNIVERSITY PRESS • EAST LANSING

♾ The paper used in this publication meets the minimum requirements
of ANSI/NISO Z39.48-1992 (R 1997) (Permanence of Paper).

Michigan State University Press
East Lansing, Michigan 48823-5245

Printed and bound in the United States of America.

19 18 17 16 15 14 13   1 2 3 4 5 6 7 8 9 10

LIBRARY OF CONGRESS CATALOGING-IN-PUBLICATION DATA
African American females : addressing challenges and nurturing the future /
edited by Eboni M. Zamani-Gallaher and Vernon C. Polite.
pages cm — (Courageous conversations series)
Includes bibliographical references.
ISBN 978-1-61186-097-9 (paper : alkaline paper) — ISBN 978-1-60917-389-0
(ebook) 1. African American women—Social conditions. 2. African American
women—Education. 3. African American women—Employment. 4. African
American women—Health and hygiene. I. Zamani-Gallaher, Eboni M., 1971–
II. Polite, Vernon C.
E185.86.A339 2013
305.48'896073—dc23
2012048403

Book design by Charlie Sharp, Sharp Des!gns, Lansing, Michigan
Cover design by David Drummond, Salamander Design, www.salamanderhill.com
Cover photo ©Flashon Studio/Shutterstock.com. All rights reserved.

Michigan State University Press is a member of the Green Press Initiative and is
committed to developing and encouraging ecologically responsible publishing
practices. For more information about the Green Press Initiative and the use
of recycled paper in book publishing, please visit *www.greenpressinitiative.org.*

Visit Michigan State University Press at *www.msupress.org*

For Deena

BLACK GIRL PAIN

My mama said life would be so hard
Growin' up days as a black girl scarred,
In so many ways though we've come so far
They just know the name they don't know the pain.
So please hold your heads up high
Don't be ashamed of yourself know I
Will carry it forth 'til the day I die
They just know the name they don't know the pain
    black girl.

—Talib Kweli

Contents

Foreword

Carol Camp Yeakey

A*frican American Females: Addressing Challenges and Nurturing the Future* is a volume long overdue. In societies all across the globe, men and women lead very different lives. Gender, defined as the biological traits that are linked to being male or female, is also linked to gender stratification, which is the unequal distribution of wealth, power, and privilege between men and women. Race intersects with both gender and class to create multiple disadvantages. It is at this intersect of race, gender, and class that this text enters. Far too often, the challenges confronting women of color, in general, and African American women, in particular, have been subsumed under strategies and programs, which have largely accommodated and benefited White women. While White women are not treated equally in our society with white men, what they do enjoy is institutional access to information, knowledge, and informal contact with power brokers, those tangible and intangible factors that facilitate social mobility in the larger society. African American women, because of their distinctive identities, coupled with crippling historical stereotypes, have no such access. As far too many recent events in U.S. society remind us, race still matters.

Because of the foregoing, women of color, and African American women in particular, are often called "twofers," a term used for those burdened with overcoming the present and past vestiges of both race and gender discrimination and the resultant societal inequalities. The synergistic combination of race, class, and gender is omnipresent in almost every societal institution, including the workplace, health and medical care, the family, marital and intimate relationships, schools, mass media, politics, religion, the military, sports, and the criminal justice system. The "'glass ceiling," which refers to the overt and covert discrimination that very effectively prevents the movement of women into the highest positions in the workplace, is still alive. Recent government data (U.S. Department of Commerce 2011) are illuminating in highlighting the interlocutory relationship between race, gender, and class. Consider the following:

- Despite the Lilly Ledbetter Fair Pay Act (2009), pay equity is far from a reality. Women are more likely to live in poverty than men, and the economic inequities for women of color are even greater.
- In 2009, the median income for non-Latino White women working full time was $39,010. However, African American women earned $31,933, or 82 percent as much, and Latino women earned $27,268, or 70 percent as much.
- Within racial and ethnic categories, in 2009, African American women earned 85 percent as much as African American men, and Latino women earned 86 percent as much as Latino men.
- Similarly, in 2009, African American women earned 62 percent as much as non-Latino White men and Latino women earned 53 percent as much as White men.

This digest provides a lens by which to view the multifaceted ways in which African American females confront, with pride, the pain and yet the promise of the challenges that serve as obstructions and barriers in their quest for social mobility and advance. Often as the sole head of households and the primary breadwinners in their families, their struggle(s) for equal access and equal opportunity have profound consequence on the future social mobility of generations of African American youth. One would think that in an advanced society such as ours, the fight against structural and institutional inequalities would be a battle long won. However, our current political climate vividly portrays how the status of women and their rights, and those of lower-status persons, are the subject of intense contemporary debate. In the twenty-first century, the fact that women and persons of color are still fighting historic wars for equality of opportunity as well as equality of results should be alarming to all who favor the full and equitable development of all humankind.

African American Females: Addressing Challenges and Nurturing the Future seeks to analyze, to understand, yet never excuse, from multiple disciplinary perspectives, the often-daunting challenges affecting African American females. The volume as constructed has tremendous applicability for other women of color in the United States and lower-status women across the globe. The issues that the chapters analyze and discuss are multifaceted and embedded within other social, political, and economic variables, which the authors carefully and skillfully craft. The editors of the book and the authors deserve tremendous praise for compiling such an intellectually exciting work that will have broad appeal for multiple audiences who care about the struggle to achieve real equality between the sexes. This book breaks the structured silence of very painful slights, debilitating stereotypes, and degrading experiences, as a vehicle to understand and confront the intransigence of a developed society as it confronts the interrelated issues of sexism, racism, and classism for African American women. Do read this gripping, yet illuminating, volume and become better informed. Then, I challenge you to act, to assist in eradicating the social, political, and economic barriers, which subvert the advancement of African American women and all lower-status women. All of society and her children will be the beneficiaries.

REFERENCE

U.S. Department of Commerce, Economics and Statistics Administration (2011). *Women in America: Indicators of social and economic well-being.* Washington, DC: U.S. Government Printing Office, Executive Office of the President; Office of Management and Budget.

Preface

$\bigvee$

On September 26, 2008, Eastern Michigan University's College of Education, the McGregor Fund, and the Office of Urban Education and Educational Equity sponsored a conference focused on African American females. The meeting was the second in the Courageous Conversations series, a follow-up to a 2006 summit that focused on African American males and that framed the development of the monograph *The State of the African American Male.* This educational conference provided an opportunity for K–12, postsecondary, healthcare, and community leaders to exchange ideas regarding programs, policies, and practices that shape the lives of African American females. One focus of the meeting was an effort to assemble key commentaries on social issues affecting Black girls and women. More than 500 participants joined in this one-day dialogue that offered insight, recommendations, and best practices for facilitating self-actualization among African American females across generations. *African American Females: Addressing Challenges and Nurturing the Future* is the product of this conference.

The following chapters illustrate the contributions of leading scholars with expertise in the areas of K–12 education, higher education, health, family, and consumer science. Each of the contributors problematizes and situates the local, state, and national context as well as recommendations for policy and practice affecting African American females.

This work would not be possible without the support of the many organizations and individuals who sponsored or otherwise supported the summit that served as initial nourishment for this undertaking. Sincere thanks are extended to C. David Campbell, president of the McGregor Fund; former governor Jennifer M. Granholm; Ypsilanti mayor Paul Schreiber; Sue Martin, president of Eastern Michigan University; State of Michigan Superintendent of Public Instruction Michael P. Flanagan; and John W. Porter, former president of Eastern Michigan University.

Additional appreciation is offered to Sharon P. Robinson, president and CEO of the American Association of Colleges for Teacher Education; Deborah Harmon; Cheryl Price; Michael Bretting; Casey Wooster; Paul Vuocolo; Erica Ginyard; Donald Loppnow; Freeman Hendrix; Caroline Sanders; Bill Miller; Kelly Quilter; and staff and students at Inkster High School and Mumford High School. Extra special gratitude is given to Sonia Sanchez for her furtherance and promotion of our efforts. Special acknowledgements are tendered to Martha Baiyee, Nancy Copeland, Marion Dokes-Brown, Doris Fields, Lynette Findley, Heather Neff, Toni Stokes Jones, M. Michelle Rosemond, Sharon Abraham, Carole Benedict, Denise Lilly, Shawn Quilter, Regina George, Beth Johnson, Virginia Harder, Jaclynn Tracy, Charnessa K. Paige, Donna K. Woodiel, and Patricia Williams-Boyd.

This text is a labor of love for several reasons. Our quest was to provide a depiction of African American females that had breadth and depth, illustrating the intersecting impact of race and gender as well as the myriad of competing influences on the lives of Black females. Early in the project, my mentor, dean, friend, and collaborator Vernon C. Polite fell ill and within months passed away. The progression of this venture was bittersweet. In him, I witnessed that hope has a face and that the difficulties of life provide opportunities for our spirits to be lifted, our faith to be renewed, and for wisdom to take root.

Vernon C. Polite was a wise man who lifted others as he climbed and a case in point for resiliency—a manifestation of African American determinism over centuries. Similar to our elders and ancestors, generations of African American women are the personification of resilience as the carriers of culture. It is my hope that the intersectionality of identities and the humanity and buoyancy of African American females comes to life for readers of this volume.

PART 1

K–12 Educational Experiences of African American Females

Trends in Cultural, Social, and Symbolic Capital Post–No Child Left Behind

IMPLICATIONS FOR AFRICAN AMERICAN FEMALE COGNITIVE AND NONCOGNITIVE ACHIEVEMENT IN MICHIGAN PUBLIC SCHOOLS

RoSusan D. Bartee

Internal and external implications of cultural, social, and symbolic capital influence the microlevel schooling process within the K–12 educational system. The individualized and collective implications associated with these distinct forms of capital affect the manner in which the context of a school culture values certain types of activities, affiliations, and knowledge (Bourdieu, 1984; Coleman, 1988; DiMaggio, 1982; Lareau & McNamara Horvat, 1999; Spillane, Hallett, & Diamond, 2003). Nonetheless, the No Child Left Behind Act of 2001 (NCLB) uses a macrolevel systematic approach to improve academic measures and foster enhanced educational outcomes for public school constituencies. Academic measures of NCLB equate school account- ability with student performance on high-stakes testing and the integration of an evidence-based curriculum. Increasing educational outcomes focus on directed control for states, communities, and parents through autonomous governance and parental choice. The emanating challenge of NCLB as a macrolevel policy, juxtaposed with forms of capital as a function of microlevel procedures, evokes competing and/or coexisting views. Examining the manner in which macro- and microlevel phenomena interact within the public schools of Michigan is important in understanding the dynamics associated with the implementation of educational policies.

Both assessment and accountability are critical components of NCLB in enhancing academic achievement. States are required to test the knowledge of students in specified content areas of reading, math, language arts, social studies, science, or a combination of them. School districts are subject to the reward or reprimand of state officials, and the latter to that of the federal government. As part of the NCLB efforts, the Michigan Department of Education developed a School Improvement Framework to provide a structure for creating an assessment model and accountability standards. Understanding the tenets of the School Improvement Framework is important because it provides insight into the types of administrative, academic, and programmatic entities that are valued within the educational system in Michigan. These entities become forms of living capital given their prioritization and integration in a framework for improving educational outcomes. In effect, the success of the students and stakeholders is measured by their ability to achieve based upon a set of prescribed standards. More specifically, for the purposes of this study, some insight is plausible from the implications of African American females in Michigan public schools and diverse forms of capital.

Indicators of assessment and accountability juxtaposed with the role of capital contain value-based implications for cognitive and noncognitive outcomes. Such implications become the basis on which the accessibility of resources, quality of relationships, and viability of results are determined. According to Bourdieu, capital is defined as "accumulated labor which, when appropriated on a private basis by agents or groups of agents, enables them to appropriate social energy in the form of reified or living labor" (1984, p. 241). Capital and its diverse forms essentially consist of exclusive assets that contain the capacity to reproduce profitable and meaningful rewards (Borrem, 2010). Bartee and Brown (2007), in their book *School Matters: Why African American Students Need Multiple Forms of Capital*, address the manner in which education exchanges diverse forms of capital within the capacities of regulator, consumer, and producer. Depending upon who is acquiring the capital and in what context affects how they operate.

The form of cultural capital refers to "acquired knowledge that stems from affiliations with particular traditions" (Bartee & Brown, 2007, p. 53). Cultural capital is acquired through academic experiences within the school, affecting administrators, teachers, students, and families (i.e., academic curriculum, professional development), and nonacademic experiences outside of the school context (i.e., leisure activities). The form of social capital is comprised of networks and associations through which access is made available (Bartee, 2011; Bartee & Brown, 2007; Coleman, 1988; Gordon, 2001). Social capital is garnered in influential relationships established for professional and personal purposes (i.e., organizational involvement, family ties). The form of symbolic capital serves as the physical representation or embodiment of legitimate forms of credential or accoutrements (Bartee, 2011; Bartee & Brown, 2007; Bourdieu, 1990; Delpit, 1988). Symbolic capital is an identifiable form of evidence to signify that skills or other relevant components are present and/or have been fulfilled (i.e., resumes, test scores).

Considering the macrolevel educational policy of NCLB in conjunction with the diverse forms of capital as operating in the microlevel tenets of schooling, important research questions need to be examined. Focusing on the cognitive and noncognitive experiences of African American high school females, the following questions within the context of the state of Michigan in purview of the larger research context of this edited volume are forwarded:

- What are the identifiable trends and subsequent implications of cultural, social, and symbolic capital for African American high school females after NCLB in the public schools of Michigan?
- What approaches can be used to enhance the quality of the dynamics between the macrolevel approach of NCLB and the microlevel functions of capital and thereby improve the overall effectiveness of NCLB and the performance levels of African American high school females?

These questions provide a useful framework for ascertaining insightful findings about the roles of a macrolevel educational policy and microlevel educational practices of capital. These questions provide a useful framework for further contextualizing female demographics within the Michigan Public Schools to include the following: American Indian / Alaskan Native (0.9 percent); Asian/Pacific Islander (2.7 percent); Black, not of Hispanic origin (20.3 percent); Hispanic (4.9 percent); White, not of Hispanic origin (71.1 percent); multiracial (0.9 percent). Forty-five percent (45.9 percent) of students from the state of Michigan are eligible to receive free and/or reduced meals (Meador, 2012).

Educational Trends of African American Females in School Settings

In today's high schools, the academic performance of African American females is consistent with the overall trends associated with the larger female population (Entwisle, Alexander, & Olson, 1997; Gregory, 1997; Ogbu, 1990). Such trends indicate that females are excelling in educational-related capacities irrespective of racial composition, which affects the transferability of their individual capital and their ability to compete on a nationwide scale.

Saunders and coauthors (2004) addressed the role of gender differences within academic performance and self-perceptions among African American high school students. Regarding self-perceptions, the focus of the study is placed on self-esteem, racial self-esteem, and academic self-efficacy, while indices for academic performance target intentions to complete the school year and grade point average (GPAs). African American females indicated stronger intentions to complete the school year than African American males, and their GPAs were higher than their African American male counterparts'. Saunders and coauthors (2004) assert the following: "Patterns of school completion are molded by the interaction of the school environment, society, and individual characteristics. It is well documented that African American males and females experience the school environment very differently" (p. 82). The manner in which teachers and peers respond to African American males is more aggressive as compared to African American females.

Entwisle, Alexander, and Olson (1997) contend that the level of success African American females in high school achieve may be associated with a broader societal view of the role of education for them. The study suggests that the stronger percep-tions of African American females in academic and nonacademic contexts are indicative of the implications of education as economically and socially beneficial. Having a positive image of what is possible and, to some extent, what is expected influences females in short- and long-term ways that have both cognitive and noncognitive rewards.

Rouse and Austin (2002) conducted a study that focused on academic performance and motivational influences of students from southwest urban school districts that are considered ethnically diverse. The article indicates that on a district-wide level, the district is implementing several initiatives and enhancement programs as well as offering a range of extracurricular activities (i.e., sports programs, Future

Business Leaders of America, cheerleading, and dance teams). Rouse and Austin (2002) assert the following perspectives:

> One of the striking differences [between African Americans and other ethnic groups] is the interaction between GPA and gender in the African American group of adolescents for three aspects of self-concept (beliefs about ability, beliefs about control, and beliefs about value/importance). No other ethnic group evidenced this interaction. More interesting is an examination of means that demonstrates that European-American females have even less motivation in these areas than the African American females, while Hispanic females have more motivation. . . . High-GPA students had more motivation in terms of their self-concept. However, in the African American sample this was evidenced in all four areas of self-concept (beliefs about ability, beliefs about environmental support, beliefs about control, and beliefs about value/importance). This was not the case for the Hispanic and Euro-American samples, though. In both of these ethnic groups, statistical significance was only evidenced in three areas: beliefs about ability, beliefs about control, and beliefs about value/importance. It seems the low-GPA African American adolescents do not feel that their academic environment is supporting them nor facilitating their achievement. (pp. 307, 311)

The finding suggests that differences exist among ethnic minorities when considering the implications of GPA. The study, too, finds that African American female adolescents who were considered as having high intellectual abilities based upon their GPAs demonstrated the most motivation about the certain beliefs about the ability, control, and importance, unlike those African American female adolescents who were considered as having low intellectual abilities, who were less likely to adapt to motivational patterns. When juxtaposing these two perspectives, it appears that a correlation is found between the motivation of African American females and their GPAs and having a positive concept of self. Each of the aforementioned studies provides interesting viewpoints about the status of African American females in schools.

Conceptual Perspectives on the School Improvement Framework in Michigan and Representation of Capital Forms

The School Improvement Framework contains the five different strands of Teaching for Learning; Leadership; Personnel and Professional Learning; School and Community Relations; and Data and Information Management. Each of the strands has corresponding standards, benchmarks, and key characteristics. According to the Michigan Department of Education, descriptions of the School Improvement Framework are as follows:

- STRAND 1: *Teaching for Learning.* The school holds high expectations for all students, identifies essential curricular content, makes certain it is sequenced appropriately and is taught effectively in the available instructional times. Assessments used are aligned to curricular content and are used to guide instructional decisions and monitor student learning.
- STRAND 2: *Leadership.* School leaders create a school environment where everyone contributes to a cumulative, purposeful, and positive effect on student learning.
- STRAND 3: *Personnel and Professional Learning.* The school has highly qualified personnel who continually acquire and use skills, knowledge, attitudes, and beliefs necessary to create a culture with high levels of learning for all.
- STRAND 4: *School and Community Relations.* The school staff maintains purposeful, active, positive relationships with families of its students and with the community in which it operates to support student learning.
- STRAND 5: *Data and Information Management.* Schools/districts have a system for management data and information in order to inform decisions to improve student achievement. (*Michigan School Improvement Framework Rubrics*, 2006)

Cognitive and/or noncognitive approaches to academic achievement are identified within descriptions of the strands. Examining the School Improvement Framework provides an important opportunity to determine whether microlevel indicators of the diverse forms of capital are included within the macrolevel conduit of NCLB. These forms of capital again must be inclusive of administrators, teachers, students, and families who are stakeholders. Likewise, if the forms of capital are not included within the governing framework of the Michigan public schools, then the implications of capital and its impact on African American high school females become invalid. The examination shows, however, that indices of cultural, social, and symbolic capital are present in the School Improvement Framework, although their presence is not consistently found in each of the strands and corresponding standards. The analyses of the strands are as follows:

- Strand 1, *Teaching for Learning*, contains indicators of cultural, social, and symbolic capital. Some of the identifiable sources of capital include the cultural capital forms of written units, lesson plans, and curriculum documents; symbolic capital forms of individual education plans, meeting agendas and minutes, competency profiles, and syllabi; and social capital forms of district-wide/school one-way communications, school accommodations, and two-way parent communications. Analyses of these different forms of data about the Teaching for Learning strand contain indicators of cultural, social, and symbolic capital within three of the standards, while two of the three standards only contain indicators of cultural and symbolic capital (see table 1).
- In strand 2, *Leadership*, an indicator of symbolic capital is found, while there are no indicators of social and cultural capital. Some of the identifiable sources of symbolic capital forms are resumes, certification requirements, observation protocols, teacher evaluations, school policies and procedures, rubrics, school improvement plans, and professional development plans. Analyses of these different forms of data related to the Leadership strand demonstrate forms of symbolic capital within the three standards, while there are no indicators of cultural and social capital within any of the three standards (see table 1).
- Strand 3, *Personnel and Professional Learning*, has indicators of cultural, social, and symbolic capital. Some of the identifiable sources of data on cultural capital forms are lesson plans, professional development plans, and unit plans, and the social capital forms of communications inviting parents to schools, teacher phone calls, e-mails to parents; and the symbolic capital forms of meeting agendas and minutes, teacher credentials, observation protocols, team policies and procedures manual, and records and reports of curriculum committees). Analyses of these different forms of data about the Personnel and Professional Learning strand contain indicators of cultural, social, and symbolic capital within one of the two standards and an indicator of symbolic capital within both of the standards (see table 1).

- Strand 4, *School and Community Relations*, also contains indicators of cultural, social, and symbolic capital. Some of the identifiable sources of data are the cultural capital forms of mentoring programs, professional development documentation, and communication system; the social capital forms of lists of parent support mechanisms, translation services, and school committee membership lists; and the symbolic capital forms of school/district websites, school calendars, walls of school, websites, and flyers. Analyses of these different forms of data regarding school and community relations' strand contain social and symbolic forms of capital within both standards, while the indicator of cultural capital is found within one of the standards (see table 1).
- Strand 5, *Data and Information Management*, has indicators of cultural, social, and symbolic capital. Some of the identifiable sources of cultural capital forms are assessment plans, intervention and/or differentiation plans, and lesson plans; and the social capital forms of staff and parent meetings, parent advisory council meetings, parent-teacher association meetings, and board of education meetings; and the symbolic capital forms of policies and procedures handbook, data arrays, and student records. Analyses of these different forms of data related to the Data and Information management Strand include cultural and symbolic capital within both of the standards, while the indicator of social capital is found in only one of the standards (see table 1).

Cultural Capital and Academic Underpreparedness

Cultural capital is based upon acquired knowledge or values that are often affiliated with certain traditions (Bartee & Brown, 2007; Bourdieu, 1984; Franklin & Savage, 2004; Olneck, 2000). These types of knowledge are often generated in families and schools and are often linked to literature, music, arts, and other culturally relevant experiences. Bourdieu (1984) suggests that for participants who acquired their cultural capital primarily from educational settings, their knowledge base and experiences are more transferable or valued within those areas that accommodate high academic qualifications. Particularly within the educational setting related to students, on the microlevel, one measure of the level of cultural capital acquired is linked to test scores in the content areas of reading and mathematics. Data from the Michigan Educational Assessment Program (MEAP) in 2011 contains some

TABLE 1. INTERSECTION OF DIVERSE FORMS OF CAPITAL WITH MICHIGAN SCHOOL IMPROVEMENT FRAMEWORK STRANDS AND STANDARDS

	STANDARDS		
	CULTURAL CAPITAL	SOCIAL CAPITAL	SYMBOLIC CAPITAL
STRAND 1: TEACHING FOR LEARNING	• Curriculum • Instruction • Assessment	• Curriculum	• Curriculum • Instruction • Assessment
STRAND 2: LEADERSHIP	• Shared leadership	• Instructional leadership • Shared leadership • Operational and resource management	• Instructional leadership • Shared leadership • Operational and resource management
STRAND 3: PERSONNEL AND PROFESSIONAL LEARNING	• Personnel qualifications • Professional learning	• Professional learning	• Personnel qualifications • Professional learning
STRAND 4: SCHOOL AND COMMUNITY RELATIONS	• Community involvement	• Parent/family involvement • Community involvement	• Parent/family involvement • Community involvement
STRAND 5: DATA AND INFORMATION MANAGEMENT	• Data management • Information management	• Information management	• Data management • Information management

interesting disaggregated findings for African Americans and females (*MEAP State Demographic Report*, 2011).

From a racial context, table 2 demonstrates how all of the racial groups have continuous decline in the content area of reading from third grade to fifth grade to eight grade, while in the content area of writing, by eighth grade, all of the racial groups show increases from the fifth grade. African American students, however, show the least amount of percentage gains. From a gender context, table 2 also indicates a decrease in the academic performance of females in the content area of reading and mathematics from third grade through eighth grade. Similar trends exist in the same content areas with males, but the females' increase in writing percentages is higher.

Inherent within this aggregate view of race and gender-specific data resonates a unique perspective about the role of cultural capital. As indicated previously, cultural capital is gained traditionally from types of knowledge often associated

TABLE 2. PERCENTAGE OF THIRD-, FIFTH-, AND EIGHTH-GRADE STUDENTS DEMONSTRATING PROFICIENCY IN READING AND MATH ON MEAP, 2011, BY GENDER AND RACE/ETHNICITY

	3RD GRADE		5TH GRADE		8TH GRADE	
	READING	MATH	READING	MATH	READING	MATH
GENDER						
Female	66	35	72	38	65	28
Male	59	38	66	42	56	31
RACE/ETHNICITY						
American Indian/Alaskan Native	59	29	59	25	54	22
Asian	74	63	81	71	76	62
Pacific Islander	73	41	81	45	59	28
Black, Not of Hispanic Origin	38	14	48	17	39	9
Hispanic	48	23	57	26	48	16
White, Not of Hispanic Origin	70	42	75	46	66	26
Multiracial	63	34	69	37	60	68

Source: MEAP State Demographic Report (2011).

with the humanities, where writing is encouraged. These findings are consistent with the literature from both a gender and discipline perspective. When considering the implications of race and capital within this model, African Americans' level of cultural capital as identified by reading and writing scores is not competitive when compared to different racial groups other than Hispanics. As early as the third grade, African American scores in these areas begin significantly lower than other racial groups. In many regards, cultural capital associated with reading and writing test scores is almost nonexistent.

Students from environments filled with cultural capital building experiences nonetheless understand the intricacies of their educational settings and they become resigned to the ideological expectations of that climate. Bourdieu (1984) asserts the following perspectives regarding scholastic and status-based capital:

The more the competences measured are recognized by the school system and the more academic the techniques used to measure them, the stronger is the relation between performance and educational qualifications. The latter, as a more or less adequate indicator of the number of years of scholastic inculcation, guarantees cultural capital more or less completely, depending on whether it is inherited from the family or acquired at school, and so it is an unequally adequate indicator of this capital. (p. 13)

The argument implies that family resources have greater impact upon academic performance than the traditional forms of education acquired in schools. Family resources contain a variety of networks that offer options and opportunities for individuals from middle, upper-class backgrounds. DiMaggio (1982) and DiMaggio and Ostrower (1990), in a classic study, argues that participation in high-cultural activities significantly influences grade performance. Those students who participate in certain activities are more likely to get better grades. Particularly, females from high-status families receive greater cultural capital returns than females from low-status backgrounds. Such findings remain consistent with the positions related to the cultural reproduction model. Findings point to a relatively low correlation between parental education and cultural capital. The quality of opportunities that is afforded by schools compensates for the lacking family resources. Table 3, providing data from the Michigan Educational Assessment Program (MEAP) in 2011, contains some interesting disaggregated findings for economically disadvantaged students, among which there is a disproportionately higher number of African American and other students of color.

Table 3 shows how the economically disadvantaged have test scores beginning substantially lower than other students in the areas of writing, reading, mathematics, and science. In effect, schools with students a greater number of whom receive free and reduced-price meals are more likely to encounter challenges with their writing test scores. The implications of the area of reading are not as pronounced in this

TABLE 3. PERCENTAGE OF FOURTH-, FIFTH-, AND EIGHTH-GRADE STUDENTS DEMONSTRATING PROFICIENCY IN READING, WRITING, MATH, AND SCIENCE ON MEAP, 2011, BY ECONOMIC STATUS

ECONOMICALLY DISADVANTAGED	4TH GRADE			5TH GRADE			8TH GRADE		
	READING	WRITING	MATH	READING	SCIENCE	MATH	READING	SCIENCE	MATH
Yes	55	31	25	56	7	25	47	8	15
No	81	58	55	81	24	54	72	24	41

Source: MEAP State Demographic Report (2011).

same context. Juxtaposing these viewpoints with the dimensions of cultural capital, data suggests that African American females within the Michigan public schools are subject to a negative impact of being African American, female, and poor. It may be true that the quality of resources available in economically disadvantaged schools is not sufficient for educating in ways that enhances and/or builds upon existing skill sets. Notwithstanding this possibility, while children from poor families populate economically disadvantaged schools, the delivery of education does not have to be conducted in a poor manner. The work of DiMaggio (1982) and DiMaggio and Ostrower (1990) serves as a reminder that no correlation exists between parental education and cultural capital. Closer examinations of the pedagogical strategies that are being used within the classrooms must be done. Nonetheless, there remains a level of academic underpreparedness for African American females to be able to compete statewide and nationwide.

Social Capital and Untapped Networks

Social capital emanates through the quality of networks and relationship that are available and resourceful (Adler & Kwon, 2002; Bartee & Brown, 2007; Coleman, 1988; Lee & Croninger, 1999; Koka & Prescott, 2002; McNeal, 1999; Spillane, Hallett, & Diamond, 2003). Social capital provides built-in tools of resources and becomes a source of convenience at any given time for any given purpose. Having direct access to forms of resources provides a comfort level for being able to navigate and negotiate different contexts. Involvement with different organizations and associations provides the needed alliances through which the quality of exchange is enhanced. Porath (1980) in his assertion of the F-connection of families, friend, and firms discusses how these exchange systems are embedded with the inherent capacity to get the desired results of what is pursued. The level of bureaucracy involved is diminished because many of these relationships are in some ways personal, but in many ways these relationships are functional.

Coleman (1990) builds upon the functionality argument of social capital in the sense that individuals belong to networks that serve a variety of functions. These functions are neither stagnant nor fluid. These functions are deliberate and purposeful. Coleman (1990) puts forth the following position related to social capital and function:

Social capital is defined by its function. It is not a single entity, but a variety of different entities having two characteristics in common: They all consist of some aspect of a social structure and they facilitate certain actions of individuals who are within the structure. Like other forms of capital, social capital is productive, making possible the achievement of certain ends that would be attainable in its absence.... Unlike other forms of capital, social capital inheres in the structure of relations between persons and among persons. It is lodged neither in individuals nor in physical implements of production. (p. 302)

The argument clearly suggests that social capital is identified by its capacity to operate in different capacities. Such capacities allow individuals to move into and out of different circles and to achieve desired outcomes. In effect, the quality of the relationship that social capital allows is measured by its ability to promote mobility and stability. Again, these relationships are formed by access that is made available through associations, networks, and organizational ties.

More specifically, social capital is nurtured through the availability of and caliber of extracurricular activities. Such activities sponsored by the school or not sponsored by the school provide the venue to establish access to influential networks and/or skill sets that become useful for gaining access to a variety of venues. It is particularly important for students from economically challenged backgrounds to have these outlets afforded by the school for developing leadership characteristics and other requisite skills. Derived from the Detroit Public Schools, which is the largest school district in Michigan and the school district with the highest percentage of African American females, aggregate data in table 4 are presented about the status of extracurricular activities (Detroit Public Schools, 2005).

The data clearly demonstrate in table 4 that the Detroit Public Schools are providing a variety of activities for students. The extracurricular program focuses on academic, cultural, and sporting activities. In 2003–2004, the report indicates, the majority of students participated in the reading component of the after-school programs, while the smallest number of students participated in the debate program. In 2004–2005, the majority of the students participated in the science, reading, math, and social studies programs, while the least number of students participated in the chess club. It is interesting to note, however, that while the number of schools with different types of social-capital-building programs increased consistently for three academic years, the number of students in those programs decreased between the

TABLE 4. BEFORE- AND AFTER-SCHOOL SPORTS, ARTS, CULTURAL, AND ACADEMIC OFFERINGS WITHIN DETROIT PUBLIC SCHOOLS, 2002–2003, 2003–2004, AND 2004–2005

	2002–2003	2003–2004	2004–2005*
NUMBER OF SCHOOLS WITH OFFERINGS	205	208	224†
TOTAL NUMBER OF OFFERINGS	426	1,370	1,594
ESTIMATED NUMBER OF STUDENTS SERVED	27,634	34,619	25,559

Source: Detroit Public Schools (2005).

*Document Sports: 2003–04 baseline—Competitive 110 schools; 5,352 students 1+ week; Document Recreational: 2003–04 baseline 87 schools, 2,574 students; Competitive: 120 schools, 4,130 students; Recreational: 76 schools, 2,249 students.

†No report from 33 sites; nil reports from 19 sites.

academic years of 2003–2004 and 2004–2005 within the Detroit Public Schools. The year in which the students encountered a decline in participation was after the enactment of No Child Left Behind. Nonetheless, while having a plethora of activities within the school would encourage more school involvement and financial support, it also important to consider the manner in which the human resources of these social-capital-building elements are utilized within the schools. Approaching social capital in multidimensional ways is important in sustaining its capacity within the schools.

Symbolic Capital and Conflicting Results

Symbolic capital serves as the physical representation or embodiment of a legitimate source of exchange (Bartee & Brown, 2007; Delpit, 1988; Bourdieu, 1984). The recognition of symbolic capital signifies the presence of a valued commodity. Symbolic capital operates as both embodied and objectified. The embodied nature of symbolic capital is the inherent value that has meaning, which is known by a select group of individuals. The objectified nature of symbolic capital is linked to something that is visualized, and its meaning is known by a wider audience. Both the embodied and objectified nature of capital demonstrates the diverse, yet meaningful, forms of symbolic capital.

From an objectified nature, symbolic capital emerges as visual identification that is known publicly and its implications are understood widely. Bourdieu (1990) identifies symbolic capital as "the form that various species of capital assume when they are perceived and recognized as legitimate" (p. 127). For schools, graduation rates, grades, AP course enrollment, and other measures serve as the objectified nature of symbolic capital. Those objectified forms of symbolic capital position students for consideration at highly selective schools and/or universities.

It remains important that students have the required test scores and grades that the school or university warrants as legitimate. While test scores, grades, and other AP courses do not necessarily connote student intelligence, they are significant to the enrollment or admissions process and are considered the measuring stick of intelligence. Having these credentials as a form of symbolic capital suggests that students are qualified and highly capable. In effect, the power to generate and produce accessibility is attached to the objectified nature of symbolic capital.

Considering the indicators of graduation and dropout rates of African American females in Michigan, the findings in table 5 indicate that African American females have significantly low graduation rates within Michigan. Such findings suggest that, overall, African American females are not academically competitive when compared to other racial groups other than Hispanics. The graduation rates of African American females in Michigan are lower than the national average of 84 percent of African American females identified by National Center for Education Statistics (Hoffman & Llagas 2003).

From an embodied nature, symbolic capital is attached to the entities that relay some type of message to connote legitimacy. In effect, this recognition is considered as private, and those who are aware of its value are those who recognize the conveyed message as being legitimate, while those who are not aware minimize or fail to recognize the level of importance. Both contexts are value-laden and signify belief systems, traditions, and other resonating ideals. The difference, however, that separates the two forms of capital is that symbolic capital assumes a greater likelihood to be transferred in different capacities. Bourdieu (1990) alludes to this viewpoint accordingly:

> It [cultural capital] thus manages to combine the prestige of innate property with the merits of acquisition. Because the social conditions of its transmission and acquisition are more disguised than those of economic capital, it is predisposed

TABLE 5. GRADUATION AND DROPOUT RATES OF FEMALE STUDENTS IN MICHIGAN PUBLIC SCHOOLS, BY RACE/ETHNICITY, 2007

	ON-TRACK GRADUATED	DROPOUT	OFF-TRACK GRADUATED	OFF-TRACK CONTINUING	OTHER COMPLETER	GRADUATION RATE AND TOTAL
American Indian/ Alaskan Native	488	106	<10	70	<10	72.40% 674
Asian/Pacific Islander	1,229	99	0	47	<10	88.86% 1383
Black, Not of Hispanic Origin	9,083	3,206	<10	1,656	57	64.83% 14,011
Hispanic	1,563	617	<10	241	34	63.54% 2,460
White, Not of Hispanic Origin	42,051	4,428	73	2,516	324	85.14% 49,392
Multiracial	265	51	<10	40	13	71.62% 370

Source: The Center for Educational Performance and Information (2008b).

to function as symbolic capital (i.e. to be recognized as capital and recognized as legitimate competence, as authority exerting an effect of (mis)recognition....

Furthermore, the specifically symbolic logic of distinction additionally secures material and symbolic profits for the possessors. (p. 245)

Some aspects of symbolic and cultural capital are interlinked and become significant in determining outcomes. Symbolic capital may or may not signify cultural capital. The prevailing attitudes and resonating ideologies, as defined by the setting, become the point of departure for assessing whether or not the capital is legitimate. For example, with respect to the statewide percentages of highly qualified teachers within the state of Michigan, table 6 details some interesting findings that reveal some insightful perspectives for consideration about symbolic and cultural capital.

Table 6 indicates that a significant percentage of classes are taught by highly qualified teachers. Having such percentage of highly qualified teachers within the schools is notable. From a broad perspective, it is presumed that the students within Michigan are being taught by the most credentialed teachers and that the quality of preparation in the class promotes student success. From a specific perspective,

TABLE 6. NUMBER AND PERCENTAGE OF CORE ACADEMIC CLASSES TAUGHT BY HIGHLY QUALIFIED TEACHERS, 2005–2006

	NUMBER OF CORE ACADEMIC CLASSES	NUMBER OF CORE ACADEMIC CLASSES TAUGHT BY HIGHLY QUALIFIED TEACHERS	PERCENTAGE OF CORE ACADEMIC CLASSES TAUGHT BY HIGHLY QUALIFIED TEACHERS
All Schools in State	*187,500*	*182,610*	*97.4%*
ELEMENTARY LEVEL			
High Poverty	7,726	7,679	99.4%
Low Poverty	10,701	10,671	99.7%
All Schools	*36,696*	*36,506*	*99.5%*
SECONDARY LEVEL			
High Poverty	20,5822	19,805	96.2%
Low Poverty	69,447	67,670	97.4%
All Schools	*150,187*	*145,519*	*96.9%*

Source: Michigan NCLB State Report Card (2005–06).

given that the majority of African American female students in Michigan are concentrated within the Detroit Public Schools and their graduation rates are less than 70 percent, the implications of having highly qualified teachers are not manifesting the expected type of competitive outcomes. Therefore, it is important to consider symbolic capital within its context to determine the various dynamics; otherwise the possibility of having conflicting results is more likely to occur.

Quality of C³ = Quality R³

From a macrolevel viewpoint, it is evident that diverse forms of capital, cultural, social, and symbolic, influence the accessibility of resources, quality of relationships, and viability of results within the educational context. The quality of capital and its capacity to be exchanged is based upon what occurs in cognitive and noncognitive arenas. Examining the School Improvement Framework as a conduit of the macrolevel NCLB in light of the perspectives on the different forms of capital and their micro-level functions, some interesting viewpoints emerge. Those viewpoints are as follows:

- Strand 1, *Teaching for Learning*, did not include social capital indicators of the standards of instruction and assessment. The key benchmarks of instruction are *planning and delivery* and the key benchmarks of assessment are *aligned to curriculum, data reporting, and use.* In both cases, given the absence of social capital indicators, consideration is needed of how extracurricular activities (school-sponsored and non-school-sponsored) can be integrated as core curricular matter. The curriculum will then need to be modified in a manner that permits aligning types of data to be collected.
- Strand 2, *Leadership*, did not fully include cultural capital related to indicators of instructional leadership, shared leadership, and operational and resource management. The key benchmarks of instructional leadership are *educational program and instructional support,* of shared leadership are *school culture and climate and continuous improvement,* and of operational and resource management are *resource allocation and operational management.* For the educational program and operational and resource management platforms, the absence of cultural capital indicators fosters a need to focus on the types of activities being used to reinforce what is being taught in class and how material and nonmaterial resources are being used to support these efforts. Bridging the gap between "theory and practice" becomes critical to creating effective measures for learning.
- Strand 3, *Personnel and Professional Learning*, did not fully include social capital indicators for the standard of personnel qualifications. The key benchmarks of personnel qualifications are *requirements and skills, knowledge, and dispositions* and the key benchmarks of professional learning are *collaboration, content and pedagogy,* and *alignment.* To encourage social capital within this standard, interest needs to be taken toward integrating some of the professional associations, community organizations, and other related social entities into the activities of the school. The affiliations of the personnel need to be considered as a resource, and efforts need to be created to engage those networks in valued ways.
- Strand 4, *School and Community Relations*, did not fully include cultural capital indicators for the standard of parent/family involvement. The key benchmarks of parent/family involvement are *communication* and *engagement.* The absence of cultural capital within this particular benchmark suggests a need to find creative ways to involve the families in activities that interest them and to conduct these activities frequently and deliberately at times when they will be available, which, in effect, builds buy-in from the families. Surveys can be

completed at these activities or by students to determine the types of activities that families would enjoy.

- Strand 5, *Data and Information Management*, did not fully include social capital indicators for the standard of data management. The key benchmarks of data management are *data generation, identification, and collection, data accessibility,* and *data support.* Issues related to social capital in this strand are based upon previous recommendations about the integration of extracurricular activities as part of the core curriculum, the treatment of personnel affiliations with professional organizations as a resource for the school, and the involvement of families within the school. A structured approach needs to be institutionalized and implemented in order to create a data-generating system to inform the policies and practices of the respective schools.

From a microlevel viewpoint, the use of particular programmatic efforts provides the practical application for capital to be generated in school settings. The Young Empowered Sisters (YES!) program is one example currently being implemented within a Michigan school that addresses the noncognitive needs of African American female adolescents. YES! uses diverse intervention measures to enhance foster increased self-awareness and consciousness in African American females attending an academically underperforming school. Thomas, Davidson, and McAdoo (2008) characterize the school-based intervention YES! program as follows:

> The goals of the intervention are to instill a healthy Black identify, promote a collectivist orientation, increase an awareness of racism, and encourage participation in liberatory activities. To achieve the goals of intervention, three overarching themes were integrated within the intervention's curriculum: cultural values, African American history, and contemporary culture. The cultural values component emphasized values and expressions of collectivism.... Participants engaged in discussions on what Black unity meant to them and how they as individuals could bring about further unity among African Americans. Participants also engaged in-group projects to facilitate collective responsibility and shared personal experiences with each other to build a sense of belong and sisterly camaraderie. The history component focused on the shared historical experiences of Black people in the United States. Participants discussed the trans-Atlantic slave trade, Black enslavement, and key historical figures in the

1960s civil rights movement. The contemporary culture component addressed present-day environmental risk factors African Americans encounter. Specifically, this component sought to increase students' awareness of their sociopolitical environment vis-à-vis racism and to inspire involvement in liberatory behaviors. … They also engaged in discussions on how to effectively cope with and overcome the effects of racism. (pp. 286–287)

The description of the YES! program indicates its integration of cultural, social, and symbolic indicators of capital in its curricular makeup. Cultural capital is acquired through the teaching of African American and American-centered values of collectivism and individualism respectively. Social capital is facilitated through the implementation of group activities to foster personal networks and friendships. Symbolic capital emerges through the exuded confidence in the dispositions of these students since they are equipped with different strategies to cope with the continuing, not-so-present implications of racial and gender discrimination.

Furthermore, it is important to note that, consistent with the goals of the YES! program, Thomas, Davidson, and McAdoo (2008) indicate that those students who participated in the YES! program had increased awareness of their racial identity and discrimination, the importance of communalism, and increased participation in activism. The study argued that both the curriculum structure and its use of group-based activities provided the framework for fostering a program to meet the holistic needs of its African American female adolescents. While the study indicates improvement in the noncognitive areas of the students, the study does not address the cognitive results of having participated in this program. However, considering the work of Saunders and coauthors (2004) and Rouse and Austin (2002) and their focus on self-esteem and academic performance, it is reasonable to conclude that there was some impact in the cognitive areas of these females' schooling experience by their having participated in the YES! program.

Implications for Research

There are various implications related to cultural, social, and symbolic capital within this important study on the interactions of the macrolevel policy of No Child Left Behind and the microlevel operating tenets of capital. From a cultural capital viewpoint, alternative measures need to be taken in the Michigan public schools to nurture cultural capital among African American females. Specific attention needs to be placed upon their current involvement in activities that are considered culturally relevant, integrating those activities within the course and using appropriate pedagogical strategies. As Gloria Ladson-Billings (1994) addresses in her book *The Dreamkeepers: Successful Teaching for African American Students*, there is significant importance in using the background and experiences of students as a teaching tool in the curriculum. Ladson-Billings (1994) comments that "students must experience academic success, students must develop and/or maintain cultural competence, and students must develop a critical consciousness through which they challenge the status quo of the current social order" (p. 160). Teachers and administrators must encourage and support these nontraditional efforts in order to build cultural capital in ways that benefit the school and the students.

Although many of these African American females may be from economically impoverished families and face the associated challenges, it still remains important to understand how their circumstances are to be used in constructive ways. Ruby Payne (1998), in her book *A Framework for Understanding Poverty*, discusses poverty as having its own language and own rules, by which it is governed. Breaking into these unspoken codes as a means to understand the population that is being served is critically important. However, Gorski (2006) uses a critical social theory lens that acknowledges the intersections of class inequities that are exacerbated by race and gender in schools. Whether or not the teacher is the same race of the student, deficit theories and thinking should not be applied; in contrast, deliberate efforts must be taken to decode and integrate the experiences of African American students (particularly females) in the curriculum in meaningful and appropriate ways.

The components of social capital are also critical to the success of African American females within the Michigan public schools. Involving persons from the community within the activities of the school encourages participation in the extracurricular activities that the schools have to offer. These individuals serve as both a material and a nonmaterial resource for the students, who may come from economically challenging backgrounds. According to Lee and Croninger (1999), social capital is considered a "resource embedded in a person's social network . . . the manner in which the structural characteristics of social groups facilitate or hinder helpful exchanges between members" (p. 6). In effect, the schools would be establishing the venue for long-term relationships to be established between the students and the mentor from external organizations and associations. These mentors would be able to offer noncognitive support to the students in essential ways for their life after school. The role of symbolic capital for African American females in Michigan public schools is critical for both public and private purposes. Within the public sphere, the level of progress that is being made is often determined by the rates and percentages that are shown. If the rates are high, then it is perceived that great strides are being made within that respective domain and vice versa. Within the private sphere, only those who are knowledgeable of what the rates and percentages are connoting understand their implications. The outcomes for African American females in Michigan public schools are dismal in both the public and private spheres. Efforts need to be taken toward bridging the gaps between the two spheres, thereby allowing the symbolic representation of the percentages and rates associated with graduation rates and highly qualified teachers to serve as representative insight into what is occurring within the schools.

The research study on trends and status of African American females within the public schools of Michigan as juxtaposed with the different forms of capital has evoked some interesting perspectives. The role of No Child Left Behind vis-à-vis the School Improvement Framework provides critical insight into the macro- and microlevel dynamics of these two competing items. Given that No Child Left Behind will continue in some capacity as the federal mandate on academic performance, it remains important to encourage and integrate capital-building elements into the governance and operations of the Michigan public schools. Nonetheless, the YES! program, as implemented in one of the Michigan schools, provides a viable example regarding how cultural, social, and symbolic capital can be integrated within a school setting. Not only will African American females benefit, but the state and nation as a whole will gain from the positive implications of producing competitive students. Academic underpreparedness, untapped resources, and conflicting results that are currently being generated as ill forms of capital can no longer be tolerated as the norm but, instead, must be considered a stepping stone for generating legitimate forms of capital.

REFERENCES

Adler, P.S., & Kwon, S. (2002). Social capital: Prospects for a new concept. *Academy of Management Review, 27*(1), 17–40

Bartee, R.D. (Ed.) (2011). *Contemporary perspectives on capital in educational contexts.* Charlotte, NC: Information Age Publishing.

Bartee, R.D., & Brown, M.C. II. (2007). *School matters: Why African American students need multiple forms of capital.* New York: Peter Lang.

Borrem, N. (2010). Teaching and teacher education for social justice: A focus on cultural assets. *Teacher Education and Practice, 23*(4), 471–474.

Bourdieu, P. (1984). The forms of capital. In J. Richardson (Ed.), *Handbook of theory and research for the sociology of education* (pp. 241–258). New York: Greenwood Press.

Bourdieu, P. (1990). *The logic of practice.* Stanford, CA: Stanford University Press.

Center for Educational Performance and Information (2008a). *State of Michigan 2007 cohort 4-year graduation and dropout rate reports.* Retrieved from http://www.michigan.gov/documents/cepi/StateFa07Total_239297_7.xls.

Center for Educational Performance and Information (2008b). *State of Michigan 2007 cohort 4-year graduation and dropout rate reports.* Retrieved from http://www.michigan.gov/documents/cepi/2007_MI_Grad-Drop_Rate_246519_7.xls.

Coleman, J.S. (1988). Social capital in the creation of human capital. *American Journal of Sociology, 94*, 95–120.

Coleman, J.S. (1990). *Foundations of social theory.* Cambridge: Belknap Press of Harvard University Press.

Delpit, L. (1988). The silenced dialogue: Power and pedagogy in educating other people's children. *Harvard Educational Review, 58*, 280–298.

Detroit Public Schools (2005). *Report on before and after school activities: For the 2002–03, 2003–04, and 2004–05 school years.* Detroit: Author, Office of Research, Evaluation, and Assessment.

DiMaggio, P. (1982). Cultural capital and school success: The impact of status culture participation on the grades of U.S. high school. *American Sociological Review, 47*, 189–201.

DiMaggio, P., & Ostrower, F. (1990). Participation in the arts by Black and

White Americans. *Social Forces, 68,* 753–778.

Entwisle, D.R., Alexander, K.L., & Olson, L.S. (1997). *Children, schools, and inequality.* Boulder, CO: Westview Press.

Franklin, V.P., & Savage, C.J. (2004). *Cultural capital and Black education: African American communities and the funding of Black schooling, 1865 to the present.* Charlotte, NC: Information Age.

Gordon, K.A. (1995). The self-concept and motivational patterns of African American high school students. *Journal of Black Psychology, 21,* 239–255.

Gordon, E.W. (2001). Affirmative development of academic abilities. *Pedagogical Inquiry and Praxis, 2,* 1–8.

Gordon Rouse, K., & Cashin, S. (2002). The assessment of academic self-concept and motivation: Results from three ethnic groups. *Measurement and Evaluation in Counseling and Development, 33,* 91–102.

Gorski, P. (2006). The classist underpinnings of Ruby Payne's framework. *Teachers College Record.* Retrieved from http://www.tcrecord.org/content. asp?contentid=12322.

Gregory, J.F. (1997). Three strikes and they're out: African American boys and American schools' responses to misbehavior. *International Journal of Adolescent Youth, 7,* 25–34.

Hoffman, K., & Llagas, C. (2003, September). *Status and trends in the education of Blacks.* Washington, DC: National Center for Education Statistics.

Janoski, T., Musick, M., & Wilson, J. (1998). Being volunteered? The impact of social participation and pro-social attitudes on volunteering. *Sociological Forum, 13,* 495–519.

Koka, B.R., & Prescott, J.E. (2002). Strategic alliances as social capital: A multidimensional view. *Strategic Management Journal, 23,* 795–816.

Ladson-Billings, G. (1994). *The Dreamkeepers: Successful teaching for African-American students.* San Francisco: Jossey-Bass.

Lareau, A., & McNamara Horvat, E. (1999). Moments of social inclusion and exclusion: Race, class, and cultural capital in family-school relationships. *Sociology of Education, 72,* 37–53.

Lareau, A., & Weininger, E.B. (2003). Cultural capital in educational research: A critical assessment. *Theory and Society, 32,* 567–606.

Lee, V., & Croninger, R. (1999). *Elements of social capital in the context of six high schools.* Office of Educational Research and Improvement, Educational

Resources Information Center. Washington, DC: U.S. Department of Education.

Meador, D. (2012). Michigan education: A profile on Michigan education and schools. *About.com.* Retrieved from http://teaching.about.com/od/ ProfilesInEducation/a/Michigan-Education.htm.

MEAP State Demographic Report (2011). Lansing: Michigan Department of Education. Retrieved from http://www.michigan.gov/documents/mde/ Fall_2011_Statewide_Demographic_Report_376775_7.pdf.

Michigan NCLB State Report Card (2005–06). Lansing: Michigan Department of Education. Retrieved from http://www.mi.gov/documents/mde/ State_Report_Card_2005-06_196112_7.pdf.

Michigan School Improvement Framework Rubrics (2006, April). Lansing: Michigan Department of Education. Retrieved from http://www.mi.gov/docu- ments/OSI_FW_Rubrics_v_157013_7.3.pdf.

Ogbu, J. (1990). Minority education in a comparative perspective. *Journal of Negro Education, 59,* 45–57.

Olneck, M. (2000). Can multicultural education change what counts as cultural capital? *American Educational Research Journal, 37,* 317–348.

Payne, R.K. (1998). A *framework for understanding poverty.* Baytown, TX: RFT Publishing.

Porath, Y. (1980). The f-connections: Families, friends, and firms and the organization of exchange. *Population and Development Review, 6,* 1–30.

Rouse, K.A.G., & Austin, J.T. (2002). The relationship of gender and academic performance to motivation: Within-ethnic group variations. *Urban Review, 34,* 292–317.

Saunders, J., Davis, L., Williams, T., & Williams, J.H. (2004). Gender differences in self-perceptions and academic outcomes: A study of African American high school students. *Journal of Youth and Adolescence, 33,* 81–90.

Spillane, J.P., Hallett, T., & Diamond, J.B. (2003). Forms of capital and the construction of leadership: Instructional leadership in urban elementary schools. *Sociology of Education, 76,* 1–17.

Thomas, O., Davidson, W., & McAdoo, H. (2008). An evaluation study of the Young Empowered Sisters (YES!) program: Promoting cultural assets among African American adolescents girls through a culturally relevant school-based intervention. *Journal of Black Psychology, 34,* 281–308.

It Can Be Done and It Must Be Done

CREATING EDUCATIONAL EXCELLENCE FOR AFRICAN AMERICAN GIRLS IN URBAN SCIENCE CLASSROOMS

Robert W. Simmons III

Recently, I was invited to speak at a Detroit high school that focused on STEM (Science, Technology, Engineering, and Math). As I spoke with the students during the lecture and when in a classroom, I began to notice a disturbing pattern. The boys seemed very involved, but far too many of the girls seemed distant. When speaking with the girls and school staff about this, it became apparent that no one had ever given this situation any thought. Some noted that the grades of the girls were okay, yet others commented on how many girls went to college.

As the majority of my K–12 teaching career was spent as a secondary science teacher in the Detroit Public Schools, I used that encounter to look back on my own experience. I had female students who were excited about science and routinely outperformed the boys on science tests, as well as in the Metro Detroit Science and Engineering Fair. However, this may not be the norm. In fact, academic success for the majority of students in the Detroit Public Schools may not be the norm. Considering that the U.S. secretary of education Arne Duncan has identified the institutional dysfunction of the public school system in Detroit as *ground zero* for urban educational reform, this is a clear indication that something is wrong.

Looking at my former female students' experiences in secondary science, this chapter aims to understand the challenges facing girls in science classrooms, as well as the specific challenges related to African American girls in science classrooms. Additionally, we will explore the various summer programs in the United States, with a more in-depth focus on summer programs that focus on girls in Michigan. Last, we will hear from secondary science teachers from various schools in Detroit.

Education in Detroit

Education in Detroit's public school system has been wrought with administrative incompetence, fiscal mismanagement, and corruption (Bergmann, 2008). Because of these issues, between 1999 and 2005 the State of Michigan "took over" the school system. With an appointed school board, city residents began to associate this development with decades-long suburb-city debate. More succinctly, and to the point, the conversation subtly rotated on a fulcrum that vacillated between discussions about the intrusion of the state into city affairs, and the ever enduring racial discourse in a largely African American city, surrounded by its mostly White suburban neighbors. While the state-appointed board ended in 2004, the public schools of Detroit have suffered through a variety of issues since then (Stover, 2006). Considering the decline in state aid, as well as the mass exodus of a significant number of students, Stover (2006) indicates that the public confidence in the public school system in Detroit has wavered.

With a lack of confidence in the public school system, many Detroiters have turned to charter schools. Originally designed to be "small, self-governing yet public institutions" (Sizer & Wood, 2008, p. 3), the role of charter schools in the education of Detroit youth has been hotly debated by educators and politicians. Both sides of the debate seem willing to acknowledge a need to improve the educational opportunities for children in Detroit, but Keith Johnson (2009), president of the Detroit Federation of Teachers. believes that charter schools are a "drain upon our school district as more and more parents begin to turn to charter schools as an alternative for the education and safety of their children" (p. 2). Regardless as to the accuracy of Johnson's assertion, 30,000 school-aged children attend 49 charter schools in Detroit (Riley, 2009).

As charter schools serve as a potential innovation in the educational conversation in Detroit, additional efforts have ignited a community conversation to discover what is needed and what should be changed. In a recent report published by Excellent Schools Detroit (2010), they discovered that community members believe teachers, students, and families need more support if education in Detroit is to work for all students. Additionally, through community meetings during November and December 2009, five significant ideas were revealed:

- More parental involvement, but schools needed to be more welcoming and proactive
- Improved safety in the schools including keeping gangs out of the schools and ensuring safety in the bathrooms
- More nonacademic services in the schools that foster greater cooperation between city/community agencies and the school community
- More diverse academic offerings
- Stronger accountability and transparency

Some would believe that the ideas discovered through the previously mentioned study are dreams lost in a city that has avoided making substantial changes to its public education system. However, the Skillman Foundation's *Good Schools Guide* (2009) clearly indicates that not all schools in Detroit situate administrative incompetence, fiscal mismanagement, and corruption as the status quo. Noting exemplary schools—public, charter, and private—the *Good Schools Guide* highlights 76 schools in Detroit whose students not only strive for excellence, but also attend schools where academic excellence is the standard.

Women and the Sciences

Over a decade has passed since women began assuming positions in fields that were traditionally male dominated (Ware & Lee, 1988). In spite of advancements, only half of the total undergraduate enrollment in schools across the United States consists of females (National Science Foundation, 2003). Notwithstanding the passage of Title IX in 1972, numerous studies suggest an imbalance between men and women in fields associated with mathematics and science (Crowley et al., 2001;

Hackett et al., 1992; Jones, Howe, & Rua, 2000; Nauta, Epperson, & Kahn, 1998; Osborne, Simon, & Collins, 2003; Thom, 2001). According to the National Science Foundation (2003), approximately 20 percent of bachelor's degrees in science and engineering were conferred to women in 1999, which was an increase of merely 4 percent since 1990. This is especially crucial as occupations within the areas of science and technology continue to expand (Sharf, 2010).

Not only is there a gap between women and men who are currently working in fields associated with mathematics and science, there still appears to be dissonance between the careers considered distinctly masculine and feminine. While some would situate this dissonance in an arena related to educational access, others would focus on the common stereotypes associated with gender. In an examination of stereotypes among college students, Nelson, Acke, and Manis (1996) found that there was a general assumption that men and women adhered to what was viewed as gender-specific occupational roles (e.g., nursing for women versus engineering for males). These assumptions remained intact even when information was presented to the contrary. According to the authors, these role stereotypes may be more implicit, thereby providing unconscious cues that affect individual perceptions. Although the students were informed that the individuals, whose career paths they were to deduce by observation alone, were not typical (e.g., man who knits) students continued to make deductions that were consistent with gender stereotypes. This suggests that individuals may not necessarily be aware of their biases and the ways in which they affect others. These unconscious processes likely affect the messages that are received, thereby influencing career and subject preferences.

As students arrive to college campuses from high schools, it would seem as if these conscious or unconscious stereotypes previously mentioned, have roots in students' prior educational experiences. The subliminal messages that are communicated to females by teachers and administrators may also influence their career choices (Ware & Lee, 1988; Sadker & Sadker, 1994; Barton, 2001). High school is an especially crucial time for females, as research suggests that one's engagement in high school math and science courses is correlated with one's intended field of study in college (Maple & Stage, 1991). In addition, Sadker and Sadker (1994) found that females were less likely to receive attention in the classroom. They also observed that males were more likely to yell out their responses, which effectively diverted the attention of the teacher and received no reprimand for such actions. When females called out their answers, the teachers were more apt, according to study findings, to correct the behavior. This phenomenon was also found to be prevalent in the homes, where parents were three times as likely to explain science-related material to boys in comparison to girls (Crowley et al., 2001).

In a world where students still perceive scientists to be White males in lab coats (Jones, Howe & Rua, 2000), it is difficult for those who deviate from this image to conceive of themselves as scientists or other occupations. Among those females who chose to engage in the sciences, a higher preponderance was found to major in biology as opposed to the physical sciences (Jones, Howe, & Rua, 2000). During the 1996–1997 school year, approximately 50 percent of the bachelor's degrees in biology were conferred to women, while only approximately 20 percent of engineering degrees were conferred (National Coalition for Women and Girls in Education, 2002). According to Jones, Howe, and Rua (2000), females may have been more averse to such sciences, as they were seen in conjunction with war and destruction, whereas biology was more concerned with the nurturance and study of life.

The educational climates for females who do choose to pursue science-related fields have also represented a barrier (Betz, 2006; National Coalition for Women and Girls in Education, 2008). Females who do decide to pursue their interests in the sciences, where they are grossly outnumbered, may encounter gender-based harassment (National Coalition for Women and Girls in Education, 2008). Research suggests that in primary and secondary schooling, girls are initially confident in their abilities to perform as well in the sciences, but they oftentimes experience ridicule by their male counterparts (Barton, 2001). The National Coalition for Women and Girls in Education (2008) cited a study by Margolis and Fisher (2002) in which their male peers in a computer science course constantly taunted females with no action taken by the teacher. The females were inevitably unwilling to participate in future computer science courses. This treatment, and lack of appropriate mentorship, may adversely affect their success in science-related programs and willingness to engage in discussions in science classrooms, and significantly affects their intention to pursue science-related fields in college (Ware & Lee, 1988; Post, Stewart, & Smith, 1994; Barton 2001).

Further complicating discussions associated with the experiences of girls in science-related courses, and their pursuit of careers in scientifically based fields, is the lack of attention given to the specific experiences of African American girls (Hanson, 2009). Extant literature has clearly shown that all girls face numerous challenges in the sciences. It is important that young African American children have examples of how science is valuable and that there is a normalization of embracing the practice of science as everyday schooling (Varelas, Kane, & Wylie, 2011). However, the intersection of race and gender for African American girls places their success, and expressed interest in science, in a scientific culture that is oftentimes hostile to anyone who is non-White and not male (Hanson, 2009).

Dating back to studies in the 1990s, the classroom experiences of female students, when delineated by race, have exposed the lack of attention, both in research and in the classroom, that African American female students have received in comparison to White female students (Sadker & Sadker, 1994). A disproportionate lack of attention, Barton (2001) contends, causes many African American female students to refuse to participate in science class as a way to communicate boredom to the teacher. Thus, these conscious acts of defiance as a method of communication may be misconstrued by some teachers as inability, thereby affecting their interactions, or lack thereof, with their female students.

Despite the differential treatment in the classroom, the gender gap between African Americans receiving bachelor's degrees in computer science was minimal in comparison to their White counterparts, with a higher preponderance of female African American students attaining bachelor's degrees in computer science at historically Black colleges and universities (Grauca, Ethington, & Pascarella, 1988; Lopez & Schultze, 2002).

Viable Solutions: The Role of Universities and K–12 Teachers

NATIONAL PROGRAMMATIC RESPONSES

Several programs have been initiated in an effort to address the disparities between males and females in the sciences (Thom, 2001). Summer bridge programs that seek to provide social and cultural capital experiences for furthering talented African American students in particular such as the Meyerhoff Summer Program embed orientation and summer enhancement programs that offer a sense of community alongside academic, social, and professional development opportunities for students (Stolle-McAllister, 2011). A majority of the programs attempt to address teacher awareness concerning their interactions with students in the classroom. One program,

Integrating Gender Equality and Reform (InGEAR), offered gender equity training for faculty on five university campuses in Georgia. A similar program in Ohio, known as Discovery, is comprised of programs, workshops, and summer institutes. These program objectives focused upon the need to be cognizant of the dynamics in the classroom as well as provide effective techniques to ensure equanimity in the classroom. While not specifically related to teachers, but more related to increasing girls' knowledge of how to do conduct research, Internet Mentoring as Girls' Imagination-Nurturing Engine (IMAGINE), hosted by Tulane University's Center for Research on Women, was developed to assist middle school and high school girls with basic Internet navigation and other similar tools.

LOCAL PROGRAMMATIC RESPONSES

Detroit Area Pre-College Engineering Program. Since 1976, the Detroit Area Pre-College Engineering Program (dapcep) has attempted to increase the number of African American, Latino, and Native American students in Detroit who are not only motivated to do well in science, technology, engineering, and math (STEM), but also prepared to pursue STEM-related jobs (Hill, 1990). At its inception, DAPCEP worked exclusively with students in the Detroit Public Schools. However, as the program developed and gained local and national recognition, summer programs and Saturday programs were developed that had participants from a broad cross-section of students from metro Detroit. Partnerships with corporations (Ford Motor Company, IBM, JP Morgan Chase), universities (Michigan State University, Wayne State University, University of Michigan–Ann Arbor), and nonprofit organizations (Tiger Woods Foundation, Black United Fund of Michigan, Detroit Youth Foundation), have contributed to the significant number of DAPCEP students who have enrolled in postsecondary education programs.

Currently, in partnership with the National Science Foundation, DAPCEP is developing a new program exclusively focused on girls—Promoting Underrepresented Girls Involvement in Research Science & Energy (PURSE). By targeting ninth-grade girls, the PURSE program hopes to spark girls' curiosity about science, engineering, and leadership in the renewable energy and energy efficiency industries. With a start date of fall 2011, PURSE requires all students to attend a residential course beginning summer 2011, as well as the active participation of parents.

POWER Organization

POWER Organization serves approximately 115 girls (60 percent of total participants) annually. 95 percent of the girls are African American. Their conferences, enrichment programs, and summer math camps introduce girls to professionals in a variety of careers, postsecondary students, and a diverse population of peers. Through these interactions, POWER has positively contributed to the way the girls view themselves academically and in social settings. The girls and their parents have noted improved confidence levels and academic progress. Additionally, female participants have noted that they are more comfortable trying math problems that they would have normally overlooked. Through partnerships with such organizations as Wayne County Community College Baker College, Pepsi Bottling Group, Edward Jones, and Comerica Bank, the female participants are becoming more assertive and engaging in meaningful dialogue about why, how, and when to use algorithms and math/science terminology.

Kettering University

Kettering University (Flint, MI) offers five programs designed to provide middle and high school students with access to STEM-related curriculum. Related to underrepresented students in STEM fields, three of the five programs specifically target girls (Discover U, Kamp Kettering, and Lives Improve through Engineering (LITE), while another focuses on African American, Hispanic, and Native American (Academically Interested Minds (AIM). Through a partnership with the Genesee Intermediate School District, Discover U is designed to support the STEM interest of girls in grades 10–12. This yearlong program allows students to utilize hands-on science activities as a way to increase their interest and knowledge of engineering, applied sciences, and applied mathematics. Selected by their teachers and counselors, the participants in this program are not only given opportunities to connect with STEM professionals, but also explore the necessary steps associated with college selection and admission. While Discover U focuses on high school girls, Kamp Kettering targets girls in grades 7 and 8. During this one-week summer enrichment program, the girls perform experiments related to chemistry, physics, and engineering and go on field trips to a variety of science and technology facilities. Last, Kettering University's Lives Improve through Engineering (LITE) is a two-week residential summer program designed for eleventh-grade girls. During this summer experience, the participants engage in critical inquiry whereby engineering principles are applied to the development of products that will improve the everyday lives of people. Be it the development of air bags or car seats for infants, participants will understand the science of solving real-world problems, but also realize that women can become successful engineers.

University of Michigan–Ann Arbor
Through the collaborative efforts of the Colleges of Engineering, Arts and Sciences, and the Office of the Vice President for Research and the Housing Division, the Women in Science and Engineering Program at the University of Michigan–Ann Arbor is designed to increase the number of girls and women interested in STEM careers. Their efforts have managed to focus on girls and women in both higher education and k–12. By reaching back and pulling young girls forward into STEM-related fields, the Women in Science and Program has managed to develop five summer programs.

- Girls in Science and Engineering provides seventh- and eighth-grade girls with an opportunity to explore the scientific field of study that they are interested in—chemistry, computer science, engineering, human genetics, physics, and robotics. Additionally, the students are given an opportunity to tour the various science labs on campus and interact with women who spend their professional time as engineers, physicians, and other STEM-related jobs.
- Engineering for Humanity and Serving Society (ENGAGE) is a nonresidential, one-week summer program that solicits the participation of tenth- and eleventh-grade girls. In this program cosponsored by the College of Engineering and the School of Natural Resources and Environmental Teaching and Inspiring Environmental Stewardship Program, students are encouraged to pursue careers in science and engineering.
- RobotC for Girls is a one-week summer program that provides girls with an opportunity to explore computer programming. Cosponsored by Google, RobotC for Girls allows girls to not only tour Google in Ann Arbor but also practice the art of programming. Through the support of University of Michigan faculty, the participants in this program will program Lego Mindstorm RobotC programming language.

Michigan State University

Sponsored by the College of Engineering, Women in Engineering (WIE) is a summer residential program set up for girls who will be entering tenth through twelfth grades. Through a partnership with DAPCEP, WIE goes to great lengths to ensure that girls of color have access to this program. By connecting the participants with women who are either engineering undergraduate students or engineering professionals, WIE engages participants in conversations related to diversity, issues affecting women in engineering, and international education opportunities.

Words from Female Science Teachers

PRIMARY CHALLENGES

African American girls in the science classrooms are very eager to learn more about many aspects of science. However, these desires are hindered in urban schools not due to the teachers or students, but due to a structural deficit. When considering the desires of the girls to learn science juxtaposed against the ability of the schools to meet this need in a twenty-first-century manner, urban schools lack the necessary technology.

> Urban schools don't have the funding for current technology, and African American girls miss out. While their counterparts in suburban schools have new computers, the latest calculators, and state-of-the-art science labs, my students have computer labs where most of the computers are outdated and not enough working ones for everyone to use without Internet connections. (Michelle)

Without access to modern technology, the "T" in STEM is lost. Thus, African American girls' interests become just a dream. When this dream is lost, the second challenge, student interest in science, decreases.

> I've never had a girl start my class and not tell me that their goal was to learn more about science. However, I have had girls who lose interest in the content when I can't provide the technology that can bring it to life. (Marsha)

Although technology is commonly associated with building a better connection between content and student interests, other factors need to be considered. Several of the teachers have spoken with a number of female students over the years and have become concerned with their emotional attachment to "drama" that can distract from their focus on academics.

> So many of my girls feel the pressure of trying to fit in. When that is the case, school ain't important. (Judy)
>
> I have found that many of my African American teenage girls are very focused on relationships with their peers and they do not think of long-term goals such as college or a career. This causes them to lose interest in science because they don't see how it will be used in the long term. (Jennifer)

Often times the "drama" associated with the students' experiences is related to boys. Perhaps the solution is single-gender schooling or at least attempting this in science classes.

> My girls oftentimes seem intimidated when they are in class. It's like they won't ask questions. I had one semester where the principal allowed me to divide my class by gender and the girls were more involved. I'm not sure that the semester was enough time to see drastic improvements in their grades, but they were definitely more involved. (Marsha)

SELF-IMAGE

What does a scientist look like? Who are scientists? These questions don't lead back to African American girls seeing themselves as scientists.

> One time I asked just the girls in my class if they saw themselves being involved in a science-related profession one day. None of them said yes. Some said it was because science was hard. Others said science and math was for Asian and White people. (Angela)
>
> I had my students draw a scientist and none of them drew images of themselves. (Ilena)

For White people? For Asian people? Where is that coming from? Perhaps one might consider that issue when framed by the motto of the Maryland chapter of 100 Black Men of America: "What they see is what they will become."

> Too many of my students have bought into the hype of Black folks [African Americans] being intellectually inferior to Whites and Asians. It's almost like they only see themselves working in the auto plant or doing manual labor. I'm not sure I can blame them because many of them are in families where that's all they know. (Benita)

Perhaps the much larger issue for African American girls is related to their overall self-esteem. A discussion of the self-esteem of African American girls in science classes seemed to evoke a lot of passion. Some teachers recognized the general idea that girls with high self-esteem in general would be more likely to see themselves as scientists. However, additional consideration must be given to their performance in other subject areas.

> If they experience many failures in several aspects of their schooling experience they are more likely to have a negative view of themselves. (Jennifer)

SOLUTIONS

Teachers play an integral role in the lives of their students. Noting previous literature that clearly indicates that girls' desire to participate in science-related fields is oftentimes mitigated by their teachers (Ware & Lee, 1988; Sadker & Sadker, 1994; Barton, 2001), we see that reframe the role of teachers is essential. Cheryl, a tenth-grade biology teacher, believes that teachers must not only encourage them to learn the content, but also think long term about their lives.

> Teachers can help these girls start thinking about life after high school and developing career goals. Also building their confidence by having these young women tutor other students. (Cheryl)

As previously mentioned, African American girls in one classroom were amazed to see African American female physicians. Part of this cause for alarm is related to images of African American women that they encounter on a daily basis. As such, when female teachers are involved in STEM-related courses, the burden is theirs. That burden is far more than reaching a particular score on a state exam or learning the latest facts associated with physics. That burden is being a role model.

> Female teachers are walking role models for girls. They are the link that many students have to the world outside of high school academics. They introduce girls to a wide variety of careers through seminars, take them camping, hiking, canoeing to give them a new experience and build a skill set. Besides the everyday teaching of content, teachers can help build confidence with these outside experiences by standing with them and saying, "Yes you can." (Nicole)

Aside from being a role model, science teachers in general need to allow these students to build upon their small successes. Too many times teachers celebrate the big successes and leave the small success stories on the sideline.

> We [teachers] need to spend more time allowing our students to feel celebrated for their small successes. So what if they only got a C. But if they had an F last time, then that's progress. Some of that behavior from teachers is because of all the damn emphasis on testing in the schools. (Jennifer)

The previously mentioned summer programs have affected numerous female students. They have impacted student interest in STEM-related professions and the way that the girls interact with other students in class.

> Several of my students went to a summer science camp for girls. They came back to school in the fall and were much more animated in class and asked more questions. It's almost like they saw themselves as competent in science. (Michelle)

Conclusion

As we aim to improve the experiences of African American girls in the sciences, we must keep in mind this is a process that will involve those in k–12 and higher education. While the programs that offer exposure to STEM-related careers are great, that is only half of the solution. As noted by the teachers, the experiences of these girls during the school day must also be reconfigured. Should we consider single-gender science classes? Should we consider internships? Regardless of the questions that we ask, or the solutions that we develop, the state of the African American female in STEM-related professions is uncertain. If we do nothing, then we should consider ourselves failures. Failures as educators. Failures as a society.

REFERENCES

Barton, A.C. (2001). Science education in urban settings: Seeking new ways of practice through critical ethnography. *Journal of Research in Science Teaching, 38*(8), 899–917.

Bergmann, L. (2008). *Getting ghost: Two young lives and the struggle for the soul of an American city.* New York: New Press.

Betz, N. (2006) Basic issues and concepts in the career development and counseling of women. In W. Walsh & M. Heppner (Eds.), *Handbook of career counseling for women* (pp. 45–74). Mahwah, NJ: Lawrence Erlbaum Associates.

Crowley, K., Callanan, M.A., Tenenbaum, H.R., & Allen, E. (2001). Parents explain more often to boys than to girls during shared scientific thinking. *Psychological Science, 12*, 258–261.

Excellent Schools Detroit (2010). *Where we stand: Community meeting survey results.* Retrieved from http://www.excellentschoolsdetroit.org.

Grauca, J.M., Ethington, C.A., & Pascarella, E.T. (1988). Intergenerational effects of college graduation on career sex atypicality in women. *Research in Higher Education, 29*(2), 99–124.

Hackett, G., Betz, N.E., Casas, J.M., & Rocha-Singh, I.A. (1992). Gender, ethnicity, and social cognitive factors predicting the academic achievement of students in engineering. *Journal of Counseling Psychology, 39*, 527–538.

Hanson, S.L. (2009). *Swimming against the tide: African American girls and science education.* Philadelphia, PA: Temple University Press.

Hill, K. (1990). The Detroit Area Pre-College Engineering Program. *Journal of Negro Education, 59*(3), 439–448.

Johnson, K. (2009, May). The facts on unionizing charters; school closures; and layoffs. *Detroit Teacher, 47*(8). Retrieved from http://mi.aft.org/dft231/index.cfm?action=cat&categoryID=ddc5f008–3872–4fe5-b490-ce9f1ffoda6a.

Jones, G., Howe, A., & Rua, M. (2000). Gender differences in students' experiences, interests, and attitudes towards science and scientists. *Science Education, 84,* 180–192.

Lopez, A., & Schultze, L. (2002) African American women in the computing sciences: A group to be studied. *SIGCSE Bulletin, 34*(1), 87–90.

Maple, S.A. & Stage, F.K. (1991). Influence on the choice of math/science major by gender and ethnicity. *American Educational Research Journal, 28*(1), 37–60.

Margolis, J., & Fisher, A. (2002). *Unlocking the clubhouse: Women in computing.* Cambridge, MA: MIT Press.

National Coalition for Women and Girls in Education (2002). *Title IX at 30: Report card on gender equity.* Retrieved from http://www.ncwge.org/pubs-reports.html.

National Coalition for Women and Girls in Education (2008). *Title IX at 35: Beyond the headlines.* Retrieved from http://www.ncwge.org/pubs-reports.html.

National Science Foundation (2003). *Women, minorities, and persons with disabilities in science and engineering: 2002.* NSF 03–312. Arlington, VA: Author.

Nauta, M.M., Epperson, D.L., & Kahn, J.H. (1998). A multiple-group analysis of higher level career aspirations among women in mathematics, science, and engineering majors. *Journal of Counseling Psychology, 45*(4), 483–496.

Nelson, T.E., Acke, M., & Manis, M. (1996). Irrepressible stereotypes. *Journal of Experimental Social Psychology, 32,* 13–38.

Osborne, J., Simon, S., & Collins, S. (2003). Attitudes towards science: A review of the literature and its implications. *International Journal of Science Education, 25,* 1049–1079.

Post, P., Stewart, M.A., & Smith, P.L. (1991). Self-efficacy, interest, and consideration of math and science and non-math and science occupations among Black freshmen. *Journal of Vocational Behavior, 38,* 178–186.

Riley, R. (2009, September 11). It's time to end the charter school fight. *Detroit Free Press,* Retrieved from http://www.freep.com/apps/pbcs.

dll/article?AID=/20090911/COL10/909110389/1319/It-s-time-to-end-charter-school-fight&template=fullarticle.

Sadker, M., & Sadker, D. (1994). *Failing at fairness: How our schools cheat girls.* New York: Touchstone.

Sharf, R.S. (2010). *Applying career development in theory to counseling* (5th ed.). Belmont, CA: Brooks/Cole.

Sizer, T., & Wood, G. (2008). Charter schools and the values of public education. In L. Dingerson, B. Miner, B. Peterson, & S. Walters (Eds.), *Keeping the promise: The debate over charter schools* (pp. 3–16). Milwaukee, WI: Rethinking Schools.

Skillman Foundation (2009). *2009 good schools guide.* Retrieved from http://www.skillman.org/publications-perspectives/.

Stolle-McAllister, K. (2011, October). The case for summer bridge: Building social and cultural capital for talented Black STEM students. *Science Educator,* 12–22.

Stover, D. (2006). Dealing with decline: For urban districts, dramatic drops in enrollment and resources leave nothing but difficult decisions ahead. *American School Board Journal, 193*(12), 42–44.

Thom, N. (2001). Young women's progress in science and technology studies: Overcoming remaining barriers. *NASSP Bulletin, 85*(628), 6–19.

Varelas, M., Kane, J.M., & Wylie, C.D. (2011, September). Young African American children's representations of self, science, and school: Making sense of difference. *Science Educator,* 824–851.

Ware, N.C. & Lee, V.E. (1988). Sex differences in choice of college science majors. *American Education Research Journal, 25*(4), 593–614.

The Experiences of Gifted African American Females

"DAMNED IF YOU ARE AND DAMNED IF YOU AREN'T"

Deborah A. Harmon *and* Donna Y. Ford

The first author was meeting with her graduate students in preparation for what was to be a highly successful and significant conference about the status of African American females when one of them made a comment that urged her to ask, "Aren't you attending the conference?" The student, an African American male, responded with, "Well, I guess I have to go because I am helping but . . . after all, it is about African American females. Why would I go—I'm a male?" I responded with, "Females attended the conference about the status of African American males. Why would males not attend this conference about African American females?" To which this intelligent young man responded, "That was different —African American men are in crisis."

At that moment, an uneasiness the first author had been feeling throughout the entire preparation of the conference revealed itself as she listened to her own graduate student devalue and diminish the importance and intent of this conference focusing on the challenges of African American females. What followed was a rigorous discussion about sexism and racism as well as the intersection of gender and race. The first author ended the minilecture determined to find out if and why such beliefs and attitudes were so pervasive among so many African American males, both students and colleagues. This chapter is the result of our collective efforts, which focus on the experiences of gifted African American females—who are the least addressed and very misunderstood when race and gender are combined.

Beginning with a literature review of African American females, it became very evident that the perceptions of African American females are biased and neglected. The research on African American females is very bleak. The majority of research in education journals paints a picture of anger, promiscuity, pregnancy, and single mothers in poverty. At best, with the exception of a few studies (e.g., Grantham & Ford, 1998; Hrabowski, Maton, & Greene, 2002; Kitano, 1998), the research on gifted African American females is almost non-existent and not comprehensive. In addition, the research on African American females, gifted or otherwise, has been minimized to real and grave issues related to African American males and White females (Ford, 1996, 2010; Kitano, 1998; Sadker & Sadker, 1994). To understand this phenomenon, this chapter begins with a discussion of the history and experiences of African American females in the United States. Next, research related to the experiences of African American females in school settings and professional settings is examined. This is followed by a discussion about the challenges of gifted African American females in schools and professional careers. The last part of the chapter provides recommendations for families and educators that support gifted African American females.

African American Female's History

Black women have always been more conscious of and more handicapped by race oppression than by sex oppression. They have been subjected to all the restrictions against Blacks and to those against women. At the same time, they have struggled in partnership with their men to keep the Black family together and to allow the Black community to survive. This dual and conflicting role has imposed great tensions on Black women and has given them unusual strength. (Lerner, 1992, p. 10)

The history of African American females differs from White and other women of color as a function of slavery. It involves more than 200 years of being denied the status of a woman. During this time, African Americans experienced the systemic absence of protection of African American males, forcing them to function in ways that were virtually indistinguishable from their male slave counterparts as gender differences between them and African American males were minimized (Davis, 1972). For the sake of their children and families, they had to play dual roles—as mothers and surrogate fathers.

African American females are and were socialized differently from African American males, even though they shared a similar history and experience of oppression. African American females were the nurturers and protectors of life, taking care of their own children as well as others (e.g., serving as nannies). As captives, if they were not working in the field or kitchen, they cared for the children and family of their owner/oppressor. It was these women, whose own children were often sold off, who developed a "fictive kinship ideology" (Richardson, 2002, p. 682), creating a collective family and community, a practice that continues to this day.

Equally noteworthy, throughout history, African American females had no choice but to find ways to protect themselves and their families, often using the knowledge of their subservient place and menial role. African American females survived because they were, by necessity, extremely hardworking; they developed perseverance, assertiveness, and self-reliance. Essentially, they continue to epitomize resilience. According to Richardson (2002):

> Historically, the Black woman has been socialized to be the backbone of African American culture. During enslavement, loved ones could be sold away and even oneself placed into new and dangerous situations at the discretion of the enslavers in the blink of an eye. Thus, the Black woman had to devise ways to live with herself, inside of her own mind. Paradoxically, from a White supremacist patriarchal perspective, she did not feel it, and even if she did, she could handle it. On the other hand, "maid" to serve as Mammy in slavery, she was socialized to be the backbone of the dominant culture. As such, the autonomous and independent Black woman is often distorted as Superwoman, someone who can be there to comfort everyone else, with no time or need to be comforted. (pp. 684–685)

African American women have always had to work to survive a reality that conflicts with White romantic ideas about women, femininity, and motherhood; with the colorblind and ill-informed often viewing African American women as "unladylike, unfit, and immoral" (Richardson, 2002, p. 683). When compared to the characteristics and behaviors of White females, African American women were cast as the antithesis of White women, especially regarding notions of femininity (Fordham, 1993). Due to the incongruence of White women's definition and image, many African American women (and other women of color) seek, unsuccessfully, to become the accepted female image in body, language, behavior, and parenting style (e.g., Davis, 1972). In essence, African American females were doubly victimized by being African American and by being female (Richardson, 2002).

Colorism

The problem of the twentieth century is the problem of the color line, the question as to how far differences of race, which show themselves chiefly in the color of the skin and the texture of the hair, are going to be made hereafter, the basis for denying to over half the world the right of sharing to their utmost ability the opportunities and privileges of modern civilization. (W.E.B. DuBois, July 1900, Pan-African Conference in London)

Over a hundred years ago, W.E.B. DuBois (1900) predicted that racial differences—most notably in skin color and hair texture—would continue to be a major basis for controlling and denying the rights and privileges of African American citizens in the United States. Colorism, (mis)belief of superiority of Whites over Blacks, and light-skinned over dark-skinned people, is a complex, multilayered, and naive process (Russell, Wilson, & Hall, 1992). "Institutionalized norms and patterns use skin color to disadvantage African Americans and Mexican Americans relative to whites; these same norms and patterns also privilege lighter skin among African Americans and Mexican Americans" (Hunter, Allen, & Telles, 2001, p. 181). Colorism and racism provided another means for (mis)dividing American society into the "haves" and "have nots" (Farley & Allen, 1989; Hochschild, 1995; Massey, 2004), with African Americans often being at the bottom of the socioeconomic ladder.

Skin color hierarchies are culturally and historically related. Colorism (how skin color is addressed within the Black community) began during slavery with the practice of White slave owners giving their illegitimate lighter-skinned offspring greater and less cumbersome opportunities than the darker-skinned slaves. These opportunities included the privileged status of house servants or becoming skilled artisans. Some were given their freedom, educated, and even participated in government. Many became leaders in free Black communities (Freeman et al., 1966).

Light-skinned African Americans became a buffer between the White and African American communities. They were also in a position to advocate for their community. After emancipation, light-skinned African Americans continued in positions of dominance with many settling into the middle and upper socioeconomic levels of the African American community (Hughes & Hertel, 1990; Williamson, 1980). The continuation of this practice concerning access to education and jobs reinforced the association of higher status with light-skinned African Americans. Within the African American community, "brown bag societies" evolved with exclusive membership limited to those whose skin was lighter than a brown paper bag (Ransford, 1970; Russell, Wilson, & Hall, 1992).

Hunter, Allen, and Telles's (2001) study on colorism found that skin color continues to be a determinant of education and socioeconomic status among African Americans, in essence determining their perceived and real possibilities. Dark skin is associated with low intellect and low education levels with the reverse being perceived for light skin (Collins, 1991; King, 1988; Russell, Wilson, & Hall, 1992). Per Hunter, Allen, and Telles (2001), "This is especially so for Blacks and for women—presumably producing an amplified compounded, multiplicative effect for Black women" (p. 181).

Stereotypes

African America females have had to construct a new definition for themselves, attempting to do so without the stigma, trials, and tribulations associated with being an African American *and* a female. Young African American females struggle to invent and reinvent themselves against the distorted and negative societal images imposed on and eventually internalized by them. Richardson (2002) discussed how "twisted images of Black womanhood have always been a pivotal element of the American economy" (p. 676). During slavery, the "mammy" figure tended to the every need of White families. Even in 2012, the First Lady Michelle Obama—also a lawyer and scholar—was depicted as such abroad on the cover page of an Italian magazine.[1] African American slave women are and have been cast as "wenches":

heartless, angry, and sexually immoral or as Jezebels: subhuman, ignorant, and incapable of love, only good for working and serving the sexual pleasure of their master. These stereotypes continue in many television shows, music videos, newspapers, magazines, and movies (Collins, 1991; hooks, 2003).

We are often dependent upon the media to inform us about the world we live in. They serve as one of the primary sources for the dissemination and reinforcement of images of African American femininity. African American females are influenced by negative stereotypes at an early age. Hip-hop music, rap music, and music videos have all served to reproduce dominant and distorted images of African America women's sexuality (Jewell, 1993). Collins (1991) stated:

> Portraying African American women as stereotypical mammies, matriarchs, welfare recipients, and hot mommas has been essential to the political economy of domination fostering Black women's oppression . . . as part of a generalized ideology of domination, these controlling images of Black womanhood take on special meaning because the authority to define these symbols is a major instrument of power . . . these controlling images are designed to make racism, sexism and poverty appear to be natural, normal, and an inevitable part of everyday life. (pp. 67–68)

SELF-ESTEEM

African American females' social, emotional, and psychological experiences differ greatly from White females and other female groups. They often assume adult responsibilities, such as caring for younger siblings and attending to household duties, at an early age. As a result, they often internalize and exude high self-confidence, self-efficacy, independence, internal strength, and resilience (Richardson, 2002). To wit and out of necessity, African American females are socialized to have both masculine and feminine sex role characteristics, displaying self-confidence, assertiveness, expressiveness, and nurturance (Harris, 1996). What this means is that African American females do not fit and may never fit the White female image of the dominant culture as passive, helpless, fragile, docile, and compliant.

Surprising to some readers, African American girls have higher self-esteem, healthier body image, and greater social assertiveness than their White counterparts do as adolescents (Akan & Grilo, 1995; Dukes & Martinez, 1994; Grantham & Ford,

1998). In one study comparing the responses of White females and African American females when asked if they thought they were attractive, 40 percent of the African American girls considered themselves attractive, compared to only 9 percent of White girls (Hrabowski, Maton, & Greene, 2002). Eating disorders, which are related to issues of self-esteem, occur less frequently in African American females than White females. In fact, 90 percent of eating disorders occur among White females. According to Carroll (1997), who studied adolescent African American girls between the ages of 12 and 20 in 12 cities, anorexia and bulimia are diseases that are a result of violent social demands that can never be met, but they often are a White issue. She suggested that

> Pondering the concept and living the reality of low self-esteem is a luxury of self-involvement that Black girls cannot afford. ... White girls have more options by way of their inherent and racially superior resources. In other words, young Black girls have neither the time nor the opportunity to concern themselves with the contemplation of self-esteem. ... However if it is not eating disorders, it is hair. Black girls, older black women alike battle with hair in a similar way that young White girls, and older white women battle with weight. Still, it is because of the white image of beauty that is constantly shoved in our faces by the media, which, like it or not, however questionable, delineates the American dream. (Carroll, 1997, pp. 141–142)

School Experiences of African American Females

Much of research that exists about the education of African American females has been guided by comparing them with White females or, on a smaller scale, comparing them to African American males. The intersection of race *and* gender shapes African American females' experiences in a multitude of ways. This experience cannot be understood by simply looking at race and gender independently.

The school environment is a major factor in the academic performance and success of African American girls. The most influential factors within the classroom for African American females are the attitudes and expectations of teachers, administrators, and staff (Ford, 1996, 2010; Harmon, 2002; Hrabowski et al., 2002; Irvine, 1996). Early research on African American girls in lower elementary grades (kindergarten to third grade) found that they are more likely to be ignored by their teachers or interact with their teachers in limited, brief, and task-related contacts (Byalick & Bersoff, 1974; Damico & Scott, 1985; Grant, 1986, 1994). They are also more likely to be asked by teachers to help other classmates with nonacademic, social, and caregiving tasks and roles with their classmates for their teachers. These roles emphasize social and maternalistic rather than academic skills. Further, compared to other culturally different female students, African American girls are more likely to fight or retaliate when confronted verbally or physically.

In upper elementary (third through sixth grades), African American girls continue to receive less positive feedback and fewer responses and opportunities from their teachers than White females (Irvine, 1986). With less and less feedback and interaction with their teachers, African American girls become socialized to expect less from their teachers (e.g., Ford, 2010; Grant, 1986; Irvine, 1986).

In the middle school grades (sixth to eighth or ninth), the earlier trend of benign negligence on behalf of teachers persists. African American females become more "invisible" and less "feminine." They are more likely to work alone as well as be left out of the network of friends (Irvine, 1986). Many feel socially isolated and excluded. In schools that are predominantly White, such as in gifted education and Advanced Placement (AP) classes, their feelings of loneliness and isolation are pronounced (Ford, 2010; Grant, 1986).

School Experiences of Gifted African American Females

African American females generally perform better in school than African American males. They have higher grade point averages, they are identified by teachers as better students, they believe that schooling is the primary means for achieving upward mobility, and they tend to have high self-esteem (Ford, 1996; 2010; Ford, Grantham, & Whiting, 2008; Fordham, 1988; Phinney, Cantu, & Kurtz, 1997; Weiler, 2000). Yet gifted African American females are at a greater risk of underachieving and dropping out of school than gifted White females and gifted African American males (Ford, 1996, 2010).

Ford (1995, 1996, 2010) identified factors that led to underachievement in elementary and middle school by gifted African American females. She reported that they felt that good or high grades led to accusations of "acting White." In fact,

Ford found that over half of African American females were teased by their peers for achieving at high levels, and one-third were accused of "acting White"—speaking Standard English, making high grades, taking AP courses. Most of the students felt their teachers did not understand them. In order to gain acceptance by their peers, they chose to underachieve. To avoid culturally insensitive and assaultive teachers, they withdrew (physically, psychologically, and emotionally) from AP courses and enrolled in lower-level courses where more African American students were enrolled. They also reported that African Americans have to work harder in school than Whites to succeed.

Grantham and Ford (1998) investigated the experiences of gifted African American females and wrote about Danisha, who epitomized their trials and tribulations. Danisha felt isolated, even though there were a few African Americans in her AP classes. In class, she felt the pressure of dispelling the negative stereotypes about African Americans being academically incompetent. She also felt pressure to be the spokesperson for her African American peers. Danisha knew she had to follow the dominant culture's social norms and use Standard English, for instance, to communicate and interact with her White peers and teachers if she wanted high grades. Danisha also had to manage friendships with her White and African American peers, limiting interactions with her White friends for fear of losing her African American friends. She worked hard to be comfortable in the gifted courses and to continue to interact with her African American peers—straddling both cultures by gender and race.

Gifted African American females, like Danisha, face superhuman expectations. They have the challenge of integrating multiple affiliations and identities—African American, female, and gifted.

Gifted African American students who see achievement as a domain of the dominant culture may believe they are denying and rejecting their race as they commit to high achievement (Fordham, 1988). These pressures can lead to high achievement but also frustration, causing students to reject school values and seek affirmation of their peer group that has adopted antischool values (e.g., Sellers et al. 1998).

For gifted African American females to deal with the unique challenges of being gifted, they must have positive self-esteem, self-concept, *and* both racial identity and gender identity. Self-esteem is critical for high-achieving African American girls (e.g., Grantham & Ford, 1998). Before entering adolescence, African

American girls usually feel self-confident and efficacious. During adolescence, girls in general tend to have few positive feelings; however, African American girls who identify strongly with their ethnicity tended to have higher self-esteem and more positive academic, physical, and social self-concepts (Ford, 2010; Ford, Grantham, & Whiting, 2008). Because of the many barriers they face, gifted African American girls have more difficulty than gifted White girls developing social and racial identity. One reason is the isolation gifted African American girls feel negotiating school and home, coupled with the isolation they experience in gifted classes, where they are often one of a few culturally different students (Ford, 2010; Grantham & Ford, 1998).

The underrepresentation of African American gifted students continues and is pervasive in gifted programs today; it is often attributed to problems associated with the testing and identification of gifted students. Although this is a major barrier to serving African Americans in gifted programs, an even greater and ignored barrier is the retention of these students in gifted programs.

Ford (1992, 2010) interviewed African American gifted students who had withdrawn or declined acceptance into gifted education programs in their schools. Among the greatest concerns associated with participating in the gifted programs for feelings of isolation from their peers, rejection from peers, pressure to assimilate, and the lack of a multicultural curriculum. Harmon (2002) interviewed African American gifted students who participated in gifted programs in elementary school but chose not to continue in middle school. When students were asked why they did not want to continue in gifted programming, they stated that teachers would not teach them or did not know how to teach them. Students shared that teachers in gifted programs did not respect their culture or believe in their ability to learn as demonstrated by low teacher expectations and the lack of a multicultural curriculum. They also believed that teachers in gifted programs could not teach to their learning style preferences. Their primary concern was that they were tired of being forced to live within two worlds—being gifted *and* being African American (Harmon, 2002). Add to these two worlds the problems associated with gender.

Experiences of Gifted African American Females in College and Graduate School: The Cycle Continues

The aforementioned problems do not end with PK–12 schooling. Fleming (1984) studied African American students attending predominantly White institutions (PWIs) and historically Black colleges and universities (HBCUs) and found differences in students' social and academic adjustment. Female students attending HBCUs were more self-reliant, while males experienced more social control (Poindexter-Cameron & Robinson, 1997). A more familiar and affirming campus environment, professors that are cultural competent, programs that better meet the needs of students, and mentoring programs with African American faculty and staff are factors that contribute to students' successful adjustment. Not having these supports and resources has the opposite outcomes.

African American students who attend PWIs have to negotiate two worlds, one related to their ethnicity, self-identity, and others, and the second world, which requires adjusting to and negotiating the values and demands of the White school environment (Fleming, 1984; Ford et al., 2008). Students who have not attended predominantly White PK–12 schools experience cultural shock. While most PWIs have programs that recruit students of color and provide academic support and even mentoring programs, very few of them address the challenges African American students face attending a PWI. Even fewer focus on the unique issues that African American female students experience.

Patterson-Stewart, Ritchie, and Sanders (1997) looked at the experiences of African American doctoral students. Similar to the experiences of gifted African American students in predominantly White PK–12 schools, graduate students discussed how they did not receive the kind of support White students received, including opportunities to participate in research and publications. African American females pursing doctoral study expressed disappointment that they were not given the same kind of attention and support that their African American male peers received. The African American males were provided with mentoring programs, study groups, and opportunities to participate in research projects. When the African American female students asked if they could participate in the same programs, they were told that they did not need those programs like their African American male counterparts; instead, they were directed to a women's graduate program.

Research on the experiences of African American women in graduate school reveals that they face significant challenges, with race overshadowing all other issues, including gender. The groundbreaking work of Tinto (1975) and Sedlacek (1987) also sheds much light on barriers to recruitment and retentions at PWIs.

To complicate matters further, research on gifted African American women who go to college indicates that they have many concerns regarding relationships with family, mates, and friends. The family and community play a critical role in the success of gifted African American females—both help these women determine their culture, what it means to be African American, and what it means to be female. It is through the supportive family that one makes sense of the world. Gifted African American females often experience fear of success from being hard-pressed to find a mate who is comfortable with and supportive of their intellect, achievement, and ambition. Maintaining contact with friends in their community is necessary to remain connected to the community (Schwartz et al., 2003) and not be perceived as acting White. Loss of friendships and rejection by family members are not uncommon.

African American gifted women pay an inordinate price for success. In order to be taken seriously and to achieve success, they must learn the cultural accoutrements of dominant culture, maintain their racial identity, and become bicultural (Pagano, 1990). Survival and resilience are dependent on the ability to live with conflict, confusion, estrangement, and isolation.

Challenges of Gifted African American Females

Ford's (1996) research on underachieving gifted African American students identified factors within the school as well as individual psychological factors that affect underachievement in gifted African American female students. Factors within the school include (1) inappropriate identification practice; (2) lack of racial diversity among students and teachers; (3) feeling alienated from classmates; (4) fear of "acting White"; (5) low teacher expectations; (6) mismatches between African American students' learning styles and teaching styles; and (7) lack of a multicultural curriculum.

Identification process

The identification of gifted students in most public schools begins with a teacher referral that includes grades, intelligence and/or achievement test scores, and a checklist. Teachers tend to rely on stereotypes about gifted students and select students with high grade point averages and test scores. Psychologists and other special education support staff administer a battery of tests, including a traditional IQ test. The results determine whether or not students qualify for gifted programming—selecting those students with high achievement and/or intelligence test scores (Harmon, 2008).

Low and negative teacher expectations

Harmon (2002) interviewed African American and Latino gifted students who participated in gifted programs in elementary school and chose not to continue in middle school. When students were asked why they did not want to continue in gifted programming, they stated that teachers would not teach them or did not know how to teach them. Students shared that teachers in gifted programs did not respect their culture or believe in their ability to learn as demonstrated by low teacher expectations.

Teachers who are not knowledgeable of cultural differences and the behaviors of gifted students will not recognize culturally different (CD) gifted behaviors. Frasier, Garcia, and Passow's (1995) informative study of barriers that prevented the identification of CD and economically disadvantaged students found race to be a significant factor impacting the expectations of teachers. Teachers who do not clearly understand the impact of environmental influences and cultural differences on gifted behavior may develop negative attitudes and low expectations for minorities and will overlook children of color (Frasier, Garcia, & Passow, 1995; Wood & Achey, 1990). Brophy (1985) observed the responses of White teachers to minority children in their classrooms and found that negative teacher beliefs or low expectations about students influence classroom practices and may adversely affect CD students.

Behavioral checklists of gifted students

As part of the assessment process, teachers and families are asked to complete a checklist of behaviors that are common in gifted students. Characteristics that can commonly be found on checklists include a keen memory, exceptional command of language, advanced vocabulary, unique expression of ideas, inquisitiveness, creative problem-solving, keen perception of patterns and relationships, strong sense of fairness, self- motivation, self-confidence, and the ability to empathize. While these characteristics may speak to the abilities and behaviors of gifted students, they are presented within the context of dominant culture (Frasier & Passow, 1994).

Behavioral characteristics of gifted students can vary depending upon the environment and culture due to the combination of individual factors, cultural factors, and economic status (Ford, 1995, 2010). Ford (1995) found many African American students with high achievement scores (e.g., 95th to 99th percentile) underrepresented in gifted education because teachers did not refer them for screening. When teacher referral is the first recruitment step and most teachers are ill informed about giftedness in culturally different students, these students are likely to be underrepresented.

While gifted African American students do share the same strengths as European American gifted students in general, they may not share certain unique characteristics of giftedness (Sternberg, 2007). Some of these characteristics of culturally different gifted students include the ability to see things that others may not, read and interpret the emotional cues and nonverbal behaviors of others, to notice discrepancies, and to confront rather than accept inequities. Gifted African American students may possess an exceptional ability for using expressive and colorful language, elaboration, and imagery to communicate feelings and emotions or affect. Many gifted African Americans feel the need for positive social relationships and are sensitive to negative feedback and rejection. They are usually very innovative and like to improvise, preferring to interact with the environment. These behaviors are usually not included in gifted behavior inventories, checklists, and nomination forms, or viewed by teachers as signs of giftedness (Passow & Frasier, 1996).

Standardized tests

Psychologists, counselors, speech therapists, and special education educators are often involved in making decisions about the placement of students in gifted programs. Lack of knowledge and training among educators and decision makers about culture and gifted students makes it unlikely that these students will be recruited and retained in gifted programs. The reliance on standardized test scores keeps the demographics of gifted programs predominantly White and middle class, as traditional intelligence tests and achievement tests effectively identify and assess European American students. Ninety percent or more of the school districts in the United States use test scores for placement decisions (Davis & Rimm, 2004). Even though they are less effective with culturally different students, they continue to be used.

While most achievement tests are administered by a special education teacher or counselors, individual intelligence tests are administered by psychologists. There is an assumption that psychologists are knowledgeable about gifted and culturally different populations. The reality is that the behavioral characteristics and the socio-emotional needs of gifted students are not necessarily part of the training of school psychologists. If psychologists are not familiar with giftedness, they may not know how to interpret the responses and behaviors of gifted students—especially culturally different students. In essence, one barrier is testing; another is referral and subjective judgments grounded with little if any training in gifted education and cultural differences.

Lack of Cultural Differences

The overwhelming presence of European American students and teachers can cause African American students to withdraw. Due to most teachers' lack of awareness and understanding about the challenges and concerns of culturally different males and females, confiding with teachers and counselors or other school personnel is not seen as an option. In the absence of a culturally different staff, students feel there is little or no support for them. Many culturally different students are unwilling to remain in gifted education programs because of the high levels of stress and anxiety they experience as a result of being the only or one of a few in a predominantly White classroom, as earlier noted.

ISOLATION AND ALIENATION

Gifted education programs often do not consider the cultural values, social experiences, and learning styles of culturally different females. Classrooms that are not designed for students become hostile learning environments. These students often experience feelings of discrimination and isolation as a result of being the only or one of a few culturally different students in the program. Ford (1995) interviewed African American gifted students who had withdrawn or declined acceptance into gifted education programs in their schools. Among the greatest concerns associated with participating in the gifted programs were feelings of isolation in these programs.

ACTING WHITE AND ANTIACHIEVEMENT ETHIC

Ford and Harris (1992) reported that gifted elementary students felt embarrassment, guilty, and confused about their academic success and how it affected their peer relationships. Culturally different students who do not hold positive racial identities may be especially vulnerable to negative peer pressures. Rejection from their peers make students with poor racial identities engage in " cultural inversion" or an oppositional social identity, viewing the behaviors of the dominant group as inappropriate for members of their own ethnic group, ultimately commonly called, "acting White" (Cartledge & Milburn, 1998; Ford, Grantham, & Whiting, 2008; Fordham & Ogbu, 1986; Fordham, 1988).

Patton and Townsend (1997) observed the development of an antiachievement ethic in many African American gifted students. The antiachievement ethic is described as

> an oppositional social identity and cultural frame of reference which, consciously and unconsciously, causes them to associate certain achievement orientations, attitudes, motivations, and behaviors (e.g., speaking standard English, getting good grades, working hard in school, and generally striving for academic excellence) as betraying African American culture and acting white. (p. 14)

African American females may develop a racelessness persona that allows them to negotiate between their perception of their own culture and their belief in the antiachievement ethic. These issues arise during the development of racial identity and in the struggle of attempting to straddle both the dominant culture and their own culture.

RACIAL IDENTITY

Racial socialization prepares children to cope with prejudice and racism through the development a positive racial identity. It is the process of raising children to be physically and emotionally healthy in an environment that is oppressive; the process occurs through both implicit and explicit teaching (Stevenson, 1995; Greene, 1992). According to Ford (1996), "An often ignored but critically important variable related to self-concept among Black students is racial identity. Racial identity development plays an important role in their psychological adjustment, academic motivation, and achievement" (p. 102). Ford, Harris, and Schuerger (1993) and Fordham (1988) state that culturally different males and females with poor racial identities are vulnerable to negative pressures and falling prey to fearing being perceived as "acting White" or "selling out."

Cross and Vandiver (2001) developed a model for the development of racial identity and African Americans. Racial identity development is the process of coming to terms with one's own racial group membership. *Pre-encounter* is where individuals view the world from the perspective of dominant White society and culture. During pre-encounter, African Americans hold one of three identities: assimilation, miseducation, or self-hatred. Assimilation identity refers to those who demonstrate low racial salience but a strong reference group orientation focused on being an "American." According to Cross (1995), it is difficult for Black people to experience the U.S. education system without being exposed to historical distortions about Africa and the African American experience. When Black females believe these distortions, they internalize negative stereotypes resulting in questioning their own self-worth, dignity, and pride as a Black person. This process is referred to as a miseducation. Self-hatred identity is manifested by Black self-hatred or extreme negative views about Black people and occurs as a result of extreme miseducation. During pre-encounter, African American females experience painful encounters from their White peers or White teachers, culminating in an awareness of their minority status and ethnic group within society (Cross, 1995). Encounters with racism affect the process of racial identity and development, influenicing new beliefs about race and identity.

Immersion-Emersion is a very dynamic phase where African American females struggle to rid themselves of their former identity and cling to their newfound identity. According to Cross and Vandiver (2001), an array of emotions are experienced, from rage to euphoria. During this phase, an individual develops identities related to the world and society: intense Black involvement or anti-White. Intense Black involvement is characterized by embracing everything Black as African American females strive to find their place in society. There is a need to learn as much as possible about African American history and culture. While this process leads to a sense of African American pride and understanding, it also involves other emotions such as rage and anxiety about White society and those African Americans that identify with White culture (Cross & Vandiver, 2001).

The anti-White identity tends to denigrate White people and the dominant culture. Individuals do not want to associate with any activities, values, or behaviors that are associated with White culture (Cross, 1995). An antiachievement ethic may unfold as there is an emphasis placed on the social self-concept more than the academic self-concept. The antiachievement ethic is the belief that certain achievement orientations, attitudes, motivations, and behaviors are associate with being "White" (Cross, 1995), a concept previously discussed.

Emersion occurs when African American female's identity is salient and a more pluralistic attitude emerges. African American females are more in control of their emotions and are able to reexamine their experiences and racial identity, abandoning both the intense Black and anti-White identities. It also signals a movement out of this stage into *internalization.*

Internalization occurs when African American females are finally at peace with who they are racially and become more pluralistic and nonracist in their thinking. During this phase, individuals experience a sense of belonging and regard themselves positively. There are three identities in this stage: Black nationalist, biculturalist, and multiculturalist. The Black nationalist engages in social and political activism within the African American community. Biculturalist females are comprised of two cultural identities—African American and American. The multiculturalist identifies with three or more cultural frames of reference, such as African American, female, and American. This final identity is a very proactive one (Cross & Vandiver, 2001). Cross suggested that an individual moves across a continuum during the process of developing a racial identity. Movement may proceed in either direction or even become arrested at any time.

Research on the impact of racial identity suggests that it leads to higher self-esteem, less stress, and less delinquency (Ford, 2010; Phinney & Kohatsu, 1997; McCreary, Slavin, & Berry, 1996; Spencer, Cunningham, & Swanson, 1995).

Racial identity is composed of three aspects: in-group identification, awareness of negative out-group perceptions, and the perception of academic achievement as part of one's racial identity (Oyserman, Harrison, & Bybee, 2001). Positive in-group identification refers to the healthy sense of connection with other African American males and females and focuses attention on compliance with productive group values and norms. Awareness of racism involves being conscious that others see you as a member of a negatively valued racial group. This realization protects self-esteem by providing counterexplanations for negative responses and low expectations. Viewing academic achievement as an in-group value helps reduce tensions between achievement and racial group membership and identity among African American females.

LACK OF A MULTICULTURAL CURRICULUM

Harmon (2002) interviewed African American gifted students who participated in gifted programs in elementary school and chose not to continue in middle school. When students were asked why they did not want to continue in gifted programming, they stated that one of the main reasons was the lack of a multicultural curriculum and that teachers would not teach them or did not know how to teach them. They believed that teachers in gifted programs could not teach to their learning style preferences, interests, and experiences (Ford & Harris, 1999).

Where Do We Go from Here: Supporting Gifted African American Females

Over 80 percent of the teachers in public schools are European Americans. Almost 50 percent of the public school population is composed of culturally different students. Teachers, in general, are not knowledgeable about cultural differences because they often live in communities that are not very diverse and do not have significant experiences in their teacher preparation with cultural diversity (Ford & Harris, 1999; Banks, 2008). Teacher education institutions provide most students with a monocultural or Eurocentric curriculum that does not prepare them to work with culturally, ethnically, and linguistically different students. What many European American teachers know about culturally different populations comes from the media that portray many of these populations through a negative lens.

Subsequently, they misunderstand cultural differences among culturally different students relative to learning, communication, and behavioral styles (Ford, Grantham, & Whiting, 2008).

Ford and Grantham (2003) found that teachers' reactions to students' racial backgrounds could influence their perceptions about definitions, policies, and practices. In addition, there is a tendency for teachers to adopt a deficit perspective about culturally different students, focusing on what students cannot do rather than what students can do (Ford, Baytops, & Harmon, 1997). Ford found that it was difficult for teachers to see positives and strengths in students who speak nonstandard English, who are poor achievers, show behavior problems, have learning disabilities, or who are different from them.

In order for teachers to identify gifted African American females, they need to understand giftedness, African American gifted students, and then specifically the needs of female African American gifted students. Knowledge about gifted students and their social-emotional and academic needs is not taught in traditional teacher preparation programs. Teacher education programs discuss giftedness within the context of a general special education course. The characteristics of gifted students, culturally different gifted students, linguistically different gifted students, economically different gifted students, and twice exceptional students (students who are gifted and have a disability) are not a part, significantly or otherwise, of the course curriculum.

CULTURAL COMPETENCY

Teachers who are not knowledgeable about cultural diversity and the behaviors of gifted students will not recognize culturally different gifted behaviors (Ford, Baytops, & Harmon, 1997; Sternberg, 2007). Frasier and Passow's (1994) study of barriers that prevented the identification of culturally different and economically disadvantaged students found race and ethnicity to be significant factors hindering or contaminating the expectations of teachers. Teachers who do not clearly understand the impact of economic, social, and environmental influences and different cultures on gifted behavior may develop negative attitudes and low expectations—and likely overlook children of color (Ford, Grantham, & Whiting, 2008; Frasier, Garcia, & Passow, 1995; Wood & Achey, 1990). According to Ford (e.g., 1996, 2010), an abundance of research and scholarly literature exists documenting the history of African Americans being rated as intellectually inferior to Whites in this country.

In order for teachers to provide a rigorous multicultural curriculum, they must become culturally competent and develop multicultural lessons and activities using culturally congruent instruction, content, and materials (Ford, 2011; Ford & Harris, 1999; Gay, 2002). Cultural competence allows educators to view the world through multicultural lens. The process of becoming culturally competent involves developing a cultural understanding of oneself and those who are different, and using that knowledge in teaching students (Harmon, 2002).

Educators who are culturally competent are better able to identify strengths rather than (perceived or preconceived) weaknesses in culturally different students. They understand that gifted behaviors can be manifested in unique and culturally specific ways. Cultural competency increases the ability of the teachers, psychologists, and counselors to recognize gifted behaviors.

Characteristics commonly found among gifted students include a keen memory, exceptional command of language, advanced vocabulary, expression of ideas, inquisitiveness, critical problem solving, keen perception of patterns and relationships, a strong sense of fairness, self-motivation, self-confidence, and the ability to empathize with others (Frasier, Garcia, & Passow, 1995). The behavioral characteristics of gifted students can vary depending upon their environment and culture. Leung (1981) argues that gifted behaviors present in culturally different students due to the combination of individual and cultural behaviors. Gifted African American females share the same strengths as European American gifted females in general. In addition to this, gifted females from different cultures share certain unique characteristics of giftedness (Ford, 1996; Frasier, Garcia, & Passow, 1995).

Some of the characteristics of gifted African American males and females include the ability to see things that others may not, read and interpret emotional cues and nonverbal behaviors of others, notice discrepancies quickly, and confront or challenge rather than accept inequities. Gifted African American females may possess an unusual ability to express feelings and emotions using expressive and colorful language, elaboration, and imagery (Boykin, 1986; Delpit, 1996; Ford, 1996, 2010). Many gifted African American females desire positive social relationships and are sensitive to negative feedback and rejection. They are usually very innovative and like to improvise and to interact with the environment (i.e., they are tactile and kinesthetic learners) (Boykin et al., 2004; Ford, 1996, 2010, 2011; Ford & Harris, 1999).

Multicultural Gifted Education

One of the most prominent barriers in retaining culturally different students in gifted programs is the curriculum. Harmon, Ford, and Grantham all found that the absence of a multicultural curriculum has proven to be an inhibitor to learning and a major barrier to culturally different students participating and succeeding in gifted programs. A monocultural curriculum lessens the possibility of reaching and engaging culturally different students. Lack of relevance decreases students' motivation and interest in school. Monocultural curriculum is less likely to engage culturally different students (Ford, Moore, & Harmon, 2005).

Ford (1992) interviewed gifted African American students who chose not to participate in gifted education programs. The concern most frequently reported about gifted education programs was the lack of an inclusive curriculum. A multicultural curriculum, according to Ford and Harris (1999) is needed to affirm individual differences and provide the inclusiveness that most gifted curricula do not provide. It is a curriculum built upon the philosophy that all people must be affirmed and given respect regardless of age, race, ethnicity, gender, socioeconomic status, language, religion, physical ability, or mental ability. The goal of a multicultural curriculum is to affirm human diversity through the elimination of prejudice and bias (Ford & Harris, 1999).

In addition to providing an inclusive multicultural curriculum, teachers must adopt strategies that will eliminate bias in the classroom. Teachers must be prepared to discuss issues about prejudice and racism with their students. An affective curriculum that facilitates the development of positive self-esteem and self-confidence is necessary. Classrooms need to develop a sense of community and belonging where students are able to participate in cooperative learning (Fordham, 1993; Ford, 1996; Ford & Harris, 1999; Frasier, Garcia, and Passow, 1995; Patton & Townsend, 1997).

Ford (2011) recommends a multicultural gifted curriculum for gifted African American students, one that integrates the goals and philosophies of both multi-cultural education and gifted education and addresses issues of cultural differences. A multicultural gifted curriculum provides the challenge and the affirmation that gifted African American students need. Gifted African American females' intense sensitivity and internal responsiveness to others can lead to ridicule and social rejection from peers. Through bibliotherapy and role-playing, concrete examples of more positive behaviors are modeled (Janos & Robinson, 1985). Most gifted African American females have fewer opportunities for positive recognition from their peers and fewer peer friendships, as they seek friendships with older children and adults. Gifted African American females need to be provided with strategies for developing new peer relationships and maintaining existing friendships.

CULTURAL CONGRUENT INSTRUCTION

The instructional methods teachers use to teach profoundly affect the way students learn. Traditional methods of instruction are based upon the dominant culture's learning style preferences but may not match the learning styles of culturally different students. Culturally congruent instruction refers to instructional strategies that capitalize on the learning style preferences of students and match a student's preferred way of learning. Teachers who use culturally congruent instruction consider the cultural learning styles of students in the activities and experiences that they provide for their students (Ford, 1995).

Boykin (2004) investigated the behavior of African American students, identified nine cultural styles that are learned in the home and manifest themselves in the learning preferences of African American children in the classroom. The cultural styles or cultural assets of African American students include spirituality, harmony, movement, verve, oral tradition, expression individualism, affect, communalism, and social time perspective. *Spirituality* is the belief in inner strength and that nonmaterial, religious forces influence people's everyday lives so that events in life occur for a reason. *Harmony* is the belief that one's fate is interrelated with other elements of nature's order and that humankind and nature are harmonically conjoined. *Movement* is a preference for kinesthetic activities that allow for movement and experiential learning while *Verve* is an inclination for relatively high levels of stimulation. *Affect* refers to an emphasis on emotions and feelings with sensitivity to emotional cues and a tendency toward emotional response. *Oral tradition* is a preference for oral modes of communication such as metaphors, analogies, graphic forms of language, and code switching. *Expressive individualism* is the need for developing a distinctive personality. The need for social connectedness, interdependence, communal learning, affiliation, and social acceptance is known as *communalism.* An orientation to time where the event is seen as more important than the time is referred to as a *social time perspective*. The combination of cultural assets of African American females with the characteristics of gifted students creates additional educational needs for teaching culturally different students. Instructional methods that are culturally congruent include cooperative learning methods, kinesthetic and tactile teaching strategies, and visual aids (Ford & Harris, 1999).

When a multicultural curriculum is offered, students of color are engaged. The combination of cultural competence and using culturally congruent instructional methods to teach a multicultural curriculum transforms a hostile classroom into a nurturing and affirming classroom. A multicultural curriculum significantly increases the retention of culturally different students in gifted education. Multicultural preparation needs to occur among all school personnel—teachers, counselors, psychologists, administrators, and support staff.

Conclusion

The underrepresentation of culturally different students in gifted education is a function of inequitable policies and practices that are pervasive within the education system. The responsibility for this lies within every part of the education system. School districts are responsible for developing the kinds of policies, programs, and practices that are culturally sensitive and inclusive and will bring parity to those populations who are underrepresented in gifted education programs. Administrators and principals are responsible for the interpretation and implementation of policies, programs, and practices to ensure equal access and opportunity to all students. They also bear the responsibility of providing teachers with the knowledge, skills, resources, and support to implement programs. Teachers, who are the gatekeepers for entry into the selection process and ultimately the providers of an appropriate education for gifted students, are directly responsible. Psychologists, counselors, and special education professionals are responsible for assessing students, supporting students, and making life-changing decisions that will affect that students' PK–12 experience. Teacher education institutions bear most of the responsibility because they prepare the administrators, principals, teachers, special educators, counselors, and psychologists for the identification and retention of gifted students. Families share some responsibility, as they are part of the decision-making process and make the final decision that may have great implications for the future of their child. Students, who have the least input, unfortunately withstand the worst of all of these policies, practices, assessments, and decisions that are made on their behalf—decisions that hopefully consider their academic, social, psychological, and cultural needs. To counter the underrepresentation of culturally different gifted students in gifted education, a systemic change needs to occur.

NOTE

1. See http://www.dailymail.co.uk/news/article-2194542/Spanish-magazine-puts-Michelle-Obamas-head-portrait-topless-slave.html.

REFERENCES

Akan, G.E., & Grilo, C.M. (1995). Sociocultural influences on eating attitudes and behaviors, body image, and psychological functioning: A comparison of African American, Asian-American, and Caucasian college women. *International Journal of Eating Disorders, 18*, 181–187.

Banks, J. (2008). *An introduction to multicultural education.* 4th ed. Boston: Pearson/Allyn and Bacon.

Boykin, A.W. (1986). The triple quandary and the schooling of Afro-American children. In U. Neisser (Ed.), *The school achievement of minority children* (pp. 55–72). Hillsdale, NJ: Lawrence Erlbaum.

Boykin, A.W., Coleman, S.T., Lilja, A.J., & Tyler, K.M. (2004). *Building on children's cultural assets in simulated classroom performance environments: Research vistas in the communal learning paradigm.* CRESPAR Technical Report Number 68.

Brophy, J. (1985). Interactions of male and female students with male and female teachers. In L.C. Wilkinson & C.B. Marrett (Eds.), *Gender influences in classroom interaction* (pp.115–142). New York: Academic Press.

Byalick, R., & Bersoff, D.N. (1974). Reinforcement practices of Black and White teachers in integrated classrooms. *Journal of Educational Psychology, 66,*

473–480.

Carroll, R. (1997). *Sugar in the raw: Voices of young Black girls in America.* New York: Crown Trade Paperbacks.

Cartledge, G., & Milburn, J. (1998). *Cultural diversity and social skills instruction: Understanding ethnic and gender differences.* Champaign, IL: Research Press.

Collins, P.H. (1991). *Black feminist thought: Knowledge, consciousness, and the politics of empowerment.* New York: Routledge.

Crenshaw, K. (1991). Mapping the margins: Intersectionality, identity politics, and violence against women of color. *Stanford Law Review, 43,* 1241–1299.

Cross, W.E., Jr. (1995). The psychology of nigrescence: Revising the Cross model. In J.G. Ponterotto, J.M. Casas, L.A. Suzuki, & C.M. Alexander (Eds.), *Handbook of multicultural counseling* (pp. 93–122). Thousand Oaks, CA: Sage.

Cross, W.E., Jr., & Vandiver, B.J. (2001). Nigrescence theory and measurement: Introducing the Cross Racial Identity Scale (CRIS). In J.G. Ponterotto, J.M. Casas, L.M. Suzuki, & C.M. Alexander (Eds.), *Handbook of multicultural counseling* (2nd ed.) (pp. 371–393). Thousand Oaks, CA: Sage.

Damico, S.B., & Scott, E. (1985, March). Comparison of *Black* and *White* females' behavior in elementary and middle schools. Paper presented at the meeting of the American Educational Research Association, Chicago.

Davis, A. (1972) Reflections on the Black woman's role in the community of slaves. *Massachusetts Review, 13*(1–2), 81–100.

Davis, G.A., & Rimm, S. (2004). *Education of the gifted and talented.* 5th ed. Boston: Pearson Education.

Delpit, L. (1996). *Other people's children: Cultural conflict in the classroom.* New York: New Press.

DuBois, W.E.B. (1900). l'Exposition Universelle de 1900 (The American Negro at Paris). *American Monthly Review of Reviews, 23*(5), 575–577.

Dukes, R.L., & Martinez, R. (1994). The impact of ethnicity and gender on self-esteem among adolescents. *Adolescence, 29*(113), 105–115.

Farley, R., & Allen, W.R. (1989). *The color line and the quality of life in America.* New York: Oxford University Press.

Fleming, J. (1984). *Blacks in college.* San Francisco: Jossey-Bass.

Ford, D.Y. (1992). Self-perceptions of underachievement and support for the achievement ideology among early adolescent African Americans.

Journal of Early Adolescence, 12(3), 228–252.

Ford, D.Y. (1995). Underachievement among gifted African American students: Implications for school counselors. *School Counselor, 42*(3), 94–106.

Ford, D.Y. (1996). *Reversing underachievement among gifted Black students: Promising practices and programs.* New York: Teachers College Press.

Ford, D.Y. (2010). *Reversing underachievement among gifted black students* (2nd ed.). Waco, TX: Prufrock Press.

Ford, D.Y. (2011). *Multicultural gifted education* (2nd ed.). Waco, TX: Prufrock Press.

Ford, D.Y., Baytops, J.L., & Harmon, D.A. (1997). Helping gifted minority students reach their potential: Recommendations for change. *Peabody Journal of Education, 72*(3–4), 201–216.

Ford, D.Y., & Grantham, T.C. (2003). Providing access for culturally diverse gifted students: From deficit to dynamic thinking. *Theory into Practice, 42*(3), 216–225.

Ford, D.Y., Grantham, T.C., & Whiting, G.W. (2008). Another look at the achievement gap. *Urban Education, 43*(22), 216–239.

Ford, D.Y., & Harris, J.J., III. (1992). The American achievement ideology and achievement differentials among preadolescent gifted and nongifted African American males and females. *Journal of Negro Education, 61*(1), 45–64.

Ford, D.Y., & Harris, J.J., III. (1999). *Multicultural gifted education.* New York: Teachers College Press.

Ford, D.Y., Harris, J.J., III, & Schuerger, J.M. (1993). Racial identity development among gifted African American students: Counseling issues and concerns. *Journal of Counseling and Development, 71*, 409–417.

Ford, D.Y., Moore, J.L., III, & Harmon, D.A. (2005). Integrating multicultural education and gifted education: A curricular framework. *Theory into Practice, 44*(2), 125–137.

Ford, D.Y., Moore, J.L., III, Whiting, G.W., & Grantham, T.C. (2008). Conducting cross-cultural research: Controversy, cautions, concerns, and considerations. *Roeper Review, 30*(2), 82–92.

Ford, D.Y., & Whiting, G.W. (2008). AP classes: Advanced placement or advancing the privileged? *Gifted Education Press Quarterly, 22*(1), 2–4.

Fordham, S. (1988). Racelessness as a strategy in Black students' school success: Pragmatic strategy or Pyrrhic victory? *Harvard Educational*

Review, 58(1), 54–84.

Fordham, S. (1993). "Those loud Black girls": (Black) women, silence, and gender "passing" in the academy. *Anthropology and Education Quarterly, 24* (1), 3–32.

Fordham, S., & Ogbu, J. (1986). Black students' school success: Coping with the burden of "acting White." *Urban Review, 18*(3), 1–31.

Ford-Harris, D.Y., Schuerger, J.M., & Harris, J.J. (1991). Meeting the psychological needs of gifted African American students: A cultural perspective. *Journal of Counseling and Development, 69*(6), 577–580.

Frasier, M., & Passow, A.H. (1994). *Toward a new paradigm for identifying talent potential.* RM94112. Storrs, CT: University of Connecticut, National Research Center on the Gifted and Talented.

Frasier, M.M., Garcia, J.H., & Passow, A.H. (1995). *A review of assessment issues in gifted education and their implications for identifying gifted minority students.* Storrs: University of Connecticut, National Research Center on the Gifted and Talented.

Freeman, H.E., Armor, D., Ross, M., & Pettigrew, T. (1966). Color gradation and attitudes among middle-income negroes. *American Sociological Review, 31,* 365–374.

Gay, G. (2002). *Preparing for culturally responsive teaching.* Retrieved from http://math4lions.com/eReserves/3Gay.pdf.

Grant, L. (1986, April). *Classroom peer relationships of minority and nonminority students.* Paper presented at the meeting of the American Educational Research Association, San Francisco.

Grant, L. (1994). Helpers, enforcers, and go-betweens: Black females in elementary school classrooms. In M.B. Zinn & B.T. Dill (Eds.), *Women of color in the U.S. society* (pp. 43–63). Philadelphia: Temple University Press.

Grantham, T.C., & Ford, D.Y. (1998). A case study of the social needs of Danisha: An underachieving gifted African American female. *Roeper Review, 21*(2), 96–101.

Grantham, C., & Ford, D.Y. (2003). Beyond self-concept and self-esteem for African American students: Improving racial identity improves achievement. *High School Journal, 87*(1), 18–29.

Greene, B.A. (1992). Racial socialization: A tool in psychotherapy with African American children. In L. Vargas & J. Koss-Chioino (Eds.), *Working with culture: Psychotherapeutic interventions with ethnic minority youth* (pp. 63–81). San Francisco: Jossey-Bass.

Harmon, D.A. (2002). They won't teach me: Voices of African American gifted students. *Roeper Review, 24*(2), 68–75.

Harmon, D.A. (2008). The underrepresentation of culturally different gifted students in the United States: Challenges and choices. *Problemy Wczesnej Edukacji, 1*(7), 59–69.

Harris, A.C. (1996). African American and Anglo-American gender identities: An empirical study. *Journal of Black Psychology, 22*, 182–194.

Hochschild, J.L. (1995). *Facing up to the American dream: Race, class and the soul of the nation.* Princeton, NJ: Princeton University Press.

hooks, b. (2003). *Rock my soul: Black people and self-esteem.* New York: Simon & Schuster.

Hrabowski, F.A., Maton, K.I., & Greene, M.L. (2002) *Overcoming the odds: Raising academically successful African American young women.* New York: Oxford University Press.

Hughes, M., & Hertel, B.R. (1990). The significance of color remains: A case study of life chances, mate selection, and ethnic consciousness among Black Americans. *Social Forces, 68*, 1105–1120.

Hunter, M., Allen, W.R., & Telles, E.E. (2001). The significance of skin color among African Americans and Mexican Americans. *African American Research Perspectives, 7*(1), 173–184.

Irvine, J.J. (1986). Teacher-student interactions: Effects of student race, sex, and grade level. *Journal of Educational Psychology, 78*, 14–21.

Irvine, J.J. (1996). Lessons learned: Implications for the education of African Americans in public schools. In J.J. Irvine & M. Foster (Eds.), *Growing up African American in Catholic Schools.* New York: Teachers College Press.

Janos, P.M., & Robinson, N.M. (1985). Psychosocial development in intellectually gifted children. In F.D. Horowiz & M. O'Brien (Eds.), *The gifted and talented: Developmental perspectives* (pp. 149–195). Washington, DC: American Psychological Association.

Jewell, K.S. (1993). *From mammy to Miss America and beyond: Cultural images and the shaping of U.S. social policy.* New York: Routledge.

King, D. (1988). Multiple jeopardy, multiple consciousness: The context of a Black feminist ideology. *Signs, 14*, 42–72.

Kitano, M.K. (1998). Gifted African American women. *Journal for the Education of the Gifted, 21*(30), 254–287.

Lerner, R.M. (1992). *Final solutions: Biology, prejudice, and genocide.* University Park: Pennsylvania State University Press.

Leung, E.K. (1981, February). The identification and social problem of the gifted bilingual-bicultural children. Paper presented at the Council for Exceptional Children Conference on the Exceptional Bilingual Child, New Orleans, LA. ERIC Document Reproduction Service No. ED 203 653.

Massey, D.S. (2004). Segregation and stratification: A biosocial perspective. *Du Bois Review: Social Science Research on Race, 1*(1), 7–25. doi:10.1017/S1742058X04040032

McCreary, M., Slavin, L., & Berry, E. (1996). Predicting problem behavior and self-esteem among African American adolescents. *Journal of Adolescent Research, 11*, 194–215.

Oyserman, D., Harrison, K., & Bybee, D. (2001). Can racial identity be promotive of academic efficacy? *International Journal of Behavioral Development, 25*, 379–385.

Pagano, J. (1990) *Exiles and communities: Teaching in the patriarchal wilderness.* Albany: State University of New York Press.

Passow, A.H., & Frasier, M.M. (1996). Toward improving identification of talent potential among minority and disadvantaged students. *Roeper Review, 18*, 198–202.

Patterson-Stewart, K.E., Ritchie, M.H., & Sanders, E.T.W. (1997). *Journal of College Student Development, 38*, 489–498.

Patton, J.M., & Townsend, B.L. (1997). Creating inclusive environments for African American children and youth with gifts and talents. *Roeper Review, 20*, 13–17.

Phinney, J., Cantu, C., & Kurtz, D. (1997). Ethnic and American identity as predictors of self-esteem among African American, Latino, and White adolescents. *Journal of Youth and Adolescence, 26*(2), 165–185.

Phinney, J., & Kohatsu, E. (1997). Ethnic and racial development and mental health. In J. Schulenberg, J. Maggs, & K. Hurrelmann (Eds.), *Health risks and developmental transitions during adolescence* (pp. 420–443). New York: Cambridge University Press.

Poindexter-Cameron, J.M., & Robinson, T.L. (1997). Relationships among racial identity attitudes, womanist identity attitudes, and self-esteem in African American college women. *Journal of College Student Development, 38*(3), 288–296.

Ransford, E. (1970). Skin color, life chances, and anti-White attitudes. *Social Problems, 18,* 164–178.

Richardson, E. (2002). "To protect and serve": African American female literacies. *College Compositions and Communication, 53*(2), 675–704.

Russell, K., Wilson, M., & Hall, R. (1992). *The color complex: The politics of African Americans.* New York: Bantam Doubleday Dell.

Sadker, M., & Sadker, D. (1994). *Failing at fairness: How America's schools cheat girls.* New York: Charles Scribner's Sons.

Schwartz, R.A., Bower, B.L., Rie, D.C., & Washington, C.M. (2003). "Ain't I a woman, too?": Tracing the experiences of African American women in graduate school. *Journal of Negro Education, 72*(3), 252–268.

Sedlacek, T.J. (1987). Blacks students on White campuses: 20 years of research. *Journal of Student Development, 40*(5), 538–550.

Sellers, R.M., Shelton, M.I., Smith, J.N., Rowley, S.A.J., & Chavous, T.M. (1998). Multidimensional model of racial identity: A reconceptualization of African American racial identity. *Personality and Social Psychology Review, 2*(1),18–39.

Spencer, M., Cunningham, M., & Swanson, D. (1995). Identity as coping: Adolescent African American males' adaptive responses to high-risk environments. In H. Harris, H. Blue, & E. Griffith (Eds.), *Racial and ethnic identity: Psychological development and creative expression* (pp. 31–52). New York: Routledge.

Sternberg, R.J. (2007). Cultural concepts of giftedness. *Roeper Review, 29*(3), 160–166.

Stevenson, H.C. (1995). Relationship of adolescent perceptions of racial socialization to racial identity. *Journal of Black Psychology, 21*(1), 49–70.

Tinto, V. (1975). Dropout from higher education: A theoretical synthesis of recent research. *Review of Educational Research, 45*(1), 89–125.

Tracey T.J., & Sedlacek, W.E. (1984). Noncognitive variables in predicting academic success by race. *Measurement and Evaluation in Guidance, 16,* 171–178.

Tracey, T.J., & Sedlacek, W.E. (1985). The relationship of noncognitive variables to academic success: A longitudinal comparison by race. *Journal of College Student Personnel, 26*, 405–410.

Weiler, J.D. (2000). *Codes and contradictions: Race, gender identity, and schooling.* Albany: State University of New York Press.

Williamson, J. (1980). *New people: Miscegenation and mulattoes in the United States.* New York: Free Press.

Wood, S.B., & Achey, V.H. (1990). Successful identification of gifted racial/ethnic group students without changing classification requirements. *Roeper Review, 13*(1), 21–26.

PART 2

Pathway to the Professions: African American Females on Both Sides of the Desk

A Needle in a Haystack

THE SEARCH FOR AFRICAN AMERICAN FEMALE
TEACHERS IN K—12 EDUCATION

Shanna L. Graves, Tamara N. Stevenson,
and Eboni M. Zamani-Gallaher

The K–12 teaching workforce, comprised primarily of White middle-class females, does not mirror the progressively diverse student population in the majority of public schools in the United States. According to the National Center for Education Statistics (NCES), during the 2007–2008 school year, there were roughly 3.5 million teachers (NCES, 2010a, 2010b). Of the 3.5 million teachers, 83 percent were White, 7 percent Black, 7 percent Hispanic, and 3 percent other (NCES, 2009).[1] In the same school year, the overall student population was 59.3 percent White, 15.3 percent Black, 19.3 percent Hispanic, 1.4 percent American Indian / Alaskan Native, and 4.6 percent Asian / Pacific Islander. These statistics reveal an unprecedented racial disparity between teachers and students. At no other time in history has this gap been so wide. Projected retirements suggest that as many as 1.5 million veteran teachers are eligible for retirement over the next eight years (NCTAF, 2010); there is little indication that the new teacher pool will be more diverse. According to Causey, Thomas, and Armento (2000), the population of preservice teachers will become more homogeneous, leaving colleges and universities to "face the daunting task of preparing predominately White middle-class college students with limited or no experience with persons from another ethnicity or social class to be effective teachers of diverse students" (p. 33).

While the shortage of teachers of color in general is a critical issue, the scarcity of African American female teachers is particularly alarming, given the historical background of this population. During the initial years following World War II, 79 percent of African American women worked as educators after college (Murnane et al., 1991). What factors have caused such a steady decline in the African American female teaching workforce? Further, what steps can be taken to restore the representation of this group for the increasingly diverse student population in today's classrooms? The authors seek to explore this critical issue, as it holds serious implications for the education of *all* students. An examination of the current literature on African American female teachers will precede a discussion of the implications for teacher preparation in Michigan and nationwide.

Historical Background

According to Gordon (1994), the shortage of African American female teachers is "embedded in a context of school desegregation" (p. 346). During Reconstruction, teaching was one of the few jobs available to literate African Americans, particularly in the South. Prior to the *Brown v. Board of Education of Topeka* Supreme Court decision in 1954, nearly 82,000 African American teachers were responsible for the education of more than two million African American children across the nation (Hawkins, 1994). Throughout that time, African American teachers were revered in Black communities, as they were viewed as role models, community leaders, and mentors (Gordon, 2000; Perkins, 1989). Many of them lived in the communities in which they taught; thus, they were able to forge strong relationships with students and their families (Milner & Howard, 2004). The earliest African American female educators were considered "*womanist*" teachers in many regards, as they epitomized ethos of care and activist instructional leading that challenged racial, class, and gender inequalities (Ramsey, 2012).

In the 10 years following the *Brown* decision, nearly half of the African American teaching population lost their jobs in 17 states (Hudson & Holmes, 1994). Many White parents were strongly opposed to having African American teachers educate their children. Therefore, the provisions that were being made to integrate minority students into majority-White schools were not always extended to African American teachers, administrators, and staff; instead, they were either dismissed or demoted in countless cases (Torres et al. 2004). In addition, with school integration came the inevitable dismantling of Black schools, which led to even more job cuts (Hawkins, 1994). For the small percentage of remaining African American female teachers, newly available job opportunities in the wake of the civil rights movement resulted in their mass exodus from teaching (Perkins, 1989). According to Gordon (2000),

> By the time the court and federal actions were initiated in the late 1960s and 1970s to prevent further displacements, the damage had already been done. Schooling became a part of the White man's world; education was undermined, taken from the community and placed in the hands of others. (p. 19)

Even though the historical influence on African American female teachers' existence in public education today is hardly questionable, several researchers are reluctant to draw a direct link between the shortage of African American female teachers and *Brown* (Hawkins, 1994; Torres et al., 2004). Empirical studies conducted over the last decade reveal a plethora of reasons why many African American females, as well as other racial/ethnic minorities, do not consider teaching a viable career option.

Why Aren't African American Females Entering the Teaching Workforce?

Upon examining statistics on college enrollment trends, one could argue that the racial disparities between teachers should be expected. While the overall undergraduate enrollment has increased by 24 percent since the year 2000 (NCES, 2010a), college participation rates of students of color continue to fall below that of their White counterparts. *The Condition of Education 2010* reports that overall college enrollment in 2008 was 63 percent White, 14 percent Black, 12 percent Hispanic, 7 percent Asian / Pacific Islander, 1 percent American Indian / Alaskan Native, and 3 percent nonresident alien. Further, the percentage of students enrolled in education degree programs reveals an even wider gap. A recent report by the American Association of Colleges for Teacher Education (AACTE) indicates that 78 percent of White students were enrolled full-time in education degree programs at the undergraduate level while only 8 percent of Black students and 6 percent of Hispanic students were enrolled at the same level (AACTE, 2010).

Gordon (1994) partly attributes the low enrollment of students of color in teacher education programs to the programs themselves, citing their lack of active recruitment and community partnerships. However, while recruitment (to be discussed later in this chapter) certainly does play a role in this critical shortage, the literature on teacher shortage reveals a bit more. In Gordon's (1994) study, she interviewed 140 teachers of color (i.e., African Americans, Latinos, Asian Americans, and Native Americans) in three large urban areas. Six questions were posed to the teachers, including, "Why do you think students of color are not going into teaching?" From this one question, three major themes emerged: (1) educational experience, (2) cultural and community concerns, and (3) social and economic obstacles. First, educational experience included not graduating from high school, lack of preparation, negative experience in school, poor student discipline / lack of respect, teachers not prepared for diversity, and lack of support in college. Second, cultural and community concerns included lack of academic encouragement, racelessness, absence of role models, low status, too much education for the return, and teaching not attractive to some ethnic groups. Third, social and economic obstacles included low pay, negative image, poor school conditions, racism, and more opportunities elsewhere.

The themes found in Gordon's research have been echoed throughout the literature on minority teacher shortages; virtually every article cites similar reasons (Basit & McNamara, 2004; Ford & Grantham, 1997; Futrell, 1999; Gonzalez, 1997; Gordon, 1994, 2000; Kane & Orsini, 2003; Quiocho & Rios, 2000; Shipp, 1999; Torres et al., 2004). Futrell (1999), for example, cited the lack of academic preparation as a major deterrent for students of color pursuing teaching careers. She argued that minorities are too often overrepresented in vocational and special education programs and underrepresented in gifted and talented, or advanced placement programs (even when they have demonstrated the capability to succeed in such programs). These injustices in the educational system are fundamental to understanding why some students choose to enter the teaching profession and others do not (Ford & Grantham, 1997; Gordon, 2000). Students' negative experiences in school can lead them to "view the teaching profession as embodying a negative daily experience" (Kane & Orsini, 2003, p. 36). Moreover, the negative experiences of students' families or community members could have the same effect. For example, Gordon (2000) suggests that an individual's choice to enter a profession is influenced by the perceptions and attitudes held by the family and community. She states:

> The distinctive qualities of one's ethnic community's experience and perception of schooling, past, present, and future, affect career decision making.... If parents or community members believed they were invalidated or misrepresented during their schooling they will not recommend teaching to their kin. If there is an assumption that participation in the perpetuation of public schooling not only undercuts one's cultural foundations but also removes one from the community, teaching will not be the vocation of choice. (p. 4)

While this idea may hold true in many cases, one could argue that students' negative experiences in the school system might actually inspire them to change the very practices that impaired their own academic growth. In such cases, these students may want to enter teaching in order to exert their own power to change future minority students' school experiences in positive ways.

Some researchers argue that poor college preparation will continue to be a major constriction in the minority teacher pipeline (Torres et al., 2004) as schools of education maintain stringent testing and admission requirements (Quiocho & Rios, 2000). Even more, once candidates are accepted into a teacher education program, they must face yet another set of state examinations—which many claim are biased and lack validity (Torres et al., 2004)—for teacher certification. Although other fields such as law, business, and science also require costly state and/or national examinations for credentialing purposes, jobs in these fields offer more prestige and financial incentives than education (Ford & Grantham, 1997). As a result, many minority students are left questioning the cost of preparing to become a teacher, especially since the return benefits are noticeably lower than other professions (Futrell, 1999). It is important to note, however, that poor college preparation is a major constriction for any field one chooses to enter. The field of education is only one of many areas that maintain stringent admission and completion requirements; in fact, one could argue that fields such as law and science are actually more academically rigorous. In this case, poor academic preparation would not seem to be a valid reason for minority teacher shortages. It could simply be the case that other career options are more appealing.

An empirical examination of the experiences of students of color in teacher education programs may yield additional insights into the lower numbers of students of color enrolling and matriculating through teacher education programs. First, negative experiences—such as sociocultural alienation and feelings of racism and powerlessness—during teacher preparation often lead to attrition (Case et al., 1988). For African American students aspiring to enter teaching careers, the context of traditional teacher education programs perpetuates the dominant culture, and racial identity does tie to the positionality of preservice candidates (Haddix, 2012). Although minority teacher candidates bring a richer multicultural knowledge base to teacher education (Sleeter, 2001), they have reported feeling devalued and excluded from the curriculum as their diverse personal and cultural backgrounds are seldom acknowledged, developed, or infused into their coursework or practicum experiences (Torres et al., 2004). Additionally, they have reported a lack of encouragement or support in teacher training; some even considered their training detrimental (Gordon, 2000).

For those who are able to successfully navigate through their teacher preparation programs and go on to graduate and secure jobs as teachers, there are another set of barriers that often lead to an early departure from teaching. According to Torres and colleagues (2004),

> Teachers, particularly in urban areas, often contend with the lowest student achievement levels, the highest dropout rates, the lowest amount of teacher resources, the highest number of discipline problems, and the lowest levels of teacher control over curricular and pedagogical decisions. (p. 15)

Teachers who find themselves in such dire situations—most often minorities—are not as eager to speak highly of the teaching profession. In fact, they are more likely to discourage others from entering the field. In Gordon's (1994) interviews with teachers of color, 75 percent said they would not recommend teaching as a career option to their students, friends, or relatives. These kinds of "negative attitudes about teaching, coming from the very people who have selected the profession, have the most powerful impact on students" (Gordon, 2000, p. 92).

Snapshot: The State of Michigan Demographics and Teacher Preparation

A report by the Association of Teacher Educators contends that universities are not adequately preparing preservice teachers for meeting the needs of divergent learners in multiethnic settings (Buttery, Haberman, & Houston, 1990). One area of the country where this is especially true is the racially segregated state of Michigan. The homogeneity in residential patterns illustrates stark contrasts, particularly in Detroit and its surrounding suburbs. While the overall population figures for the state of Michigan are 81.2 percent White, 14.2 percent Black, 4.2 percent Hispanic, 2.4 percent Asian, 1.6 percent bi- or multiracial, and 0.06 percent Native American, residents of Detroit do not mirror the state demographics (U.S. Census Bureau, 2010). More specifically, in 2008, 8 percent of Detroit residents were White non-Hispanic, whereas 83 percent were African American / Black, 6 percent were Hispanic,[2] and 4 percent indicated some other race; 1 percent were Asian, 1 percent reported two or more races, less than 0.5 percent were American Indian and Alaskan Native, and less than 0.5 percent were Native Hawaiian and Pacific Islander. When looking at the educational attainment overall, between 2006 and 2008, 24 percent of Detroit residents were high school dropouts, the vast majority being African Americans; however, 11 percent of Detroit residents had a bachelor's degree or higher (U.S. Census Bureau, 2006–2008 American Community Survey).

The current composition of public elementary and secondary (K–12) institutions in the state of Michigan consists of 551 local school districts, 57 intermediate school districts, and 227 public school academies (i.e., charter schools) serving over 1.6 million students. These institutions collectively employ more than 345,000 school personnel inclusive of administrators, teachers, substitute teachers, paraprofessionals/aides, substitute paraprofessionals/aides, and noninstructional staff. Approximately one-third (92,691) of school personnel are general education, career/technical education, and special education teachers (State of Michigan, Center for Educational Performance and Information, 2008). Table 1 displays interesting demographic characteristics of Michigan public school teachers by race/ethnicity and gender (State of Michigan, Center for Educational Performance and Information, 2012).

Michigan's public K–12 teachers in fall 2011 were predominantly White (90.48 percent) and female (76.35 percent), and the largest number of Michigan public school teachers were between the ages of 40 and 70 (little over one-third), while

TABLE 1. RACE/ETHNICITY OF PUBLIC K–12 TEACHERS IN THE STATE OF MICHIGAN, 2011–2012

	NUMBER	PERCENTAGE
American Indian/Alaskan Native	230	0.23
Asian	718	0.71
African American/Black	7,351	7.23
Hispanic/Latino	1,052	1.03
Multiracial	237	0.23
Native Hawaiian/Other Pacific Islander	90	0.09
White	92,019	90.48
Total	*101,697*	*100.00*

Source: Adapted from State of Michigan, Center for Educational Performance and Information (2012).

nearly 30 percent were between 30 and 39 years of age. African American women comprised approximately 7 percent of all k–12 teachers in Michigan in fall 2011, including local and intermediate school districts, as well as charter schools (State of Michigan, Center for Educational Performance and Information, 2012). In 2008, the Detroit Public School District had the largest concentration of African American female teachers in the state with 3,763. Southfield Public Schools had the next highest number of Black female teachers at 240. Other school districts with at least 100 Black female teachers included the cities of Flint, Pontiac, Grand Rapids, Ann Arbor, Saginaw, and Lansing. Paradoxically, many African American students attend majority-minority schools in cities such as Detroit, Flint, and Pontiac. However, each of the school districts is in communities with a critical mass of African American residents with notable underrepresentation of African American teachers proportionate to the student population (U.S. Census Bureau, American Community Survey, 2008).

Of the 7,274 Black female teachers in the state of Michigan as of fall 2008, approximately half are located in the Detroit Public School District. Other public school districts and charter schools with relative concentrations of African American female teachers are in those cities and counties with high African American populations. The percentage of the total population in Detroit who identified as Black is the highest nationally among places with populations of 100,000 or more (U.S. Census Bureau, American Community Survey, 2008). Wayne County is home to the city of Detroit, and two-fifths of Wayne County is comprised of African Americans (U.S. Census Bureau, 2012). Nearly 5,000 Black women teach in public k–12 schools and academies in Wayne County. The African American population in Genesee County, which includes the city of Flint, totals 20.9 percent. With 330 Black female teachers at various public school districts and charter schools located in the county, 233 teach in the Flint Public School District. In Saginaw County, 151 teachers are African American females; 105 teach in the Saginaw City School District. At 19.4 percent, Saginaw County has the third highest Black population in the state. At 15.6 percent, Berrien County has the State of Michigan's fourth largest African American population. Of its 78 African American female schoolteachers, 49 teach with Benton Harbor Area Schools. Muskegon's population of African American citizens total 14.6 percent, the fifth largest of the state. With 75 Black female schoolteachers, 66 teach in the Muskegon City and Muskegon Heights School Districts (U.S. Census Bureau, American Community Survey, 2008; U.S. Census Bureau, 2012).

TEACHER PREPARATION PROGRAMS IN THE STATE OF MICHIGAN

Currently, teacher education programs at 32 colleges and universities are approved by the Michigan State Board of Education to prepare teachers and recommend certification to teach. Another four institutions have received preliminary approval and are assigned to mentor institutions (Michigan Department of Education, Office of Professional Preparation Services, 2010). An estimated 8,000 new teachers are prepared through these programs yearly (Michigan Department of Education, 2009).

In compliance with state and federal requirements to establish performance

TABLE 2. RACE AND GENDER OF PUBLIC K–12 TEACHERS IN THE STATE OF MICHIGAN, FALL 2008

	FEMALE		MALE	
	NUMBER	PERCENTAGE	NUMBER	PERCENTAGE
American Indian/Alaskan Native	173	0.16%	64	0.06%
Asian	465	0.42%	127	0.12%
African American/Black	7,274	6.59%	1,763	1.60%
Hispanic/Latino	700	0.63%	261	0.24%
Multiracial	24	0.02%	4	0.00%
Native Hawaiian/Other Pacific Islander	63	0.06%	18	0.02%
White	75,028	67.99%	24,380	22.09%
Total	*83,727*	*75.88%*	*26,617*	*24.12%*

Source: Adapted from State of Michigan, Center for Educational Performance and Information (2008).

measures for teacher preparation institutions, the Michigan Department of Education's Office of Professional Preparation Services developed a set of criteria to determine program effectiveness, consisting of a six-part scoring system (with a highest possible score of 70) for placement in one of four Title II performance categories: exemplary, satisfactory, at-risk, or low-performing. The six criteria include test pass rate (specialty content areas) (30 points), program review (endorsement program status) (10 points), program completion (candidate eligibility for recommendation) (10 points), candidate and supervisor survey (perceived readiness) (10 points), institutional responsiveness to state need (diversity and high-need subject areas) (10 points), and teaching success rate (number of placed new teachers at satisfactory or better; points to be determined).

Highlighting the diversity component in the institutional responsiveness to state need (worth 5 of the 10 points in this section) as indicated in the *Report on the Teacher Preparation Institution Performance Scores for Academic Year 2010–11*, institutions received 5 points if 10 percent or more of their recommended candidates (regardless of the number of individuals in the group) in the current academic year were from a racial/ethnic minority group (defined as Black / African American, Hispanic, Asian, Native American, Pacific Islander, and multiracial). Three points were given to institutions with the number of ethnic minority candidates ranging from 5 to 9 percent (State Board of Education, 2011). Both public and private colleges/universities are tracked in the Title II performance category. Only six institutions received exemplary ratings (i.e., 5 points) for diversity of teacher candidates and overall scores from 63–70 ranking exemplary for teacher education across categories (which also included teacher exit surveys, program completion rate, supervisor surveys, program review status, high-need content, and principal feedback).

The *Report on Teacher Preparation Institution Performance Scores for Academic Year 2010–11* noted that racial/ethnic minorities numbered less than 10 percent of Michigan's k–12 teachers. This figure has remained virtually unchanged since 2004. Approximately 8 percent of Michigan teachers are African American (6.59 percent female; 1.60 percent male) (Michigan Department of Education, 2007). The Michigan Department of Education report on teacher quality, attrition, and retention in the state asserts that regionalism has influenced employment patterns of teachers along with the production of new teachers throughout the state. Urban, suburban, and rural school districts look to their respective local teacher preparation institutions to fill teaching positions, and conversely, new teachers pursue opportunities to work in school districts in proximity to their teacher preparation programs.

> On average, of all new teachers in Michigan, 18.5 percent were trained in the same county in which they currently teach. Excluding teachers who were trained out of state, this proportion increases to 21.3 percent. This social and institutional effect can be seen across all types of districts, from suburban to rural to urban. ... Through this data, we characterize the State of Michigan teaching labor markets as regional, or sub-regional. We claim "sub-regions" since districts seem strongly polarized to the closest school, even when the larger region claims other certification institutions. These sub-regional markets appear to influence the flow of teachers into districts. (Michigan Department of Education, 2007, pp. 17, 19)

For example, as noted in the April 2007 Michigan Department of Education report on teacher quality and turnover, 29 percent of new teachers to the Detroit Public Schools were from Wayne State University, located in the city of Detroit. In addition, 12 percent of new teachers to the Detroit Public Schools were from Eastern Michigan University and 8 percent from the University of Detroit–Mercy. Similar patterns were observed in both suburban and rural districts. In Portage Public Schools, a local school district in a suburb of Kalamazoo, Michigan, nearly 69 percent of new teachers came from Western Michigan University. In the rural Upper Peninsula, 82 percent of new teachers to Gwinn Area Community Schools were from Northern Michigan University. In addition, about 13 percent of new teachers were hired to public school academies (or charter schools) throughout the state.

The Importance of African American Female Teachers

The premise that the presence of African American female teachers is critical—particularly for African American students—rests mainly on the idea that they will be role models and empathetic toward these students, thus enhancing their academic performance (Hess & Leal, 1997). While there may be little empirical evidence to support this idea (Cizek, 1995; Hess & Leal, 1997; King, 1993; Kirby, Berends, & Naftel, 1999), one cannot simply ignore this notion given the disheartening statistics on

African American students' academic performance, especially when compared to their White counterparts. Data collected from the National Center for Education Statistics (NCES) reveal that African American students in elementary and secondary grades continue to lag behind White students (and in some cases, every other racial group) in core subject areas (NCES, 2010a). Further, the disproportionate representation of African American students in special education is an even greater concern (Valles, 1998) as national patterns over the last 40 years continue to show African American students overrepresented in categories of mental retardation and emotional disturbance, and underrepresented in gifted and talented (Hosp & Reschly, 2004).

If teacher referral is a strong predictor of special education eligibility (Hosp & Reschly, 2004), and African American students are likely to be taught more by White teachers throughout their schooling, then what does this really say about the importance of placing students in classrooms with teachers from similar backgrounds? Dee (2005) discusses two ways in which the demographic matches between teachers and students could influence educational outcomes. First, the "passive" teacher effects refer to the presence of a demographically (i.e., racial/ ethnic, gender) similar teacher. It does not include explicit teacher behaviors. Essentially, students' academic motivation and expectations increase simply by being in the presence of a teacher who looks like them. Second, the "active" teacher effects refer more to explicit behaviors or interactions with students from different backgrounds. These effects may include unintended biases in a teacher's expectations of certain students. In other words, a teacher may offer less assistance or provide less positive feedback to students who are demographically different or vice versa. This, in turn, could affect students' performance in negative or positive ways. In his research, Dee found that "the odds of a student being seen as disruptive by a teacher are 1.36 times as large when the teacher does not share the student's racial/ethnic designation" (p. 162). Additionally, he found that a student who had a teacher from a different racial background was at least 33 percent more likely to be seen as inattentive and the student's odds of rarely completing homework increased by at least 22 percent.

Perhaps it seems rather impractical, even discriminatory, to suggest that African American students only be taught by African American teachers or that White students only be taught by White teachers. Such an approach would surely do a great disservice to all students, especially in our growing multicultural society. At the same time, it is important to create a balance of sorts. African American female teachers have so much to bring to the classroom, from their rich sociocultural experiences to the cultural mediation skills they have developed to bridge school and home (Quiocho & Rios, 2000). African American female teachers often go beyond the subject matter and subsequently their position as teachers and role models to minority students who at times call them to act as surrogate parents, disciplinarians, and counselors (Ford & Grantham, 1997). There is a relational quality inherent in most African American female teachers that allows them to influence children, particularly minorities, far beyond the classroom walls. This aspect of teaching reflects cultural congruence that is critical given its potential to have a positive influence on student performance.

> If we do not have some knowledge of children's lives outside of the realms of paper-and-pencil work, and even outside of their classrooms, then we cannot know their strengths. Not knowing students' strengths leads to our "teaching down" to children from communities that are culturally different from that of the teachers in school. (Delpit, 1992, p. 242)

It is also important to note the significance of African American female teachers for students from all backgrounds. They can be role models to all students, across racial/ethnic groups, as they shape these students' images of what African American people can achieve (Kane & Orsini, 2003). It is important that all children have the opportunity to see positive images of African Americans in professional or leadership roles. "Positive role models and the removal of stereotypes are as important for White children as for children of color" (Gordon, 2000, p. 2).

Increasing the Pipeline of African American Female Teachers

School districts, colleges of education, and departments of education each play a part in the recruitment and support of African American teachers to ensure that the disparity between teachers and students of color does not become even greater (Futrell, 1999; Kane & Orsini, 2003; Quiocho & Rios, 2000). Most of the empirical literature on minority teacher recruitment and retention, however, can be found at the university level, as it focuses mainly on teacher preparation programs.

Nonetheless, there is available information on recruitment at other levels (i.e., school districts, the U.S. Department of Education, private sectors).

RECRUITMENT AT THE SCHOOL LEVEL

School policies and practices in relation to teacher recruitment should be examined to ensure that equal opportunity is afforded to every prospective teacher. Ford and Grantham (1997) pose a number of questions for consideration: (1) How committed are administrators to increasing teacher diversity? (2) What measures do educational leaders take to ensure that minority teachers are not disproportionately assigned to low tracks and low ability groups? (3) What strategies are used to elevate the status of teaching as a profession in the eyes of minority groups? These questions force school leaders to critically analyze their current practices in relation to hiring and retaining African American female teachers. If districts are truly committed to hiring African American female teachers—or minorities in general—then what are they are actually doing to help administrators accomplish this goal?

In Quiocho and Rios's (2000) review of the research on minority teachers, they found several studies that revealed differential experiences in the employment process for minorities. For example, recruitment teams composed of only White recruiters visited colleges to interview teacher candidates. Minority candidates reported that they were not given enough time and were not treated courteously during the interview process. What is even more disturbing is that many of the people responsible for hiring were unaware of their biases against African Americans. Brar's (1991) work, conducted in London, illustrates the cross-cultural context pertaining to concern over underrepresentation of Black teachers in schools abroad as well. Head teachers were asked why there was a lack of Black teachers. Their responses were compiled into five categories: (1) there is no problem; (2) there are no Black applicants; (3) problematizing the Black teacher; (4) passing the buck; and (5) institutional racism. Many of the responses were disconcerting (to say the least) and provide further evidence that there is a lack of commitment to recruiting or retaining African American female teachers. One head teacher stated:

> Black teachers in this country are a new concept. Today's parents remember their teachers who were White. The problem is one of the acceptance of Black teachers. White parents meet Black people in the shops, etc., and see them as

having a poor command of English. They fear that with Black people as good teachers, good English will not be learnt. (p. 42)

While such discriminatory practices and/or ideologies may not occur in every school district, it is important to note the impact that biased attitudes and behaviors can have on the recruitment and retention of minority teachers. School leaders must be committed to creating a more diverse teaching workforce. They must ensure that recruiters are ethical in their interviewing and hiring practices. They must be ready to defend good minority teachers when confronted with closed-minded parents. Finally, school districts need to develop real partnerships with universities and colleges, especially Black colleges, to ensure that African American female teachers are connected to the same formal and informal hiring networks as their White counterparts.

RECRUITMENT AT THE UNIVERSITY LEVEL

The body of research related to the recruitment of African American female teacher candidates at the university level includes a number of empirical studies of university initiatives over the last two decades. In the late 1980s, the Southern Education Foundation (SEF)—with support from a planning grant from the Bell South Foundation—collaborated with six historically Black colleges and universities (HBCUs) and three graduate institutions of education to address the critical need for African American teachers (Goodwin, 1991). This consortium of SEF and the nine institutions created various programs on the campuses of these institutions, including the Teacher Cadet Program, the Summer Enrichment Program for Future Teachers, the Summer Scholars Program, Faculty Exchange and Enrichment, the Minority Leadership Center, and Collaborative Research and Evaluation. Goodwin (1991) reported the results of such initiatives, revealing an increase in the number of students majoring in education. According to Goodwin, "in the words of one faculty member, the programs have been very visible on HBCU campuses and have helped to raise 'the consciousness of the other majors (students)' about teaching and to project 'a positive image of teaching'" (p. 35).

Gonzalez (1997) conducted a study of six preservice preparation programs in three regions of the United States, documenting students' perceptions of the program features that were most successful in attracting and retaining them. Results of his study indicated several program components that had a positive effect on minority students' recruitment, retention, and graduation. Some of the program features included (1) the human dimension, (2) peer recruitment, (3) bridging into college, and (4) monitoring progress.

First, the "human dimension" of a program was important, as students appreciated the presence of a caring and nurturing environment and noted that it kept them focused on their mission to persist. Second, "peer recruitment" was critical in attracting prospective candidates. Students who were currently enrolled in a teacher preparation program were employed as recruiters and visited high schools and community colleges. This recruitment approach was instrumental in prospective candidates' decision to apply for admission. Additionally, the student recruiters reported that their role in urging others to become teachers was a growth experience for them. Third, "bridging into college" was an approach designed to ease entry into the university environment. Some programs began bridging during students' junior and senior years in high school, while some were implemented as early as the eighth grade. Bridging experiences ranged from three-week residential programs on college campuses during the summer to field trips to colleges and universities and weekend college activities. Students recognized the value of the bridging experience, reporting that they may not have aspired to earn a baccalaureate degree or enter the profession on their own. Last, "monitoring progress" was critical in retaining and graduating students. This included the structured and systematic monitoring of students' progress. Students set monthly learning goals and would meet one-on-one with professors every month.

Futrell (1999) suggests several strategies that may help in the recruitment of African American and other students of color into teaching. Among her suggestions are (1) develop marketing and recruitment campaigns to attract more minority candidates; (2) design outreach programs, such as Future Teachers of America, Teacher Cadets, and Grow a Teacher, to inform middle and high school students about the value of teaching (in these programs, students would be given the opportunity to work with experienced teachers as interns); (3) develop programs to bring first-generation college students to college campuses to learn about campus life; (4) provide financial aid in the form of forgiveness loans in which students would be credited with one year of repayment for each year they teach; (5) develop mentoring programs for minority teacher candidates and first-year teachers; (6) develop partnerships with school districts to identify minority students who may be able to teach in critical shortage areas such as math, science, and bilingual education; and (7) work to enhance salary and working conditions of teachers in order to be more competitive with other professions.

RECRUITMENT AT OTHER LEVELS

Minority teacher recruitment initiatives have been implemented at all levels—federal, state, and local. However, the successes of these initiatives remain to be seen, as the number of African American female teachers continues to decline. Currently, the U.S. Department of Education offers grants through programs such as Teacher Quality Partnerships, Transition to Teaching, and Troops to Teachers. Additionally, the National Education Association's (NEA) Recruitment and Retention of Educators (RRE) program addresses the minority teacher shortage by providing grants to local affiliates for the recruitment and retention of teachers. Private sector recruitment initiatives include a number of programs funded by the Ford Foundation, Carnegie Corporation of New York, Pew Charitable Trusts, and Rockefeller Brothers Fund.

Conclusions and Implications for Practice

The shortage of African American female teachers is a critical issue that has yet to be resolved. A myriad of recruitment and retention efforts have been initiated for more than 20 years; however, the percentage of African American female teachers in K–12 education has reached an all-time low. While school districts and departments of education hold some responsibility in the efforts to secure African American female teachers, teacher preparation programs are ultimately held accountable for producing qualified teachers who can handle the challenges of being a classroom teacher in today's society. These programs must ensure that prospective candidates understand the realities of today's classrooms and are equipped with the knowledge, skills, and dispositions to be successful teachers. How can teacher preparation programs make a significant difference in the current teacher workforce? What can be done at the university level to ensure that more African American female teachers enter and remain in the teaching workforce?

First, African American female candidates need to feel supported throughout their teacher training. The importance of establishing nurturing communities of practice that support the professional development of African American female candidates cannot be emphasized (Quiocho & Rios, 2000). As stated previously, the human dimension of a teacher preparation program is critical, particularly for minorities (Gonzalez, 1997). In order to support African American female candidates, university faculty should be available as mentors for these students. However, the challenge rests in the availability of mentors from minority backgrounds. Most higher education institutions, similar to public school districts, are staffed by predominately White faculties. As of 2007, the racial/ethnic background of full-time faculty in professional education programs was 78 percent White, 10 percent Black, 4 percent Hispanic, 4 percent Asian / Pacific Islander, 1 percent American Indian, 1 percent nonresident alien, and 2 percent race unknown (AACTE, 2010). While African American female candidates would certainly benefit from the mentorship of faculty who genuinely care, having minority faculty members serving as models and mentors would be invaluable. Minority faculty may be more privy to effective teaching techniques and strategies for diverse students. According to Zeichner (2003),

> The White, monolingual, English-speaking teacher education professors and staff who are responsible for educating teachers for diversity often lack experience themselves in teaching in culturally diverse elementary and secondary schools, and the lack of diversity among faculty, staff and students in many teacher education programs undermines efforts to prepare interculturally competent teachers. (p. 493)

Another important factor for African American female candidates in teacher preparation is the quality and relevance of their experience in the program. Lack of attention to diversity issues can leave candidates feeling ill prepared to deal with diversity within a school context (Quiocho & Rios, 2000). According to Ladson-Billings (2000), there has been widely expressed dissatisfaction with teacher education coursework, particularly in its lack of attention to the perspectives and concerns of African Americans. Futrell (1999), as well, argues that culturally responsive pedagogy should be integrated into all aspects of preparation programs in order to ensure that prospective candidates utilize effective teaching strategies for all students.

In closing, teacher preparation programs must restructure coursework to reflect multicultural issues and ensure that teacher candidates gain experience outside of university classrooms in a variety of diverse settings. Additionally, numerous and diverse teacher education programs exist at community colleges nationwide. Given the critical mass of African American students participating in postsecondary education through attendance at community colleges (i.e., close to half of all African American collegians attend two-year institutions of higher learning), teacher preparation programs should strengthen partnerships with two-year institutions in recruiting more diverse potential teacher candidates.

There are various paths to a teaching career, such as through two-year attendance with vertical transfer, traditional four-year attendance with declared education major, and so on. As such, there are African American females that could be attracted to teaching and recruited through postbaccalaureate programs in teacher education. Thus, institutions of higher learning have to provide professional development and career opportunities for diverse candidates that are not just targeted to the traditional age (i.e., 18–24).

Research has demonstrated that it is imperative to the professional development of teachers to have field placement in diverse settings for their clinical experiences (Kauchak & Burbank, 2003). It is through these placements that schools with significant minority student populations can have teachers who mirror their image, affirm their presence, and provide a safe place to explore issues of race, language, and culture. The shifting demographics of the instructional core of American schools have not kept pace with the growing diversity of school-age children. Hence, the racial/ethnic composition of the teaching workforce needs to align with the population of divergent learners seeking access to educational opportunities. African American female teachers can provide additional cultural capital to children of color in the classroom. Their presence is required and necessary in curbing deculturalization, increasing expectancy, and improving outcomes for culturally diverse learners.

NOTES

1. Other refers to Asian, Native American, Hawaiian / Pacific Islander, American Indian / Alaskan Native, and two or more races.

2. People of Hispanic origin may be of any race.

REFERENCES

American Association of Colleges for Teacher Education (AACTE) (2010). *An emerging picture of the teacher preparation pipeline.* Washington, DC: Author.

Basit, T.N., & McNamara, O. (2004). Equal opportunities or affirmative action? The induction of minority ethnic teachers. *Journal of Education for Teaching, 30*(2), 97–115.

Brar, H.S. (1991). Unequal opportunities: The recruitment, selection and promotion prospects for Black teachers. In G. Grace & M. Lawn (Eds.), *Teacher supply and teacher quality: Issues for the 1990s* (pp. 34–46). Clevedon: Multilingual Matters.

Buttery, T.J., Haberman, M., & Houston, W.R. (1990). First annual ATE survey of critical issues in teacher education. *Action in Teacher Education, 12*(2), 1–7.

Case, C.W., Shive R.J., Ingebretson, K., & Spiegel, V.M. (1988). Minority teacher education: Recruitment and retention methods. *Journal of Teacher Education, 39,* 54–57.

Causey, V.E., Thomas, C.D., & Armento, B.J. (2000). Cultural diversity is basically a foreign term to me: The challenges of diversity for preservice teacher education. *Teaching and Teacher Education, 16,* 33–45.

Cizek, G.J. (1995). On the limited presence of African American teachers: An assessment of research, synthesis, and policy implications. *Review of Educational Research, 65*(1), 78–92.

Dee, T.S. (2005). A teacher like me: Does race, ethnicity, or gender matter? *American Economic Review, 95*(2), 158–165.

Delpit, L.D. (1992). Education in a multicultural society: Our future's greatest challenge. *Journal of Negro Education, 61*(3), 237–249.

Ford, D.Y., & Grantham, T.C. (1997). The recruitment and retention of minority teachers in gifted education. *Roeper Review, 19*(4), 213–220.

Futrell, M.H. (1999). Recruiting minority teachers. *Educational Leadership, 56*(8), 30–33.

Gonzalez, J.M. (1997). Recruiting and training minority teachers: Student views of the preservice program. *Equity & Excellence in Education, 30*(1), 56–64.

Goodwin, A.L. (1991). Problems, process, and promise: Reflections on a collaborative approach to the solution of the minority teacher shortage.

Journal of Teacher Education, 42(1), 28–36.

Gordon, J.A. (1994). Why students of color are not entering teaching: Reflections from minority teachers. *Journal of Teacher Education, 45*(5), 346–353.

Gordon, J.A. (2000). *The color of teaching.* New York: RoutledgeFalmer.

Haddix, M. (2012). Talkin' in the company of my sistas: The counterlanguages and deliberate silences of Black female students in teacher education. *Linguistics and Education, 23*(2), 169–181.

Hawkins, B.D. (1994). Casualties: Losses among Black educators were high after *Brown. Black Issues in Higher Education, 10*(23), 26–31.

Hess, F.M., & Leal, D.L. (1997). Minority teachers, minority students, and college matriculation: A new look at the role-modeling hypothesis. *Policy Studies Journal, 25,* 235–248.

Hosp, J.L., & Reschly, D.J. (2004). Disproportionate representation of minority students in special education: Academic, demographic, and economic predictors. *Exceptional Children, 70*(2), 185–199.

Hudson, M.J., & Holmes, B.J. (1994). Missing teachers, impaired communities: The unanticipated consequences of *Brown v. Board of Education* on the African American teaching force at the precollegiate level. *Journal of Negro Education, 63*(3), 388–393.

Kane, P.R., & Orsini, A.J. (Eds.). (2003). *The colors of excellence: Hiring and keeping teachers of color in independent schools.* New York: Teachers College Press.

Kauchak, D., & Burbank, M.D. (2003). Voices in the classroom: Case studies of minority teacher candidates. *Action Teacher Education, 25*(1), 63–75.

King, S.H. (1993). The limited presence of African American teachers. *Review of Educational Research, 63*(2), 115–149.

Kirby, S.N., Berends, M., & Naftel, S. (1999). Supply and demand of minority teachers in Texas: Problems and prospects. *Educational Evaluation and Policy Analysis, 21*(1), 47–66.

Ladson-Billings, G. (2000). Fighting for our lives: Preparing teachers to teach African American students. *Journal of Teacher Education, 51*(3), 206–214.

Michigan Department of Education (2007, April). Teacher quality and turnover in the State of Michigan. University of Michigan Public Policy Class 632.

Michigan Department of Education (2009). *Report of the NCLB Teacher Equity Plan.* Retrieved from http://www2.ed.gov/programs/teacherqual/ hqtplans/revisedmicequ1109.doc.

Michigan Department of Education (2010). Office of Professional Preparation Services. *Approved teacher preparation programs.* Retrieved from https://mdoe.state.mi.us/proprep/.

Milner, H.R., & Howard, T.C. (2004). Black teachers, Black students, Black communities, and *Brown:* Perspectives and insights from experts. *Journal of Negro Education, 73*(3), 285–297.

Murnane, R.J., Singer, J.D., Willett, J.B., Kemple, J.J., & Olsen, R.J. (1991). *Who will teach? Policies that matter.* Cambridge: Harvard University Press.

National Center for Education Statistics (NCES). (2009). *Characteristics of public school districts in the United States: Results from the 2007–2008 schools and staffing survey (NCES 2009-320).* Washington, DC: Author.

National Center for Education Statistics (NCES). (2010a). *Digest of Education Statistics (NCES 2010-013).* Washington, DC: Author.

National Center for Education Statistics (NCES). (2010b). *The Condition of Education 2010 (NCES 2010-028).* Washington, DC: Author.

National Commission on Teaching and America's Future (NCTAF). (2010). *Who will teach? Experience matters.* Washington, DC: Author. Retrieved from http://nctaf.org/wp-content/uploads/2012/01/NCTAF-Who-Will-Teach-Experience-Matters-2010-Report.pdf.

Perkins, L.M. (1989). The history of Blacks in teaching: Growth and decline within the profession. In D. Warren (Ed.), *American teachers: Histories of a profession at work* (pp. 344–369). New York: Macmillan.

Quiocho, A., & Rios, F. (2000). The power of their presence: Minority group teachers and schooling. *Review of Educational Research, 70*(4), 485–528.

Ramsey, S. (2012). Caring is activism: Black southern womanist teachers theorizing and the careers of Kathleen Crosby and Bertha Maxwell-Roddey, 1946–1986. *Educational Studies: Journal of the American Educational Studies Associations, 48*(3), 244–265.

Shipp, V.H. (1999). Factors influencing the career choices of African American collegians: Implications for minority teacher recruitment. *Journal of Negro Education, 68*(3), 343–351.

Sleeter, C.E. (2001). Preparing teachers for culturally diverse schools: Research and the overwhelming presence of whiteness. *Journal of Teacher Education, 52*(2), 94–106.

State Board of Education (2012). *Report on the teacher preparation institution performance scores for academic year 2011–12.* Retrieved from http:// www.freep.com/assets/freep/pdf/C4193359814.PDF.

State of Michigan, Center for Educational Performance and Information (2008). *Registry of Educational Personnel Summary Report.* Retrieved from http:// www.michigan.gov/cepi/0,1607,7-113-21423_30446-,00.html.

State of Michigan, Center for Educational Performance and Information (2012). *Registry of Educational Personnel Summary Report.* Retrieved from http:// www.michigan.gov/cepi/0,4546,7-113-21423_30446-,00.html.

Torres, J., Santos, J., Peck, N.L., & Cortes, L. (2004). *Minority teacher recruitment, development, and retention.* Retrieved from http://www.alliance.brown. edu/pubs/minority_teacher/minteachrcrt.pdf.

U.S. Census Bureau (2006–2008). Detroit city, Michigan population, and housing narrative profile: 2006–2008. *American Community Survey.* Retrieved from http://factfinder.census.gov/servlet/NPTable?_bm=y&- geo_id=16000US2622000&-qr_name=ACS_2008_3YR_G00_NP01&- ds_name=&-redoLog=false.

U.S. Census Bureau (2010, November 4). State and County Quick Facts. Data derived from Population Estimates, Census of Population and Housing, Small Area Income and Poverty Estimates, State and County Housing Unit Estimates, County Business Patterns, Nonemployer Statistics, Economic Census, Survey of Business Owners, Building Permits, Consolidated Federal Funds Report. Washington, DC: Author.

U.S. Census Bureau (2012). *State and county quick facts.* Retrieved from http:// quickfacts.census.gov/qfd/states/26000.html.

U.S. Census Bureau, American Fact Finder (2008). GCT0202. Percent of the total population who are Black or African American Alone. *American Community Survey.* Retrieved from http://factfinder.census.gov/.

Valles, E.C. (1998). The disproportionate representation of minority students in special education: Responding to the problem. *Journal of Special Education, 32*(1), 52–54.

Zeichner, K.M. (2003). The adequacies and inadequacies of three current strategies to recruit, prepare, and retain the best teachers for all students. *Teachers College Record, 105*(3), 490–519.

Preparing for the Knowledge Society

LESSONS FROM DETROIT'S EARLY AFRICAN AMERICAN
FEMALE TEACHERS

LINDA G. WILLIAMS

The knowledge society, or postcapitalist society, as described by Drucker (1993), requires new ways to think about education, schooling, and work. As the United States transitions from an industrial culture to a knowledge-based society, the depth of change is felt deeply in industrial cities such as Detroit. Rapid technological and social change, however, is the stuff from which "rust belt" cities such as Detroit are made.

There is an intersectionality of literacy, identity, and lived experiences relative to pedagogical practices and educational realities (Wissman, 2011). It is the premise of this research that there are lessons to be learned from those who have experienced previous economic and cultural upheavals. One such group is Detroit's early African American teachers.

New economies call for new literacies. This was no less true when Fannie Richards walked into the offices of the Detroit Public Schools nearly 150 years ago and applied for a position as a teacher in the soon to be opened Colored School No. 2. She was successful in her pursuit, thus becoming the first African American employee of the Detroit Public Schools. In a Midwestern city of less than 50,000 people, of whom less than 3 percent were African American, this was quite an accomplishment, and it set the stage for the further development of Detroit's Black community in general, and the professional class specifically.

Fannie Richards and successive generations of Detroit's early Black teachers shared a deep belief in the value of literacy and its ability to transform and transcend personal circumstances and societal restrictions. However, the literacy that these women shared through generations was not a stable, autonomous skill limited to reading and writing. Rather, literacy was nurtured in very specific and strategic ways to navigate the rough waters of intense social and economic change. It would be more appropriate to call this knowledge "literacies," for it was multifaceted and wide-ranging. Fannie Richards and later teachers understood that gaining these literacies was a necessary and empowering requisite for racial uplift, community development, and economic freedom.

In this chapter, I explore some of the literacy practices of the family and communities of two early Detroit teachers: Fannie Richards (1840–1922) and Freida Browne (1918–) (pseudonym). Through historical, archival, and interview data gathered over the past five years, I developed life history accounts of these and several other women who taught in Detroit Public Schools. Using the constructs of critical social theory (Weiler, 1988), critical race theory (Ladson-Billings, 2000), and Black feminist thought (Collins, 2000) as a guide, I culled through the data, noting specific themes for analysis. In addition, Brandt's (2001) examination of the relationship of literacy to self-development and economic systems gave insight into the transformation of literacies through various social and economic settings. I conclude with thoughts about how the literacies of these African American women were developed and adjusted to respond to the social, economic, and technological changes experienced in their lifetimes—and what we can learn from them in today's rapidly changing world.

Fannie Richards

Fannie Richards's decision to apply for the position of teacher within the segregated public schools of Detroit in 1865 was strategic and purposeful. Just as Rosa Parks had been prepared through her membership in the NAACP and attendance at the Highlander Folk School for her fateful moment in 1955, Fannie Richards had been prepared to become a public school teacher. She was ready to apply at the first opportunity.

Richards's odyssey began in Fredericksburg, Virginia, where she was born into a free African American family in 1840. She was the youngest daughter of Maria Louise Moore Richards and Adolphus Richards, both of whom were also born free. Richards's mother was of mixed parentage and had come to Fredericksburg from Toronto. Her father was from Guadalupe.

Tensions abounded for free Black families in antebellum Virginia. This was especially true in the towns and small cities where most of them lived. Competition for jobs was stiff as free Blacks, enslaved Blacks, and Whites competed for work in the declining agricultural economy. Richards's father was an artisan who made furniture and was well respected in the community (Fitzgerald, 1979; Hartgrove, 1916). However, as laws became stricter in Virginia as to the rights and status of free Blacks, even his good reputation could not insulate the family from encroaching restrictions. By the time Fannie was born, it had become illegal for any person of color to become educated in the state and illegal for anyone to teach them. This legislation was largely in response to slave rebellions. Gabriel Prosser, who led a significant revolt in 1805, had been a free, literate Black. Rebellion leader Nat Turner, although enslaved, could also read and write when he led his revolution in 1831. Virginian legislators recognized the influence of literacy on instigating rebellion, and sought to close down all avenues for Blacks (free or enslaved) to obtain an education. It had been further legislated that African American children who had been sent out of state for an education could not return to Virginia. Thus, one of Richards's older brothers, John, was not allowed to return to his home and family after he had been educated in Washington, DC.

The situation around Richards's family only inspired activism. According to Hartgrove (1916), Maria Louise Moore Richards educated the children at home when they were younger. The Richards also sent their children to several clandestine schools that were run by various free Blacks and Whites (Hartgove, 1916). Adolphus Richards's signature appears on a petition from 1836 where he joined with other free Black men in Fredericksburg to appeal the state legislature of Virginia to create a school for free children of color. This petition, however, was rejected (Schweninger, 2001).

After Mr. Richards's sudden death in 1850, Mrs. Richards sold her property, and she and her children departed Virginia for the politically friendlier climes of Detroit. Other "well-to-do" families of the free Black artisan and professional classes followed shortly thereafter, including the Lees, Cooks, Williamses, and DeBaptistes. The Pelham family, from nearby Petersburg, followed a few years later (Hartgrove, 1916; Katzman, 1973). It was from these families that the first and second generations of Detroit Black teachers came.

With the addition of a few other families from other states (the Thompson, Cole, and Shewcraft families), these families formed the African American elite in Detroit, also known as the "Cultured 40," a name the press bestowed, or the "Old Detroiters," a name they adopted themselves. Reid (1996) describes what was significant about these families. First, the families were free. Either through manumission, birth, or immigrant status, the Old Detroiter families had enjoyed at least one generation of freedom before their children were born. This was significant because free status often helped when applying to become an apprentice or craft worker, a significant avenue of work at the time. Second, the families were gainfully employed in the South and migrated to Detroit with a reasonable amount of capital. This accumulation of capital continued in Detroit, and most of the families invested heavily in real estate, as well as education for their children. That Fannie Richards's mother had capital from the sale of their home in Fredericksburg was significant in helping the family become established in Detroit. Last, the families had a history of dealing with the civic and legal system. To maintain one's state of freedom in the South, it was necessary to interact with often hostile civic and legal institutions. Relationships had to be established with reputable Whites who could furnish letters of reference or vouch for Blacks in court. The ownership of land, furniture, tools, and technology (such as clocks) was accounted for and taxed. Petitions and appeals to the courts, while not commonplace, certainly happened often enough. These families also had a history of agitating for education that they saw as essential for controlling their own destinies. For them, literacy was a necessity that helped to maintain their status.

Fannie Richards arrived in Detroit at about the age of 10 and more than likely attended the private school operated at Second Baptist Church, the central Black institution in the city. Some newspaper accounts say she received her teacher training at the Toronto Normal School. When she returned to the city, she opened her own private school for children of color, until she applied for a teaching position at the new Colored School No. 2 that was being opened in response to parent demands that Colored School No. 1 was too far from their homes and inadequate (Katzman, 1973).

The family history of agitating for better conditions was reflected in Miss Richards joining with her brother, politico John Richards, and school board member John Bagley, to support a legislative bill to eliminate segregated schools in Michigan (Pebbles, 1981). When the bill was finally passed, Fannie Richards led her group of children from Colored School No. 2 to the Everett School, where she taught for 44 years (Hartgrove, 1916; Pebbles, 1981; Reid, 1996).

While at Everett, Miss Richards set up the city's first Froebel Kindergarten in 1872. It is not clear where or how she received her Froebel Kindergarten training, (a possibility is she took one of the short courses offered in St. Louis). Miss Richards's work establishing the kindergarten predated the National Association of Colored Women's Clubs (NACWC) call for support of the kindergarten by nearly 20 years. Dombkowski (2002) describes how

> NACWC mounted a tireless campaign to draw young middle-class African American women in kindergartening, based on the belief that middle-class women had a responsibility to use their material and intellectual advantages in order to socially and morally uplift the African American community through (among other programmes) the kindergarten. (p. 481)

This work intersected Miss Richards's major arena of activist literacy—that of her clubwoman endeavors. The theme of moral and social uplift permeates the clubwomen's work that Fannie Richards and her teaching colleagues, as well as her social peers, saw as necessary. Besides the kindergarten work that Miss Richards undertook professionally, she was also instrumental in establishing the Detroit chapter of the Phyllis Wheatley Home for the Colored Aged in 1901, a home that served the aged poor, many of whom were former slaves. Her name is also listed as a member of the Original Willing Workers, and the Michigan State Association of Colored Women. An obituary also mentions that Fannie Richards taught Sunday school at Second Baptist Church for over 50 years.

Fannie Barrier Williams, a well-known African American activist and writer from Chicago, detailed some of the developments of the Black women's club movement of the late nineteenth and early twentieth centuries (Williams, 1900).

She acknowledged how important church work was to learning how to conduct work in women's clubs:

> The training that first enabled colored women to organize and successfully carry on club work was originally obtained in church work. These churches have been and still are the great preparatory schools in which the primary lessons of social order, mutual trustfulness, and united effort have been taught. The churches have been sustained, enlarged, and beautified principally through the organized efforts of their women members. The meaning of unity of effort for the common good, the development of social sympathies grew into woman's consciousness through the privileges of church work. (p. 383)

Thus, the church served as an important place for developing the organizational and management literacy necessary to form effective social organizations. Fannie Richards used this knowledge to perform work within the growing urban world in which she lived.

Shaw (1996) in her research on Black professional women at the turn of the century pointed out that African American families were aware that their daughters would have to work to support their families. In fact, the only way to avoid domestic or agricultural work was to become a professional—and virtually the only profession available at the time in the South and in cities was school teaching. Shaw's research shows how young Black women of the elite and middle class were often socialized to be successful through family sacrifices that made formal education possible. In turn, these young women were expected to use their skills in support of the community. This notion of "socially responsible individualism," as discussed by Shaw (p. 2), was apparent in the family structures of both Miss Richards and other members of her cohort. This construct had the effect of not only reinforcing class, but also acknowledging the racialized and gendered environment in which the women participated. That these daughters of the elite were educated for professions meant that they would work in female-dominated occupations, and that they could also cross racialized boundaries and teach not only African American children, but other children as well, including the racialized immigrants arriving from different parts of Europe.

Their education also allowed them to be active leaders in their communities, and their club work, social work, literary pursuits, and musical endeavors laid the foundation for developing a leadership class of educated Black women that coexisted with the leading African American males. Miss Richards, then, was not only the first African American schoolteacher—she was also probably the first African American female professional in Detroit. Thus, she and the other women who followed stepped over a threshold into leadership and family development that had previously been limited to males (Katzman, 1973; Osterberg, 2003; Thomas, 1992; Wolcott, 2001). In addition, their activities brought them into daily contact with White children, parents, and colleagues, and this contact probably further defined their social class and position within the African American community.

During Fannie Richards's nearly 50 years of employment with the Detroit Public Schools, the population of Detroit grew from 63,000 to over 730,000. A frontier town when Richards began teaching, the city transformed into an economic powerhouse within 40 years, mostly due to the manufacturing of steel products and railroad cars. Detroit's African American population grew from approximately 1,800 to just under 6,000 people. However, the actual proportion of African Americans fell to about 1 percent as European immigration accounted for the vast majority of the population surge (Metzger & Booza, 2002). In fact, Fannie Richards taught very few children of color in her tenure with the Detroit Public Schools.

From 1865 through 1930, about a dozen African American women entered the teaching force in Detroit. These women, almost without exception, were daughters, granddaughters, or nieces of the elite class of African Americans that settled in Detroit with the Richardses from 1850 to 1880. They attended normal schools, at most (equivalent to present day junior colleges), and a few made lifelong careers of teaching. It is important to remember that this occurred at a time when even high school attendance was rare in the society. It would not be until the 1920s that high school attendance would reach more than half of the general population (Spring, 2004).

Ford's assembly line, the subsequent $5 a day salary, and the flow of White and Black workers from the south (after World War I stymied European immigration) changed Detroit drastically. "By 1930, Detroit had 1.5 million inhabitants . . . and its factories produced two billion dollars' worth of goods, more than any other American city except New York and Chicago" (Boyle & Getis, 1997, p. 12). The schools had changed also. By the 1920s, the Detroit Public Schools followed the progressive mandates of the time and had become one of the finest school systems in the world (Mirel, 1999). These schools educated the next generation of Detroit's Black schoolteachers.

Freida Browne

Mrs. Browne, born in 1918, just three years after Fannie Richards retired, represents the next generation of Detroit's African American teachers. Mrs. Browne was born in the South and arrived in Detroit in her midteens, in the early 1930s. I interviewed Mrs. Browne when she was in her mid-80s. Her recollections were clear and sharp, and she had much to say about her tenure as a Detroit Public Schools teacher and administrator.

As the migration of southern Black and White workers to Detroit grew and World War I closed the borders to immigration from Europe, a new African American elite emerged as the community expanded in size and stature. This elite group of people was comprised of successful Black entrepreneurs and professionals who served the burgeoning Black community. The daughters and sons of this new middle class were prepared to become professionals, and many of them chose the teaching profession, among few other choices. The school system they entered as teachers, however, was substantially different from the school system of the 1920s where many of them received their education.

Mirel (1999) convincingly argues that the strength of the Detroit Public Schools in the 1920s drew from the consensus among political conservatives, business interests, organized labor, and liberal allies in defining what a school system is for, whom it should serve, and how should it serve. This consensus fell away in the dire financial environment of the Great Depression. Positions hardened across the divide between business and labor and a financially strapped city and Board of Education that sought to staunch the loss of revenue.

A hiring freeze put in place in 1931 lasted for four years, resulting in fewer teachers and more students. In addition, curricular changes were enacted to keep more students in school and out of the employment lines. These changes resulted in watering down the general track, a situation that remained in place decades past the crisis days of the Depression (Mirel, 1999). Finally, school construction was halted, and overcrowded classrooms and unmaintained buildings became common in Detroit schools deep into the 1940s. The most significant change, however, for African American teachers was the Black community activism that became more visible in the 1930s, and the Detroit Public Schools became a focal point as segregation and discrimination in the schools became more apparent.

Mrs. Browne's family migrated to Detroit from Oklahoma City in 1929, shortly before the stock market crash. Her father was a janitor in Oklahoma and came to Detroit at the invitation of his brother, who was concerned about the educational opportunities available to his brother's four children, of which Mrs. Browne was the youngest. Mrs. Browne remembers overhearing the conversation between her father and his brother:

> And he said, this uncle said, "Well, I can give you a job, but you'll never be able to educate these children down here in a segregated society, and you don't make enough money to send them away. So, if you want to bring your family to Detroit, I could see that you manage very well."

Mrs. Browne's uncle convinced her father that the educational opportunities were much better in Detroit. He also ran a popular barbeque business downtown and was certain that he could provide adequate work for his brother.

An aunt secured a rented house for them on the west side of the city—in an area that was becoming increasingly African American as some families began to move out of Black Bottom, the poor and overcrowded ghetto on the near eastside. This particular portion of the Westside was racially mixed, with primarily Polish residents surrounding a Black enclave. The block to which the Brownes moved had only Negro residents according to the 1930 census. A working-class, upwardly mobile neighborhood, the Brownes' block featured a mixture of autoworkers, house cleaners, chauffeurs, and a few proprietors. Evidence of the striving character of the block was the presence of a music teacher, a mail carrier, and a porter for the railroads (U.S. Department of Commerce, 1930), all three of which were considered middle-class positions in the African American community at the time.

There were several aunts and uncles already in Detroit when the Brownes arrived in 1929. These connections helped the family secure employment that kept the family afloat and together through the turbulent economic times of the 1930s. One of Mrs. Browne's aunts, her mother's sister, was a licensed beautician who eventually owned six beauty shops. According to Mrs. Browne,

> She had passed as White at one time and learned beauty culture. . . . She learned everything there except how to straighten hair. She knew how to shampoo; she knew how to give facials and manicures, and dye hair and everything. But she

was fair enough that she could pass. So, after she finished her training, she went to work in one of the shops that was recommended, and she worked there long enough to get herself together and finally, she and her husband decided that they were going to be able to open up a beauty shop. So she opened it up in her basement on Boxwood near Tireman Avenue.

At a time when beautician licenses were not granted to Black women, Mrs. Browne's aunt was able to "infiltrate" the industry and obtain her own licensure. Mrs. Browne's mother and later Mrs. Browne herself would help in the shop and through this "apprenticeship" learn enough skills to bring in extra money to the household. Mrs. Browne's mother eventually opened her own shop in her basement, working as an unlicensed beautician. Jacqueline Jones (1995) explains the exceptional place of Black beauty parlors in the African American community:

> As a type of Black enterprise, beauty parlors were unique. Owned and staffed almost exclusively by women, they created jobs, offered highly valued services, and functioned as social centers in many neighborhoods. Their operators worked on a somewhat informal basis, often in their own homes or in a small rented booth in a store, and kept irregular hours in order to accommodate the schedules of patrons who were domestic servants. Hair pressers and stylists prided themselves on their skills, "fashioning beautifully arranged coiffures of smooth and pleasing waves." (J. Jones, 1995, p. 214)

Hence, Mrs. Browne, her mother, and her aunt used their acquired skills to maintain and support their families and interests through a type of female entrepreneurship that was crucial to sustaining Black working-class (and some middle-class) families. The service was exclusive to other African American women in the community, and thus it was an important economic mainstay where Black dollars were circulated among the Black community. It also provided an important alternative to domestic service that offered independence and community respect. Mrs. Browne's mother used the money to help pay for her house and college for her children. Mrs. Browne relates:

> She wanted us to go to college because she did not have the experience. And you know she kept a running finance note at a finance company up on Grand River. It never got paid out until the last one of us was out of school. She just

kept renewing it and renewing it so that we could go to school. And she curled hair to pay for it.

Mrs. Browne related another story that speaks to the place of Black women and work in Detroit in the 1930s. She was the youngest girl in a family of four and had one brother and two sisters. Mrs. Browne was a year younger than her closest sister was, and all of the sisters graduated from the local junior high within a year or two of their arrival in Detroit. The middle sister decided she wanted to become a nurse, so she chose to attend Cass Technical High School, instead of the much closer Northwestern High School, where Mrs. Browne and her oldest sister went. "And my sister had always wanted to be a nurse, so my mother let her transfer to Cass High School where they had pre-nursing, pre-dental, pre-everything." But the proximity of Cass Technical High School to the downtown business district led to Mrs. Browne's sister making a new choice:

And so when she went to Cass, she hadn't been there very long—I don't know what made her do this. She started leaving Cass every afternoon, going down to J. L. Hudson's [Detroit's largest department store at the time] and finally, Bill Hall, who hired all the Black people for J. L. Hudson's, hired her to run an elevator. And it was weeks before the Board of Education notified my mother that my sister was not in school.

My own family lore includes stories from my mother and aunts about how difficult it was to obtain a job at Hudson's Department Store. African American clerks were not hired in downtown Detroit stores until the 1950s or 1960s. The only position available for a Black woman at Hudson's was elevator operator. Even for that position, she had to pass the "paper bag test," meaning, her skin could not be darker than a brown paper bag. If she passed the test, she might be offered a position in the front banks of elevators. Women with darker skin worked the service and freight elevators, if they were hired at all.

Mrs. Browne's sister had specific reasons why she sought employment:

And [when confronted] my sister said, "You've got Theresa already in college and Freida's right behind her. And I'm not going to leave my job. You need every bit of help you can get." So she continued to work at Hudson's.

Mrs. Browne reported that her sister's employment downtown was beneficial to the rest of the family. "She could get a decent pair of shoes for $2.99 downtown and she helped us in many ways because money was so short." Eventually, this sister did fulfill her dream of becoming a nurse. She received her nursing degree from Sinai Hospital many years later.

The fact that Mrs. Browne's sister dropped out of high school to pursue employment was not that unusual. In fact, staying in high school was a much less frequent occurrence for males or females, Black or White at the time. Nationally, the high school completion rate was about 30 percent (Grossnickle, 1986; Tyack, 1974). This sister's story, however, illuminates how race and gender restricted the type of work available to young working women in the Detroit of the 1930s. Nevertheless, the sister was able to make a significant contribution to the family's financial situation, and by doing so, ensured that her younger siblings would go to college.

Employment proved to be a tenuous proposition for Mrs. Browne's father. When the Brownes arrived in Detroit, he was the main wage earner, but his brother's barbeque business where he was employed soon went under in the throes of the Depression. Unemployed for a while, he eventually landed a job at Ford Motor Company, with the help of his wife's family connections:

> My mother had at that time another brother who had come from Oklahoma. The only job he ever had was doorman at the Detroit Athletic Club downtown. He knew every big figure in the metropolitan area. When my father had nothing to do, all he [my uncle] did was speak to somebody who was walking in that door at the Detroit Athletic Club and said, "I have a brother-in-law who needs a job," and that's when my father went to work at Ford's.

At the time, Ford Motor Company was the largest employer of Black men in the Detroit area (Thomas, 1992). This vignette points to how important family and social networks were for all new migrants. Families with such networks did not have to rely as heavily on such agencies as the Urban League or church programs, or simply on luck. In this respect, Mrs. Browne's family bore resemblance to the families mentioned earlier in this study, all of whom supported each other by finding and/or sharing housing, developing and sustaining independent businesses, and by obtaining employment in either Detroit's diverse and burgeoning industries or with the city government. This family network provided a depth of support that allowed the children of migrants to pursue college educations.

There were other factors, however, that assisted Mrs. Browne and other Blacks in obtaining positions with the Detroit Public Schools. Within the African American community there was a growing dissatisfaction with not only the apparent segregation of schools, but also the lack of Black teachers and other employees within the Detroit Public Schools (Mirel, 1999).

The problem of school segregation became evident as the number of Blacks in the city increased. Prior to the 1930s, Detroit, like other northern cities, had school populations that were integrated (Homel, 1984; Perlmann, 1988). During the 1920s, only two of Detroit's 141 elementary schools were majority Black, and both of these schools were over 40 percent White (Mirel, 1999). By the 1930s, however, the number of Blacks in the city had increased to about 8 percent of the population, and as evidenced in the experiences of Mrs. Browne, the African American community began to spread away from the conscribed, congested area of the near eastside.

Black leaders began to call attention to the low numbers of Black elementary teachers and the fact that there were no African American high school teachers. They also noted that the Board of Education policy of placing Black teachers with only Black students was discriminatory. Segregation of pupils, however, became a larger issue. Mirel (1999) encapsulates the situation:

> By the mid-1930s, there was growing evidence that the school system was again becoming racially segregated.... During the late 1920s and early 1930s, many of the schools that previously had been integrated became almost completely Black. Unquestionably, this trend was largely due to the changing racial composition of neighborhoods and practices such as restrictive real estate covenants. (p. 188)

School segregation, plus the larger economic and social issues of teacher hiring and teacher placement, received hardly any attention from the Detroit chapter of the NAACP, one of the largest chapters in the country at the time (Thomas, 1992). Instead, the NAACP was occupied with housing issues (including the Sweet trial in 1925) and union issues, as the drive toward labor organizing was met with heavy resistance in the Black community (Thomas, 1992).

Snow Grigsby, a college-educated Detroiter who worked at the post office and Rev. William Peck, the founder of the Booker T. Washington Trade Association (a Black middle-class entrepreneurial business association) formed the Detroit Civic Rights Committee. There were few if any positions for college-educated Black men in Detroit at the time; hence the Detroit Civic Rights Committee openly challenged the hiring practices of many organizations, including the Detroit Board of Education. Targeting organizations that were financed by public funds, the Civic Rights Committee published pamphlets and held programs in African American churches to publicize the lack of Black employment in taxpayer-funded organizations. Their pivotal position was that the percentage of personnel hired in publicly funded agencies should reflect the demographics of the city. In other words, if nearly 8 percent of the city population was Negro, then nearly 8 percent of the personnel hired in these agencies should also be Negro (Grigsby, 1967; Mirel, 1999; Thomas, 1992).

In 1933, the committee confronted the Board of Education on its dismal hiring record, and the board responded by assigning Mr. Cody, the superintendent, to meet with the committee. The instructions were if qualified people were found, they should be hired. In a later interview, Mr. Grigsby recounted:

> To our surprise, we got 19 jobs that day, and within a year, the Board hired almost a hundred, whereas before they hadn't hired one a year in the past 91 years. (Grigsby, 1967)

While Grigsby is correct in saying that the board put some effort into hiring more African Americans, Thomas (1992) points out that by 1936 only 57 Blacks worked as regular teachers, out of a total number of 7,408 teachers. Black teachers remained less than 1 percent of the total teaching force. African American employment did increase, however, in other occupations for the board. Most notably, Lloyd Cofer was hired in 1934 as the first Black male professional and first Black secondary counselor (at Miller High), and William St. Clair Billups gained employment as the first African American school secretary for the Board of Education (C.K. Jones, 1970; Kurth, 2005). These pioneering African American men ushered in an era of rapid advancement for the few Black males who gained entry into the Detroit Public Schools.

Mrs. Browne was graduating from high school when these events occurred, and found her entrance into teacher preparation relatively unhindered. She was accepted to the State Normal School at Ypsilanti (now Eastern Michigan

University), with financial assistance provided by the Federal Emergency Relief Act (FERA), the beginning of President Franklin Roosevelt's "New Deal." Among the many emergency education programs of the FERA was the college student aid program. Participating colleges provided part-time employment for low-income or unemployed students" (Federal Emergency Relief Administration, 2003). Mrs. Browne remembers:

> [It was in] '34. And I went straight to college, out at [what is now called] Eastern, because at that time the federal government had some kind of special program, I went out for my first year, and I worked.... The campus was nothing like it is today. They had no hospital; they had nothing to service the students. And all the kids lived in private homes, as we did. Well, out there they had what they called "Health Cottage."... And my federal job was to work at Health Cottage, and all I did was keep those files, but I got my first year's tuition paid by doing that.

This federal assistance job helped Mrs. Browne develop clerical skills, and she expressed supreme satisfaction with her classes at the State Normal School. However, she was unable to remain at the school past the first year. Lack of family finances brought her back to Detroit.

At first disappointed at the transfer home, Mrs. Browne came to consider that the trip home was a fortunate event. She soon found out that the only way she could become a teacher in Detroit was to go to City College (now Wayne State University). According to Mrs. Browne, the Detroit Board of Education "ran City College," and those prospective teachers from other teacher education institutions had to have exceptional credentials in order to be hired by the Detroit Public Schools. She reported that students from the Normal School in Ypsilanti were frequently sent to "substandard" school systems in more rural school districts.

The one pivotal event that Mrs. Browne described about her years at City College was the invitation to join Delta Sigma Theta, an African American female sorority. She was very proud to have been invited to join the newly recognized chapter and during our interview boasted of her 70-year anniversary with the sorority.

Sororities, for this generation, were important places of self- and professional development. Unlike other organizations with racial goals, sororities were created to change and benefit individuals, and through the development of individual Black women, serve society (Giddings, 1988; Graham, 1999). "The sorority has also been an important source of leadership training for African American women, whose opportunities to exercise such skills in formal organizations are few" (Giddings, 1988, p. 16). Membership was based on successful college attendance, and women were sought who shared social bonds and experiences. Mrs. Browne's enthusiasm for joining the Deltas was linked to how honored she felt to be asked to join. Many of the members were the wealthier daughters of Detroit's elite and entrepreneurial class, a group she aspired to.

The connections forged in sororities served the women well as they entered the Detroit Public Schools. A kinship was shared among the other few Black schoolteachers who were also sorority sisters that proved helpful as opportunities for advancement opened up for African American women in the Detroit Public Schools in the 1950s and 1960s. As the national and local sororities expanded their commitment to community and political service, they began to supplant the national and local club work that women in previous generations had participated in (Giddings, 1988).

Mrs. Browne was required to substitute for two years before receiving a position with the Detroit Public Schools. She thought the experience gave her a good overview of the school system, although she acknowledged that she was only sent to schools with high African American enrollment. Mrs. Browne proclaimed, "I could tell you every Black teacher in the system, 'cause that's the only place they would send me—where there were Black teachers." Mrs. Browne named four elementary schools on the lower eastside, Barstow, Lincoln, Trowbridge, and Duffield—where the majority of Detroit's Black students and teachers attended and taught. Mrs. Browne finally landed a permanent position teaching second grade at Lincoln School.

Freida Browne's journey highlights the struggles that were faced by many in a rapidly changing social and economic world. As part of a large wave of migration from rural and semiurban locales to Detroit, Mrs. Browne and her family experienced many of the challenges and benefits of learning new ways of work and education. Her father became an assembly line worker, and was able to provide a steady income for the family. Her mother became an entrepreneur and as such could support her daughters' aspirations for a college education. Her sister took on service work in order to support the family further. Freida Greene learned "new literacies" in college—through employment, her sorority work, and her education. Later she spoke about her career as a teacher and how she learned to manage a classroom, and later a school as an assistant principal. She remained devoted to social causes, civic organizations, and the arts throughout her life, and she credits her parents with having the foresight to move to a more vibrant city like Detroit when she was a girl.

New Literacies

From the 1865 birth of Black female professionals in Detroit to the women entering teaching in the 1940s, there is evidence that there were many community and familial supports that helped these women become successful despite the rapidly changing cultural and economic environment around them. The women documented in this study—Fannie Richards and Freida Browne—moved from rural and semiurban communities to the industrialized North, just as the industrial revolution was reaching its peak in productivity. Is there anything about their experience that would be useful to Black women now who face a society changing from an industrial base to a knowledge economy?

When Richards and Browne were coming of age, they too faced extraordinary circumstances in extraordinary times. Both of these women acquired new skills, developed and participated in private, religious, and public institutions, and used their foresight to bring the skills and depositions needed for an urban environment to a younger generation. I contend that parallels can be drawn between the capacities and skills they developed and the capacities and skills needed as this culture transitions to the twenty-first-century knowledge economy.

Drucker (1993) points to the most important aspect of the knowledge economy: Knowledge becomes the means of production. Whereas previously the means of production was capital, natural resources, or labor, it is now knowledge, knowledge that can be applied to systems, processes, and organizations. Fannie Richards, Freida Browne, and other Black women in their cohorts used knowledge production in an activist way. They were intensely involved in efforts to define themselves and their peers as professional Black women who were active in the spheres of community building and education. This knowledge-building process was essential as the women worked against the prevailing stereotypes of African American women that were persistent in the media and public perceptions. In order to battle these images, early Black teachers worked tirelessly at developing a deep sense of respectability that was enhanced by knowledge about who they were and how they wanted to be perceived.

Another capacity that early Black teachers developed was the ability to plan and anticipate changes in the social, cultural, and economic environment. Because of the subjugated status of their families and communities, these professional women learned to anticipate, investigate, and solve problems. Like knowledge workers of today, they were able to locate, gather, analyze, and organize information. By doing so, they were able to adapt to a range of situations and take calculated risks to fulfill their vision. For example, after Fannie Richards was employed by the Detroit Public Schools, she took up the work of investigating how she might assist in the desegregation of the school system. Her efforts including study of the legal constructs around segregation, as well as a consideration of what might happen if she did or did not participate in the process. Her analysis allowed her to take a calculated risk and achieve success.

Early African American teachers also learned how to learn. Neither Fannie Richards nor Freida Browne thought their education ended with formal schooling. They were both in organizations that put them on the front line of new knowledge. They took advantage of learning situations provided through continuing education, and they undertook quite a bit of self-education. Freida Browne was offered a chance to accompany her husband to Germany during the Korean War. She took the opportunity as an officer's wife to learn to tutor the many Black and White American soldiers there who were barely literate. Later she applied for a teaching position in the American Department of Defense Schools. Her application was accepted, but when someone at the agency met her, the offer was withdrawn. The employer did not realize that Freida Browne was African American. After some negotiating, she was given the position and enjoyed much success in her position, proudly stating she was the first Black teacher the Department of Defense hired overseas. For both Browne and Richards, knowledge was not static and was not confined to the narrow halls of their own schooling experiences.

Browne, Richards, and their peers knew the importance of working in teams with others, an aspect that knowledge workers of today are called upon to do. Leu and coauthors (2007) point out that the new literacies are "multiple, multimodal, and multifaceted" and "they increase the complexity of analysis that seeks to understand them" (p. 43). This level of complexity suggests that multiple viewpoints are necessary to understand them and that further study might advance best in interdisciplinary teams. Richards, Browne, and others in their cohort worked in a variety of situations where multiple viewpoints were expressed. This diversity of opinion helped shaped club work, church work, and other social endeavors, as well as professional tasks. In addition, a tradition of community support and agitation made teaching jobs available. Even though professional work for African American women was limited to teaching (and later, social work and nursing), community agitation was necessary to open up these fields more widely to Black women and men.

The final capacity of these women of these that should be mentioned was their strong foundation in the basic communication skills of the time that was enhanced by the dedicated literate families that supported the education of their daughters. The insurance of a strong education prepared these women for successful college and professional careers at a time when other Black women were still confined to domestic work and when other White women were being prepared for clerical and sales positions unavailable to Black women. Families were willing to relocate to places where education was available and thus, essentially, changed their class status from the lower working class to the striving lower rungs of the professional class by moving their daughters into positions where they could become educated and teach. Some families took on more entrepreneurial work such as hairdressing or real estate sales, while others developed and relied on professional and patronage positions that were the result of past social and education investments. This flexibility and vision required and inspired innovative thinking and risk taking.

The lives of Fannie Richards and Freida Browne are two examples of early African American teachers in Detroit who were able to pursue and establish productive careers in the Detroit Public Schools. Their lessons still serve as inspiration and hope to a fresh generation facing turbulent times.

REFERENCES

Boyle, K., & Getis, V. (1997). *Muddy boots and ragged aprons: Images of working-class Detroit, 1900–1930*. Detroit: Wayne State University Press.

Brandt, D. (2001). *Literacy in American lives*. Cambridge: Cambridge University Press.

Collins, P.H. (2000). *Black feminist thought.* New York: Routledge.

Colored teacher loved children and enjoyed 44 years in service. (June 20, 1915). *News Tribune.*

Deegan, M.J. (Ed.). (2002). *The new woman of color: The collected writings of Fannie Barrier Williams, 1893–1918.* DeKalb: Northern Illinois University Press.

Dombkowski, K. (2002). Kindergarten teacher training in England and the United States 1850–1918. *History of Education, 31*(5), 475–489.

Drucker, P.F. (1993). *Post-capitalist society.* New York: Harper Business.

Federal Emergency Relief Administration (2003). University of Washington Special Collections Division. Retrieved from http://content.lib. washington.edu/feraweb/about.html.

Fitzgerald, R.C. (1979). *A different story: A Black history of Fredericksburg, Stafford and Spotsylvania, Virginia.* Greensboro, NC: Unicorn Press.

Giddings, P. (1988). *In search of sisterhood: Delta Sigma Theta and the challenge of the Black Sorority movement.* New York: William Morrow.

Graham, L.O. (1999). *Our kind of people: Inside America's Black upper class.* New York: HarperCollins.

Grigsby, S. (1967). Interview of Snow Grigsby by Roberta McBride. Archives of Labor History and Urban Affairs, Wayne State University.

Grossnickle, D. (1986). *High school dropouts: Causes, consequences, and cure.* Fastback #242. Bloomington, IN: Phi Delta Kappa Educational Foundation.

Hartgrove, W.B. (1916). The story of Maria Louise Moore and Fannie M. Richards. *Journal of Negro History, 1*, 23–33.

Higginbotham, E. (1987). Employment for professional Black women in the twentieth century. In C. Bose & G. Spitze (Eds.), *Ingredients for women's employment policy* (pp. 74–92). Albany: State University of New York Press.

Hine, D.C. (1994). *Hine sight: Black women and the re-construction of American history.* Bloomington: Indiana University Press.

Homel, M. (1984). *Down from equality: Black Chicagoans and the public schools, 1920–41.* Urbana: University of Illinois Press.

Jones, C.K. (1970). The historify of Sidney D. Miller High School with particular exploration into those factors which resulted in the inordinately high incidences of pupil successes considering, and despite, existing socioeconomic factors which are perceived as being prime predictors of high incidences of pupil failure. 1919–1957. Ed.D. diss., Wayne State University.

Jones, J. (1995). *Labor of love, labor of sorrow*. New York: Random House.

Katzman, D.M. (1973). *Before the ghetto: Black Detroit in the nineteenth century*. Urbana: University of Illinois Press.

Kurth, J. (2005, March 31). Educator rose above the specter of racism to make his mark. *Detroit News*.

Ladson-Billings, G. (2000). Racialized discourses and ethnic epistemologies. In N.K. Denzin & Y.S. Lincoln (Eds.), *Handbook of qualitative research* (pp. 257–277). Thousand Oaks, CA: Sage.

Leu, D.J., Zawilinski, L, Castek, J., et al. (2007). What is new about the new literacies of online reading comprehension. In L.S. Rush, A.J. Eakle, & A. Berger (Eds.), *Secondary school literacy: What research reveals for classroom practice* (pp. 37–68). Urbana, IL: National Council of Teachers of English.

Metzger, K., & Booza, J. (2002). *African Americans in the United States, Michigan, and Metropolitan Detroit*. Detroit: Wayne State University, College of Urban, Labor, and Metropolitan Affairs.

Mirel, J. (1999). *The rise and fall of an urban school system: Detroit, 1907–1981*. 2nd ed. Ann Arbor: University of Michigan Press.

Osterberg, B. G. (2003). *Our silent song: The true story of an American family*. Baltimore: PublishAmerica.

Pebbles, R. (1981). Fannie Richards and the integration of the Detroit Public Schools. *Michigan History Magazine, 65*, 25–26.

Perlmann, J. (1988). *Ethnic differences: Schooling and social structures among Irish, Italians, Jews and Blacks in an American city, 1880–1935*. New York: Cambridge University Press.

Reid, J.B. (1996). Race, class, gender, and the teaching profession: African American schoolteachers of the urban Midwest, 1865–1950. Ph.D. diss., Michigan State University.

Royster, J.J. (1994). *Traces of a stream: Literacy and social change among African American women*. Pittsburgh: University of Pittsburgh Press.

Shaw, S.J. (1996). *What a woman ought to be and to do: Black professional women workers during the Jim Crow era*. Chicago: University of Chicago Press.

Schweninger, L. (2001). *The southern debate over slavery*. Vol. 1: *Petitions to southern legislatures, 1778–1864*. Urbana: University of Illinois Press.

Spring, J. (2004). *The American school: 1642–2004*. New York: McGraw Hill.

Sugrue, T.J. (1996). *The origins of the urban crisis: Race and inequality in postwar*

Detroit. Princeton: Princeton University Press.

Thomas, R.W. (1992). *Life for us is what we make it: Building Black community in Detroit, 1915–1945.* Bloomington: Indiana University Press.

Tyack, D.B. (1974). *The one best system: A history of American urban education.* Cambridge: Harvard University Press.

U.S. Department of Commerce, Bureau of the Census (1930). *Fifteenth Census of the United States: 1930 Population Schedule.* Retrieved from www.ancestry.com.

Washington, B.T. (Ed.). *A new Negro for a new century.* Chicago: American Publishing House.

Weiler, K. (1988). *Women teaching for change.* Westport, CT: Bergin & Garvey.

Williams, F.B. (1900). The club woman movement among colored women of America. In B. T. Washington, F.B. Williams, & N.B. Wood (Eds.), *A new Negro for a new century: An accurate and up-to-date record of the upward struggles of the Negro race* (pp. 379–405). Chicago: American Publishing House.

Wissman, K.K. (2011). "Rise up!" Literacies, lived experiences, and identities within an in-school "other space." *Research in the Teaching of English, 45*(4), 405–438.

Wolcott, V.W. (2001). *Remaking respectability: African American women in interwar Detroit.* Chapel Hill: University of North Carolina Press.

Poverty, Postsecondary Education, and Child Care

THE IMPACT OF "WORK FIRST" POLICIES ON AFRICAN AMERICAN SINGLE MOTHERS IN MICHIGAN

VALERIE POLAKOW

But you know even if I'm in that survival mode, I still want that education for my child—I don't want that cheap day care lady down the block, we want our kids to be safe and taught like in the preschool.... You don't always get that.... When I started back in school, my worker she cut my aid, and then they denied me the subsidies.

—*Brandy, a divorced student mother of two young children*

I mean it's just like such a struggle to deal with them [the Department of Human Services].... I made the dean's list at the community college, but now I'm just struggling to maintain my grades and do the work hours.... I lost my first job because the worker would not give me child care.... I told her I want a hearing because I called the lawyer and he said I'm entitled to that [child care] subsidy as long as I'm working.

—*Tina, a returning student and single mother of two young children*

I couldn't find someone to watch my baby.... I've just been trying to go to work and trying to pretend it's not even there. When I come home I still call [child care providers], but I mean nothing's changed. I feel like I ain't getting nowhere.

—*Jasmine, a 19-year-old single mother of a toddler*

These are the voices of African American mothers in poverty in Michigan—divorced, single, and teen parents. All share in common experiences of harsh inflexible treatment from a welfare system that systematically discourages them from pursuing postsecondary education and, with its "Work First" emphasis, coerces the women to take jobs, no matter how bad the pay or working conditions, in order to receive any benefits. As the women are mothers of young children, their lives are made more complicated by the lack of affordable, high-quality child care, and the inadequate child care subsidies to which they are entitled are frequently and arbitrarily denied and seldom pay the full cost of care. Struggling to earn, to learn, and to parent their children, Brandy, Tina, and Jasmine are emblematic of poor women across the country whose lives and the lives of their children have been constricted, harmed, and diminished because of public policies that work against, not for, poor mothers. The fact that they are poor African American women means that they confront disproportionate obstacles as they struggle to survive against the double burdens of racial and gender discrimination.

For the past 20 years, I have been documenting the obstacles confronted by poor women who, as mothers, encounter an extraordinarily hostile social welfare system and often indifferent and/or inhospitable higher education institutions, as they struggle to complete both vocational and postsecondary education, with limited or no access to good-quality child care, housing, and health care.[1] In this chapter, I focus on the devastating federal and state impacts of poverty and "welfare reform" on college aspirations during the period from the inception of welfare reform in 1996 to the election of President Obama in 2008. Additionally, this chapter examines the consequences of restricted access to postsecondary education and child care that threatens the viability of low-income single-mother families in general, and African American single-mother families in particular, and the constant crisis of care that erupts when good-quality child care is neither accessible nor affordable.

A Brief History

In 1996, a Republican-controlled Congress passed, and President Bill Clinton signed into law, one of the most far-reaching and damaging pieces of social legislation—the Personal Responsibility and Work Opportunity Reconciliation Act (PRWORA), otherwise known as welfare reform. PRWORA was the culmination of several decades of rhetorical and legislative assaults against poor women, particularly women of color, and their children—for whom welfare (minimal though it was) served as an essential safety net. In the racially coded debates preceding the passage of PRWORA, poor women were denounced in Congress by Republican legislators as "breeding mules" "monkeys," and "alligators." Representative Clay Shaw, House Ways and Means chairman, who ensured passage of the legislation through the House stated, "It may be like hitting a mule with a two by four but you've got to get their attention" (DeParle, 1994). When the bill reached the Senate, Senator Phil Gramm (famous for his "America is a nation of whiners" comment during the economic crisis in September 2008) stated, "We've got to get a provision that denies more and more cash benefits to women who have more and more babies while on welfare" (Toner, 1995). This racially coded and demonizing discourse about poor single mothers in the United States was part of a long and ignominious history of "welfare racism," where race has largely shaped who is poor, who is (or will be) denied public assistance, whose children are disproportionately harmed, and who are constructed as sexually promiscuous and work-aversive (Abramowitz, 2001; Mink, 1998; Neubeck & Casenave, 2001; Piven, 1998). Former president Ronald Reagan, in the presidential primary campaign of 1976, immortalized such pernicious images when he denounced the Cadillac-driving "welfare queen" supposedly defrauding the nation:

> She has 80 names, 30 addresses, 12 Social Security cards and is collecting veteran's benefits on four non-existing deceased husbands. And she is collecting Social Security on her cards. She's got Medicaid, getting food stamps, and she is collecting welfare under each of her names. (Gilliam, 1999)

Hence, the groundwork for the demonization of poor mothers was well embedded in the media and public consciousness when President Clinton, who campaigned on a pledge to "end welfare as we know it," formed an unholy alliance with right-wing Republicans who controlled the House and Senate to "point to poor women, especially minority women, as the source of America's troubles. Welfare and the women who depend on it have been cast as the locus of a kind of moral rot" (Piven, 1995, p. xiii).

The welfare reform legislation of 1996 rescinded Title IVA of the 1935 Social Security Act and repealed the statutory entitlement to income security through Aid to Families with Dependent Children (AFDC) that guaranteed assistance for poor mothers and their children. While the AFDC program historically had discriminated against African American women and immigrants using exclusionary "moral fitness" provisions, a broad expansion of access for women of color did take place during the War on Poverty in the 1960s, fueled by activists in the Poor People's Campaign and the National Welfare Rights Organization (Amott, 1990; Piven & Cloward, 1998). Although the expanded welfare provisions were never adequate to sustain single-mother families, AFDC was a vital entitlement that supported poor women and their children with minimal cash benefits and served as a residual safety net from destitution. However, PRWORA dismantled these minimal entitlements and replaced AFDC with state-administered block grants, Temporary Assistance for Needy Families (TANF). The TANF grants made assistance conditional on fulfilling mandatory Work First requirements, thereby forcing millions of poor mothers with infants, toddlers, and very young children into the low-wage labor market, precipitating a child care crisis (Polakow, 2007). These punitive reforms, argues Mink, "pressure[d] poor single mothers to surrender their civil rights as a condition of economic assistance ... [and] punish[ed] poor single mothers for bearing and caring for children by compelling them to work outside the home" (1998, p. 2). State TANF grants were time-limited to two consecutive years and a lifetime limit of five years. It was left up to the states to decide how welfare clients would meet Work First requirements; but only six states (Maine, Kentucky, Illinois, Iowa, Wyoming, and Kentucky) permitted some postsecondary education as a countable work activity for a limited period. While the 1996 PRWORA legislation mandated a minimum of 20 hours of work a week for mothers with children between one and six years old, and up to 35 hours a week for those with children over six, some states, such as Michigan, instituted even harsher TANF requirements (as did Ohio, Massachusetts, Wisconsin, and New York) mandating that women with infants 12 weeks and older also be required to meet Work First mandatory requirements.

Under the threat of benefit cutoffs for failure to comply, poor women were denied the right to make critical parental decisions about their out-of-home care for their young children (Kahn & Polakow, 2000a, 2004; Mink, 1998). Faced with bad choices for cheap child care or no welfare benefits, the emotional well-being and safety of their children had to be weighed against family survival needs due to the inflexibility of the Work First mandates. The demand for child care, particularly for infants and toddlers, increased exponentially under PRWORA, but the limited funds allocated for child care subsidies for mothers in welfare-to-work programs did little to alleviate the growing child care crisis of quality, access, and affordability.

During the years immediately following the passage of welfare reform, there was a precipitous drop in the number of families receiving welfare—from 5 million in 1994, to 4 million in 1996, and down to just 2 million by 2002 (U.S. Department of Health and Human Services, 2003). The proportion of families receiving food stamps dropped as well, and African American women who left welfare for low-wage work fared far worse than other ethnic groups, experiencing deeper poverty and increased hardships (Institute for Women's Policy Research, 2003). While politicians triumphantly extolled the rapid decline in welfare caseloads, it should be remembered that two-thirds of welfare recipients are children; hence, the immediate aftermath was an increase of 1.1 million children falling into extreme poverty and destitution. The workforce participation of single mothers living in extreme poverty increased by 50 percent. Nonetheless, they lost access to other benefits such as health care and food stamps (and often child care); they found themselves poorer, with less monthly income, and increasingly destitute under the new TANF Work First policies (Lyter et al., 2004; Super et al., 1996).

The ensuing consequences wreaked further havoc on single-mother families with very young children—as more and more mothers with infants and toddlers were pushed off welfare into the low-wage workforce, unable to access affordable, infant care as they struggled to meet mandatory work requirements. However, national reports and ethnographic studies pointed to a growing crisis of care for very young children, characterized by lack of access and inferior quality with disproportionate negative impacts on young African American and Latino children (Chaudry, 2004; Ebb, 1994; Galinsky et al., 1994; Polakow, 2007).

When President Bush announced his plans for the reauthorization of PRWORA in 2002, he declared the 1996 welfare legislation "a resounding success" and proposed further expansion of mandatory work requirements. The new work requirements stipulated that welfare recipients work 40 hours per week to retain any benefits—a workweek that exceeds the average of *all* mothers with children under 18 (Institute for Women's Policy Research, 2002). Sixteen of the 40 hours permitted recipients to engage in "constructive activities" such as short-term job training; but postsecondary education was clearly not an option. Noticeably absent from the plan were investments in income and job supports, investment in postsecondary education, and additional funding for child care subsidies. As Marian Wright Edelman, director of the Children's Defense Fund put it: "The President requires more hours of work, but not one dime more for child care.... Right now only one in seven children eligible for federal child care assistance gets it" (Toner & Pear, 2002, p. A18).

Women who leave welfare for work are generally employed in minimum wage jobs with little opportunity for advancement or benefits. Such jobs offer few exits from poverty and little hope for family self-sufficiency, particularly among African American mothers. Nationally African American women work more hours than White women work, but earn less, and are disproportionately affected by layoffs and job losses. In 2005, the unemployment rate for African American women was double that of White women (Institute for Women's Policy Research, 2005). The effects of the Great Recession (2007–2009) were significantly worse for women than men, and a higher number of African American and Hispanic women experienced unemployment spells (36 percent and 35 percent, respectively) in contrast to 20 percent of White women (Hayes & Hartman, 2011). For the period under study in this chapter, national data indicate that the wages of women who had left welfare and were employed averaged just $6.51 per hour, with only 23 percent of employers providing health insurance. Additional studies showed that more than two-thirds of adults terminated from welfare were employed at jobs paying $7.50 an hour with few if any benefits; these unstable jobs meant that those who transitioned off welfare frequently ended up back on welfare, reporting housing and food insecurity as key hardships (Brauner & Lopest, 1999; Kahn et al., 2004; Sherman et al., 1998).

However, the most severe impacts of the erosion of welfare entitlements must be judged against the backdrop of the United States' shameful record of child poverty: the highest child poverty rates among 19 wealthy industrialized countries (Innocenti Research Centre, 2007). By 2008, 13.3 million children were living in poverty and 28 million were in low-income families.[2] This coincided with the Bush administration's social spending cuts and exacerbated the harsh strictures of "welfare reform" as child poverty increased dramatically by 1.2 million, and almost a million of the newly poor children were under-threes living in extreme poverty. With 9.4 million children lacking any form of health insurance and 12.6 million estimated to be hungry or living on the edge of hunger, children of color (African American, Latino, and American Indian) experienced disproportionate impacts, with the highest percentage of African American children—36 percent—living in poor families, in contrast to 10 percent of White children. The poorest children (69 percent) lived in single-parent families that were predominantly female-headed. African American single mothers with young children continued to represent the most vulnerable subgroup in the United States, with persistent poverty a pervasive threat to their well-being and healthy development (Food Research and Action Center, 2007; National Center for Children in Poverty, 2008a; National Urban League Policy Institute, 2007). Employment in low-wage work was also no buffer against poverty; 56 percent of children lived in low-income families where a parent actually worked full-time (Douglas-Hall & Chau, 2007; Fass & Cauthen, 2008). Since the severe recession of 2008, economic inequality has increased exponentially and child poverty rates have soared. Currently, there are 15.5 million children living below the federal poverty level, with a total of 31.9 million children living in low-income families (Addy & Wight, 2012).

Poverty and Child Care

With almost 12 million children under the age of five in some form of public or private child care, low-income single mothers with young children continued to face an acute child care crisis. Furthermore, the desperate demand for child care resulted in women on welfare competing for scarce resources with low-income women surviving just above the poverty line. Demand for child care far exceeds the supply across the country, and has led states into a race to the bottom, in order to provide the cheapest of publicly subsidized care. There are long waiting lists for child care subsidies in 22 states, and only 1 in 6 of all income-eligible children actually receives them—even then, subsidies do not pay the full cost of care (Helburn & Bergmann, 2002; National Association of Child Care Resource and Referral Agencies, 2012; National Women's Law Center, 2011; Polakow, 2007). Child care costs are so high that they often exceed the cost of college tuition at most public universities, ranging from $3,900 to $11,700 a year for full-time center-based care for a preschool child, and from $4,600 to $15,000 for an infant (National Association of Child Care Resource and Referral Agencies, 2012). While costs are considerably cheaper in family day care homes, many are unlicensed, and lack of regulation and monitoring substantially increases the risks for young children. The American Recovery and Reinvestment Act of 2009 did temporarily make a dent in the acute crisis of child care as states gained a $2 billion increase in child care funds, but as budget deficits grew, early childhood budgets shrank, and programs were cut after the funds were exhausted by the end of 2010 (National Women's Law Center, 2011).

Because there is no federal regulation of private child care, it is up to the states to set minimum standards for child care centers: but minimum translates to less than minimal in terms of regulating the quality of care. Low-income parents encounter greater hurdles obtaining licensed care; as lack of resources diminishes choices, there is less access in poor neighborhoods to higher-quality care, and unstable, odd-hour work schedules make child care arrangements very difficult (Boushey & Wright, 2004; Chaudry, 2004; Presser & Cox, 1997). Consequently, mothers must rely on makeshift and multiple care arrangements that create further instability in a young child's life. There are 6 million infants and toddlers in child care, and they are most likely to experience multiple care arrangements with the infants of single mothers spending double the time in out-of-home care in comparison with two-parent families (Ehrle, Adams, & Tout, 2001). Large numbers of poor African American and Latino children spend their earliest years not only in cheap, inferior, licensed care settings, but also in the largely invisible underworld of unregulated care. Helburn and Bergmann (2002) estimate that about one-third of children in child care from birth to five are in the unregulated sector.

The developmentally damaging conditions that exist nationwide for millions of vulnerable young children in their most formative stages of development have been extensively documented for more than a decade. More specifically, widespread lack of regulation, unaffordable care, bad working conditions with low pay, high turnover, high ratios of children to staff, and substandard care that disproportionately impact low-income children and children of color (Helburn & Bergmann, 2002; Ebb, 1994; Galinsky et al., 1994; Helburn, 1995; Polakow, 2007; Schulman, 2000). While high-quality child care results in long-lasting social and educational impacts that are particularly significant for low-income children, they are also far more sensitive to the negative effects of bad child care (Klein & Knitzer, 2007; Peisner-Feinberg et al., 1999).

Yet, despite the accumulating body of research that clearly points to what supports and enriches young children's lives and what *harms*, poor children have no *entitlement* to good-quality early care. In the absence of such rights, their lives, like those of their parents, are largely expendable; and when poverty, low-wage work, and lack of child care coalesce, an acute crisis of care is the consequence of welfare reform policies and its Work First mandates.

Work First versus Postsecondary Education

The passage of PRWORA severely restricted the access of low-income single mothers to postsecondary education, and with its explicit Work First paradigm, many student mothers were forced to "drop out" of college and move into the low-wage workforce as a condition of receiving benefits. This resulted in a dramatic decline of low-income student mothers enrolled in college. Post-1996 numbers point to drops in enrollments nationwide ranging from 29 percent to 82 percent (Institute for Women's Policy Research, 1998; Kahn et al., 2004). Most states permit only time-limited vocational education for up to a year, with little flexibility for two- and four-year degrees, and just a few—California, Illinois, Iowa, Kentucky, and Wyoming—permit postsecondary education as an allowable work activity for a two-year period. Maine's Parents as Scholars program is a notable exception, permitting welfare recipients to enroll in both two- and four-year degree programs, while providing wraparound services including child care (Deprez, Butler, & Smith, 2004). Michigan, under former governor Engler, introduced one of the harshest Work First programs, effectively shutting down access to college. In a survey conducted in Michigan in 2002, only 2 percent of single mothers receiving welfare assistance were enrolled in college (Coalition for Independence through Education, 2002).

The importance of postsecondary education for women, particularly single mothers, has been documented in numerous studies during the past two decades. Higher education provides a buffer against job loss during economic downturns. Over half of the jobs lost during the 2001 recession occurred in those industries that had employed former welfare recipients. Job losses and dislocation disproportionately harm those with the lowest levels of education. Women who fail to complete high school are 43 percent more likely to live in poverty than men without a high school diploma. On the other hand, women's earnings increase exponentially with each year of college, and completion of a four-year college degree definitively reduces women's chances of being poor. Completion of an associate's degree increases earnings by 60 percent, but for women who complete a bachelor's degree the "education premium" is even more dramatic—there is a 182 percent increase in *lifetime* earnings in comparison to women who have not graduated from high school (Jones-DeWeever & Gault, 2006; U.S. Department of Commerce, Bureau of the Census, 2003). The income advantages for college-educated women over high school graduates are dramatic, particularly for women of color. White women with a four-year degree have a 77 percent earnings increase over White high school graduates; but for African American women there is a 92 percent increase in income in comparison to African American high school graduates (Jones-DeWeever & Gault, 2006).

Yet, despite the dramatic educational data, pointing to increased earning power and exits from poverty for low-income women (Gittel, Schehl, & Fareri, 1990; Gittel et al., 1996; Gittel, Ortega-Bustamante, & Steffy, 2000), in most states mothers on welfare have not been permitted to count postsecondary education in lieu of mandatory Work First requirements. Hence, not only must they struggle to stay in school and succeed, but they are also required to work 30–40 hours a week, and parent their children, alone, on tightly stretched budgets. Work First policies, as framed by national and state legislation and implemented in the practices of social service and welfare-to-work agencies, have built a nearly insurmountable wall of obstacles to student mothers' pursuit of two-year and four-year degrees, as they try to study while working and parenting in conditions of poverty. Welfare reform thus presents a striking paradox. On one hand, Work First policies and practices create increasing pressure on women to find jobs; any jobs no matter how low the pay and how bad the working conditions, under threat of benefit termination and sanctions. On the other hand, the same policies and practices threaten their access to postsecondary education, which *could* ensure long-term economic self-sufficiency for their families (American Psychological Association, 1998; Polakow et al., 2004).

Access and Impact of Postsecondary Education

It is clear that postsecondary education is a key social capital investment in low-income female-headed families, yet the research on the access of the poor to higher education has paid scant attention to the distinctive obstacles experienced by low-income single mothers (Levine & Nidiffer, 1996). Heller and Bjorklund (2004), reviewing the empirical research on the impact of financial aid on all low-income students, point out that the beneficial impacts of financial aid are greatest for the poorest students, and that there is strong evidence that aid, particularly scholarships and grants, facilitates college enrollment and retention. Financial aid assessments, however, usually disadvantage low-income student *parents* as they face greater amounts of "unmet need," which is calculated as " the difference between the cost of attending college and the resources available to meet those costs" (p. 134). Low-income single mothers, a nontraditional student constituency, receive disproportionately less aid, as their financial aid packages do not adjust for dependent children; and the high costs of child care and parenting are frequently not taken into account because those particular costs are not viewed as central to the completion of a student's program of study. Yet, for single parent students, child care often constitutes the biggest hurdle in terms of college completion (Gittell et al., 1996; Kahn & Polakow, 2004; Polakow, 2007). Federal student aid favors full-time students, or students taking at least six hours a semester, but many low-income single mothers who work can only attend school part-time; hence, their opportunities to benefit from more generous financial aid packages are circumscribed (Heller & Bjorklund, 2004).

Postsecondary education does not just increase the earning power of poor mothers, but reaps dividends for families and communities. In mixed-method and qualitative studies conducted in New York, California, Maine, Massachusetts, Michigan, and Iowa, the positive effects of a college education for welfare recipients and their children point to higher standards of living, economic self-sufficiency, greater self-esteem, increased social capital and community engagement, civic participation, and aspirations to send their own children to college (Jones-DeWeever & Gault, 2006; Deprez, Butler, & Smith, 2004; Gittell et al., 1996; Kahn & Polakow, 2004; Polakow, 2007). In the California study, two-thirds of women graduates chose to work in their own communities, and the majority reported increased levels of community and civic participation (Jones-DeWeever & Gault, 2006). Maine, which implemented a unique statewide, postsecondary education program for welfare recipients in response to PRWORA's restrictions on college access, developed the Parents as Scholars program. Student participants reported that college had broadened their horizons, personally empowered them, and transformed their lives as well as their relationships with their children (Deprez, Butler, & Smith, 2004). In Massachusetts, participants in the Women in Community Development program, which promoted college access and leadership, described their high motivation, increased social capital, and community leadership skills developed in the program and supported by staff and peers (Clarke & Peterson, 2004). And in Michigan, where access to college has been fraught with obstacles for student mothers receiving welfare, student mothers have persevered in the face of a hostile welfare bureaucracy, lack of child care supports, and mandatory work requirements that due to arbitrary application in different counties has resulted in a considerable number of mothers of young children being forced to work up to 40 hours a week, despite the reduced federal work requirement of 20 hours for those with children under six. Yet, despite the obstacles, many succeed. As one young African American student mother who has persevered remarked during an interview:

> My goal was to . . . finish school and make a better life for them [her twins] to try to provide for them and be a good mother. I never anticipated taking care of two infants and trying to go to school and then trying to work these outrageous hours and then going home and not being able to rest, not being able to sleep. (Kahn & Polakow, 2000b, p. 18)

Haveman and Wolfe argue that one of the most important factors shaping children's academic success in school is the educational level of the mother, where level of schooling "may proxy for a wide variety of maternal-and family-activities of an investment character," contributing to motivation and performance in school and imparting to their children the value of learning (1994, p. 99). Jones-DeWeever and Gault (2006), in documenting the changed lives of welfare recipients enrolled in college, point to the positive impact of college on student mothers' children. Mothers report that their children's study habits changed, they developed positive relationships in school, and their educational achievement improved. It is clear that mothers' well-being, increased levels of education, and a stable family life positively affect low-income children in a multitude of ways, fostering school success and contributing to overall child well-being. Young children's literacy, one of the key factors influencing educational achievement in school, is strongly influenced by mothers' educational levels (Institute for Women's Policy Research, 2002). Hence, college education is one of the most "powerful and dependable ways to interrupt the intergenerational transmission of poverty" (American Psychological Association, 1998, p. 15).

Michigan's Welfare-to-Work Regime: Policies That Fail Low-Income Student Mothers and Their Children

In the following section the struggles of three African American single mothers, who are juggling low-wage jobs, school, and parenting, are portrayed. The lives of Brandy, Tina, and Jasmine are juxtaposed against the harsh and unremitting work requirements of Michigan's TANF program, which constricts the women's educational opportunities and threatens their family viability. The three brief narratives that follow are drawn from qualitative interviews with the mothers conducted in Michigan between 1999 and 2004 and illuminate the systemic obstacles to self-sufficiency and educational progress that they have encountered.[3]

BRANDY

Brandy is a 29-year-old single mother of two sons, a toddler and a seven-year-old. For the past eight years, she has been struggling to complete a four-year bachelor's degree in business at a university in southeast Michigan. Enrolled part-time in school and working 30 hours a week in a low-wage, retail job with no benefits, Brandy has experienced ongoing harassment in pursuit of her educational goals. Her caseworker threatened to cut her benefits if she did not work 40 hours a week, despite the fact that she has a child under six, which, according to Michigan Public Act 280 of 2001 required her to meet the federal minimum requirement of 20 hours a week but did not specify a 40-hour workweek (J. Doig, personal communication, December 22, 2008, Center for Civil Justice) although many caseworkers chose to interpret the requirements that way. The family's food stamps were inexplicably cut when Brandy protested, and only with the help of an advocate at a community center were they restored two months later. Brandy was erroneously informed that she could only receive child care subsidies for work, but not for class time at school. In addition, the child subsidy payments to the child care provider were chronically late, causing Brandy extreme anxiety and stress, which affected her health, resulting in frequent and debilitating migraines. The mounting deficit of child care subsidies ricocheted and threatened to destabilize her young family as Brandy fell further behind in child care tuition payments. After three months, the child care center informed her that they would proceed with disenrollment of her son unless she paid the balance up front.

Brandy, who recognizes the importance of high-quality child care, has chosen to send her toddler son to an accredited child care center that costs $850 a month in Wayne County. Even with the child care subsidies, she must still shoulder a high copay of approximately $366 a month, as the child care subsidies pay only partial tuition, based on outdated market rates. Heavily in debt, with a maximum of student loans, Brandy is at a tipping point. Her caseworker reprimands her for choosing a high-quality center for her toddler, saying, "We're not going to pay to send your child to that center—find a cheaper provider!" Brandy has also had to reduce her school hours due to an increase in her work requirements to 35 hours a week; therefore, her financial aid package has also been reduced. Her older son has been hospitalized twice in the past four months with severe asthma and subsequently misses many days of school, threatening Brandy's job, as she frequently has to pick him up from school when he is ill. With no extended family in the area, and few support networks, Brandi is living on the edges:

> It's so hard . . . it's just been so hard. My caseworker does not care about me being in school—she keeps telling me I shouldn't ask for help because other people need it more. . . . She says I should drop out and get a better job and get off of welfare, but how can I find a good job without my education? I want my kids to see their mom can do it!

TINA

Tina is a 25-year-old single mother with an eight-year-old son and four-year-old daughter. She recently transferred from a local community college in a large urban area to a four-year institution pursuing a degree in criminal justice. Tina feels isolated on the new campus, away from her family with no ready support system to help her with her two children. Although she is working 20 hours a week, for several months she has been denied cash assistance and child care subsidies as her caseworker has told her she is required to work 35 hours a week. The ensuing stress of finding child care for her daughter has caused her grades to plummet and interfered with her class attendance, and she temporarily drops out of school for one semester. Taking a job at a department store, Tina relates how, with no child care, she was forced to take her daughter to work with her:

> I lost my first job because the worker would not give me child care. I just lost my job … because I had brought my daughter to work with me. I know I shouldn't had done it … but I missed so many days that they told me the next time I missed a day they were going to fire me. I was a cashier and … I set my daughter on the bench, and you know at the time she was four years old. … The manager she told me you can't bring your child to work and stuff, but she said I can come back once I find a day care center for my child. … So then I went to the Work First program and the Work First counselor called my worker and she said, "Well we can't give her day care until they verify employment and she gets a receipt for a first check."

Terminated from her job because she has no child care, Tina finds herself caught in a bizarre catch-22—no money for child care, yet no job without child care, and no child care without a first check! Tina returns to school, finds an on-campus job, and begins to pursue her rights to child care. However, she encounters continuing harassment from a second caseworker, who twice loses her forms and course verifications. Finally, with the help of a legal aid attorney who calls for a hearing, Tina receives her child care subsidies, but the whole process has taken six months. Tina has found a food service job on campus with flexible hours and a supportive employer, and she receives a child care scholarship, which partially subsidizes a place for her daughter at the on-campus child care center, but the caseworker now demands that she seek an off-campus job with longer hours and higher pay.

> I tried to explain to the worker everything is centered around here. If you get a job outside you have to have transportation … but I keep telling her it's the convenience. … But she keeps saying I should be looking for a better job … but to my mind, this job is doing what it supposed to do. It's helping me out a whole lot. It's on campus and I have really good employers. … Like if my child gets sick they will come to my class and tell me, and they picked up my daughter for me. I mean they are real good … and they really support me being in school, and my employer she said to me when I was really down, "Hang in there … it will be so much better for you and your kids when you graduate."

Not only has Tina experienced constant harassment about her on-campus job, but her caseworker has also disregarded both her work and school schedules when setting up bimonthly home visits, creating another source of ongoing stress for Tina. On numerous occasions, the caseworker has sent a notice to Tina informing her of a mandatory home visit during the time that Tina attends class or is working on campus. Despite the ongoing harassment and punitive treatment, she experiences from the local DHS welfare agency, Tina is determined to stay in school and succeed. As the first in her family to attend college, she has a vision of a different future and sees the promise of postsecondary education as the route out of poverty for herself and her two children:

> That is not how I want to live. Every time I just want to stop and not go to school—it's like, OK, I came all this way and I gotta do this. . . . My kids need a chance to grow up different!

JASMINE

Jasmine is a 19-year-old single mother of a toddler. Abused at home, Jasmine ran away at age 15. After living on the streets for several months, she found her way to a local nonprofit community agency for runaway teens and was placed in a group home in another city. Enrolled in school and doing well academically, Jasmine's troubled young life began to stabilize. However, during her eleventh-grade year, she became embroiled in an abusive relationship with a violent boyfriend and soon afterward became pregnant. With no educational interventions for pregnant teens in place at her high school, 17-year-old Jasmine dropped out and soon afterward gave birth to her son. With the help of a supportive social worker at the nonprofit community agency that had assisted her previously, Jasmine and her baby moved into a subsidized rental unit in a nearby town and received a welfare grant. However, when her baby was three months old, Jasmine was ordered to report to the Work First agency in her Michigan county, despite the fact that she had not located any child care. Jasmine failed to comply, and her assistance was cut.

Desperate and alone, Jasmine asks her younger sister (who is a senior in high school) to move in with her temporarily to take care of the baby, while Jasmine searches for work. After finding a housekeeping job for 40 hours a week at minimum wage and no benefits, she begins a futile search for child care. "It's been so hard," she says. "I been looking and looking for child care. If it's not the area, it's the amount of money. If it's not the amount of money, it's the transportation." Meanwhile her sister's own educational progress is jeopardized as she misses several weeks of school while taking care of her nephew.

Over the next year, Jasmine's toddler son cycles through seven unstable child care placements: relatives, her violent boyfriend (who is the father of her son and against whom she has a protection order), the boyfriend's aunt, Jasmine's younger sister, a neighbor, a friend from Milwaukee, and a neighborhood provider who is not licensed and proves to be unreliable and careless with the children in her care. Jasmine's application for child care subsidies was initially denied due to her failure to attend a mandatory Work First orientation; however a local Michigan 4C (Community Coordinated Child Care Association) provides Jasmine with a temporary child care scholarship while they assist her in processing another request for state child care subsidies. After a delay of seven months, Jasmine is approved for child care subsidies, but they do not pay the full cost of child care at a licensed center, so Jasmine is forced to look for cheap care in the informal, unregulated sector. Despite these mounting obstructions, Jasmine is determined to complete her education:

> I'm going to go back to school and I'm going to get my diploma [GED]. In addition, I want a car so transportation wouldn't be so hard and a better-paying job to be able to pay my day care. . . . I want to go to college so bad and move on with my life, but they [welfare] they don't want me in school, they want me in these pay-nothing jobs where I'm basically cleaning bathrooms all my life. Me and my son, we want a better life.

Yet Jasmine's hopes for a better life are derailed when she loses her job in housekeeping due to her many work absences. With her education plans on hold, an eviction for unpaid rent looming, and no stable child care in sight, Jasmine, young, isolated, and poor, has nowhere to turn.

Poverty, Postsecondary Education, and Child Care
under Michigan's Welfare Regime

Low-income student parents in Michigan continue to confront a plethora of obstacles to their educational aspirations. Brandy, Tina, and Jasmine, like thousands of other student mothers in Michigan, have experienced routinized violations of their rights. Postsecondary education is devalued, family stability is disrupted, and work, any work, not matter how demeaning or disruptive, forms part of the coercive environment that welfare-reliant mothers must confront. Improper denials of child care subsidies, punitive sanctions and arbitrary enforcement of mandatory work hours in different counties, threats, home surveillance, and harassment by workers create a situation "that removes poor single mothers from the welfare state to a police state" (Mink, 1998, p. 133).

Michigan inherited a particularly damaging legacy from former governor John Engler. During the Engler administration (1991–2002) aided by a Republican-dominated legislature, the Michigan "model" rapidly decreased welfare caseloads under a particularly harsh and punitive approach to welfare reform. Work First was seen as the exclusive remedy to push poor single mothers into the labor force under the mantra of personal responsibility, but with minimal public responsibility for the harmful consequences. In 1991, Engler cut General Assistance for unemployed childless adults (many of whom were disabled) and throughout the 1990s, he slashed social spending and required single mothers to work more than the federally prescribed mandatory requirements in the PRWORA legislation of 1996. Welfare caseloads declined by almost 70 percent, and by 2000, 34 percent of children in the state were living in households below 200 percent of the federal poverty threshold (Michigan League for Human Services, 2001). Many women in Michigan's TANF program, seeking to pursue vocational or postsecondary education, were actively discouraged by caseworkers, and there was no effort to provide educational resources and support to single mothers.

When Governor Granholm assumed the governorship in 2003, a culture of hostility and dysfunctionality was endemic in the Department of Human Services and hostility to postsecondary education widespread (Kahn & Polakow, 2004). While there have been some attempts to change the institutional culture, student mothers on the ground are still encountering obstacles to postsecondary education, delayed subsidy payments, and punitive sanctions when they fail to work their mandatory requirements.

The reauthorization of TANF in 2002 under the Bush administration tightened work requirements, mandating a 40-hour workweek with 24 hours of direct employment, and 16 hours allotted for job training and vocational education, permitting only a three-month waiver from work requirements every two years, and four-year degrees were explicitly prohibited. This further endangered the educational aspirations of welfare-reliant student parents; and Michigan's rigid promotion of Work First policies extended the 40-hour workweek to parents of children under six, despite a federal requirement of only 20 hours (Institute for Women's Policy Research, 2003; J. Doig, personal communication, December 22, 2008, Center for Civil Justice).

In response to continuing pressure and criticism of this punitive legislation, the Department of Health and Human Services issued a federal final rule (effective October 2008). This rule permitted TANF recipients to count participation in a two- or four-year degree program as vocational educational training for up to 12 months, and if core work requirements were met, there was the possibility of expansion to 24 months. The final rule also permitted study time as a countable work activity, but was of little help to women pursuing four-year degrees as the focus is on vocational, not postsecondary, education, favoring immediate attachment to the low-wage labor force with short-term job training. As of 2011, Michigan TANF recipients must meet "core" work requirements of 20 hours a week, and must engage in "non-core" activities for the remaining 10–20 hours a week. Postsecondary education may only be counted as an allowable "non-core" activity if it can be characterized as job skills training leading to labor market attachment. However, there is a 12- month limit—effectively obstructing women's capacity to pursue a two or four-year degree (J. Doig, personal communication, December 13, 2012, Center for Civil Justice).

MICHIGAN AND CHILD CARE

The latest available data for Michigan indicates that there are 471,636 children under the age of six in need of child care, but income eligibility for state child care assistance is limited to those with an annual income of $23,880 (129 percent of the federal poverty level (FPL) (Child Care Aware, 2012). The need for child care is particularly acute for low-income parents of infants and toddlers and for those children requiring after-hours care. In 2011, the monthly cost (calculated at the 75th percentile of market rates) for full-time center-based care for a four-year-old in Michigan was $974 or $11,688 a year with costs considerably higher for infants. However, Michigan's monthly state subsidy reimbursement rate for center-based care was $433—leaving parents in poverty with a monthly copay of $541 (National Women's Law Center, 2012). Increased work requirements have led to increased demand for child care assistance, but subsidies reach just over one-third of income-eligible children, and the subsidies are based on outdated market surveys. While subsidies should be reimbursed at the 75th percentile of current market rates, two-thirds of providers who care for infants and toddlers, and over 90 percent of those providing care for children over two and a half years old, are reimbursed at less than 50 percent of current market rates. In Brandy's situation described earlier, she was paying $366 a month in Wayne County in the early 2000s; and Wayne County had one of the highest gaps between actual market costs and subsidy reimbursement among 50 metro areas across the country (Michigan League for Human Services, 2006). In addition, past surveys of centers and providers indicate that only 47 percent of licensed centers and just over 50 percent of licensed family child care homes in the state accepted subsidies (Urban Institute 1999), creating further stratification of care for children of the poor, who are denied access to may centers because they are "subsidy" children.

During the period documented in this chapter, the child care crisis for low-income families and particularly for single-parent households increased dramatically as unemployment, home foreclosures, and loss of benefits hit working poor families, with 35 percent of single-parent families living below the poverty threshold. Half a million Michigan children (468,000) were living in poverty, and of that number, 44 percent were African American, in contrast to 13 percent of White children. Even more disturbing was the high number of children, 229,000, whose families were living below 50 percent of the FPL ($8,800 for a family of three) (Kids Count, 2008). Since 2008, the number of children in poverty in Michigan has increased to over half a million (560,000) and, at 25 percent, Michigan's child poverty rate now exceeds the U.S. child poverty rate of 23 percent (Addy & Wight, 2012; Kids Count, 2011).

Parental education (particularly the mother's level of education) plays a significant role in alleviating children's poverty: 61 percent of children whose parents have not completed high school and 31 percent of children whose parents have a high school diploma but no college live in poverty; but only 8 percent of children whose parents have some college education are poor (National Center for Children in Poverty, 2008b), pointing to postsecondary education as one of the most potent antipoverty measures for families with children. Given the high rates of poverty in single-mother African American households in Michigan and nationally, postsecondary education is not only a human capital investment in women, but in their children as well.

Michigan, in many ways, is the face of the nation: high unemployment, extremely high levels of child poverty, large numbers of single-parent families, and public policies that have exacerbated family poverty, with disproportionate impacts on children of color. The well-being of children is inextricably intertwined with the social and educational capital of their mothers. European Union countries have recognized this through the promotion of strong family support polices for working parents that primarily benefit mothers—universal child care, universal health care, paid maternity and parental leave policies, and opportunities and incentives for postsecondary and vocational education (Gornick & Meyers, 2003; Polakow, 2007).

Education matters. It matters for infant and toddlers, it matters for schoolchildren; it matters most for those who have experienced chronic injustices in their lives. Moreover, it matters for single parents, with life-changing consequences for the entire family. What is overlooked and tuned to lower frequencies in educational and social policy discourse is the early systemic inequality that shadows children born into poverty, as their mothers encounter inferior and unstable child care, chronic employment stress, and lack of access to postsecondary education. These systemic inequalities are both racialized and gendered—exacerbating the growing feminization of poverty with its snowball effects on African American and Latino families. Public policy is as much about the *unmaking*, as it is about the *making*, of people's lives. Recent public policies have coalesced to promote an alarming rise in poverty among women and children. In addition, for women and children of color, the United States is currently one of the most *growth-harming* democracies to live in—if you are a poor, single mother with young children.

There is reason to hope for a transformation of public policy as President Obama's second term begins, bringing promise of sustained investments in the early lives of young children and the college aspirations of their mothers; so that it will yet be possible, through education, to move up and out of poverty. As Tanya, an African American single mother who moved to Iowa with her children in order to complete her college education, puts it:

> Education is something you will always have. No one can take that away from you, and it is education that will help you succeed! (Polakow, 2007, p. 127)

NOTES

1. I have conducted much of this research in collaboration with Peggy Kahn, and together we have written several reports, articles, and book chapters documenting the derailing of postsecondary educational opportunities for low-income women under Michigan's welfare regime and in the broader national context. In particular, see Kahn & Polakow, 2000; Kahn & Polakow, 2004; Polakow et al., 2004.

2. In 2008, the federal poverty level (FPL) was calculated to be $21,200 and in 2011, $22,350 for a family of four according to the Department of Health and Human Services. The FPL is considered outdated, inaccurate, and out of step with the widely accepted international measure of relative poverty (less than 50 percent of the national median income). A low-income household is categorized as 200 percent of the FPL—currently about $44,700 for a family of four. This measure is generally accepted as a more accurate indicator of actual child poverty in the United States.

3. Brandy's story is constructed from interviews conducted in 2004. Part of Tina's story appears in Kahn & Polakow, 2004; Jasmine's story is an update on an excerpt published in Polakow, 2007.

REFERENCES

Abramowitz, M. (2001, May). Race, class, and welfare reform. NASW Welfare Reform Task Force. Retrieved from http://www.naswnyc.org/w14.html.
American Psychological Association (1998). *Making "welfare to work" really*

work: Report of the task force on women, poverty, and public assistance.
Washington, DC: Author.

Addy, S., & Wight, V. (2012, February). *Basic facts about low- income children, 2010.* New York: National Center for Children in Poverty. Retrieved from http://www.nccp.org/publications/pub_1049.html.

Amott, T. (1990). Black women and AFDC: Making entitlement out of necessity. In L. Gordon, (Ed.), *Women, the state, and welfare* (pp. 280–298). Madison: University of Wisconsin Press.

Boushey, H., & Wright, J. (2004, May 5). *Working moms and child care.* (No. 3). Washington, DC: Center for Economic and Policy Research. Retrieved from http://www.cepr.net/index.php/publications/reports/working-moms-and-child-care/.

Brauner, S., & Loprest, P. (1999, May). *Where are they now? What states' studies of people who left welfare tell us.* No. A-32. Washington, DC: Urban Institute.

Coalition for Independence through Education (2002, February). *Access and barriers to post-secondary education under Michigan's welfare-to-work policies.* Ann Arbor: Center for the Education of Women.

Chaudry, A. (2004). *Putting children first: How low-wage working mothers manage child care.* New York: Russell Sage Foundation.

Child Care Aware of America (2012). *2012 Child care in the state of: Michigan.* Retrieved from http://www.naccrra.org/sites/default/files/default_site_pages/2012/michigan_060612-3.pdf.

Children's Defense Fund (2005, April). *Child care basics 2005.* Retrieved from http://www.childrensdefense.org/site/DocServer/child_care_basics_2005.pdf.

Clarke, D., & Peterson, L. (2004). College access and leadership-building for low-income women: Boston's women in community development (WICD). In V. Polakow, S. Butler, L.S. Deprez, & P. Kahn (Eds.), *Shut out: Low income mothers and higher education in post-welfare America* (pp. 189–202). Albany: State University of New York Press.

DeParle, J. (1994, November 13). Momentum builds for cutting back welfare system. *New York Times.* Retrieved from http://query.nytimes.com/gst/fullpage.html?res=9F03E0D71731F930A25752C1A962958260&sec=&spon=&pagewanted=all.

Deprez, L S., Butler, S., & Smith, R.J. (2004). Securing higher education for women on welfare in Maine. In V. Polakow, S. Butler, L.S. Deprez, & P. Kahn (Eds.), *Shut out: Low income mothers and higher education in post-welfare America* (pp. 217–236). Albany: State University of New York Press

Douglas-Hall, A., & Chau, M. (2007, November). *Most low-income parents are employed.* Retrieved from http://www.nccp.org/publications/pub_784.html.

Ebb, N. (1994, January). *Child care tradeoffs: States make painful choices.* Washington, DC: Children's Defense Fund.

Ehrle, J., Adams, G., & Tout, K. (2001). *Who's caring for our youngest children? Child care patterns of infants and toddlers.* No. 42. Washington, DC: Urban Institute. Retrieved from http://www.urban.org/Uploaded-PDF/310029_occa42.pdf.

Fass, S., & Cauthen, N. (2008, October). *Who are America's poor children? The official story.* New York: National Center for Children in Poverty. Retrieved from http://www.nccp.org/publications/pub_843.html.

Food Research and Action Center (2007, January). *Hunger in the U.S.* Retrieved from http://www.frac.org/html/hunger_in_the_us/hunger_index.html.

Galinsky, E., Howes, C., Kontos, S., & Shinn, M. (1994). *The study of children in family care and relative care: Highlights of findings.* New York: Families and Work Institute.

Gilliam, F.D. (1999, Summer). The "welfare queen" experiment. *Nieman Reports, 53*(2). Retrieved from http://www.nieman.harvard.edu/reports/99–2NRsummer99/Gilliam.html.

Gittell, M., Schehl, M., & Fareri, C. (1990). *From welfare to independence: The college option: A report to the Ford Foundation.* New York: Howard Samuels State Management and Policy Center.

Gittell, M., Vandersall, K., Holdaway, J., & Newman, K. (1996). *Creating social capital at CUNY: A comparison of higher education programs for AFDC recipients.* New York: Howard Samuels State Management and Policy Center.

Gittell, M., Ortega-Bustamante, I., & Steffy, T. (2000). Social capital and social change: Women's community activism. *Urban Affairs Review, 36*(2), 123–147.

Gornick, J., & Meyers, M. (2003). *Families that work.* New York: Russell Sage.

Haveman, R., & Wolfe, B. (1994). *Succeeding generations: On the effects of investments in children.* New York: Russell Sage Foundation

Hayes, J., & Hartmann, H. (2011, September). *Women and men living on the edge: Economic insecurity after the Great Recession.* Washington, DC: Institute for Women's Policy Research. Retrieved from http://www.iwpr.org/ initiatives/poverty/#publications.

Helburn, S.W. (Ed.) (1995, June). *Cost, quality and child outcomes in child care centers. Technical Report.* ED 386 297. Denver: Center for Research in Economic and Social Policy, University of Colorado.

Helburn, S.W., & Bergmann, B. (2002). *America's child care problem: The way out.* New York: Palgrave Macmillan.

Heller, D., & Bjorklund, S. (2004). Student financial aid and low income mothers. In V. Polakow, S. Butler, L.S. Deprez, & P. Kahn (Eds.), *Shut out: Low income mothers and higher education in post-welfare America* (pp. 129–148). Albany: State University of New York Press.

Innocenti Research Centre (2007). *Child poverty in perspective. An overview of child well-being in rich countries.* Retrieved from www.unicef-irc.org.

Institute for Women's Policy Research (1998, April). Welfare reform and postsecondary education: Research and policy update. *Welfare Reform Network News, 2*(1). Retrieved from http://www.eric.ed.gov/ERICWeb-Portal/search/detailmini.jsp?_nfpb=true&_&ERICExtSearch_SearchV alue_0=ED445134&ERICExtSearch_SearchType_0=no&accno=ED4.

Institute for Women's Policy Research (2002, April). *Education and job training build strong families.* Retrieved from http://www.iwpr.org/pdf/b238.pdf.

Institute for Women's Policy Research (2003, June). *Before and after welfare reform: The work and well-being of low-income single parent families.* Retrieved from http://www.iwpr.org/pdf/D454.pdf.

Institute for Women's Policy Research (2005, March 29). *African American women work more, earn less.* Retrieved from http://www.iwpr.org/pdf/ IWPRRelease3_29_05.pdf.

Lyter, D., Sills, M., Oh, G., & Jones-DeWeever, A. (2004). *The children left behind: Deeper poverty, fewer supports.* Washington, DC: Institute for Women's Policy Research. Retrieved from http://www.iwpr.org/pdf/D457a.pdf.

Jones-DeWeever, A., & Gault, B. (2006, April). *Resilient and reaching for more: Challenge and benefits of higher education for welfare participants and their children.* No. D466. Washington, DC: Institute for Women's Policy

Research. Retrieved from http://www.iwpr.org/pdf/D466.pdf.

Kahn, P., Butler, S., Deprez, L.S., & Polakow, V. (2004). Introduction. In P. Kahn, S. Butler, L.S. Deprez, & V. Polakow (Eds.), *Shut out: Low income mothers and higher education in post-welfare America* (pp. 1–17). Albany: State University of New York Press.

Kahn, P., & Polakow, V. (2000a). Mothering denied: Commodification and caregiving under new US welfare laws. *SAGE Race Relations Abstracts*, 25(1), 7–25

Kahn, P., & Polakow, V. (2000b). *Struggling to stay in school: Obstacles to postsecondary education under the welfare-to-work regime in Michigan.* Ann Arbor: University of Michigan, Center for the Education of Women.

Kahn, P., & Polakow, V. (2004). That's not how I want to live: Student mothers fight to stay in school under Michigan's welfare-to-work regime. In V. Polakow, S. Butler, L. Deprez, & P. Kahn (Eds.), *Shut out: Low income mothers and higher education in post-welfare America* (pp. 75–96). Albany: State University of New York

Kids Count (2008). *Kids Count Data Center: Profiles by geographic area, Michigan.* Retrieved from http://datacenter.kidscount.org/data/bystate/stateprofile. aspx?state=MI.

Kids Count (2011). *Kids Count Data Center: Data across states.* Retrieved from http://datacenter.kidscount.org/data/acrossstates/Rankings.aspx?loct =2&by=a&order=a&ind=43&dtm=322&tf=867.

Klein, L., & Knitzer, J. (2007, January). *Promoting effective early learning: What every policymaker and educator should know.* Retrieved from http://www. nccp.org/publications/pub_695.html.

Levine, A., & Nidiffer, J. (1996). *Beating the odds: How the poor get to college.* San Francisco: Jossey-Bass.

Lin, J., & Bernstein, J. (2008, October 29). What we need to get by. Briefing Paper No. 224. Washington, DC: Economic Policy Institute. Retrieved from http://www.epi.org/content.cfm/bp224.

Michigan 4C Association (2006, February). 2006 child care in the state of Michigan. Retrieved from http://www.naccrra.org/docs/data/MI.pdf.

Michigan League for Human Services (2001, September). *A snapshot of family well-being: A focus on Michigan.* Lansing, MI: Author.

Michigan League for Human Services (2007, May). *Michigan child care assistance*

policies: 2006. Retrieved from http://www.milhs.org/Media/EDocs/
ChildCareAssistPoliciesOct07REV2.pdf.

Michigan League for Human Services (2008, May). *Recent TANF changes are
favorable to education and training.* Retrieved from http://www.milhs.
org/Media/EDocs/TANFnewrulespaper1.pdf.

Mink, G. (1998). *Welfare's end.* Ithaca, NY: Cornell University Press.

National Association of Child Care Resource and Referral Agencies (2008).
Parents and the high price of child care: 2008 update. Retrieved from http://
www.naccrra.org/.

National Association of Child Care Resource and Referral Agencies (2012).
Parents and the high cost of child care: 2012 Report. Retrieved from
http://www.naccrra.org/sites/default/files/default_site_pages/2012/
cost_report_2012-_executive_summary_081012_1.pdf.

National Center for Children in Poverty (2008a). *'07 issues portend continued
hard times in '08 for low-income working Americans: Trends seen in housing,
wages, health care, family leave.* Retrieved from http://www.nccp.org/
media/releases/release_37.html.

National Center for Children in Poverty (2008b). *Michigan: Demographics of
poor children.* Retrieved from http://www.nccp.org/profiles/state_profile.
php?state=MI&id=7.

National Women's Law Center (2011, October). *State child care assistance
policies 2011: Reduced support for families in challenging times.* Retrieved
from http://www.nwlc.org/sites/default/files/pdfs/state_child_care_as-
sistance_policies_report2011_final.pdf

National Women's Law Center (2012). *Downward slide: State child care assistance
policies 2012.* Retrieved from http://www.nwlc.org/sites/default/files/
pdfs/NWLC2012_StateChildCareAssistanceReport.pdf.

National Urban League Policy Institute (2007, July). *The opportunity compact:
Blueprint for economic equality.* Retrieved from http://www.nul.org/.

Neubeck, K., & Casenave (2001). *Welfare racism: Playing the race card against
America's poor.* New York: Routledge

Peisner-Feinberg, E.S., Burchinal, M.R., Clifford, R.M., et al. (1999, June). *The
children of the Cost, Quality, and Outcomes Study go to school: Executive
summary.* Chapel Hill: University of North Carolina at Chapel Hill,
Frank Porter Graham Child Development Center.

Piven, F.F. (1995). Foreword. In S. Schram, *Words of welfare: The poverty of social science and the social science of poverty* (pp. ix–xv). Minneapolis: University of Minnesota Press.

Piven, F.F. (1998). Welfare and work. *Social Justice, 25*(1), 67–81.

Piven, F.F., & Cloward, R.A. (1998). *The breaking of the American social compact.* New York: New Press.

Polakow, V. (2007). *Who cares for our children? The child care crisis in the other America.* New York: Teachers College Press.

Polakow, V., Butler, S., Deprez, L.S., & Kahn, P. (Eds.). (2004). *Shut out: Low income mothers and higher education in post-welfare America.* Albany: State University of New York Press.

Presser, H., & Cox, A.G. (1997, April). The work schedules of low-educated American women and welfare reform. *Monthly Labor Review, 120*(4), 25–34

Schulman, K. (2000). *The high cost of child care puts quality care out of reach for many families.* Washington, DC: Children's Defense Fund.

Sherman, A., Amey, C., Duffield, B., Ebb, N., & Weinstein, D. (1998, December). *Welfare to what: Early findings on family hardship and well-being.* Washington, DC: Children's Defense Fund and National Coalition for the Homeless.

Super, D., Parrott, S., Steinmetz, S., & Mann, C. (1996). *The new welfare law.* Washington, DC: Center on Budget and Policy Priorities

Toner, R. (1995, September 20). Senate approves welfare plan that would end aid guarantee. *New York Times.* Retrieved from http://query.nytimes.com/gst/fullpage.html?res=990CEEDE163BF933A1575AC0A963958260&sec=&spon=&pagewanted=2.

Toner, R., & Pear, R. (2002, February 27). Bush urges work and marriage programs in welfare plan. *New York Times,* p. A18.

Urban Institute (1999). *Child care in Michigan: A short report on subsidies, affordability, and supply.* Washington, DC: U.S. Department of Health and Human Services.

U.S. Department of Commerce, Bureau of the Census (2005, March). Table a-3. Mean earnings of workers 18 years and over, by educational attainment, race, Hispanic origin, and sex: 1975 to 2003, *U.S. Census Bureau, Current Population Survey.* Washington, DC. Retrieved from http://www.census.

gov/population/socdemo/education/tabA-3.pdf.

U.S. Department of Health and Human Services (2003, September 17). *Temporary assistance for needy families program information memorandum: Work participation rates for FY 2002* (No. TANF-ACF-IM-2003–02). Washington, DC: Author.

U.S. Department of Health and Human Services (2011). *The 2011 HHS Poverty Guidelines.* Retrieved from http://aspe.hhs.gov/poverty/11poverty.shtml.

Examining African American Female Students' Decision to Pursue the Doctorate

CARMEN M. MCCALLUM

African Americans have made great advancements in postsecondary education. Over the last 30 years, enrollment and degree attainment has increased over 65 percent at undergraduate and graduate degree levels (National Center for Education Statistics, 2008). In 1976, barely 111,000 African Americans participated in higher education. Today, over 2.4 million have enrolled or obtained a college degree, and projections indicate that enrollment and degree attainment will continue to increase well into the twenty-first century (NCES, 2008).

The increase in participation over the last 10 years is partially reflective of the momentous gains African American women have made in pursuing graduate education. From 1990 to 2007, the number of African American women who earned their doctorate increased by 74 percent (NCES, 2008). Prior to the 1990s, African American women were 40 percent less likely to obtain a doctorate in comparison to African American men (NCES, 2008). However, by the beginning of the twenty-first century, African American women accounted for over 60 percent of the doctorates conferred to African Americans (NCES, 2008). Yet, despite these gains, researchers have paid little attention to the experiences of African American women who pursue graduate education. Scholars have explored the experiences of African Americans

• **155**

in general with no regard to gender, or they have focused on African American women only in comparison to the experiences of White women, with the focus being on White women. However, few studies have focused exclusively on the experiences of African American women who pursue graduate education. Thus, scholars agree that there is no general understanding of the factors that influence African American women to pursue graduate education (Carter, Pearson, & Shavilik, 1988; Henry, 1985; Howard-Vital, 1989; Johnson-Bailey, 1998, 2004; Louque, 1999; Ward, 1997; Williams et al., 2005).

This exploratory study will examine the factors that affect first-generation African American women in their decision to pursue the doctorate. The study specifically focuses on doctoral students, as the decision to enroll in master's or professional programs may be different from the process that students engage in when pursuing the doctoral education ("Trends in Graduate Enrollment," 2006). The study also specifically focuses on first-generation African American women, as a significant number of doctoral students identify as first-generation (Hoffer et al., 2005). According to a report by the Survey of Earned Doctorates, approximately 36 percent of those who earned the doctorate reported neither parent had earned more than a high school diploma (Hoffer et al. 2005). Hoffer and coauthors (2002) concluded, "These students are likely to have faced special challenges in the course of earning the doctorate, for their parents are likely to have . . . less knowledge to share about how to negotiate college and graduate school" (p. 34). Moreover, in a study of first-generation minority students' decision to pursue higher education, participants described their parents as "cheerleaders" in the decision process (Noeth & Wimberly, 2002), that is, extremely supportive but unable to provide "the necessary tools and resources to help them with postsecondary planning," as they had not attended college (Noeth & Wimberly, p. 15). Therefore, for the purpose of this study, first-generation is defined as being the first in the family to pursue the doctorate. Considering the characteristics of being first-generation and an African American woman is critical in distinguishing how this population makes the decision to pursue doctoral education.

First-generation students in general face unique challenges when deciding to pursue higher education when compared to students who have college-educated parents (Terenzini et al., 1996). They are more likely to come from low-income families and score lower on college entrance exams than students who parents have earned a bachelor's degree (Warburton, Bugarin, & Nunez, 2001). The question remains if first-generation African American women also experience similar challenges when deciding to pursue the doctorate. This study will explore how first-generation African American women make the decision to pursue doctoral education while considering the role of family, undergraduate experiences, and financial concerns embedded in the decision process.

The remainder of this chapter is as follows: The following section reviews relevant studies that examine factors that influence the decision to pursue graduate education, as studies specifically focusing on the enrollment in doctoral education are sparse. After reviewing the prior literature, a theoretical and conceptual framework describes how related factors may contribute to the decision process. Given the conceptual framework, a qualitative research project further explores the phenomenon and gives voice to African American women pursuing the doctorate.

Related Literature

The literature that addresses the decision to pursue graduate education is fractured and limited. Educational aspirations, the application and admission processes, completion, and attrition concerns have been studied (Bowen & Rudenstine, 1992; Gardner, 2009; Golde, 2005; Lovitts, 2001; Malaney, 1987; Olson & King, 1985; Poock, 1999, 2000; Stoecker, 1991). However, researchers agree that a comprehensive theoretical framework that encompasses the multiple factors that influence enrollment decisions in graduate education does not exist in the current literature (Gardner, 2009; Malaney, 1987; Olson & King, 1985; Poock, 1999, 2000; Stoecker, 1991). Additionally, scholars have also neglected to investigate the cultural and environmental influences that affect African American women graduate school decisions. It is not clear whether researchers have discounted the importance of environment and identity, or have simply not had access to sufficient sources of data and information to examine their influence upon students' decisions (Millett, 2003). Nevertheless, this review highlights factors identified as influential in the graduate school decision process: background characteristics, financial concerns, academic self-efficacy, outcome expectations, learning experiences, and environmental influences.

BACKGROUND CHARACTERISTICS

Parents influence many aspects of their children's education, including decisions about whether to pursue a given level of schooling, which institution to attend, and even choice of major at the undergraduate level (Karrker, 1992; Leppel, Williams, & Waldauer, 2001). At the graduate level, however, the influence of parents is extremely complex. Students have experienced college and have gained a sense of independence—a possible indirect effect of an undergraduate education. This independence frequently clouds the connection between their decision to go to graduate school and their background characteristics. Thus, it is not surprising that scholars have found conflicting results. Several indicate that SES—parents' income and education—influences graduate school attendance (Fox, 1992; Stolzenberg, 1994; Zhang, 2005), while others maintain the effects of SES disappear at the graduate level (Ethington & Smart, 1986; Kallio, 1994; Stolzenberg 1994). To address this discrepancy, Stolzenberg (1994) analyzed causal models that compared a composite of SES with its distinct components. Results suggest that the connection between SES and graduate degree aspirations found in other studies have been misinterpreted (Stolzenberg, 1994). According to Stolzenberg, educational aspirations only function as a conduit through which parental background effects on graduate education are transmitted. Thus, there is not a direct connection between SES and graduate school aspiration (Stolzenberg, 1994).

On the other hand, Mullen, Goyette, and Soares (2003) examined the effects of parents' education specifically on enrollment in doctoral programs. They concluded that parents' education does influence one's likelihood of enrolling in doctoral education. Students from highly educated families are more likely to enroll in doctoral programs than students whose parents have less education—some college or high school diploma (Ethington & Smart, 1986; Karraker, 1992; Mullen, Goyette, & Soares, 2003). Mullen, Goyette, and Soares (2003) also confirm the need to examine the components of SES and graduate degree levels separately. The influence of parents' education on enrollment was specific to doctoral programs (Mullen, Goyette, and Soares, 2003). Parents' education did not influence enrollment in master of business administration (MBA) or other graduate programs.

FINANCIAL CONCERNS

Financial concerns also factored into the decision to attend graduate school. Although some parents assume the financial burden of paying for their students' undergraduate education, often students accumulate personal student loans, leaving them in debt upon graduation. The possibility of accruing additional debt combined with the uncertainty of financial gain upon completion of a graduate degree can deter qualified students from pursuing graduate education (Brazziel & Brazziel, 2001).

In contrast, scholars have found that undergraduate debt does not deter students from pursuing graduate education (Fox, 1992; Heller, 2001; Weiler, 1994). Fox (1992) examined the impact of undergraduate debt on the propensity to enroll in graduate education. The empirical analysis revealed that undergraduate debt discouraged women slightly from pursuing graduate education but had no impact upon men. Weiler (1994) confirmed that a relationship does not exist between a student's actual undergraduate debt and the decision to pursue graduate education. Using the third follow-up from the 1980 High School and Beyond data sample of seniors who graduated from a four-year university, Weiler (1994) concluded that students take into consideration their interests, abilities, SES, and the perceived cost of and benefits of graduate education when making their enrollment decisions. However, actual undergraduate debt does not deter students from pursuing graduate education.

Although researchers generally agree that past debt alone does not influence the decision to attend graduate school, financial aid or financial assistance from graduate institutions appears to increase the likelihood of enrollment (Cardon & Rogers, 2002; Ethington & Smart, 1986; Kallio, 1994; Olson & King, 1985). According to Ethington and Smart (1986), of all influences affecting the graduate school decision process, financial aid has the greatest impact on enrollment decisions. St. John's (2007) qualitative analysis of interviews from the Gates Millennium Scholars Program (GMS) indicated that the promise of GMS financial awards increased the chances that undergraduate GMS recipients will attend graduate school.

ACADEMIC SELF-EFFICACY

Academic self-efficacy is a person's belief in her ability to perform well academically (Zimmerman 1995). Undergraduate students who perform well academically generally have a greater interest in attending graduate school (Hearn, 1987; Mullen,

Goyette, & Soares, 2003). Students who perform well in their course work typically perform well on college admissions tests, which are necessary in order to be admissible in most graduate programs (Mullen, Goyette, & Soares, 2003). Academic success leads to academic confidence; therefore, academically successful students tend to consider graduate school a viable option.

OUTCOME EXPECTATIONS/GOALS

Heller (2001) utilized a national data set to explore what factors influence graduate school attendance. A logistic regression model indicated that graduate school aspirations were the most influential factor in the decision process. Those who aspired and set a goal to earn the doctorate or a professional degree were more likely to attend graduate school than those who did not set a goal. Cardon and Rogers (2002) found that personal goals and the desire to be top in the field were major influences for master's and doctoral students (Anderson & Swazey, 1998; Malaney, 1987). Likewise, potential career advancement, the desire for knowledge, and the possibility to gain research experience were also important influences (Anderson & Swazey, 1998; Stiber, 2000).

LEARNING EXPERIENCES

The selectivity of the undergraduate institution and the experiences students have while attending greatly influences decisions to pursue graduate education (Ethington & Smart, 1986; Heller, 2001; Mullen, Goyette, & Soares, 2003). Specifically, "The greater the social and academic involvement of students in the undergraduate institution, the more likely they are to extend their education by attending graduate school" (Ethington & Smart, 1983, p. 298). Students can become engaged by participating in student organizations (Patton & Bonner, 2001; Schuh et al., 1992; Harper, Byars, & Jelke, 2005), socializing with faculty (Hathaway, Nagda, & Gregerman, 2002; Lammers, 2001), participating in graduate preparatory programs (Ishiyama & Hopkins, 2003), or participating in undergraduate research projects (Barlow & Villarejo, 2004; Hathaway, Nagda, and Gregerman, 2002; Huss et al., 2002; Ridgwell & Creamer, 2003). All of the aforementioned activities have been associated with influencing graduate school aspirations and plans.

PERCEIVED ENVIRONMENTAL INFLUENCES

In general, characteristics of the graduate institution play an important role in the decision process. The quality and reputation of the program and its faculty strongly influences students' decisions (Cardon & Rogers, 2002; Kallio, 1994; Olson & King, 1985). The geographic location and the time to degree completion factor into student enrollment decisions as well (Cardon & Rogers, 2002; Olson & King, 1985; Mullen, Goyette, & Soares, 2003).

Theoretical Overview

Social cognitive career theory (SCCT) complements and builds conceptual linkages with existing career theories to explore decision-making processes (Lent, Brown, & Hackett, 1994). Grounded in Bandura's (1986) revised social cognitive theory, SCCT focuses specifically on the processes through which "(a) academic and career interests develop, (b) interests, in concert with other variables, promote career-relevant choices, and (c) people attain varying levels of performance and persistence in their educational and career pursuits" (Lent, Brown, & Hackett, 1994, p. 311). The SCCT causal model includes background characteristics, learning experiences, self-efficacy, outcome expectations, interests, and environmental influences that simultaneously affect goals, choices, and ultimate decisions. "The cognitive personal variables allow individuals to have agency in their choice about their career interest while the environmental variables acknowledge that person, environment, and behavior variables affect one another through complex and reciprocal linkages" (Lent, Brown, & Hackett, 1994, p. 85).

Among the key factors—self-efficacy, outcome expectations, and goals—self-efficacy refers to the level of confidence a person uses to organize and execute courses of actions (Bandura, 1986). A person's level of confidence can be affected by interactions with other people, the environment, or one's own behavior. SCCT defines self-efficacy as a person's expectations about her confidence to negotiate various career-related tasks and pursuits (Lent, Brown, & Hackett, 1994). Students who have demonstrated self-efficacy in their academic ability are more likely to pursue further education as a career path (Hearn, 1987; Mullen, Goyette, & Soares, 2003).

Outcome expectations are beliefs related to the consequences of performing a specific behavior (Bandura, 1986). This construct focuses on the consequences some believe will occur if a particular behavior is performed. Typically, outcome expectations are developed through past learning experiences, either direct or vicarious, and the perceived results of those experiences. The experiences are influenced by self-efficacy. Thus, SCCT assumes individuals are more likely to choose a particular academic or vocational path if they envision favorable outcomes resulting from that behavior. The expectation that education will lead to social mobility historically has been an expectation for students of color (Louque, 1999; Walpole, 2003).

Goals play a primary role in behavior. They inspire and help facilitate academic and vocational plans. They assist with aspirations to complete a certain task. In SCCT, goals are defined as the decision to begin a particular activity or future academic or career plan (Lent, Brown, & Hackett, 1994). They are a function of self-efficacy and outcome expectations. Typically, there are several goals associated with obtaining a graduate degree for African American students. Obtaining social mobility, career advancement, and having the means to give back to the community are prevalent in the literature (Louque, 1999, Walpole, 2003).

In addition to cognitive person-variables, SCCT also assumes that environmental factors, objective or perceived, influence vocational and academic choices (Lent, Brown, & Hackett, 1994). A doctoral program can be considered an objective environmental factor. How one interprets that environment, whether it is positive or negative, can be viewed as a perceived environmental factor.

THEORETICAL FRAMEWORK AND CONCEPTUAL MODEL

The literature review of factors that influence graduate school decisions and SCCT provides a framework for understanding how students make the decision to pursue doctoral education. The model focuses on the individual decision to pursue the doctorate while taking into account the external influences that can affect such decisions. Building upon the work of Lent, Brown, and Hackett (1994), this study will utilize SCCT as a lens to understand how students make the decision to pursue graduate education. Specifically, pursuing the doctorate will be considered a career decision. This study will use academic self-efficacy to focus the concept of self-efficacy in the original model, and it will be defined as a student's beliefs about his or her ability to complete academic tasks (Zimmerman, 1995). In general,

FIGURE 1. A SOCIAL-COGNITIVE MODEL OF THE GRADUATE SCHOOL DECISION

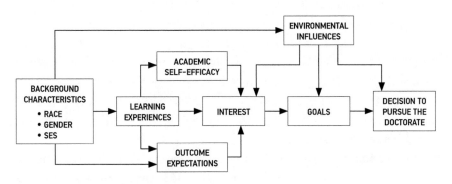

Source: Lent, R.W., Brown, S.D. & Hackett, G. (1994).

this study assumes background characteristics, learning experiences, academic self-efficacy, and outcome expectations form students' career and educational goals, which lead to the decision to pursue doctoral education. An illustration of the conceptual model is given in figure 1.

METHODOLOGICAL APPROACH

This exploratory study seeks to understand how first-generation African American women made the decision to pursue doctoral education. As mentioned earlier, first-generation doctoral students are defined as students whose parents did not attend a doctoral program. Few studies examine the decision to pursue graduate education. Currently, no studies specifically explore the decision to pursue doctoral education of first-generation African American women. This study aims to add to the scholarly literature by recognizing the influence that being first-generation and an African American woman can have on the decision process.

This study specifically focuses on doctoral students rather than master's or professional (e.g., law, medicine) students. Graduate programs differ dramatically in the commitment required and the rewards gained from them. Master's degree programs sometimes require two years of study with limited research required. However, doctoral programs require a greater level of time commitment and are typically research-intensive. Since there is no theoretical evidence that connects the experience of master's, doctoral, and professional students, and since by all indications the experiences of students differ significantly, this study will focus exclusively on doctoral students.

Studies investigating the decision to pursue graduate education often employ quantitative approaches to link background characteristics, self-efficacy, and expectations. The quantitative approach often focuses on uncovering relationships between inputs and outputs through statistical analysis (Stage & Manning, 2003). The strength of a quantitative approach lies in its ability to support statistically sound conclusions about general behavior within the context of theory based on a sizable number of observations.

Conclusions from quantitative studies provide valuable information about general phenomena occurring during the decision-making process. However, when findings are generalized to a student population, the range of what can be said about one individual student or small group experience is limited (Stage & Manning, 2003). Because quantitative research tends to collapse theoretical concepts and predetermine categories, an accurate understanding of the complex nature of individuals becomes almost unobtainable (Stage & Manning, 2003). Consequently, segments of the population that do not reflect the prevailing norms of the larger population are unevenly influenced.

> Individuals in the sample who differ significantly from average (for example, older students, or ethnic minority students on a predominately White research campus) are unlikely to find their experiences represented unless the data are collected in a manner that deliberately seeks to represent large numbers of these students. (Stage & Manning, 2003, p. 25)

Since the primary purpose of this study is to understand the process by which first-generation African American women make the decision to pursue doctoral education, a qualitative approach is necessary. The strength of qualitative research is the ability to provide an account of the means by which individual outcomes are achieved, considering both environmental context and participant meaning rather than focusing on the relationship between predefined independent variables. It allows the researcher to understand and explain the social phenomena of a given inquiry (Stage & Manning, 2003). The approach allows for in-depth analysis of factors that may be influencing the decision process.

A qualitative study is especially appropriate for defining important relationships and identifying new ideas in an area of critical need (Merriman, 1998). "It allows the researcher to get an inner experience of participants, to determine how meanings are formed through and in culture, and to discover rather than test variables" (Corbin & Strauss, 2008, p. 12). A qualitative approach is appropriate because I desire to step beyond the known and enter into the world of the participants, to see the world from their perspective and in doing so make discoveries that will contribute to the development of empirical knowledge (Corbin & Strauss, 2008). The following questions serve to guide this study:

- What factors into the decision to pursue advanced graduate education among first-generation doctoral students?
- More specifically, what are the processes that first-generation students use to decide to pursue doctoral education?
- What role do family background, educational background, and expectancy have on the decision to embark on doctoral study?
- What are the perceived costs and benefits associated with pursuing doctoral education for first-generation students?
- What barriers do students perceive in their pursuit of doctoral education?

The phenomenological approach of qualitative research will guide my interest in understanding the meaning individuals have constructed about their decision-making process (Merriam, 1998). In qualitative inquiry, the researcher becomes the instrument through which participants' perspectives are interpreted and analyzed. Researchers interact with participants and cannot function apart from the context (Creswell, 2003). The participants in the research construct realities, and multiple realities exist (Creswell, 2003). Using a phenomenological approach, it will be my responsibility to interpret the essence of students' shared experiences in the decision-making process (Merriman, 1998).

Research Design

In order to explore and explain the decision to pursue doctoral education for first-generation African American women, I utilized purposive sampling to conduct 10 in-depth, semistructured interviews with African American doctoral students at a doctoral extensive research university as defined by the Carnegie Foundation Classifications, 2000. However, only data from the five female participants is utilized in this exploratory pilot study. I chose to conduct interviews for their utility in investigating past events (Merriman, 1998). Semistructured interviews elicit detailed descriptions about the decision process in participants' own words, adding value to the overall process (Merriman, 1998). The method allowed participants to tell their story as they saw fit. I asked clarifying questions only after students finished with their narrative, synchronizing their voice with the research process (Corbin & Strauss, 2008). I am interested in identifying the decision processes from inception to enrollment; therefore, semistructured interviews were appropriate.

DATA COLLECTION

Building upon the conceptual model, I created an interview protocol that assisted in building rapport with participants (Stage & Manning, 2003). A qualitative methodologist validated the protocol before it was used in this study. The methodologist examined whether the protocol had clear wording, sufficient detail, or irrelevant questions. I made adjustments accordingly. The protocol did not ask specifically about race; however, I paid special attention to the way race and gender were reflected in the narratives of the participants and how they made meaning from their respective experiences in deciding to pursue the doctorate.

I interviewed each participant once for approximately 60 minutes. The 60-minute period allowed enough time for participants to discuss issues in depth (Stage & Manning, 2003). I informed participants that they might be contacted for follow-up interviews later. I conducted interviews during the 2008 winter semester and digitally recorded each with the consent of the participant. In addition, I transcribed all interviews verbatim and gave each participant a pseudonym.

SAMPLING

In order to participate in the study, participants had to self-identify as "first-generation" and as an "African American." Participants also had to be currently enrolled in a social science or education doctoral program. According to the National Center for Educational Statistics (2008), over the last 10 years, education and social science fields have produced the largest percentage of doctoral degrees conferred on African Americans. Research also indicates that students in the social sciences approach graduate education differently than students in science, math, and engineering fields (Sax, 1996). Thus, science, math, and engineering students were excluded from the sample.

The purposive networking sampling approach requires all participants within a specific group to meet specific characteristics of that group in order to participate. "This type of non-random sampling is done to increase the utility of the information obtained in that participants are chosen because they are likely to be knowledgeable and informative about the phenomenon of interest" (Padula & Miller, 1999). In this study, race, first-generation status, and enrollment in an education or social science doctoral program were used as criteria to recruit participants. The sampling technique provided information-rich interviews as I engaged with participants and solicited additional interviewees (Merriman, 1998).

Every effort was made to be completely transparent with participants concerning this study. I sent an e-mail to all participants, soliciting participation and a consent form indicating the purpose of the study. I took measures to ensure confidentiality and anonymity, the researcher's role, procedures for safe data storage, exit procedures, and reciprocity. I assured participants that their identities would not be exposed in the report of the findings. For example, their institution or doctoral program would be omitted or referred to in general terms. I kept the transcribed interviews and field notes in a locked storage container, and in the future, should a participant choose not to participate, I will destroy her materials or return to them to the participant.

ROLE OF RESEARCHER

The relationship between the researcher and the subject under investigation is a critical threat to internal validity (Merriman, 1998; Stage & Manning, 2003). The relationship requires independent consideration. As the instrument through which data analysis flows, qualitative investigators are encouraged to confront their subjectivity through reflectivity—articulation and clarification of assumptions, experiences, and orientation that may influence study (Merriman, 1998).

I am aware and acknowledge the subjectivity noted in my identity as a first-generation African American doctoral student. I understand that my presence may alter the information provided by participants due to visible cues and characteristics they may have identified (Stage & Manning, 2003), but I also acknowledge the value of being an insider in the community I have chosen to study. Several scholars (Marshall & Rossman, 1999; Maxwell, 2005; Strauss & Corbin, 1990) have stated that "recognizing personal ties to the study you want to conduct can provide you with a valuable source of insight, theory, and data about the phenomena you are studying" (Maxwell, 2005, p. 35). Maxwell refers to this as experimental knowledge and states that it is the most important yet most neglected concept in qualitative studies. Strauss concurs:

> These experimental data should not be ignored because of the usual canons governing research (which regard personal experiences and data as likely to bias the research), for these canons lead to the squashing of valuable experimental data. We say, rather, "Mine your experience, there is potential gold there!" (1987, p. 11 as quoted in Maxwell, 2005, p. 38)

Therefore, I acknowledge that my identity and subjectivity has the potential to bias the study, but I argue that various ascribed characteristics (e.g., race, gender) mediate the design and interpretation of all research endeavors, and as such, my study is no different. Nonetheless, I will take steps to amplify trustworthiness and minimize my own inherent biases and assumptions so that alternative viewpoints and disconfirming evidence are recognized and given equal consideration and voice in the analysis and reporting of the results.

TRUSTWORTHINESS

I used multiple strategies in order to provide trustworthiness and support the validity of my findings (Merriman, 1998; Stage & Manning, 2003). These strategies included rich, thick descriptions, peer debriefing, and the presentation of discrepant information (Creswell, 2003). As new and emergent themes became present in the data, I selected samples of participants' transcripts to be reviewed by the participants for accuracy. I also solicited a colleague who served as a peer debriefer. Their role was to ask questions about the qualitative study to ensure that the accounts will resonate with people other than the researcher. I compared, contrasted, and situated findings with existing literature.

The Participants

Amber is a 24-year-old African American woman pursuing a doctorate in psychology. She is a third-year student. She began her doctoral program immediately following her bachelor's degree. She self-identifies as a first-generation doctoral student because she is the first in her family to receive a college degree.

Kristina is a 27-year-old African American woman also pursuing her doctorate in psychology. She is a fourth-year student who began her graduate career pursuing a master's degree. Kristina applied and enrolled in the doctoral program prior to completing the master's requirements. She identifies as a first-generation doctoral student because her parents have not earned the doctorate. Her mother has a master's in education and her father received his bachelor's degree while Kristina was in high school.

April is a 23-year-old African American woman pursuing a joint doctorate in political science and sociology. She self-identifies as a first-generation doctoral student because she is the first in her family to receive a college degree. She is also the first among her siblings to pursue the Ph.D. At the time of this interview, April did not have a master's degree. She is a second-year student in her doctoral program.

Karen is a 29-year-old African American woman pursuing a dual degree in public health and education. She is a third-year student and considers herself a first-generation doctoral student because her parents have not earned the doctorate. Karen's father did not attend college and her mother earned a bachelor's degree in art but never utilized the degree for employment purposes. She began her graduate education as a master's student and is currently looking forward to completing the doctorate.

Janice is African American and does not have a master's degree. She is 25 years old and is currently pursuing her doctorate in sociology. Janice is the oldest of four siblings and the first to attend college in her family. Neither her mother nor father has earned a bachelor's degree. She is currently a second-year student in her program.

Analysis

The data are analyzed in a multistep process, which included open, axial, and selective coding mechanisms recommended by Creswell (2003) and Corbin and Strauss (2008). Although open and axial coding are presented here as separate steps, for clarity, I considered open and axial coding as one step.

> The distinction made between the two types of coding [is] "'artificial" and for explanatory purposes only, to indicate to the reader that though we break data apart, and identify concepts to stand for data, we also have to put it back together again by relating these concepts. (Corbin & Strauss, 2008, p. 198)

First, I read two transcripts while looking for emerging themes and connections to the conceptual model. Second, after labeling observed patterns, I created a set of codes for sorting, comparing, and contrasting the data. Third, I grouped the codes into themes and subthemes and summarized them while looking for emergent themes. Next I gave the coded transcripts and the codes to a peer debriefer. The peer debriefer recommended expanding the codes into broader categories. The new codes were utilized to code all five transcripts. Then I gave one of the initial transcripts with the new codes and overall themes to a second peer debriefer who made recommendations. Finally, I reread all transcripts utilizing the final themes and subthemes. I utilized peer reviewers to ensure internal validity (Merriman, 1998).

Limitations

Inherent to qualitative research is the potential for undue interviewer bias. Although all attempts to secure validity were made, I recognize that my biases may have influenced data collection and analysis. I believe higher education institutions are not making enough efforts to inform and encourage first-generation African American students to pursue the doctorate. In order to be true to findings, I must be open to alternative explanations. One strategy employed involved the identification of my motivations, assumptions, and hypotheses associated with this study. For future interviews, I will periodically prepare research memos to chronicle my journey with the project and create a conversation of sorts around the topic and emergent themes.

Another limitation to this study was the participants. Participants were relying on memory to reconstruct original complex factors including attitudes, beliefs, and perceptions that influenced them to decide to enter a doctoral program. The quality of the data collection was limited to the participants' abilities to be introspective and to recall those perceptions. Frequently participants would discuss issues or concerns they are currently experiencing in their doctoral programs rather than the processes that occurred prior to enrollment.

Due to the in-depth nature of this qualitative study, financial concerns, and time constraints, smaller samples were used than with a typical quantitative study. This may have implications for generalizing to a larger population. Although the goal of qualitative research is not to seek generalizability of findings but to provide perspective rather than truth, it could still be considered a limitation of this study (Merriman, 1998). It is imperative that readers remember that this is an exploratory study conducted to inform future research on the factors, which affect the doctoral decision for first-generation African American women. Future studies will have a more robust sample.

Finally, studies of students' experiences cannot account for every factor that may influence the decision to pursue doctoral education. Other environmental or contextual developments not identified may specifically influence the decision process. For example, doctoral students in psychology may have very different experiences than students pursuing the doctorate in education. Readers should consider the unique environment and context of each particular discipline when considering the conclusions offered in this study. Despite the limitations, distinct factors identified as influencing first-generation African American women's decisions to pursue doctoral education will have implications for future research and policy development.

Emergent Themes

An analysis of the data revealed five major themes that influenced the participant's decision to pursue the doctorate: (1) encouragement, (2) instrumental support, (3) outcome expectations: intergenerational mobility (4) race and gender concerns, and (5) sacrifices.

The thematic code of encouragement refers to the variety of support and reinforcement students perceived regarding their education and career plans (Fisher & Padmawidjaja, 1999). Participants revealed that they believed they could successfully enroll in a doctoral program because family, friends, and faculty members all consistently encouraged them to succeed. All participants indicated that encouragement made a difference in their decision process. Kristina explains how her father's encouragement at an early age influenced her decision to pursue doctoral education:

> My dad was constantly, like, "Take education as far as you can take it." He was very concerned about our grades and what we were learning in school. I guess I had this perception—I don't know if it was from school or from my parent that, you know, you're smart so you should pursue graduate education or something, with something with some status, go as far as you can in education as you can, so that was kind of instilled in me . . . to pursue a graduate degree.

Amber described the little things family members would do to help her stay focused on her educational goals as encouragement. She smiled as she described the encouragement she received from her mother:

> She's supportive in the ways she can be. She tried not to call me as much because she's like, "I know you're busy," so she was supportive in the ways she could be. She would call and say, "I just wanted to call and say hi," you know. She called to check on me, make sure I'm going to church, make sure I'm eating right . . . ya know . . . the things that a lot of mothers do. . . . Yeah, she really wants to see me succeed.

In addition to encouragement by family members, the majority of participants felt encouraged by faculty in their academic endeavors and identified a two-way relationship between themselves and faculty members. In other words, because the women presented themselves as good students they believed faculty members singled them out and encouraged them to participate in graduate school preparatory programs. For example, Amber talked about the encouragement and support she received in the McNair program because of a faculty referral:

> I would say McNair was the most helpful because we had a really committed program director and she was just wonderful. She was really, truly honestly invested in us being successful, so we would have late nights with her working on studying for GRE. . . . I mean . . . I was studying for the GRE as a sophomore in college! She was really invested in helping us, developing essays, personal issues—anything you can think of, she was supportive in that.

Kristina agreed as she reflected on her own experiences:

> The former chair of the department, I took a class from her in educational psychology and she was also advisor to Psi Chi, the national honor society in psychology, so I got to know her very well. She sought me out and was like, "Look, are you planning on going to graduate school? 'Cause I really think you would do well and flourish there." . . . That made a difference.

Both Amber's and Kristina's statements illustrate the faculty and institutional encouragement they experienced while deciding to pursue the doctorate.

Encouragement is often overlooked and viewed as an intangible source of assistance; however, a few scholars have documented its importance in the scholarly literature (Blustein et al., 1991; Fisher & Griggs, 1995; Kenny, 1990). For these participants, encouragement was viewed as a key variable that provided the motivation needed to pursue the doctorate. Knowing that important individuals (e.g., family, friends) cared and believed they could succeed provided participants the motivation they needed to pursue their goals of pursuing an advance degree.

INSTRUMENTAL SUPPORT

Although participants felt strongly encouraged, one of the barriers identified was a lack of instrumental support. Instrumental support, often referred to as "tangible support," differs from encouragement or emotional support. It is the specifics needed to complete a given task. Providing students with information on how to write a personal statement, seek funding, or connecting students with faculty are tasks identified as instrumental support (Ortiz-Walters & Gilson, 2005). When asked, "Did your family members have any advice about you applying to a doctoral program?" or "How did your family members help you with the decision process?" each participant stated their family members were not able to provide instrumental support. Amber reflects on a conversation she had with her mother when she was frustrated about the application process:

> She just told me to make sure that I continued to work hard. Yeah, that was pretty much it, 'cause she didn't know, she doesn't really know what the process is, so she's just like, "If you need anything, we're here if you need help," and I'm, like, OK. So you know they offer. Her and my sisters, they offer themselves to help me but . . . (sigh).

Amber specifically connects the incapability of her parents to provide instrumental support to her first-generation doctoral status:

> I think it's different for first-generation grad students because you don't really have those people to talk to, like in your family, so even though you have professors who may be very supportive of that kind of thing [providing information about grad school], you don't have anyone directly from your background that can relate. So even though I had a lot of supportive advisors or faculty from [my school], a lot of them may not have identified with my financial background or my family background, so I think that might be something different than someone who might have had a parent or someone who also has a graduate degree. . . . They could provide more concrete advice.

Kristina agreed with the importance of instrumental support, especially at the institutional level. Her desire to pursue the doctorate began early in her undergraduate career, yet she did not gain the skills necessary to navigate the enrollment process during her undergraduate studies. Her statement reflects the consequences of not having institutional instrumental support:

> I knew I wanted to get into graduate school but I really didn't know how, so at first I had to apply to graduate school a couple times before I got in because I

didn't know the know-how. You need to talk to people from other universities, find out what research they are working on.... You need undergraduate research experiences.... I'm a good student. I had good GRE scores. I thought I should be able to get in, but I didn't realize how much went behind that, so I had to apply a couple of times before I learned those finer points. Looking back now, I think that some of that was knowing how to ask the right questions, so I don't think I was asking the right questions. They [faculty] were saying, "You can do this. You would be really suited," but I didn't know about the intricacies of having them look over my personal statement and give feedback or having them advise me on contacting people.... I was not asking those, the right questions.

Other participants confirmed they did not get specific information from faculty at their undergraduate institution about the process of pursuing doctoral programs. Lack of instrumental support is particularly problematic for first-generation African American women who do not have alternative communities to turn to for guidance. Results indicate that first-generation African American women are not being provided the "insiders' knowledge" necessary to gain access to social networks—social capital—needed to ease the process of pursuing the doctorate (Bourdieu, 1977).

OUTCOME: INTERGENERATIONAL MOBILITY

Intergenerational mobility refers to an individual's capability to achieve a higher social and economic status than previous generations. Often referred to as "achieving the American Dream," intergenerational mobility is the goal of many college students and their families. Participants agreed that opportunity for intergenerational mobility motivated them, and Karen's statement defines the essence of the theme:

I've noticed a theme in talking with other students as well as with myself, almost like this call to action that is bigger than a personal issue. It's almost like a call to action for social change. So ... I think it has to be something more than wanting to be called doctor for myself that got me through the application process in the end. It was the ideal that my entire family status may change because I made the decision to pursue this degree.

Amber reflects on her family's financial status and desires to improve her economic status:

> I definitely wanted to do something so that I would be able to make more money. ... My father raised us making $25,000 and there were seven of us in the house. ... My parents made miracles ... so I knew I didn't want to struggle. I wanted to do better. ... The degree will allow me to do better.

Kristina was not as concerned about the economic gains of the doctoral degree as she was the social mobility it would provide her and her family:

> I think part of it had to do with social comparison with the peers that I was with in high school, people claiming they were going to med school or become a lawyer. I think social comparison sort of limited the options. I had to do something that would require a lot of education and be very specialized and I knew that I didn't want to be a doctor ... lawyer ... hmm ... I don't know. Something about that doesn't appeal to me ... I mean ... that [is] really how simplistic it was ... for me in high school ... doctor, lawyer ... Oh well ... I guess I am going to get my Ph.D. ... I will be just as good if [I get it].

Students who pursue the doctorate in an effort to achieve intergenerational mobility often feel overwhelmed with the responsibility and obligation to succeed. Unlike students who have family members who have earned the doctorate, first-generation students feel as if they are embarking into new territory, not only for themselves, but also for their family and their entire race. This burden of success may discourage some undergraduates from pursuing the doctorate, but further research is needed to understand the nuances at work in this regard.

RACE AND GENDER

Participants were not asked directly about the influence of race and gender in their decision, but all five woman mentioned race and gender when reflecting on their decision to pursue the doctorate. For example, Karen stated:

> I talked to other Black women in Ph.D. programs [about family life] and they were like, "'Why don't you just hang it up?" (laughs) "Be prepared to wait like five to

seven years." I didn't know if [having a family] was something I wanted to give up. I began negotiating—family or Ph.D.—and then and other people were like "What are you thinking, get the PhD, freeze some eggs."

Karen's concern about her role as a student, wife, and mother is a concern typically experienced by woman pursuing higher education (Home, 1992).

All participants discussed their desire to improve societal conditions for African Americans through their research agendas. Williams and coauthors (2005) state, "There remains a vigilant need for African American women to 'pass it forward' or give back to other African American women." By educating themselves, African American women strive to enrich their community and make a difference (Louque, 1999; Schwartz et al., 2003; Williams et al., 2005). All five participants indicated their personal statements reflected their interest in pursuing research with African American populations. April described her agenda as follows:

> I'm interested in looking at race, class, and gender and intersectionality more broadly. I wanted to look at polarization of the Black middle class and how, on a local level, local representatives navigate between their needs and concerns of poorer groups of society versus more affluent Black members of society.

SACRIFICES

The decision to pursue doctoral education is not made in isolation. The participants frequently reflected on the sacrifices they had to make in order to pursue the doctorate. They recalled how they considered the hardships their families may experience due to their "selfish decision" and how that knowledge weighs heavily on whether or not you should pursue a degree as time consuming as the doctorate. Karen explained how she weighed the potential sacrifices:

> I think that's a major issues for deciding whether or not to do graduate school ... You are signing yourself up for five or more years living at the poverty level ... especially if you have other responsibilities.... Like I still have to help my mother out.... That becomes a source of stress, in it of itself ... because I can barely survive off the money that I have here, so to help her out with things is a challenge.... I have a 16-year-old sister that I have to make sure she is fed and clothed and you know what I mean.... So that's another thing 'cause I have to

make sure. . . . I have to support her as well, and then she is going to college . .
. and this could be just as complicated as going to graduate school away from
your family . . . just [because of] all of the things I'm missing.

April agreed that deciding to pursue the doctorate required many sacrifices but was
adamant that this was the one time in her life where she was entitled to be selfish:

This was the one area that I felt I could be selfish . . . that I had to do whatever was
best for me even if it was not in the best interest of other people. . . . Like it was not
in the best interest of my mom because I didn't help her with my grandmother
or I didn't help stay at home and pay bills. . . . It was all about me (sigh).

The sacrifices students make to pursue the doctorate range from financial to
emotional. This theme acknowledges the external influences that are involved in
the decision to pursue the doctorate. It suggests that the well-being of the family,
both immediate and extended, should be considered when attempting to recruit
African American students. Resources, which help address some of the emotional
and financial sacrifices, should also be considered when encouraging first-generation
students to pursue doctoral education.

Conclusion

This study adds new information to the growing body of literature on first-generation
African American women. One obvious advantage of utilizing a qualitative approach
in studying this phenomenon is it affords us the opportunity to use the words and
behaviors of those actually experiencing the situation (Padula & Miller, 1999).
The rich thick description of common themes among the participants increases
the likelihood that others may be able to relate to the findings and apply them to
their particular context.

Participants reflected on family background characteristics, academic self-
efficacy, goals, and outcome expectations associated with pursuing the doctorate.
All are mechanisms of the social cognitive career theory linear model; therefore,
SCCT appears to be a useful lens to examine first-generation African American
women doctoral students. However, the findings also suggest that SCCT should

not be the only theory considered when exploring the doctoral decision process. The theme *sacrifices* was prevalent, but SCCT gives relatively limited attention to lived experiences that constrain or facilitate individuals' opportunities, such as finances, support from significant others, and other social conditions related specifically to the individual (Vondracek, Lerner, & Schulenberg, 1986). Researchers could consider *sacrifices* as an environmental influence, but the environmental component of the theory has been criticized for being underdeveloped. Arbona (1995) questions the cultural validity of SCCT, although it is important to note that scholars have just begun examining the sociocultural contexts surrounding the decision to pursue the doctorate.

Overall, the findings suggest that factors that are culturally connected to the lives of African American women influence their decision to pursue doctoral education. Several scholars have utilized Collins's (2000) Black feminist thought (BFT) as a theoretical framework to understand the lived experiences of African American women (Coker, 2003; Grant, 2012; Johnson-Bailey, 2004; Williams et al., 2005). The theory provides a framework for examining the intersectionality of race, class, and gender. Its capability for understanding the doctoral decision for African American women should be explored in future studies.

This study also expanded the definition of "first-generation student" and exposed some of the factors that influence African American women as they aspire to obtain the doctorate. All participants verbalized the importance of encouragement while referring to their first-generation status. Surprisingly, participants whose parents have earned a master's degree, more frequently than those who parents did not, indicated they lacked instrumental family support when making the decision to apply. This finding is contradictory to our general understanding of social networking, which hypothesizes that individuals benefit from social contacts. Although participants had parents who had attended graduate school, they were unable to assist with the decision to pursue the doctorate. This finding further suggests that the pursuit of doctorate is a unique task in comparison to pursuit of other terminal degrees.

Intergenerational mobility was one of the expected outcomes of earning the degree. All participants described their immediate family economic status as being poor or lower middle class and connected that status to their doctoral decision. This finding indicates that research should further examine the influences of socioeconomic status of first-generation doctoral students and perhaps the impact of African American traditions on the doctoral decision.

In summary, these findings suggest that despite the attainment of a bachelor's degree, and sometimes even a master's degree, students are still unsure of the pathway to pursue the doctorate. In response, institutions should begin introducing students to the idea of pursuing doctoral education early in their academic career. Freshman or sophomore seminars should be structured to encourage students to reflect on their academic plans and career goals, which could lead to consideration of the doctorate.

Our examination of factors that influence African American women to pursue doctoral education has many implications for further research. Kallio (1994) summarized the thoughts of many scholars: "The implications for further research are many, but [they] can be reduced to a simple plea for more research on graduate students, period" (p. 122). This study has confirmed that pursuing a doctoral degree is a complex decision that involves multiple constituents. In order to unravel its intricacies, further research, both quantitative and qualitative, should examine what additional factors influence first-generation African American women to pursue the doctorate.

REFERENCES

Anderson, M.S., & Swazey, J.P. (1998). Reflections on the graduate student experience: An overview. *New Directions for Higher Education, 101,* 3–13.

Arbona, C. (1995). Cultural awareness and ethnic loyalty: Dimensions of cultural variability among Mexican American college students. *Journal of Counseling & Development. 73*(6), 610–614.

Bandura, A. (1986). Social foundations of thought and action: A social cognitive theory. Englewood Cliffs, NJ: Prentice-Hall.

Barlow, A.E.L., & Villarejo, M. (2004). Making a difference for minorities: Evaluation of an educational enrichment program. *Journal of Research in Science Teaching,* 41(9), 861–881.

Blustein, D.L., Walbridge, M.M., Friedlander, M.L., & Palladino, D.E. (1991). Contributions of psychological separation and parental attachment to the career development process. *Journal of Counseling Psychology, 38,* 39–50.

Bourdieu, P. (1977). *The logic of practice.* Stanford, CA: Stanford University Press.

Bowen, W.G., & Rudenstine, N.L. (1992). *In pursuit of the Ph.D.* Princeton, NJ: Princeton University Press.

Brazziel, M.E., & Brazziel, W.F. (2001). Factors in decisions of underrepresented minorities to forego science and engineering doctoral study: A pilot study. *Journal of Science and Technology, 10*(3), 273–281.

Cardon, P., & Rogers, G. (2002). Technology education graduate education: Factors influencing participation. East Lansing, MI: National Center for Research on Teaching Learning. ERIC Document Reproduction Service No. ED462615.

Carter, D., Pearson, C., & Shavilik, D. (1988). Double jeopardy: Women of color in higher education. *Educational Record, 69*, 98–103.

Coker, A. (2003). African American female adult learners: Motivations, challenges, and coping strategies. *Journal of Black Studies, 33*(5), 654–674.

Collins, P.H. (2001). *Black feminist thought: Knowledge, consciousness, and the politics of empowerment.* New York: Routledge.

Corbin, J., & Strauss, A. (2008). Basics of qualitative research: Techniques and procedures for developing grounded theory. United Kingdom: Sage Publications.

Creswell, J. (2003). Research design: Qualitative, quantitative, and mixed methods approaches. Thousand Oaks, CA: Sage.

Ethington, C., & Smart, J. (1986). Persistence to graduate education. *Research in Higher Education, 24*(35), 287–303.

Fox, M. (1992). Student debt and enrollment in graduate and professional school. *Applied Economics, 24*, 669–677.

Fisher, T.A., & Griggs, M.B. (1995). Factors that influence career development of African American and Latino youth. *Journal of Vocational Education Research, 20*, 57–72.

Fisher, T.A., & Padmawidjaja, I. (1999). Parental influences on career development perceived by African American and Mexican American college students. *Journal of Multicultural Counseling and Development, 27*(3), 136–152.

Gardner, S.K. (2009). The development of doctoral students: Phases of challenge and support. ASHE Higher Education Report: 1551-6970. San Francisco: Jossey-Bass.

Golde, C.M. (2005). The role of the department and discipline in doctoral student attrition: Lessons from four departments. *Journal of Higher Education, 76,* 669–700.

Grant, C.M. (2012). Advancing our legacy: A Black feminist perspective on the significance of mentoring for African American women in educational leadership. *International Journal of Qualitative Studies in Education, 25*(1), 101–117.

Harper, S.R., Patton, L.D., & Wooden, O.S. (2009). Access and equity for African America students in higher education: A critical race historical analysis. *Journal of Higher Education, 80*(4), 299–414.

Harper, S. R., Byars, L. F., & Jelke, T. B. (2005). How membership affects college adjustment and African American undergraduate student outcomes. In T. L. Brown, G. S. Parks, & C. M. Phillips (Eds.), *African American fraternities and sororities: The legacy and the vision* (pp. 393–416). Lexington: University Press of Kentucky.

Hathaway, R.S., Nagda, B.R., & Gregerman, S.R. (2002). The relationship of undergraduate research participation to graduate and professional education pursuit: An empirical study. *Journal of College Student Development, 43*(5), 614–631.

Hearn, J. (1987). The impact of undergraduate experiences on aspirations and plans for graduate and professional education. *Research in Higher Education, 27*(2), 119–141.

Heller, D. (2001). Debts and decisions: Student loans and their relationship to graduate school and career choice. East Lansing, MI: National Center for Research on Teaching Learning. ERIC Document Reproduction Service No. ED453722.

Henry, M.D. (1985). Black reentry females: Their concerns and needs. *Journal of the National Association of Women Deans and Counselors, 48*(4), 5–10.

Hoffer, T.B., Sederstrom, S., Selfa, L., Welch, V., Hess, M., Brown, S., Reyes, S., Webber, K., & Guzman-Barron, I. (2002). *Doctorate recipients from United States universities: Summary report 2002.* Chicago: National Opinion Research Center.

Hoffer, T.B., Welch, V., Webber, K., Williams, K., Lisek, B., Hess, M., et al. (2006). *Doctorate recipients from United States universities: Summary report 2005.* Chicago: National Opinion Research Center.

Home, A. (1992). Women facing the multiple role challenge. Adult women studying social work and adult education in Canada: A study of their multiple role experiences ad of supports available to them. East Lansing, MI: National Center for Research on Teaching Learning. ERIC Document Reproduction Service No. ED 369909.

Howard-Vital, M.R. (1989). African-American women in higher education: Struggling to gain identity. *Journal of Black Studies, 20*(2), 180–191.

Huss, M.T., Randall, B.A., Davis, S.F., & Hansen, D.J. (2002). Factors influencing self-rated preparedness for graduate school: A survey of graduate students. *Teaching of Psychology, 29*(4), 275–281.

Ishiyama, J.T. & Hopkins, V.M. (2003). Assessing the impact of a graduate school preparation program on first-generation, low income college students at a public liberal arts university. *Journal of College Student Retention, 4*(4), 393–405.

Johnson-Bailey, J. (1998). Black reentry women in the academy: Making a way out of no way. *Initiatives, 58*(4), 37–48.

Johnson-Bailey, J. (2004). Hitting and climbing the proverbial wall: Participation and retention issues for Black graduate women. *Race Ethnicity and Education, 7*(4), 331–349.

Kallio, R. (1994). Factors influencing the college choice decisions of graduate students. East Lansing, MI: National Center for Research on Teaching Learning. ERIC Document Reproduction Service No. ED373640.

Karraker, M. (1992). Socioeconomic or race differences? Explaining Black and White adolescent females' plans for schooling. *Urban Education, 27*(1), 41–58.

Kenny, M.E. (1990). Education and function of parental attachment among first-year college students. *Journal of Youth and Adolescence, 16,* 17–29.

Lammers, W.J. (2001). An informal seminar to prepare the best undergraduates for doctoral programs in psychology. *Teaching of Psychology, 28*(1), 58–59.

Lent, R.W., Brown, S.D., & Hackett, G. (1994). Sociocognitive mechanisms of personal agency on career development: Pantheoretical prospects. In M.L. Savikas and R.W. Lent (Eds.), *Convergence in career development and theories* (pp. 77–102). Palo Alto, CA: CCP Books.

Leppel, K., Williams, M., & Waldauer, C. (2001). The impact of parental occupations and socioeconomic status on choice of college major. *Journal of Family and Economic Issues, 22*(4), 373–93.

Louque, A. (1999). Factors influencing academic attainment for African American women Ph.D. recipients: An ethnographic study of their persistence. *Negro Educational Review, 50*(3), 101–108.

Lovitts, B.E. (2001). *Leaving the ivory tower: The causes and consequences of departure from doctoral study.* Boston: Rowman & Littlefield.

Malaney, G. (1987). Why students pursue graduate education, how they find out about a program and why they apply to a specific school. *College and University, 62*(3), 247–258.

Marshall, C., & Rossman, G.B. (1999). *Designing qualitative research.* 3rd ed. Thousand Oaks, CA: Sage.

Maxwell, J.A. (2005). *Qualitative research design: An interactive approach.* Vol. 41. Thousand Oaks, CA: Sage.

Merriman, S.B. (1998). *Qualitative research and case study applications in education.* San Francisco: Jossey-Bass.

Millett, C.M. (2003). How undergraduate loan debt affects application and enrollment in graduate or first professional school. *Journal of Higher Education, 74*(4), 386–415.

Mullen, A., Goyette, K., & Soares, J. (2003). Who goes to grad school? Social and academic correlates of educational continuation after college. *Sociology of Education, 76*(2), 143–169.

Noeth, R.J., & Wimberly, G.L. (2002). *Creating seamless educational transitions for urban African American and Hispanic students.* (Rep.). Iowa City, IA: ACT.

Olson, C., & King, M. (1985). A preliminary analysis of the decision process of graduate students in college choice. *College and University, 60*(4), 304–315.

Ortiz-Walters R, Gilson L.L. (2005). Mentoring in academia: An examination of the experiences of protégés of color. *Journal of Vocational Behavior, 67*(3), 459–475.

Padula, M., & Miller, D. (1999). Understanding graduate women's reentry experiences. *Psychology of Women Quarterly, 23*(2), 327–343.

Patton, L.A., & Bonner, F.A. II (2001). Advising the historically Black Greek letter organization (HBGLO): A reason for angst or euphoria? *National Association of Student Affairs Professionals Journal, 4*(1), 17–30.

Poock, M.C. (1999). Students of color and doctoral programs: Factors influencing the application decision in higher education. *College and University, 74*(3), 2–7.

Poock, M.C. (2000). African American students and the decision to attend doctoral programs in higher education administration. *College Student Affairs Journal, 19*(2), 51–59.

Ridgwell, D.M., & Creamer, E.G. (2003). Institutional culture and the advanced degree aspirations of students attending women's colleges. *College Student Affairs Journal, 23*(1), 77–90.

St. John, E.P. (2007). Student voices and graduate school choices: the role of finances in the lives of low-income, high-achieving students of color. In E.P. St. John, & P.K. Stillman (Eds.), *Readings on Equal Education.* Vol. 22: *Confronting educational inequality: reframing, building understanding, and making change* (pp. 85–107). Brooklyn, NY: AMS Press.

Sax, L.J. (1996). Understanding science majors: Gender differences in who goes to graduate school. *Review of Higher Education, 24*(2), 152–172.

Schuh, J., Triponey, V.L., Heim, L.L., & Nishimura, K. (1992). Student involvement in historically Black greek letter organizations. National Association of Student Personnel Association Journal, *29*(6), 274–282.

Schwartz, R.A., Bower, B.L., Rice, D.C., & Washington, C.M. (2003). Ain't I a woman, too? Tracing the experiences of African American women in graduate school. *Journal of Negro Education, 72*(3), 252–268.

Stage, F.K., & Manning, K. (2003). Research in the college context: Approaches and methods. New York: Brunner-Routledge.

Strauss, A., & Corbin, J. (1990). Basics of qualitative research: Grounded theory procedures and techniques. Newbury Park, CA: Sage Publications .

Stiber, G.F. (2000). Characterizing the decision process leading to enrollment in doctoral programs: Theory, application, and practice. *Journal of Marketing for Higher Education, 10,* 13–26.

Stoecker, J. (1991). Factors influencing the decision to return to graduate school for professional students. *Research in Higher Education, 32*(6), 689–701.

Stolzenberg, R. (1994). Educational continuation by college graduates. *American Journal of Sociology, 99*(4), 1042–77.

Terenzini, P.T., Springer, L., Yaeger, P.M., Pascarella, E.T., & Nora, A. (1996). Research in Higher Education. *Research in Higher Education, 37*(1), 1–22.

Tinto, V. (1975). *Leaving college: Rethinking the causes and cures of student attrition.* Chicago: University of Chicago Press.

Trends in graduate enrollment and degree. (2006, January/February). *Council of Graduate Schools Newsletter: The Communicator.* Retrieved from http://www.cgsnet.org/portals/o/pdf/DataSources_2006_01.pdf.

National Center for Educational Statistics, U.S. Department of Education (NCES). (2008). *Digest of Educational Statistics,* 2008.

Vondracek, F., Lerner, R., & Schulenberg, J. (1986). *Career development: A life-span developmental approach.* Hillsdale, NJ: Erlbaum Associates.

Walpole, M. (2003). Socioeconomic status and college: How SES affects college experiences and outcomes. *Review of Higher Education, 27*(1), 45–73.

Warburton, E.C., Bugarin, R., & Nunez, A.M. (2001). *Bridging the gap: Academic preparation and postsecondary success of first-generation students.* Rep. No. NCES 2001–153. Washington, DC: U.S. Department of Education, National Center for Education Statistics.

Ward, W.G. (1997). Black female graduate students in the academy: Re-moving the masks. Report no. 503669 East Lansing, MI: National Center for Research on Teacher Learning. ERIC Document Reproduction Service No. ED410779.

Weiler, W. (1994). Expectations, undergraduate debt and the decision to attend graduate school: A simultaneous model of student choice. *Economics of Education Review, 13*(1), 29–41.

Williams, M.R., Brewley, D.N., Reed, R.J., White, D.Y., & Davis-Haley, R.T. (2005). Learning to read each other: Black female graduate students share their experience at a White Research I institution. *Urban Review, 37*(3), 181- 199.

Zhang, L. (2005). Advance to graduate education: The effect of college quality and undergraduate majors. *Review of Higher Education, 28*(3), 313–338.

Zimmerman, B.J. (1995). Self-Regulation involves more than metacognition: A social cognitive perspective. *Educational Psychologist, 30*(4), 217–221.

It's My Prerogative

BLACK WOMEN ADMINISTRATORS SHARE
THEIR CHALLENGES OF RACE AND GENDER AT
PREDOMINATELY WHITE MICHIGAN INSTITUTIONS

DENISE O'NEIL GREEN *and* RAMONA MERAZ LEWIS

With the passage of the Michigan Civil Rights Initiative, better known as Proposal 2, in 2006, race-conscious and gender-conscious policies and programs garnered much attention and review because Proposal 2 made such efforts illegal due to their exclusive and preferential practices (Michigan Civil Rights Commission, 2007). Women of color in Michigan, specifically African American women, find themselves in a peculiar situation because neither their race nor gender can be recognized in efforts to improve their status in the state, whether it is in terms of securing government contracts, government jobs, access to selective Michigan institutions, or merit scholarships. However, prior to the passage of Proposal 2, African American women have always had ongoing challenges due to their double jeopardy status (Moses, 1989).

In the arena of higher education, African American women of Michigan, before and after the advent of Proposal 2, have faced multiple challenges. Whether Black women are in the role of student, faculty member, or staff member, they face a regular dose of behavioral and psychological assaults that question their right to occupy spaces at predominately White institutions (PWIs) (Clayborne & Hamrick,

2007; Holmes, 2003; Moses, 1989). Understanding that there are commonalities to these challenges (Collins, 2005), we in this chapter will focus on African American female administrators and draw attention to the issues they confront being Black women at PWIs.

Many challenges that African American female administrators face today are similar to challenges of the 1970s, when large numbers of African American students matriculated at predominately White institutions. Ironically, who advocates for and represents the interests of junior, midlevel, and senior-level Black female administrators? Where are the safe spaces and systems of support for them? When their administrative titles are designated "minority," "diversity," "affirmative action," or "multicultural," are there added burdens and concerns? The goal of this chapter is not to generalize that all Black women administrators share the same experiences, but to give voice to the challenges and coping strategies of 10 African American female administrators on predominately White campuses in the state of Michigan. Additionally, this chapter advances several policy recommendations and discusses implications for practice with respect to navigating predominately White campuses and allowing institutions to place greater value on what African American women administrators bring to college campuses.

Black Female Administrators in Higher Education

Throughout the educational pipeline, rates of degree attainment for women of color, including African American women, have risen at all levels (American Council on Education, 2008 & 2006). Although the numbers of African American women securing bachelor's, master's, doctoral, and professional degrees steadily increased between 1995 and 2005, African American women still hold a small percentage (5.7 percent) of full-time administrative positions in higher education (American Council on Education, 2008). At each transition point throughout the education pipeline, African American women lose ground, along with other minorities, while Whites continue to hold the majority (81 percent) of positions in both private and public institutions (American Council on Education, 2008). As a result of this attrition and lack of representation, Black female administrators continue to find themselves in unwelcoming and hostile environments that lead to isolation, marginalization, tokenism, stereotyping, and few mentoring opportunities

(Blackhurst, 2000; Clayborne & Hamrick, 2007; Collins, 2005; Holmes, 2003; Moses, 1989; Turner, 2002).

Extant literature discusses the multifaceted experiences of African American male and female administrators in academe (Becks-Moody, 2004; Benjamin, 1997; Clayborne & Hamrick, 2007; Edwards & Camblin, 1998; Garner, 2004; Jackson, 2001, 2003, 2004; Lloyd-Jones, 2009; Jones, 2001; Holmes, 2003; Mitchell-Crump, 2000; Patitu & Hinton, 2003; Watson, 2001). The experiences of African American administrators vary. Historically, the climate for African American females in the administrative ranks has been shaped by institutional type. For example, at predominately White institutions, African American administrators have often been viewed as "window dressers" or "tokens" with diminished authority and power (Hoskins, 1978, p. 5). On the other hand, at historically Black colleges and universities, African American administrators have often earned their status by working their way up the ranks. Hence, while administrative positions can often be highly esteemed positions for Black administrators, the opportunity does come at a price (Howard-Hamilton, 2003).

When the focus is specifically on African American women, the intersectionality of race and gender becomes salient and plays a vital role in their experiences and how they navigate PWIs (Clayborne & Hamrick, 2007; Collins, 2005; Holmes, 2003; Moses, 1989; Zamani, 2003). According to the paucity of literature that speaks to the experiences of African American female administrators, either in part or as a primary topic, Black women face and confront a plethora of roadblocks, challenges, and assaults on their humanity in these spaces, as they work in a system that provides very little institutional support and few rewards for what they uniquely bring to the environment (Blackhurst, 2000; Clayborne & Hamrick, 2007; Holmes, 2003; Lindsay, 1999; Moses, 1989, Patitu & Hinton, 2003; Turner, 2002).

Universities benefit from a diverse workforce. The experiences and perspectives of African American women bring to the workplace are of increasing importance given the changing demographics of students in institutions of higher education (Jackson & O'Callaghan, 2009). Although the percentages of African American students obtaining college degrees is still below White students, the *Chronicle of Higher Education 2010 Almanac* (2010a) reports more than a 50 percent increase of African American female students at institutions of higher education between 1998 and 2008. African American women hold only 11.3 percent of executive, administrative, and managerial positions on college campuses compared to the

79.5 percent held by their Whites colleagues (*Chronicle of Higher Education 2010 Almanac*, 2010b). Detailed discussion on the most recent findings on the presence of African American administrators and faculty in higher education is provided by Jackson and O'Callaghan (2009).

The rate of growth of administrators of color must keep pace with the changing student demographic; students need to see representative reflections of themselves. Retention and persistence rates of African American students are positively associated with the numbers of African American administrators and faculty at PWIs (Jackson & O'Callaghan, 2009; Patitu & Hinton, 2003). The presence of Black administrators sends an important message to students and more specifically, the presence of Black female administrators and faculty provides more opportunities for mentoring the increasing number of African American female students entering the ivory tower (Patton & Harper, 2003). Unfortunately, African Americans females hold significantly fewer professional positions than their White colleagues at colleges/universities (Jackson & O'Callaghan, 2009).

Black Women in the State of Michigan

Locating specifics on the numbers of African American female administrators in higher education in the state of Michigan proves extremely difficult. In Michigan, African American women hold significantly less (11.5 percent) executive, midlevel manager, and professional jobs across all professions than their White female counterparts, although more than African American men (Equal Employment Opportunity Commission, 2008a). The EEOC also reports aggregates for the number of positions held by Black women in executive, midlevel manager, and professional positions in the broad terminology of educational services as 55 percent, whereas their White female colleagues hold 68 percent of those same positions. These findings indicated that African American women still hold proportionately lower number of mid- to high-level positions in the state of Michigan. It is not an anomaly that we see so few African Americans in mid- to high-level positions in Michigan, as the aforementioned aggregate numbers for higher education indicate. Jackson and O'Callaghan (2009) indicate that "location matters" and point out the geographic distribution of administrators of color (p. 30). Across all racial groups leadership tends to clustered in areas of the country where there are the greatest numbers of concentration of their own specific groups; for example, African American leadership tends to be clustered highest in the Southeast (Jackson & O'Callaghan, 2009). There continues to be a lack of significant representation of both African American faculty and administrators of color in institutions across the country and in Michigan.

Theoretical Framework

The framework informing this essay was centered on the "four dimensions of the campus racial climate," coined by Hurtado (1992) and later expanded on by Hurtado and coauthors (1998). Those four dimensions include exploration of the following: "an institution's historical legacy of inclusion or exclusion of various racial ethnic groups, its structural diversity in terms of numerical representation of various racial/ethnic groups, the psychological climate . . . , and the behavioral climate" (p. 3). Applying the tenets of the aforementioned dimensions allowed Hurtado and coauthors (1998) to analyze, interpret, and explain the type of campus climate for students of color, and informs the current authors' understanding of the world that African American administrators exist in, navigate, and experience daily in higher education. Moreover, the campus climate affects personal congruence, satisfaction, and the desire to remain in one's environment. Furthermore, the severity and number of both overt and subtle incidents of prejudice, racism, and racial microaggressions made toward African Americans and other persons of color is often a direct result of the campus climate (Harper & Hurtado, 2007; Hurtado et al. 1998; Solorzano, Ceja, & Yosso, 2000).

Racial microaggressions are a manifestation of racism that happens in society and on our college campuses. Microaggressions can be subtle or overt, "automatic," "intentional," or "unintentional" comments or behaviors that serve to undermine persons of color (Constantine & Sue, 2007; Constantine et al., 2008; Sue, Capodilupo, & Holder, 2008). Sue & Constantine (2007) divide microaggressions into three categories. *Microassaults* are purposeful behaviors or words such as "explicit . . . name calling" or avoiding someone that are offensive and hurtful (p. 137). *Microinsults* are both words and actions that convey "rudeness, insensitivity, or demeaning attitudes" (p. 138). These microinsults can also be underlying demeaning statements. Finally, *microinvalidations* that serve to "exclude" and "negate" the experiences or feelings of people of color (p. 138). Racial microaggressions occur frequently and are such a hidden part of dialogue and behavior that they are often overlooked by not only the hearer but by the perpetrator. Research indicates that these constant, nagging racial attacks lead to emotional distress and reduced self-esteem, which result in "sapping the spiritual and psychological energies" from the recipients (Sue, , Capodilupo, & Holder, 2008, p. 329).

Methods

PHENOMENOLOGY

As stated, the purpose of this study is to explore the experiences of Black female administrators at PWIs in the state of Michigan to understand their challenges and coping strategies. Specifically, what are their challenges and how do they thrive in higher education environments, particularly PWIs. Similar to other studies (Clayborne & Hamrick, 2007; Holmes, 2003; Lindsay, 1999; Moses, 1989; Turner, 2002, 2007) that have examined the experiences of African American women in higher education, a qualitative, phenomenological approach was used to explore their stories to uncover the essence of their lived experiences (Creswell, 2007; Marshall & Rossman, 2006; Moustakas, 1994). The phenomenological tradition relies "on the assumption that there is a structure and essence to shared experiences that can be narrated" (Marshall & Rossman, 2006, p. 104). As such, the phenomenon or meaning of the core concept emerges from the articulation and construction of their shared experiences, experiences that expose the salience of race and gender.

PARTICIPANTS

Purposeful sampling was done to recruit participants who could speak to the experiences that are at the center of this study (Creswell, 2007; Merriam, 1997). Eleven colleagues in the state of Michigan were contacted via e-mail or telephone to participate in the study. A total of 10 African American women (Sharon, Hannah, Florence, Anne, Suzette, Diane, Rose, Marie, Beverly, and Alison—assigned pseudonyms) represent two four-year institutions in Michigan; however, collectively these women have worked in several higher education institutions as well as corporate America and government. Their higher education positions, past and present, included entry, midlevel, and senior-level positions (i.e., associate director, assistant dean, associate vice president, and director). Five are native to Michigan. Three of the participants were married, three divorced, and five were mothers. Years of work experience ranged from five to thirty-plus. In order to maintain confidentiality, references to their former or present institutions will not be used.

DATA COLLECTION AND DATA ANALYSIS

Each respondent was encouraged to provide feedback on several open-ended questions, through either electronic mail or informal face-to-face or telephone interviews. Most chose to respond by replying by e-mail. Their responses were collected over the course of two spring semesters, 2004 and 2009. The respondents were assigned pseudonyms to protect their professional and personal identities, and all identifying information was deleted from their written and verbal statements. Finally, a thematic analysis was conducted (Miles & Huberman, 1994). Member-checking (Lincoln & Guba, 1985) assisted us with the study's rigor and ensured that our articulation of the respondents' voices and ideas were shared in ways that protected as well as honored their experiences.

Findings

Consistent with the literature, participants in this study have also faced numerous challenges, dealt with unwelcoming campus climates, encountered racial microaggressions, and have routinely relied on coping strategies to survive in such hostile environments. Three prominent themes emerged that clearly illustrate the type of challenges these women consistently tackle at PWIs: (1) the lack of access to mentoring experiences, (2) isolation and marginalization, and (3) the lack of respect and recognition of credentials. Each theme exemplifies the nature of their battles, but also points to the necessary tactics or strategies that must be employed to provide temporary relief. Although several strategies were broached and discussed, three salient coping strategies resonated most with them: (1) aggressively seek out mentoring experiences beyond their departments or campuses; (2) spirituality; and (3) working with associations, whether on or off campus. This combination of challenges and strategies frames their administrative experiences.

CHALLENGES

At the time of the interviews, all women were serving midlevel to senior-level positions in PWIs in Michigan and faced a myriad of challenges. The following narratives highlight the common themes of experience including lack of mentoring opportunities, isolation and marginalization, and lack of respect of their professional roles.

Lack of access to mentoring opportunities

While aggregate numbers indicate that Black female administrators outnumber Black female faculty on predominately White campuses (American Council on Education, 2008), they lack mentoring opportunities that one typically would assume are available to them. To the contrary, from middle to senior levels, the participants reported difficulty in finding such opportunities because either their gender or race posed a barrier. Dr. Cunningham/Sharon explained mentoring this way:

> I find that mentoring comes in unexpected places and unpredictable forms. It's hard to identify a mentor that looks like me because they are few. I have made a conscious effort to attend functions (i.e. workshops or events) that are attended by those individuals. I admire and with whom I desire to establish a mentor-mentee relationship. . . . Establishing contact, expressing genuine interest in needing support and being willing to go the extra mile to situate oneself in settings, on or off campus, to increase the possibility of meeting a mentor, are constant challenges for midlevel Black administrators.

Since establishing a mentoring relationship with another African American woman was difficult or not feasible, Sharon turned to her peers as an alternative. She said, "I have other colleagues at similar or greater levels of responsibility at other institutions who have established great mentoring relationships. A couple of times, I have benefited from wisdom shared with my colleagues by their mentors." Sharon continued to share that when students or junior-level colleagues approached her that she would "try to emulate the type of mentor" she wished she had.

There were instances, however, when Black female administrators established mentoring relationships throughout their professional careers through networking with White colleagues. This approach benefited these women in ways that bolstered their professional status and enabled them to provide opportunities for others, including people of color and women. Hannah disclosed:

> I was very fortunate to receive excellent mentoring in my first professional position as a higher education professional. The program director did all she could to informally and formally recognize my professional experiences coming into my first position, but there were prohibitive institutional policies to acknowledging my skill set and professional work experiences with salary and other formal recognition. Most of my mentoring has come directly from my former program director. There were very few African American women in like positions at my institution and almost none in more positions that are senior. In fact, my former director was the first to formally create an assistant director position and then fill it with an African American.

Additional aspects of mentoring relationships involved trust and making oneself vulnerable, but with limited safe spaces on predominately White campuses for Black female administrators, there existed among the participants a level of apprehension to making oneself vulnerable because it led to disappointment in the past. Florence, who spoke to this type of fear, explained her mentoring experience this way:

> My experiences... are limited. Many midlevel African American administrators assume that they will receive mentoring from higher-level African American administrators. This is usually not the case. I believe this is true because high-level African American administrators fear that they will not reach their highest potential if they are perceived as associating with other African Americans. So, they instead choose to mentor others outside of their racial identity to prove that they are "global" individuals. Higher-level African American administrators may fear, also, that mentoring other African Americans will give the perception that they are "bringing in too many people of their kind."

Florence noted that in her experience race functioned as a dividing versus a uniting factor. She explained why selecting a mentor outside of one's race is often inevitable for personal career survival or advancement purposes. Distancing oneself from others, even from other Black administrators, male or female, served as a means of survival.

Another dimension of mentoring relationships was convenience. Often, there is a void of viable options for mentors, irrespective of racial background. Due to campus size and/or demanding responsibilities, it was noted that in order to receive assistance these women must actively seek out mentoring opportunities external to their unit, department, college, or institution. Anne affirmed this reality:

> Mentoring has not occurred during the 20 years in my ... current position. I am basically self-taught. I have availed myself of professional development meetings, conferences, institutes, and classes. It would have been great to have a mentor. One faculty member, now retired, said to me one day, "I see you have taught yourself how to run the ... office."

Anne's interview hints at the detriment of not having a mentor—someone to teach us about the culture of academia or our institutions. This is further illuminated in the comments by Florence, who recognized the importance of the navigating the political landscape. "I think that the biggest problem for midlevel African Americans in higher education is a lack of or limited knowledge of the political environment and how that limited knowledge can impact professional growth and promotion." Mentors play an instrumental role in teaching mentees how to navigate these sometimes tumultuous administrative waters, but as the interviewees point out, there is a lack of mentors. Mentoring relationships are invaluable resources for both women and people of color in higher education (Allen, Jacobson, & Lomotey, 1995; Blackhurst, 2000; Davidson & Foster-Johnson, 2001; Moses, 1989; Patton & Harper, 2003). In particular, the Black women in this study expressed the myriad ways in which meaningful mentoring experiences either escaped them or became a part of their career path.

Isolation and marginalization

With such a small number and proportion of Black female administrators in PWIs in Michigan and across the nation, alienation and isolation are natural outcomes. Such isolation can be debilitating, requiring a resolve to survive, fight, and flourish. Sharon offered this commentary:

> Isolation is one of the most difficult challenges as a midlevel manager of color. I was once told by a former boss that I was lucky to be one of the few [people

of color] at my level. This was his comment when I approached him regarding pay equity, as I was the lowest-paid, highest-educated person at that pay grade classification. I didn't have anyone that I could share this information with [on campus] or obtain a reality check regarding his opinion. I felt further isolation after I inquired with the Human Resources department.

As shown in the above passage, not only was Sharon isolated as a function of her race, she was also expected to be grateful that she was one of a few but was rewarded with the least pay in spite of her educational achievements. This comment made by her former boss was a microinsult—a demeaning and insensitive attack.

Hannah, however, was able to connect with other African Americans on campus who were willing to share resources and coping strategies, inevitably making those relationships indispensable. Hannah explained:

When I first began my career in higher education at an academic/student affairs program office, there was an African American male working in the office. He provided me with direct mentorship [showing me] the basics of everything, to office culture, and expectations to writing in a business environment, to supervising student employees. This employee [along with] the inclusive, multicultural nature of the program I worked for translated into feeling little or no isolation with regard to race. What I did find isolating was the combination of my age, race, and gender. As a general rule, most of my student/academic affairs colleagues were White. Of the individuals who were African American or other people of color, most were male. Furthermore, most of my peers (staff in like positions) were 10–25 years my senior, making age a social identity I had to navigate very carefully.

While Hannah's experience of isolation was first due to race, she found some connection though mentorship, and through the positive office climate—where her colleagues helped create a safe space. However, her experience of isolation continued because of the gender differences and generational gaps. Socioeconomic status, geographical/regional differences, and level of professional position also appear to have played roles in the isolation of the other women in this study. Rose underestimated the geographic difference, specifically how much of an "impact" it would make moving to a campus where there were fewer persons of color than at her previous institution. She describes the "culture shock" she felt, explaining that "some of the isolation" had to do with the geographic location, a small town with few people of color. She continues:

> I remember not fitting in with any of my peers and the ones I should have fit in with did not extend the invitations. . . . I did not fit in . . . because I was not married, had no children, and I did not fit into the one last category of being Catholic/attending their places of worship.

Sadly, Rose says that feeling of isolation led to feelings of insecurity in her job. She explains, "Being the only African American in my department, I often felt my job was not secure. I did not fit in/I was not in the circle, and my boss had uncomfortable communication with me." Suzette explained isolation does happen but it is not a great concern to her:

> There is some isolation, but I feel that it's more from the work that I do in affirmative action, which is not popular, rather than myself as a Black female. It doesn't bother me because if I want to do something or be somewhere or say something, I will generally do it. So not inviting me to participate in a meeting or activity is not important to me. I have enough to think about without worrying if someone doesn't want to include me. I have a high self-esteem (thanks to God and my mom), so I'm not concerned about being excluded for the most part.

In comparison to Suzette, isolation was much more poignant for Diane. From her perspective, isolation is a by-product of being excluded, which is difficult to swallow because it permeates both dimensions of one's professional and private life.

> Working every day and feeling like you are always on your own—like everyone else is included and you are on the "outskirts," i.e., people have lunch together, meeting and having life and relationships outside of work. Feeling like you are only included in "formal" meetings where by the title of your position they can't avoid including you. Even when you are in a meeting, having people not listen to or acknowledge your voice—only to have someone else say the same thing and others excitedly agree to the wise opinion. If you speak up, then you are labeled "difficult" or abrasive.

Not being invited to meeting or functions was also raised by Anne, who said that she often had to "initiate interaction with Whites to avoid isolation because Whites rarely [invited her] to join them, except for a handful of known liberal Whites." This type of isolation was not as problematic for Florence because she had a unique work situation. As she explained, "I have not experienced isolation at the University. . . . This is true primarily because I have worked in two departments where the directors were African Americans. This is a unique experience."

Outside of Florence, all of the women experienced degrees of isolation at their respective institutions. Whether isolation was due to working in an environment with a small population of Black colleagues who are supportive or colleagues who challenge one's identity as a young, professional woman; or to job responsibilities that lead to isolation and/or White colleagues who are more inclined to exclude versus include their Black female colleagues, the challenge remained the same, a marginalized existence.

Lack of respect and recognition of credentials

In higher education, educational degrees and expertise are very highly respected. The profession is driven by degree attainment and professionalism that signifies the importance of knowing and being skilled in a field of study. As such, it is easy to assume that those who possess advanced degrees, are pursing advanced degrees, or have a significant level of expertise in a particular line of work would receive respect and support from their peers and supervisors.

For all the Black women who shared their challenges, whether at midlevel management or upper level of the administration, support and respect were essential for maintaining positive experiences. However, there were varying degrees at which each placed importance on respect. While a few believed that the lack of respect was not crucial to them, others expressed how their academic credentials or expertise were minimized or ignored, overtly or covertly. Anne indicated how little her degree at a historically Black college was valued:

I was told by a previous associate dean of my current PWI that this institution does not calculate GPAs earned at HBCUs such as my undergraduate institution. I was applying for admission to the doctoral program . . . and was surprised to hear that the college would not recognize my bachelor's GPA from my undergraduate institution. They did, however, recognize my master's degree GPA earned at a PWI.

On another campus, Marie, director of a unit with high visibility, pursued her doctorate, and upon completion, a White male colleague told her that she now had to leave her institution to be called "doctor." At the same time, Marie noticed that White students called her by her first name but went to someone else's office and acknowledged their credentials by addressing him or her as doctor. While Marie focused on students and colleagues, Rose expressed how parents and her immediate supervisor would question her judgment and not afford her respect that others were given:

> My concerns in this area as a hall director would come from parents. My name, as I put it, is "race neutral," and my experience with speaking on the phone versus the first time meeting after speaking on the phone differed dramatically. Especially in discipline situations that involved their children. They would appear shocked to see an African American person and they would then approach the situation with their child with skepticism once their idea of the person on the phone did not match the reality of the person standing before them. . . .
>
> My own experience with my boss was the discomfort he experienced with talking to me. In situations, I felt as though he too did not trust my judgment when it came to the discipline decisions I had to make with non–students of color. He would ignore/overlook their behavior as playful, and ask that I give them a chance and have more educational discussions. With students of color, there was always a discussion about safety and the impact of their behavior on the floor community.

Sharon, an administrator from a different PWI, who routinely had to prove her expertise, stated:

> On a regular basis, in my former job and my current position, I am challenged to prove that I know what I know, which is both frustrating and time-consuming. Very little of what I say is taken at face value or as credible without extensive documentation or confirmation from another (usually White person) source. In my current position, I submit an annual data report in three parts. . . . The raw data for each of these reports is extracted from three separate university databases. The second year that I submitted these reports to [my supervisor] he returned them to me immediately and asked me to redo them because they didn't "look"

Spirituality

Faith and spirituality have been known to play a central role in the lives and coping strategies of many African American women (Andrews, 1993; Edwards & Camblin, 1998; Becks-Moody, 2004; Mattis, 2002; Watt, 2003). These women called upon their inner reserves—their faith and spirituality—to help them through times of trouble and instability in the workplace. Sharon says that spirituality keeps her alive, as she explains.

> My faith has been an important component of my survival. I use silent prayer and meditation when situations seem to need a greater intervention than I have the strength to muster. I observe actions by people with whom I work that appear to be mean-spirited, rude, or lacking ethics. It's during those times I decide if it's worth my time and energy to explore the situation to see if I can be a positive influence or if I just say a prayer and let the situation take care of itself.

Similar to Sharon who has had to push away the hurtful words of others, Hannah says that her spirituality is what "grounds" her, particularly in times when she is bombarded by negative external messages as she explains.

> My spirituality grounds my life. Further, my faith is the motivation for my work in trying to make the institutions I work for more inclusive and diverse. Without my spiritual beliefs and practices, I would certainly have internalized the negative messages sent from a poor institutional climate for young African American women. The lessons my family taught me—from a very early age—about race and gender have stayed with me—I have understood from quite some time that others negative reactions to my race or gender is not about me, my worth as person, my capabilities or talents.

Interestingly both of these women discuss the important role that spirituality has played in helping them maintain a sense of self-respect despite attacks of racial microaggressions by of colleagues and acquaintances, and the negative and unsupportive institutional racial climate.

Networking

Having multiple avenues of support can help to ensure success for African American female administrators. Networking is crucial in not only navigating the workplace, but it in receiving answers to professional questions, as well as getting tasks accomplished quickly and efficiently and helping to ward off isolation (Patitu & Hinton, 2003). Sharon points out networking has been her life preserver; she calls out to others for help and within "minutes" receives invaluable professional advice. She explains the importance of her network. "My ability to effectively network has been the saving grace on many occasions. It's not that I need to be connected broadly and deeply, just strategically." Suzette's network extends beyond the workplace, and she explains that it is a "good outlet." She talks about the joy she receives from both spending time with her network of friends as well as seeing them succeed.

> I enjoy networking with colleagues; my investment club, my book club; at conferences; and any gatherings I may want to attend. I like to hear others' ideas, and hear of their accomplishments. It makes me feel good to see my sisters being successful.

Both Suzette and Sharon have reached out to others and been successful, but Diane has not been as lucky. Her personality and busy schedule seem to hold her back, and unfortunately, that leads to having a much smaller reserve of individuals to pull from when she needs help.

> I have attempted to bring women together when I can. I try to reach out to others when possible. I am not great at professional networking. I know how but really have trouble balancing additional relationships and taking advantage of opportunities. Taking classes is the biggest prohibitory to going to additional conferences and connecting beyond my current program and circle.

Although individuals may want to reach out to others, networking is not always easy as Anne explains. "Networking within PWIs is very challenging, because you have to work extremely hard at initiating and reaching out to them, because they seldom reciprocated and reach out to you." Again we hear the theme of vulnerability, because to put oneself out there and to not be accepted leads to reminders of being on the outside. Similar to the mentoring, the burden seems to lie with these women; they seek out others, they invest the time and the energy into building new relationships, and when it works the result is positive.

Discussion

The narratives illuminate the challenges African American female administrators face on college campuses. The experiences vary for each woman because of their institutional context and climate and because of their own personal characteristics. First, considering the introductory framework of institutional racial climate we hear that these women all experience a lack of structural diversity—there are relatively few African American administrators on their campuses. Furthermore they all experience the consequences of negative climates—degrading comments from co-workers—microinsults; the exclusion from collegial and personal interactions—microassualts; and the lack of respect given for their positions and experience—microinvalidations. Despite these negative experiences, women found ways to survive and thrive at their institutions.

Women in this study pushed themselves to find colleagues and friends who could either mentor them or be a part of their support network. Sometimes they found those individuals on campus and other times it was off campus. Several authors discuss the concept of "counterspaces" in relationship to college students coping with microaggressions (Solorzano, Ceja, & Yosso, 2000; Solorzano & Villalpando, 1998). Counterspaces are the safe spaces where persons of color can join to have positive dialogue and interactions with others of like minds. These havens are places to go where their points of view can be affirmed and validated. Essentially these women have created their own "counterspaces," by finding and creating networks where they feel safe and valued.

Repeated racial microaggressions, both subtle and overt, lead to the feelings of isolation and marginalization in their workplaces and communities as evidenced by these women's narratives (Sue, Capodilupo, & Holder, 2008; Solarzano et al., 2000). A lack of mentors from the same racial background, the low numbers of Black colleagues at their institutions, and the exclusion by White and Black colleagues all added to their feelings of marginalization. These women, refusing to accept isolation, reached deep within themselves to their spiritual center and reached out to their spiritual family of friends. Managing to maintain their sense of self-worth and self-respect is key to their resiliency and retention in the workplace.

The narratives also point out repeated microinsults and microinvalidations and their impacts on the women. Not only are having professional expertise repeatedly challenged and being disrespected by peers, supervisors, clients, and students central themes here, but similar experiences exist throughout the literature on the experiences of not only Black administrators but also Black faculty and managers (Constantine et al., 2008; Constantine & Sue, 2007; Sue, , Capodilupo, & Holder, 2008; Lloyd-Jones, 2009). Without understanding the rich history of Africans and later African Americans, who take pride and value in respect, it is easy for White administrators and others to credit respect as an attribute only worthy to a specific population, primarily, White people. Historically, laws, policies, and social forces (such as Jim Crow and Black Codes), as well as a culture of entitlement that many White people hold, have restricted the rights of Black people to have civil liberties in several spectrums of society while simultaneously affording to Whites generational wealth and privilege (Anderson, 1988; Cruse, 2005; Thompson & Louque, 2005; Wise, 2005).

GENDER

Gender, akin to race, is another social construct in America. Higher education is not exempt from discriminatory practices against people of color and/or women (Collins, 2000; Feagin, 2001; hooks, 1981; Smith, Altbach, & Lomotey, 2002). Women and people of color have been considered second- and even third-class citizens in regards to their positions and social order within the United States. For Black women in particular, their identities as Black and female have placed them behind White males, White females, and Black males (hooks, 1981; Collins, 2000). Another experience for Black female administrators, if not being constantly questioned about their competency or labeled as the "sapphire" or "angry Black" woman who speaks out of place in meetings (Collins, 2000; hooks, 1981), is being objectified to a sexual being and dealt with accordingly.

Implications for Practice and Policy Recommendations

Although this chapter shares insights from a few African American practitioners, their comments covered a myriad of topics that can aid other practitioners and institutional leaders in understanding the nature of challenges faced by Black administrators. Collectively, they give voice to and expose their realities at PWIs, revealing how these challenges shape their experiences and ways they manage assaults in order to increase opportunities for themselves and future practitioners of color.

Understanding the diverse challenges placed before administrators of color at PWIs. Once a person understands the campus norms/cultures and the local community, one is better equipped to respond to the limitations of the environment, using several strategies:

- Depersonalizing campus issues of discrimination and prejudice by not allowing others to limit your contributions and capabilities to diversity issues. Although addressing inequalities is critical, owning campus diversity as your sole responsibility is detrimental to one's personal and professional growth.
- Identify spaces (i.e., safe havens or support systems) to minimize isolation. Establishing social networks where individuals share similar interests, concerns, and values, decreases or in some cases alleviates feelings of isolation and despair for Black administrators.
- Actively seeking and establishing both formal and informal mentoring relationships. Whether the connection is among peers or established with colleagues who hold higher-ranking positions within or outside your institution, mentoring continues to be a worthwhile investment.
- Preserving and protecting your mental, physical, emotional, and spiritual well-being by establishing and maintaining both professional and personal boundaries.

Nevertheless, these soldiers continue to find ways to be successful. Extant literature discusses best practices for responding to the opposition that African American administrators encounter in the academy (Elam & NAEOHE, 1989; Harvey, 1999; Jones, 2001; Rusher, 1996). A plethora of strategies and recommendations can be applied to enhance the quality of experiences that African American administrators have in PWIs. For example, Guillory (2001, pp. 111–123) suggests seven "Strategies for Administrators of Color." Of those seven, three strategies complimented the four dimensions of campus racial climate that Hurtado and coauthors addressed, as well as speaking directly to the respondents' shared experiences in this study. The three strategies included the following.

Aligning oneself with an accomplished mentor

Here Guillory (2001) encourages administrators of color to be proactive about the connections of support needed for their survival in higher education. The author particularly addressed the importance of mentoring relationships with other African American administrators who have acquired multiple levels of success within higher education and who possess the ability to assist you in accomplishing your goals and objectives. Equally critical to having other successful African American mentors is having their firsthand knowledge of survival on predominantly White campuses. Here, Hurtado and coauthors (1998) would contend that examining the history of exclusion as well as the impact of structural diversity would help Black administrators gain knowledge from the past. Such information of how former people of color combated discriminatory practices may allow future Black administrators to apply strategies that serve in resisting prejudice and discrimination. The respondents shared examples of such useful tools, including depersonalizing the hateful acts of others as well as the importance of having mentors.

Enhancing one's credibility

Guillory (2001) discusses working toward educational and professional credentials beyond the baseline requirements and/or expectations of one's current position. This recommendation would equip Black administrators with a greater sense of confidence and accomplishment while also giving them freedom in that if opportunities presented themselves internally or external to the institution, they would be prepared to assume the role for career advancement. Hurtado and coauthors (1998) would offer that it is fundamental to challenge and reframe the psychological and behavioral tendencies of complacency that may keep Black administrators in fear and in constant threat of losing their job. Rather, Black administrators would have the chance to alter the views that not only Whites have of them but also the limitations that society has taught Black people to have/place on themselves. The respondents discussed such evolutions of thought when they applied their faith and spirituality to challenging situations. By doing so, Black administrators were able to transcend the aftermath of racism and focus on improving their skills, helping others and reclaiming the power of their voices and positions on campus.

Avoiding marginalization

Guillory (2001) contends that by diversifying one's areas of expertise and broadening the scope of one's job and the people that one assist, African American administrators demonstrate that they have the ability to contribute their talents and expertise beyond the scope of their current position or role. Hurtado and coauthors (1998) discusses the historic stigma that has been placed on African Americans as well as other groups who have been traditionally underrepresented in academia. By extending their focus, concern, time toward issues pertaining not only to African American students but also to other students, Black administrators can demonstrate that the improvement of the campus racial climate affects students of color in addition to all constituents of the institution. Respondents disclosed that while they feel that it is their responsibility to assist other African Americans, be they peers or students, their goal is to illustrate the necessity of their role on campus. They want to be validated for their hard work and dedication and to receive recognition for the visibility that their diverse identities bring to the institution—they desire to be seen as assets rather than approached as deficits. In short, the Black administrators want to be seen, heard, validated, recognized, rewarded for their contributions and supported in their efforts that help make the campus climate inclusive for all students, faculty, staff, and administrators who seek advancement through research interests, academic achievement, and social and professional development.

An institutional climate that strives to be inclusive of all members provides a campus culture that offers much-needed support and respect. The preceding recommendations emphasize what individual midlevel Black administrators can do to cope with hostile and unwelcoming institutional environments. For campus leaders wishing to transform their campus communities into places and spaces that are inclusive and accepting of Black administrators and their unique roles, returning to the four dimensions of campus climate is critical—historical, structural, psychological, and behavioral (Hurtado et al., 1998). Addressing each dimension with the intention of improving the climate for administrators of color is the most appropriate place to begin.

Examine the historical legacy of the institution with respect to traditions, values, hiring practices, and programs that promote inclusion or exclusion. Also, leaders should consider ways to address historical elements in order to preserve tradition without marginalizing administrators of color, specifically midlevel Black administrators. Structural diversity points to a relatively simple solution that speaks to fostering a critical mass of administrators of colors who can bring diversified perspectives to the campus community while contributing to all facets of the educational enterprise. Both psychological and behavioral dimensions are difficult to resolve because they are driven by misinformation, myths, and stereotypical thinking (Hurtado et al., 1998). However, if leaders are willing to assess the status of these dimensions, solutions will emerge from a campus-driven assessment that does not simply focus on students, but incorporates all contexts of the campus climate. As such, institutional strategies can potentially be devised to reduce isolation, foster mentorship relationships, provide opportunities for advancement, and ultimately recognize and value the many contributions of administrators of color.

Limitations

Statistics on specific numbers of African American females working in midlevel managerial positions in the state of Michigan are difficult to access. This study could have clearly benefited from more readily available, organized, and systematic data points. The goal of qualitative research is not to generalize, but rather to give voice to the participants and acknowledge experiences and challenges; due to the small sample size there is limited generalizability. However, the findings in this research study mirror findings in similar aforementioned studies. Furthermore, the participants of this study are all self-selected. We are up-front about our positionality in this research, noting that our own experiences as African American female administrators certainly inform our inquiry. We as researchers had to attend to our subjectivities to ensure trustworthy and authenticity in the research (Peshkin, 1988; Glesne, 2011).

Suggestions for Future Research

There is a paucity of research on African American female administrators in higher education. First, limited data is available on the numbers and functions of African American female administrators and particularly by state. Future studies could (*a*) address quantitative measures of satisfaction and experience by African American midlevel administrators, (*b*) explore the exit of Black female administrators in the workplace, and (*c*) explore the intersection of resiliency as it relates to coping strategies in response to racial microaggressions in the workplace.

REFERENCES

American Council on Education (2006). *Minorities in higher education twenty-second annual status report.* Washington, DC.

American Council on Education (2008). *Minorities in higher education 2008: twenty-third status report.* Washington, DC:

Allen, K., Jacobson, S., & Lomotey, K. (1995). African American women in educational administration: The importance of mentors and sponsors. *Journal of Negro Education, 64*(4), 409–422.

Alridge, D.P. (2001). Redefining and refining scholarship for the academy: Standing on the shoulders of our elders and giving credence to African American voice and agency. In L. Jones (Ed.), *Retaining African Americans in higher education: Challenging paradigms for retaining students faculty & administrators* (pp. 193–206). Sterling, VA: Stylus.

Anderson, J.D. (1988). *The education of Blacks in the South, 1860–1935.* Chapel Hill: University of North Carolina Press.

Andrews, A.R. (1993). Balancing the personal and the professional. In J. James & R. Farmer (Eds.), *Spirit, space, and survival: African American women in (White) academe* (pp. 179–195). New York: Routledge.

Becks-Moody, G.M. (2004). African American women administrators in higher education: Exploring the challenges and experiences at Louisiana public colleges and universities. Ph.D. diss., Louisiana State University.

Benjamin, L. (1997). *Black women in the academy: Promises and perils.* Gainesville: University of Florida Press.

Blackhurst, A.E. (2000). Career satisfaction and perceptions of sex discrimination among women student affairs professionals. *NASPA Journal, 37,* 399–413.

Chronicle of Higher Education Almanac (2010a). *Enrollment growth, 1998–2008: More minorities, more women.* Retrieved from: http://chronicle.com/article/Graphic-Enrollment-Growth/124069/.

Chronicle of Higher Education Almanac (2010b). *Employees in colleges and universities by racial and ethnic group, fall 2007.* Retrieved from http://chronicle.com/article/Employees-in-Colleges-and/123999/.

Clayborne, H.L., & Hamrick, F.A. (2007). Rearticulating the leadership experiences of African American women in midlevel student affairs administration. *NASPA Journal, 44*(1), 123–146.

Collins, P.H. (2000). *Black feminist thought: Knowledge, consciousness, and the politics of empowerment.* New York: Routledge.

Collins, P.H. (2005). *Black sexual politics: African Americans, gender, and the new racism.* New York: Routledge.

Constantine, M.G., Smith, L, Redington, R.M., & Owens, D. (2008). Racial microaggressions against Black counseling and counseling psychology faculty: A central challenge in the multicultural counseling movement. *Journal of Counseling and Development, 86*(3), 348–355.

Constantine, M.G., & Sue, D.W. (2007). Perceptions of racial microaggressions among Black supervisees in cross-racial dyads. *Journal of Counseling Psychology, 54*(2), 142–153.

Creswell, J.W. (2007). *Qualitative inquiry and research design: Choosing among five traditions.* 2nd ed. Thousand Oaks, CA: Sage.

Cruse, H. (2005). *The crisis of the Negro intellectual: A historical analysis of the failure of Black leadership.* New York: New York Review of Books.

Davidson, M.N., & Foster-Johnson, L. (2001). Mentoring in the preparation of graduate researchers of color. *Review of Educational Research, 7*(1), 549–574.

Edwards, J., & Camblin, L. (1998). Assorted adaptations by African American administrators. *Women in Higher Education, 7*(11), 33–34.

Elam, J.C., & National Association for Equal Opportunity in Higher Education (U.S.) (NAEOHE) (1989). *Blacks in higher education: Overcoming the odds.* Lanham, MD: University Press of America.

Equal Employment Opportunity Commission (2008a). *Job patterns for minori-ties and women in private industry, 2008: Aggregate report for Michigan.* Retrieved from http://www.eeoc.gov/eeoc/statistics/employment/ jobpat-eeo1/2008/state/Michigan/index.html.

Equal Employment Opportunity Commission (2008b). *Job patterns for minorities and women in private industry, 2008: EEO-1 national aggregate report for state by NAICS-2.* Retrieved from: http://www.eeoc.gov/eeoc/statistics/ employment/jobpat-eeo1/2008/state_nac2/Michigan/Educational%20 Services.html.

Feagin, J.R. (2001). *Racist America: Roots, current realities, and future reparations.* New York: Routledge.

Fontana, A., & Frey, J.H. (1994). Interviewing: The art of science. In N.K. Denzin & Y.S. Lincoln (Eds.), *Handbook of qualitative research* (pp. 47–48). Thousand Oaks, CA: Sage.

Garner, R. (2004). *Contesting the terrain of the ivory tower: Spiritual leadership of African American women in the academy.* New York: Routledge.

Glesne, C. (2011). *Becoming qualitative researchers* (4th ed.). Boston, MA: Pearson Education.

Guillory, R.M. (2001). Strategies for overcoming the barriers of being an African American administrator on a predominantly White campus. In L. Jones (Ed.), *Retaining African Americans in higher education: Challenging paradigms for retaining students faculty and administrators* (pp. 111–123). Sterling, VA: Stylus.

Harper, S.R., & Hurtado, S. (2007). Nine themes in campus racial climates and implications for institutional transformation. In S.R. Harper, & L.D. Patton (Eds.), *Responding to the realities of race on campus* (pp. 7–24). New Directions for Student Services, No. 120. San Francisco, CA: Jossey-Bass.

Harvey, W.B. (1999). *Grass roots and glass ceilings: African American administra-tors in predominately while colleges and universities.* Albany: SUNY Press.

Holmes, S.L. (2003). Black female administrators speak out: Narratives on race and gender in higher education. *National Association of Student Affairs Professionals Journal, 6*(1), 45–65.

hooks, b. (1981). *Ain't I a woman: Black women and feminism.* Boston: South End.

Hoskins, R.L. (1978). *Black administrators in higher education: Conditions and perceptions* Westport, CT: Praeger.

Howard-Hamilton, M.F. (2003). Theoretical frameworks for African American women. In M.F. Howard-Hamilton (Eds.), *Meeting the needs of African American women* (pp. 19–29). New Directions for Student Services, no. 104. San Francisco: Jossey-Bass.

Hurtado, S. (1992). The campus racial climate: Contexts of conflict. *Journal of Higher Education, 63*(5), 539–569.

Hurtado, S., Milem, J., Clayton-Pedersen, A., & Allen, W. (1998). Enhancing campus racial/ethnic diversity: Educational policy and practice. *Review of Higher Education, 21*(3), 279–302.

Jackson, J.F.L. (2001). A new test for diversity: Retaining African American administrators at predominantly White institutions. In L. Jones (Ed.), *Retaining African Americans in higher education: Challenging paradigms for retaining students, faculty, and administrators* (pp. 93–109). Sterling, VA: Stylus.

Jackson, J.F.L. (2004). Engaging, retaining, and advancing African Americans in executive-level positions: A descriptive and trend analysis of academic administrators in higher and postsecondary education. *Journal of Negro Education, 73*(1), 4–20.

Jackson, J.F.L., & O'Callaghan, E.M. (2009). *Ethnic and racial administrative diversity: Understanding work life realities and experiences in higher education.* ASHE Higher Education Report, vol. 35. San Francisco: Jossey-Bass.

Jackson, J.F.L., & Terrell, M.C. (Eds.). (2003). Diversifying student affairs: Engaging, retaining, and advancing African Americans in the profession. *National Association of Student Affairs Professionals Journal, 6*(1), 9–24.

Jones, L. (2001) *Retaining African Americans in higher education: Challenging paradigms for retaining students faculty & administrators.* Sterling, VA: Stylus.

Lincoln, Y.S., & Guba, E.G. (1985). *Naturalistic inquiry.* Beverly Hills, CA: Sage.

Lloyd-Jones, B. (2009). Implications of race and gender in higher administration: An African American woman's perspective. *Advances in Developing Human Resources, 11*(5) 606–618.

King, J.E. (2006). *Gender equity in higher education: 2006.* Washington, DC: American Council on Education.

Lindsay, B. (1999). Women chief executives and their approaches toward equity in American universities. *Comparative Education, 35,* 187–200.

Marshall, C., & Rossman, G. (2006). *Designing qualitative research.* 4th ed. Thousand Oaks, CA: Sage.

Mattis, J.S. (2002). Religion and spirituality in the meaning-making and coping experiences of African American women: A qualitative analysis. *Psychology of Women Quarterly, 26*(4), 309–321.

Merriam, S. (1997). *Qualitative research and case study applications in education: Revised and expanded from case study research in education.* San Francisco: Jossey-Bass.

Michigan Civil Rights Commission (2007, March 7). *"One Michigan" at the Crossroads: An Assessment of the Impact of Proposal 06-02.* Retrieved from http://www.michigan.gov/documents/mdcr/FinalCommissionReport3–07_1_189266_7.pdf.

Miles, M.B., & Huberman, A.M. (Eds.). (1994). *Qualitative analysis: An expanded workbook.* Thousand Oaks, CA: Sage.

Mitchell-Crump, P.J. (2000). Mid-level African American women administrators in higher education institutions: Struggles and strategies. Ph.D. diss. UMI no. 9978529.

Moses, Y.T. (1989). *Black women in academe: Issues and strategies.* Washington, DC: Association of American Colleges.

Moustakas, C. (1994). *Phenomenological research methods.* Thousand Oaks, CA: Sage.

Patitu, C.L., & Hinton, K.G. (2003). The experiences of women and administrators in higher education: Has anything changed? In M.F. Howard-Hamilton (Ed.), *Meeting the needs of African American women* (pp. 79–93). New Directions for Student Services, no. 104. San Francisco: Jossey-Bass.

Patton, L.D., & Harper, S.R. (2003). Mentoring relationships among African American women in graduate and professional schools. In M.F. Howard-Hamilton (Ed.), *Meeting the needs of African American women* (pp. 67–78). New Directions for Student Services, no. 104. San Francisco: Jossey-Bass.

Peshkin, A. (1988). In search of subjectivity: One's own. *Educational Researcher, 17*(7), 17–22.

Rudolph, R. (1990). *The American college and university: A history.* 2nd ed. Athens: University of Georgia Press.

Rusher, A.W. (1996). *African American Women Administrators.* New York: University Press of America.

Smith, W.A., Altbach, P.G., & Lomotey, K. (Eds.). (2002). *The racial crisis in America: Continuing challenges for the twenty-first century.* Albany: SUNY Press.

Smith, D.G. (1996). Organizational implications of diversity in higher education. In M. Chemers, S. Oskamp, and M. Costanzo, (Eds.), *Diversity in organizations* (pp. 191–219). Newbury Park, CA: Sage.

Solorzano, D., Ceja, M., & Yosso, T. (2000). Critical race theory, racial microaggressions, and campus racial climate: The experience of African American college students. *Journal of Negro Education, 69*(1–2), 60–73.

Solorzano, D., & Villalpando, O. (1998). Critical race theory, marginality, and the experience of minority students in higher education. In C. Torres & T. Mitchell (Eds.), *Emerging issues in the sociology of education: Comparative perspectives* (pp. 211–224). Albany: SUNY Press.

Sue, D.W., Capodilupo, C.M., & Holder, A.M. (2008). Racial microaggressions in the life experience of Black Americans. *Professional Psychology Research and Practice, 39*(3), 329–336.

Sue, D.W., & Constantine, M.G. (2007). Racial microaggressions as instigators of difficult dialogues on race: Implications for student affairs educators and students. *College Student Affairs Journal, 26*(2), 136–143.

Thompson, G.L., & Louque, A.C. (2005). *Exposing the "culture of arrogance" in the academy.* Sterling, VA: Stylus.

Turner, C.S. (2002). Women of color in academe: Living with multiple marginality. *Journal of Higher Education, 73*(1), 74–93.

Turner, C.S. (2007). Pathways to the presidency: Biographical sketches of women of color firsts. *Harvard Educational Review, 77*, 1–38.

Watson, L.W. (2001). In their voices: A glimpse of African-American women administrators in higher education. *National Association of Student Affairs Professionals Journal, 4*(1),7–16.

Watt, S.K. (2003) Come to the river: Using spirituality to cope, resist, and develop identity. In M.F. Howard-Hamilton (Ed.), *Meeting the needs of African American women* (pp. 29–40). New Directions for Student Services, no. 104. San Francisco: Jossey-Bass.

Wise. T.J. (2005). *Affirmative action: Racial preference in Black and White.* New York: Routledge.

Zamani, E.M. (2003) African American women in higher education. In M.F. Howard-Hamilton (Ed.), *Meeting the needs of African American women* (pp. 5–18). New Directions for Student Services, no. 104. San Francisco: Jossey-Bass.

PART 3

Social and Cultural Issues Affecting African American Females

An Exploratory Study of Social Issues Facing African American High School Female Adolescents in Detroit

DELILA OWENS, RHONDA M. BRYANT, *and* DIANA THOMAS

Recent statistics indicate that approximately two-thirds of girls who occupy the juvenile justice system are students of color, primarily African American and Latina adolescent females (American Bar Association and National Bar Association, 2001). In addition, a study conducted by Girls Incorporated (2006) found that ethnic minority young women in grades 9–12 were more likely to report getting into a physical altercation in the last 12 months than their nonethnic minority counterparts: African American (39 percent), Latina (34 percent), and White (22 percent). Based on these statistics, it is important that the educators better understand the schooling experiences of urban African American female adolescents so that this population may be more effectively supported in its development. Counselors who have the opportunity to guide these students must recognize and respond to the unique concerns that motivate their thoughts and behaviors.

There are still many gaps in the literature with regard to both African American males and females. Traditionally, African Americans have been reluctant to talk about their lives with trained professionals (Temkin-Greener & Clark, 1988). Thus, it is not surprising that there is a significant paucity of published research devoted specifically to counseling African American girls and women (Coker, 2002; Jones & Shorter-Gooden, 2003). To assess their needs, it is essential that researchers address the issues that these adolescents feel are most salient in their lives. On the whole, African American women and girls have been left out of the social science research. Most of the social science research focuses on the plight of young African American males (Ferguson, 2000; hooks, 2004; Lopez, 2003; Rollock, 2007).

There may be a certain amount of reluctance on the part of this group to utilize psychological services for several reasons. One factor contributing to this reluctance is the absence of counselors of color who might be in a better position to assist. The majority of counselors in the United States are Caucasian (Sue & Sue, 2003, 2008), and historically, persons of color tend to consider seeking support for psychological concerns as a European endeavor (Sue & Sue, 2003, 2008). However, in order for counseling to be effective with African American females, counselors must give specific attention to African American girls' cultural context. This setting and its social norms are often highly influential in the development of the belief systems of girls and often relied upon to make critical life decisions (Gregg, 2005). Proper understanding of African American women and girls' issues from a cultural context will have a beneficial effect on counselors' case conceptualization as well as the selection of treatment approaches appropriately tailored to their clients' needs (Williams-Braun, 2005). Recognizing cultural differences will also assist counselors with understanding coping rituals and customs of diverse groups of individuals. In addition, culturally sensitive counselors more easily adapt to cultural norms, thereby avoiding automatic application of so-called "universal" treatment approaches when assisting clients with their presenting problems.

There is a growing recognition of the need to explore the experiences of African American female students. To understand and support African American female students, counselors must be aware of the issues that they are facing. Feeling misunderstood and invisible can lead to loneliness and profound unhappiness (Jones & Shorter-Gooden, 2003). This exploratory study is an effort to bring together some of the findings of our research on the social issues that urban African American girls face. In addition, this research adds to the limited knowledge on the schooling experiences of urban African American girls. This chapter is intended to give voice to the issues that African American girls face in urban school settings. The research is also part of a larger project that will explore social issues and academic outcomes in African American female adolescents.

In general, African American children can receive messages, become socialized, and internalize the dominate culture (Bigler & Liben, 2007). These experiences may include but are not limited to an adoption of individualism, accumulation of material things, and an affinity for competition, all of which have been historically associated with the White culture (Day-Vines, Patton, & Baytops, 2003). Early in life, African American children may adopt the belief that being African American predisposes them to certain forms of discrimination. Due to the constancy of their minority status, students may also begin to devalue their own race/ethnicity and internalize negative images (Day-Vines, Patton, & Baytops, 2003; Hirschfeld, 2008).

Navigating through the demands of life while consciously aware of and reminded of the influence of both gender and race in one's life can have a tremendous impact on African American girls and their sense of self (Jones & Shorter-Gooden, 2003). For African Americans in general, seeking support for psychological issues is inconsistent with cultural norms that value reliance on elders, religious leaders, and inner fortitude. More specifically, in culturally oppressive surroundings, African Americans girls can struggle to maintain a positive sense of self (Coker, 2003). Sue (1978) wrote that "cultural oppression occurs when this world view is blindly imposed upon the culturally different client" (34). The author refers to a worldview that does not affirm or take a strengths-based orientation to African American culture.-

This chapter seeks to contribute to the literature on the social issues facing African American girls in urban schools. We offer implications for practice and suggestions on how professional school counselors can better assist African American girls in urban settings.

The purpose of this pilot study is to explore the experiences of African American female adolescents at a high school in the Midwest. Our aim was to gain an understanding of the social issues they face in school. The authors argue that although African American high school female adolescents face barriers in the pursuit of academic success, removing systemic barriers to accessing culturally responsive counseling can improve these students' educational outcomes. That previous and current literature understudies the educational experiences of African American female adolescents belies the importance of this topic and the needs of this group.

Methodology

PARTICIPANTS

Participants were selected based on two criteria: (*a*) Each had to identify as being an African American female, and (*b*) each had to be currently enrolled in the urban public high school where the study was conducted.

Administrators (i.e., the principal and assistant principal) were contacted at a large urban high school in the Midwest. They were given an overview of the study and asked to help identify participants. The lead investigator was asked to schedule an initial meeting with the principal to go over the procedures of the study. After the initial meeting, the researchers gave the principal a list of 10 African American female adolescents who volunteered to participate in the study. The lead investigator then had an initial meeting with all 10 students and explained the purpose of the study. Once the purpose of the study was clear, each interested participant was given a parental permission slip to take home for parent(s) to sign. The lead researcher received eight of the 10 parental permission slips distributed and moved forward with scheduling appointments to interview the participants.

Although 10 students initially agreed to participate, only eight African American female students actually participated in the study. Two students decided to withdraw their participation because of other school-related commitments. The median age for participants was 15 years old. The majority of participants in the study were tenth-graders. Most participants reported living in female- headed households. The total enrollment at the high school for the 2010–2011 academic year was 1,130; hence, the student-to-counselor ratio was approximately 1:440. It is important to note that the American School Counselor Association recommends a student counselor ratio of 1:250 (American School Counselor Association, 2012) and that the school's ratio exceeds best practice recommendations.

PROCEDURES

Face-to-face, semi-structured interviews were conducted with each participant. However, as a necessary prerequisite, initial contact was made with each individual to ensure her willingness to volunteer for the study. Once participants agreed to volunteer, permission slips were sent home to parents to attain parental consent prior to the scheduling the interviews. Each participant was interviewed for approximately 30–45 minutes in a private office inside of the school's counseling center. The interviews were recorded for later transcription and data analysis. The transcribing was done by the lead investigator. No follow-up interviews were conducted.

INTERVIEW GUIDE

The researchers used a standard open-ended interview guide. The researchers selected two main factors for exploration of African American high school girls: (*a*) social issues that they were facing in school, and (*b*) perceptions of how school administrators could assist with social issues. The standard open-ended interview guide contained two questions composed by the lead researcher and developed from a review of the limited literature on African American female adolescents. Each participant responded to the items in the exact same order.

Data Analysis

Data in our qualitative study were analyzed using interpretative phenomenological analysis. This approach was used because we were interested in how the participants made sense of their experiences in school as African American females. Interpretative phenomenological analysis focused on the participants' experiences, views, and understanding of being an African American female in an urban school setting. This approach allows participants to give an account of their various experiences and how they made sense of these experiences (Brocki & Wearden, 2006).

In addition, we wanted to focus on the uniqueness of the students' thoughts and experiences in an urban school setting (Shaw, 2001). More specifically, we wanted to allow the readers of this chapter to understand the "lived" schooling experiences of urban African American girls by incorporating personal accounts in their own words.

For reliability and credibility purposes, the lead author taped each interview and took notes. Once the researchers had transcribed the taped sessions, the lead author compared the written notes taken during the interviews with the transcript of the session.

Findings

In the analysis of the study's data, we focused on the themes presented by the majority of the participants. Hence, when the term "participants" is used in the results section, the reader can assume that most of the students discussed or mentioned the theme during their interviews. The three themes that emerged from the data analysis: (1) relationship issues with other African American females and significant others, (2) perceptions of beauty, and (3) the students' expressed need for the development of programs specifically tailored to African American girls.

RELATIONSHIPS

The identities of African American women and girls seem largely tied to their ability to maintain relationship ties with others (Miller & Stiver, 1998). During adolescence, friendship ties often take precedence over relationships with one's own family (Bell, 1981). Research shows that once adolescent girls reach high school, they value social support and friendship over boys (Kilpatrick-Demaray & Kerres-Malecki, 2003). Friendships are critical in developing adolescent's identity. In the words of one participant, "I love my friends, but we really have problems getting along sometimes. But they are important to me." One study on African American adolescent social relationships concluded that African American youth are more peer-oriented than their White counterparts because peer support is related to a more positive self-concept (Felner et al., 1985). In contrast, Giordano, Cernkovich, and DeMaris (1993) found that African American youth reported significantly higher levels of intimacy among family members than within friendships, perceived less peer support from friends, and reported lower needs of peer approval than their White counterparts. In the words of one participant, "All of the cattiness and fighting and stuff . . . it is hard because it is like you really do not know who you can trust." Another participant stated, "Since I have come to this school, it seems like nobody really likes me. I just keep to myself. It is easier than having a lot of friends."

There are countless issues that may contribute to relationship breakdowns for African American girls. For example, Brown (2003) posits that girls compete and show aggression toward each other because of their lack of genuine empowerment in the American society. The author contends that for girls there are few positions of popularity within their circles. In order to attain this coveted status and feelings of empowerment, they must compete with each other (Brown, 2003). In the words of one participant, "We [Black girls] have a problem getting along sometimes. I think that we just need to grow up and stop all this gossiping and stuff. That is what the teachers and stuff think of us, that we are loud and gossip and fight a lot. But not all of us are like that." Even though the literature describes difficulties in relationships between girls, this participant's comments reflect a willingness and maturity to work through problems that may include behaviors based on cultural ways of relating and being.

PHYSICAL ATTRACTIVENESS

The theme of "beauty" in this sample was ever-present. Historically, researchers have found that the women typically focus more on appearance than men do (Cash & Henry, 1995). However, most of the quantitative research on beauty and attractiveness has been limited to White populations (Hall, 1995). Skin tone and hair texture has been an ongoing issue in the African American community (Robinson & Howard-Hamilton, 2000). One participant stated, "Really, it is the biracial girls that have the most problems because they are pretty and I think if you have certain characteristics about your shape or your hair, people just get jealous." This issue may stem from slavery when slave masters extended preferential treatment to their offspring or biracial children. These children usually had lighter skin and a certain hair texture (Okazawa-Rey, Robinson, & Ward, 1987). Long after slavery ended, many African Americans continue to place a premium on those among them who look more Eurocentric. These may be values that have been integrated into a cultural subconscious. One student painted a verbal picture of the issue of skin tone and hair texture in Black girls: "I mean it seems the popular girls are the ones that are pretty with long, good hair. Some of the guys just use them, but they are the ones that get most of the attention from the boys." Another participant stated, "I feel like some of the other girls hate me because of the way I dress and look."

While a preoccupation with skin color and beauty has remained salient in American culture throughout recorded history, it was not until the late 1930s that psychologists began researching the effects of skin tone on the perceptions of African American children (Clark & Clark, 1940). A study was conducted on

African American children using a Black doll and a White doll. Researchers posed the question to the African American children: "Which doll is the pretty doll?" The children overwhelming chose the White doll. Researchers over the years have inferred that societal images can have negative effects on the self-concept of African American children (Hall, 1995; Hirschfeld, 2008). It is important to note that Clark's research was a key deciding factor in the 1954 *Brown v. Board of Education* case, a landmark case that challenged school segregation (Patterson, 2001). In addition, the portrayal of African American women in the media can contribute to stereotypes and ethnically biased standards of attractiveness. Coltrane and Messineo (2000) found that television commercials that were geared toward African American audiences contained equally stereotypical images of African Americans as those commercials that targeted White audiences.

The media saturates the environment with images of how a beautiful person is supposed to look like (Poran, 2002). Authors Jones and Shorter-Gooden (2003) found that for African American women, the pressure to conform to traditional European standards of beauty was present from adolescence through adulthood. In the words of one participant, "I mean if you watch BET and stuff like that, it makes us feel like if you don't look a certain way or dress a certain way you are not sexy or pretty. All of the girls have long hair and are tall with nice shapes. If you watch TV enough, you feel like if you don't look like that, you are not pretty. I am good at trying to not let all of that stuff affect me though." Hence, when counseling African American girls, school counselors may have to reinforce within them a personal sense of self and unique beauty. In addition, counselors should challenge young girls' ideas about physical attractiveness and assist them with developing skills to combat negative internalizing messages that are presented through various forms of media (Day-Vines, Patton, & Baytops, 2003; Duke, 2002).

STUDENTS' NEED FOR PROGRAM DEVELOPMENT

Hudley (2001) pleads with researchers to address the issues facing underserved populations. The author calls for the development and implementation of programs especially for urban students and particularly girls. As one participant stated, "I think it would help to have programs in the school that help us deal with relationships and girl stuff." Another participant commented, "There are really no programs that help Black girls talk in a positive way. We usually get together and talk on our own."

Another stated, "We need stuff that we can relate to and programs that would help us communicate and maybe get along better. Really most of the programs here that school counselors sometimes do are not interesting to us." Program development was a theme that was often mentioned during the interviews with African American girls. Most girls cited the need to be actively involved in programs that addressed their issues. Another participant stated, "Most of the programs are not specifically for Black girls, you know."

Discussion and Implications for School Counselors Based on Our Findings

Findings from this study provide insight into the schooling experiences of urban African American girls attending one particular school in the Midwest. In particular, results fell into three thematic areas that should be addressed when working with African American girls. The three core themes found in this study were relationships with each other and significant others, addressing standards of beauty, and urban African American high school girls' need for further program development. These findings indicate that when counseling African American girls, central attention should to be paid to images of beauty, relationship development, and the introduction of unique programs to aid in student development.

With respect to the ways in which girls and women develop in relationships (Leadbeater & Way, 2007), the findings that apply to relationship conflicts in this study have several implications. First, school counselors must be aware of the relationship dynamics among urban African American girls. Although the dynamics of relationship issues are not unique to urban African American girls, it was commonly cited by those participating in our study. Finally, this finding supports the notion that students in school counselor education programs as well as current school counselors must develop the necessary skills to assist students in negotiating relationships. According to the American School Counselor Association (2005), school counselors must be ready to address the needs of the population that they serve.

It is important that counselors have an adequate level of familiarity (meaning they must understand and know how to intervene) with the issues faced by school-aged, urban African American girls. Counselors must be aware of the intersection between race, class, and gender in assisting African American girls

(Evans-Winters, 2005; Glenn, 2002). Having this awareness will assist counselors with dealing with students based on a systemic approach. As Constantine (2002) wrote, "Current models of mental health care often do not allow for the processes by which individuals with multiple oppressed identities arrive at a positive overall sense of cultural identity" (p. 211). Internalized oppression for African American women is a theme that has previously been addressed in the literature (Gainer, 1992; Tinsley-Jones, 2003). Findings related to physical attractiveness in this study support the need for further research in this area.

Program development is essential in addressing some of the social issues that African American girls face in schools. Program development for these students can highlight the importance of cohesiveness and teamwork, identify cultural biases, and address standards of beauty. Program development is accepted and mandated by the ethical standards for school counselors (American School Counselor Association, 2005).

LIMITATIONS OF THE STUDY

One limitation of this study is its sample size as eight participants are simply not enough to generalize the findings to urban high school girls across the country. The goal of this study was to make a preliminary inquiry with the expectation of expanding the study's sample size in the future. It is also important to note that the data was collected from a select group of individuals attending one urban high school in the Midwest. Finally, another problematic limitation of the study was the fact that data were collected toward the end of the academic school year. Students may carry heavier responsibilities at this time (e.g., preparing for final exams, attending awards banquets, and preparing for graduation), which may have impacted the total number of those willing to participate in the study as well as the degree of effort put forth by the ones who did.

In addition, the interview length could have been a limitation. Students had restricted time to discuss their schooling experiences (maximum 50 minutes, or one class period). If the interviewer would have had more time to discuss schooling experiences, richer data may have been acquired. Finally, no follow-up interviews were conducted, and doing so may have been helpful in testing the reliability of the three themes gathered from the data.

Future Research

The findings in this study can be further explored in future research. School counselors must be trained to meet the social and emotional needs of the students that they serve (American School Counselor Association, 2005). An additional area that might warrant further research is the extent to which school counselors are aware of the multitude of issues that urban African American female adolescents face in schools. Also, how might these social issues influence self-concept for African American girls? The racial identity of African American female adolescents and their psychological well-being are crucial areas to investigate. Prior research has shown a correlation between positive racial identity (i.e., strong connection with one's racial and ethnic group) and academic achievement (Oyserman, Harrison, & Bybee, 2001; Resnicow et al., 1999). Future research should also focus on the potential strength of Black girls and coping styles in the face of multiple oppressions.

Conclusion

In a field where communication is so important, school counselors must be equipped with the necessary skills to guide African American girls and develop programs to address their specific developmental needs. For example, the introduction of programs that explore society's standard of beauty as well as those dealing with relationship conflicts might be beneficial. They should focus on showing young African Americans girls how to avoid adopting external, culturally inappropriate scales of self-worth. Additionally, they should be encouraged to utilize their own individual sense of beauty and style; with the expectation that counseling services may not always be available, African American girls should be taught how to support one another in this regard based upon shared participation in a number of common struggles. Finally, as school counselors design programs to meet the diverse needs of students, forging partnerships with community organizations are critical in providing support to counselors in meeting the needs of African American female adolescents.

REFERENCES

American Bar Association and National Bar Association (2001). *Justice by gender: The lack of appropriate prevention, diversion and treatment alternatives for girls in the justice system.* Washington, DC: Authors.

American School Counselor Association (2005). *The ASCA national model: A framework for school counseling programs.* 2nd ed. Alexandria, VA: Author.

American School Counselor Association. (2012). The role of the professional school counselor. Retrieved from http://www.schoolcounselor.org/content.asp?contentid=240.

Bell, R.R. (1981). *Worlds of friendships.* Beverly Hills, CA: Sage.

Bigler, R. S., & Liben, L.S. (2007). Developmental intergroup theory: Explaining and reducing children's social stereotyping and prejudice. *Current Directions in Psychological Science, 16,* 162–166.

Brocki, J.M., & Wearden, A.J. (2006). A critical evaluation of the use of interpretative phenomenological analysis in health psychology. *Psychology and Health, 21,* 87–108.

Brown, L.M. (2003). *Girlfighting: Betrayal and rejection among girls.* New York: New York University Press.

Coltrane, S., & Messineo, M. (2000). The perpetuation of subtle prejudice: Race and gender imagery in 1990s television advertising. *Sex Roles, 42,* 363–389

Cash, T.F., & Henry, P.E. (1995). Women's body images: The results of a national survey in the U.S.A. *Sex Roles, 33,* 19–28.

Clark, K., & Clark, M. (1940). Skin color as a factor in racial identification of Negro school children. *Journal of Social Psychology, 11,* 159–169.

Coker, A.D. (2002). *Racial tasks of African American clients: Understanding historical cultural values as a means of developing appropriate counseling interventions.* Paper presented at the Thirty-Sixth Annual Conference, Alabama Counseling Association, Mobile, Alabama.

Coker, A.D. (2003). *African American woman and the utilization of counseling services.* A presentation made at the Sixth Annual Meeting of the American Association of Behavioral and Social Sciences, Las Vegas, Nevada.

Constantine, M.G. (2002). The intersection of race, ethnicity, gender and social class in counseling: Examining selves in cultural contexts. *Journal of*

Multicultural Counseling and Development, 30(4), 210–215.

Day-Vines, N.L., Patton, J.M., & Baytops, J.L. (2003). Counseling African American adolescents: The impact of race, culture and middle class status. *Professional School Counseling, 7*, 40–51.

Duke, L. (2002). Get real!: Cultural relevance and resistance to the mediated feminine ideal. *Psychology & Marketing, 19*(2), 211–233.

Evans-Winters, V. (2005). *Teaching Black girls: Resiliency in urban classrooms.* New York: Peter Lang.

Felner, R.D., Aber, M.S., Primavera, L., & Cauce, A.M. (1985). Adaptation and vulnerability in high-risk adolescents: An examination of environmental mediators. *American Journal of Community Psychology, 13*(4), 365–379.

Ferguson, A.A. (2000). *Bad boys: Public schools in the making of Black masculinity.* Ann Arbor: University of Michigan Press.

Gainer, K.A. (1992). Internalized oppression as a barrier to effective group work with Black women. *Journal for Specialists in Group Work, 17*(4), 235–242.

Glenn, E.N. (2002). *Unequal freedom: How race and gender shaped American citizenship and labor.* Cambridge, MA: Harvard University Press.

Giordano, P.C., Cernkovich, S.A., & DeMaris, A. (1993). The family and peer relationships of Black adolescents. *Journal of Marriage and the Family, 55*(2) 277–287.

Girls Incorporated (2006). *The supergirl dilemma: Girls grapple with the mounting pressure of expectations.* New York: Author.

Gregg, G.S. (2005). *The Middle East: A cultural psychology.* New York: Oxford University Press.

hooks, b. (2004). *We real cool: Black men and masculinity.* New York: Routledge.

Hall, C. (1995). Beauty is in the soul of the beholder: Psychological implications of beauty and African American women. *Cultural Diversity and Mental Health, 1*(2), 125–137.

Hirschfeld, L. A. (2008). Children's developing conceptions of race. In S.M. Quintana & C. McKown (Eds.), *Handbook of race, racism, and the developing child* (pp. 37–54). Hoboken, NJ: John Wiley & Sons.

Hudley, C., (2001, March 4). *The role of culture in prevention research.* Prevention and Treatment. Retrieved from http://www.journals.apa.org/prevention/volume4/pre0040005c.html.

Jones, C., & Shorter-Gooden, K. (2003). *Shifting: The double lives of Black women in America.* New York: HarperCollins.

Kilpatrick-Demaray, M., & Kerres-Malecki, C. (2003). Importance ratings of socially supportive behaviors by children and adolescents. *School Psychology Review, 32*(1), 108–131.

Leadbeater, B.J.R., & Way, N. (Eds.) (2007). *Urban girls revisited: Building strengths.* New York: New York University Press.

Lopez, N. (2003). *Hopeful girls, troubled boys.* New York: Routledge.

Miller, J.B. & Stiver, L. (1998). *The healing connection.* Boston: Beacon Press.

Okazawa-Rey, M., Robinson, T., & Ward, J. (1987). Black women and the politics of skin color and hair. *Women and Therapy, 6,* 89–102.

Oyserman, D., Harrison, K., & Bybee, D. (2001). Can racial identity be promotive of academic efficacy? *International Journal of Behavioral Development, 25,* 379–385.

Patterson, J.T. (2001). *Brown v. Board of Education: A civil rights milestone and its troubled legacy.* Oxford: University Press.

Poran, M.A. (2002). Denying diversity: Perceptions of beauty and social comparisons processes among Latina, Black, and White women. *Sex Roles, 47,* 65–81.

Resnicow, K., Soler, R.E., Braithwaite, R.L., Selassie, M.B., & Smith, M. (1999). Development of a racial and ethnic identity scale for African American adolescents: The survey of Black life. *Journal of Black Psychology, 25,* 171–188.

Robinson, T.L., & Howard-Hamilton, M. (2000). *The convergence of race, ethnicity, and gender.* Upper Saddle River, NJ: Prentice-Hall.

Rollock, N. (2007). Why Black girls don't matter: exploring how race and gender shape academic success in an inner city school. *Support for Learning, 22*(4).197–202.

Shaw, R.L. (2001). Why use interpretative phenomenological analysis in health psychology? *Health Psychology Update, 10*(4), 48–52.

Sue, D.W. (1978). Eliminating cultural oppression in counseling: Toward a general theory. *Journal of Counseling Psychology, 25*(5), 419–428.

Sue, D.W., & Sue, D. (2003). *Counseling the culturally diverse.* New York: Wiley.

Sue, D. W., & Sue, D. (2008). *Counseling the culturally diverse: Theory and practice.* 5th ed. Hoboken, NJ: John Wiley & Sons.

Temkin-Greener, H., & Clark, K.T. (1988). Ethnicity, gender, and utilization of mental health services in a Medicaid population. *Social Science and Medicine, 26,* 989–996.

Tinsley-Jones, H. (2003). Racism: Calling a spade a spade. *Psychotherapy: Theory, Research, Practice, & Training, 40,* 179–186.

Williams-Braun (2005). Counseling African American woman: Multiple identities—multiple constraints. *Journal of Counseling and Development, 83*(3), 278–283.

Critical Race Theory and African Womanism

THEORIZING BLACK GIRLS' EDUCATION
AT THE LOCAL AND GLOBAL LEVELS

VENUS E. EVANS-WINTERS

I f educational policymakers and critics are truly committed to moving the education of Black girls forward, first we must begin by looking at how the educational conditions of U.S. Black female students are connected to larger economic, social, and political injustices that Black women and girls encounter across the African Diaspora. For example, scholars and practitioners alike must seek to understand more about the beliefs, behaviors, languages, and traditions of Black girls at the local level, while simultaneously, seeking to understand the ways in which cultural knowledge(s) are historically situated and transmitted across contexts and spaces. Most educational theorists continue to research, ponder, and theorize Black girls experiences locally, but tend to overlook the influence of global factors on Black girls' opportunities and choices.

For instance, rarely do educational researchers, especially those who employ traditional White feminist's theoretical models, contemplate the effects of colonization, the African slave trade and holocaust, slavery, segregation, lynching campaigns, and apartheid schooling on Black girls' bodies and psyches. Similarly, raced-based models that are absent of a gendered analysis fail to seek to understand how rape, genital mutilation, domestic violence, and abusive welfare policies effect Black girls and women's development across lands and spaces. Therefore, there is a need for frameworks that are more theoretical research methodologies and for analytical interpretations in the social sciences that conscientiously illuminate the present state of Black girls' education to historical practices, while simultaneously shifting the discourse on Black girls' education from the local to the global to the local again. More specifically and to the point, there is a need for race-based and gender-based theoretical frameworks that examine the influence of globalization on the state of localized race, class, and gender experiences in schools.

For the purposes of this discussion, a distinction should be made between globalization and internationalization. In alignment with Africana scholar Filomina Chioma Steady (2002), when theorizing the education of Black girls, the author takes the stance that "Internationalization facilitates communication, international travel, multilateral cooperation, global education, and other opportunities" (p. 37). By most scholarly viewpoints, internationalization is the transfer and sharing of knowledge, ideas, and cultural understanding between different groups of people. In contrast, "Globalization or corporal globalization is viewed as "a modern, high-tech, and in many ways a brutal form of re-colonization. Its main objective is the integration and domination of economic markets by transnational capital through corporations whose centers of gravity are in the North," according to Steady (2002, p. 37). For some at the bottom of the sedimentation of inequality (Oliver & Shapiro, 2006), globalization is an economic and political force that exploits the poor, undereducated, women, and Black and brown people. Arguments in this chapter coincide with the stance that women who live at the intersections of race, class, and gender oppression inside and outside of the United States are the most at-risk of the devastating effects of globalization.

That being said, educational researchers interested in critically examining and ameliorating education on behalf of Black female students in the United States (and abroad) should begin with the following set of questions: How are school curriculums and teaching practices striving to meet the demands of economic globalization, and how are Black girls schooling implicated in such efforts? In other words, in what ways are Black girls being prepared to participate and compete in the global marketplace? Furthermore, how are Black girls in local contexts socially and economically affected by shifts and trends in the global economic structure? Additionally, how are Black girls being portrayed in the global world, especially through cultural aesthetic forms like print, visual, or sound media (e.g., hip-hop, rap, or talk shows)? Moreover, in what ways have young Black women contributed to the growth and dissemination of African and African American cultural forms and material goods in the global context? Finally, how can educational scholars and social justice advocates ensure that young Black women do not become invisible or obsolete in the current global/internationalization sociopolitical economy? Together these sets of questions view Black girls and women as consumers as well as producers of material and cultural goods.

To begin to respond to the above questions, educational theorists need to draw upon the disciplines of sociology, women studies, Black studies, history, and economics. Black girls and women's social realities are situated at the nexus of race, class, and gender exclusion, which makes their life circumstances often very variegated; thus, any proposed frameworks in education must also be just as multifaceted and dynamic. African womanism and critical race theory, coupled as a theoretical framework, by design seek to understand, explain, and affirm the complex realities of Black girls' lives. Together African womanism and critical race theory have the potential to yield educational policy and frameworks for practice that are beneficial to the social, cultural, psychological, and economic needs of female students of African descent.

Globalization

From a minimalist perspective, globalization is defined as the exchange and movement of goods, services, money, ideas, and people across national borders. Broadly speaking, globalization represents economic interconnectedness and the development of information technology, international integration, free trade, and open borders. Even though many scholars estimate that economic globalization began circa World War I, some African scholars argue that globalization (as internationalization) has been around at least since or even prior to the African slave trade. Prior to European exploration and exploitation of African lands and peoples on the African continent, African peoples explored, traded, and exchanged information and ideas across cultural and physical borders (Asante, 2007). After European conquest and colonization, African peoples (and their ideas) were traded, stolen, and sold across national borders as a form of chattel.

Notwithstanding this significant historical dereliction, in the so-called postmodern era it is common to consider the digitization of information, along with the rapid mass transmission of commerce within and across North American, European, Asian, and African countries, as the marking the beginning (and end) of globalization. Most economists and political scientists give little attention to when, where, and how globalization begins and ends, which might have dire consequences for those living at the margins of society. In particular, at this historical moment not enough is known about the social and economic opportunities or dangers that globalization will present for young Black women of African descent.

The intent here is not to argue that globalization is good or bad for Black females, for such a discussion would go beyond the scope of this chapter; however, suffice it to say for the purposes of this volume that Black girls and women on all seven continents have been and will be further impacted by economic globalization. Therefore, in this chapter I call for theoretical frameworks and methodologies in education that seek to understand how Black girls and women across the diaspora are being prepared to participate in and/or resist the dynamics of globalization.

EDUCATION AND GLOBALIZATION

Recent studies have pointed out a few predictable consequences of globalization, such as (1) a decrease in the demand for repetitive, low-skilled labor, (2) an increase in demand for highly skilled laborers, and (3) an increase in economic uncertainty. In the new world order, there will be a need for workers who are highly educated, have the ability to respond quickly to solve complex problems, communicate effectively, manage information, and work in teams and produce knowledge (Partnership for 21st Century Skills, 2008; Stromquist, 2006). Across the globe, education is being propagated as the equalizing force in closing social and economic gaps between diverse social groups, and between men and women, in particular (Stromquist, 2006).

Formal educational institutions predictably will play a central role in developing human and cultural capital. Those in the business and higher education fields have pointed out the skills, knowledge, and dispositions that will be of value in the present and near future for individual and group progress in the global economy. According to the educational advocacy group Partnership for 21st Century Skills (2008), the following skill sets and abilities will be an asset in the next century for students and workers:

- Basic skills in math, science, reading, and writing
- Critical thinking and problem-solving skills
- The ability to solve complex and multidisciplinary problems
- The ability to communicate and collaborate across diverse groups
- Knowledge of human cultures and the natural world
- Information, media, and technology skills
- Financial, economic, business, and entrepreneurial literacy
- Creativity and innovation skills
- Important life and career skills (e.g., flexibility and adaptability; initiative and self-direction; social and cross-cultural competency; productivity and accountability; leadership and responsibility)

Because education is being touted as the socioeconomic equalizer, it is critically important that educational researchers, preservice and in-service educators, policymakers, and educational advocates expand the conversation on Black girls' education to include inquiry on what is being done in classrooms and outside of school settings to prepare girls with the necessary marketability, employability, and life skills necessary to compete in the postindustrial economy. No longer is it worthwhile to compare Black girls' (and boys') academic progress to White middle-class girls and boys in the United States alone. Sadly, there is evidence that suggest that even the most academically privileged U.S. students are not adequately prepared to compete with their international peers in the areas of math and science literacy. For instance, in 2006, the average U.S. score in mathematics literacy was 474 on a scale from 0 to 1,000, which was more than 20 points lower than the world average score of 498. According to NCES data, 31 jurisdictions had a higher average score than the United States in mathematics literacy in 2006. In addition, U.S. students scored lower in science literacy than their peers in 16 of the other 29 OECD jurisdictions and six of the 27 non-OECD jurisdictions (see NCES, 2006). Thus, the so-called achievement gap is a U.S. problem, and not simply a Black or low-income "problem." In other words, research and advocacy efforts in education must focus on closing the achievement gap between Black female students and students worldwide.

For economic stability and overall health and well-being, policy formation needs to bring attention to African American female students' access to early childhood education and elementary and secondary schooling, and improve access to and attainment of postsecondary education. However, as pointed out by Stromquist (2006), with local and global competition on the rise, access to education and the accumulation of educational credentials is not enough; instead, the focus needs to be for Black female students (grades pre-K through 22) to have access to quality education. Quality education includes curriculum and classroom practices that enhance basic skills in the core curriculum (e.g. math, science, and reading), as well as attention to building students' competency in critical thinking skills, information gathering, technology, and media literacy.

In addition, as articulated by Nembhard (2005), "Increased education and better test scores are necessary but not sufficient conditions for increased economic well-being" (p. 239). African American young women require access to educational opportunities that serve the purpose of community-building, transforming the economic system, and building their entrepreneurship capacity (Nembhard, 2005). I add to Nembhard's observation the need for curriculum and pedagogy that focuses on connecting Black American youth to their African ancestry and knowledge of the African Diaspora. Many Black youth in the United States feel isolated and confused about their racial/ethnic identity. Consequently, they fail to appreciate their connection to the larger social world outside of their own families, peer groups, or neighborhoods. Globalization presents the opportunity for cultural bridge building within and across borders. This historical moment presents the opportunity to facilitate and encourage Black youths' sense of personal and cultural identity, as well as educate them on their cultural bond with African youth worldwide.

Theoretical Perspectives

Based on previous research on the schooling experiences of African American female students (Evans-Winters, 2005; Evans-Winters & Esposito, 2010; O'Connor, 1997), more is known about how the family, community, and school simultaneously affects the academic development of Black girls. Moreover, we know that the biggest challenge confronting Black girls in local settings and globally is not necessarily the achievement gap between themselves and White girls or White boys, for that matter. Most theorists of African descent assert unequivocally the biggest challenges confronting young Black women of African ancestry are residential segregation and isolation (Frazer, 2008; Kozol, 1996; Massey & Denton, 1993; Wilson, 1996) and poverty and exclusion from top-tier jobs in the formal economy (Feagin, 2001; Oliver & Shapiro, 1997). Racial segregation problems are further complicated by unhealthy environmental conditions and corporate disinvestment in Black urban and rural communities (Frazer, 2008; see Kozol 1996 and 2012 for discussion on the relevancy of urban pollution to children's educational development).

Many young Black women's socio-emotional development, in particular, is further negatively influenced by the lack of access to adequate health care, safe and affordable reproductive health care, and mental health education (Cozier et al., 2007; Hearst, Oakes, & Johnson, 2008; Jones, Cross, & DeFour, 2007), transracial teaching, and the lack of access to free and appropriate curriculum and teaching practices. Another challenge facing women of African ancestry is the objectification and commodification of Black women's bodies and sexuality in the mainstream media, and the bombardment of Eurocentric standards of beauty (hooks, 1992; Collins, 2004). There simply are not many positive images in mainstream media that serve to affirm Black girls racial/ethnic identity or African identity. Too many young Black women are living like a third-world underclass in their own communities and nations.

As pointed out by Ladson-Billings (2006), when educational scholars and others narrowly focus on the academic achievement gap between Whites and Blacks, or males and females, attention is speciously redirected from the gap in other areas that influence educational outcomes, such as housing patterns, the criminal justice system, economic discrimination, and school-funding disparities. With these kinds of social, legal, and educational problems confronting them, young Black women in the United States are especially destined in the international market to face severe poverty, disease, and economic illiteracy.

AFRICAN WOMANISM

African womanism and a critical race theory lens offer new perspectives to discuss, critique, and explore methodological and theoretical directions in the study of Black female students. Black feminism has traditionally been the dominant lens leading the discourse on the educational experiences of females of African descent in the United States. As a theoretical lens, Black feminism seeks to understand how race, class, and gender affect women's experiences (Collins, 2000). Scholars inside and outside of U.S. borders have critiqued U.S. Black feminists for not bringing attention to the social and economic conditions confronting Black women outside of the U.S. context, especially those on the continent of Africa.

African womanism is also concerned with how racism, sexism, and classism work together to shape women's experiences, but its focus is more on women on the continent of Africa and processes of colonization and postcolonization. African womanism has been influenced by the theoretical and advocacy work of Black female scholars in the United States and abroad. In fact, at times, this chapter uses the terms *African feminism* and *African womanism* interchangeably; the shift between terms denotes their strong historical, political, and cultural bond.

In this chapter, it is suggested that theorists interested and invested in the educational development of Black female students may benefit more from a combination of Black feminism and African womanism. It seems that African womanism allows the opportunity to shift Black girls' social, economic, and cultural experiences back and forth between the local and the global. In reference to the theoretical association between Black feminism/womanism and African womanism/feminism, Steady (2002, p. 22) declares:

> Both intersectionality and African feminism bring us closer to our present while being part of the general quest for explanations of dominance. For purposes of understanding the process of engendering racism, both offer some interesting insights. Intersectionality looks at how race, class, and gender interactions work and why they are important in the social construction of power and domination. African feminism uses a global and human-centered perspective to examine how and why these converging elements have interacted within the context of historical processes of colonization, racial domination, globalization, and cultural realities.

In agreement with Steady, this chapter argues that African womanism provides a critical lens for interrogating the role of past and present gendered racism (e.g., colonization, apartheid, and segregation) and its influence on the schooling experiences and outcomes of women of African descent from a global perspective. Thus, a large part of my argument is that much can be learned from connecting educational inequality in the United States to race, class, and gender inequality in other parts of the world. Even more, for policy formulation and implementation purposes, it is time for those researchers who claim to do race, class, and gender work to demonstrate the ways in which educational development is strongly influenced by larger economic trends and political decisions often beyond the power of individual agency.

CRITICAL RACE THEORY

Educational scholars Ladson-Billings and Tate (1995) as well as Dixson and Rosseau (2006) have illustrated the usefulness of critical race theory to education. Critical race theory (CRT) has five tenets that have the potential for informing educational research, curriculum, and policy formation, which are of particular interests to research with and on behalf of Black girls and women. CRT (1) asserts that race and racism are central, endemic, permanent, and fundamental in defining and explaining how U.S. society functions, (2) challenges dominant ideologies and claims of race neutrality, objectivity, meritocracy, color-blindness, and equal opportunity, (3) is activist in nature and propagates a commitment to social justice, (4) centers the experiences and voices of the marginalized and oppressed, and (5) is necessarily interdisciplinary in scope and function (Delgado Bernal, 2002; Delgado & Stefancic, 2000; Solorzano & Yosso, 2002).

Legal scholar Bell (2000) informs us that the *Brown v. Board of Education* (1954) decision brought to an end state-mandated racial segregation. As pointed out by the legal scholar, the case was decided on the basis that legal racial segregation benefited the interests of Whites, while actively excluding and discriminating against Black citizens. At the time of *Brown v. Board of Education*, civil rights scholars successfully argued that legal segregation was a violation of the Fourteenth Amendment's equal protection clause. Nonetheless, argues Bell (1995), the *Brown* decision and other social and legal issues decided by the courts are only brought forth when they appease the White populace. Therefore, any legal remedies as they relate to educational reform will necessarily "secure, advance, or at least not harm" (Bell, 1995, p. 22) the state of affairs for Whites. Bell refers to the tendency of the judicial system of maintaining or not treading on the privileges of White citizens, in the interest of Black citizens, as the principle of interest convergence.

Bell's (1995) interest convergence theory is more than relevant to discussions on the plight of Black girls' education. For example, research shows that public schools located in central cities are more racially segregated than they have been in the past, and the majority of African American and Latino/a students attend predominately minority schools (Orfield, 2001), where the student population is non-White. The problem is not with minority children attending school with other minority children, nor is the problem with minority children not attending schools with White children. The problem is that many White middle-class families on the surface have no interest assisting in providing social and financial support to low-income and working-class students (who are disproportionally minority) with a quality education (Kozol, 2006). Consequently, the interests of the White middle class may not converge with the interests of Blacks attending public schools.

If one takes a closer look inside our nation's public schools, especially schools serving low-income families in African American communities, more than likely one would notice that Black girls outnumber the boys in these classrooms. Black girls are left to fend for themselves in desegregated public urban and private school classrooms, more than likely with White female middle-class teachers from family and economic backgrounds different from their own (Cochran-Smith & Fries, 2005; NCES, 2004). What interest does the White middle class have in meeting the needs of Black female students? From a convergence theory perspective, where do the needs of Whites and males intersect with the needs of African American female students? There may not be an answer to this question, without, of course, considering the question and its possible response from a human rights perspective. All U.S. citizens have the right to a free and appropriate education.

Yet, from a social justice perspective, it will be difficult to argue for educational reform from a legal or legislative perspective, considering women of African descent were left out of the Constitution as women and as Black Africans (Ruth, 1990; Hine, 1988). In fact, considering that African American women go on to college at greater rates than their Black male and Latino/a peers, young Black women may be perceived as competition in the marketplace to some Whites. As for younger Black women who have not had the privilege of formal schooling, they have served as the scapegoat for everything that is morally wrong with the U.S. social welfare system (Augustin, 1997; Collins, 2004; Monnat, 2007). Thus, Bell's (1995) interest convergence theory suggests that there may be a bind for those who pursue educational efforts on behalf of Black girls.

Furthermore, Peller (1995) contends that race and racism in mainstream American politics have been articulated and contested primarily through an integrationist ideology. Such an ideology, according to the legal scholar, views race and racism as a set of beliefs situated in the notions of prejudice and stereotypes based on skin color, which positions racial "progress with the transcendence of a racial consciousness" (p. 127). As outlined by Peller (1995), the consequences of a integrationist ideology has resulted in the suppression of White racism; Black nationalism being equated with White supremacy; race consciousness on the part of Whites or Blacks deemed as unintelligent and culturally backward; and the publicly consumed opinion that racism can be replaced by knowledge of and contact with the "other."

Accordingly, efforts toward racial justice from an integrationist perspective downplay the significance of race, while propagating a stance of neutrality, objectivity, and White middle-class normativity (Peller, 1995). For example, Black girls are encouraged to think that deep down all children are the same, regardless of race or location; however, Peller points out that such a notion is shortsighted and too idealistic and only proliferates Whiteness as the norm or White middle-class values as the ideal ways of thinking or behaving. Instead, there is a need for curriculum and pedagogical practices that sets out to affirm Black girls' unique racial and cultural identities.

Peller (1998) further asserts that schools have become technocratic, impersonal, and dominated by White middle-class perspectives on teaching and learning. On the other hand, education is mantled as racially and culturally neutral, and politically objective. Therefore, educational theorists and advocates will have to exert an enormous amount of effort and sophistication when arguing for educational reform at the intersections, because it would be nearly impossible for young Black women, especially those from lower- and working-class backgrounds, to integrate racially or otherwise into mainstream society. In the state of Michigan, policymakers and educational reformists must contemplate an educational plan that serves to ensure that Black female students have substantial opportunities for full participation in the local educational, political, and business marketplace.

Historically, young Black women have been socially constructed as the epitome of exactly what whiteness (as maleness) and femininity (as whiteness) is not: dark, sinister, raunchy, belligerent, burly, and licentious. In the U.S. context, White femininity is sacrosanct to patriarchy and vice versa. An integrationist approach to educational equity would only further marginalize the majority of African American female students, because full integration may not be an option, for White middle-class identity is constructed around young Black women's identity as the "other." Considering critical race theorists have unveiled the legacy of whiteness as property (Harris, 1997) and educational theorists have outlined its ramifications in the history of Black education in the United States (Ladson-Billings & Tate, 1995), the state of young Black women's educational development may be at further risk, if left solely in the hands in the White middle-class majority. Harris (1997) contends that whiteness or White identity comes with a set of private and public privileges in America that has been protected, affirmed, and legitimated by the law.

Under the institutionalization of slavery, Blacks became equated with property, while Whiteness became a tangible and intangible protection against slavery; therefore, whiteness became an asset to be acquired, protected, and cosseted. As this relates to Black women, under the institution of slavery, Black women's bodies were deemed a vessel for increasing property; thus, profit. Thomas Jefferson made the following statement in an 1805 letter: "I consider the labor of a breeding woman as no object, and that a child raised every 2 years is of more profit than the crop of the best laboring man" (as cited in Stanton, n.d.). During slavery, Black women were viewed as property that begets property, and any possibility of her humanity was only tied to her ability to "breed" more labor for the White dominant elite.

If the state of Michigan is committed to educational reform, it is appropriate for the following question to be raised: If a young Black woman's worth is measured through her aptitude for reproducing the next generation's labor (i.e., capital), what would be the interest of the privileged class in assisting in the development of her educational well-being through self-empowerment or social and financial support? Once more, where does the interest of Michigan's White, middle-class, educated populace converge with the interest of young women of African descent? With Bell's (1995) interest convergence theory, Peller's (1995) reflections on the limitations of integrationist ideology, and Harris's (1997) averment of whiteness as property in mind, how will the educational community and Black community work together to develop and implement curricula, pedagogies, and educational policies aimed at *intersectionalities*.

For instance, women of color's social and political needs have traditionally been positioned in between the needs of a feminist agenda and antiracist efforts. White feminism politicizes the experiences of women, while antiracist efforts are inclined to emphasize the experiences of people of color. Crenshaw (1995) claims that identity politics often overlooks intragroup differences. The experiences and political concerns of women of color tend to fall through the cracks with those focused on solely gender-based initiatives or race-based initiatives. Crenshaw asserts that women of color's lived experiences are influenced by their identities as both women and persons of color. "Because women of color experience racism in ways not always the same as experienced by men of color and sexism in ways not always paralleled to experiences of white women, antiracism and feminism are limited, even on their own terms," articulates Crenshaw (1995, p. 360).

Mainstream social and political efforts usually fail to address the concerns of women of color, because White women define the feminist agenda and men conceptualize the antiracist agenda. This analysis suggests a need for social, political, economic, and educational reform initiatives and pedagogies that consider and interrogate the specific academic needs of Black women. African American female students have educational experiences that are simultaneously similar to, albeit divergent from, the needs and experiences of White girls and boys of color. This is why discussions such as the one taken up in this book are important, because the project validates Black women in Michigan's experiences as woman, Black, and as Black woman. Hopefully, this chapter sets the foundation on how to transform and lead this conversation in a meaningful way for all involved in the project.

Critical Race Feminism / African Womanism in Education

Critical race feminism (CRF) is a branch of CRT. As a movement, CRT grew out of critical legal studies, which was dominated by the voices of White male legal academics (Wing, 1997). Legal scholars involved in the CRT movement advanced legal issues and strategies affecting people of color. In an overview of the history of race feminism, Wing (1997) explains that CRT scholars have taken up diverse issues, such as de facto segregation discrimination, affirmation action, and federal Indian law. Often CRT was dominated by men's experiences, excluding the perspectives of women of color. Additionally, feminist legal theorists highlighted the viewpoints of White and upper-class women, but assumed that the gendered experiences of White women and women of color were identical in character. Because of its unapologetic examination of the intersection of race, class, and gender in the legal sphere and the broad experiences of women of color, the premises of critical race feminism are distinct from, but at times, intersect with CRT. Critical race feminism in education (Evans-Winters & Esposito, 2010) is beneficial to investigation and theory building around educational issues impacting Black girls in the following ways:

- Critical race feminism as a theoretical lens and movement purports that women of color's experiences, thus perspectives, are different from the experiences of men of color and those of White women.
- Critical race feminism focuses on the lives of women of color who face multiple forms of discrimination, due to the intersections of race, class, and gender within a system of White male patriarchy and racist oppression.
- Critical race feminism asserts the multiple identities and consciousness of women of color (i.e., antiessentialist).
- Critical race feminism is interdisciplinary in scope and breadth.
- Critical race feminism calls for theories and practices that simultaneously study and fight against gender and racial oppression.

Along with an African womanist perspective, CRF (see Crenshaw, 1995 and Wing, 1997 for a thorough discussion on the emergence and legal cases associated with CRF) is currently the most useful lens for studying, analyzing, critiquing, and celebrating the educational experiences of African American female students, as indicated in the above outline.

First, White feminists have tended to overlook or ignore Black girls' experiences in schools (Ladner, 1987); thus, feminist frameworks alone cannot address the pervasiveness of racism or the lived experiences and educational concerns of Black girls (Vonzell & Karanxha, 2012). Also, the social and educational problems challenging African American boys' educational development should not be conflated with the gendered trials and tribulations confronting Black girls. There is little doubt that Black boys face cruel realities of the school-to-prison pipeline (Duncan, 2000) and institutionalized separate and equal education (Dunbar, 2001). Black girls have also faced their own share of exclusion and marginalization in the educational system. Research shows that Black girls are more likely to be reprimanded or praised for social behaviors in the classroom as opposed to being provided adequate feedback on their academic pursuits (Evans-Winters, 2005). In addition, teacher expectations are lower for Black girls than White girls, and findings show that Black girls are more likely to experience racist remarks from their peers (Evans-Winters & Esposito, 2010). Sadly, other research in the social sciences point out that Black women's bodies, inside and outside of school environments, are policed, controlled, and heckled, while at the same time the Black woman's body is a site of spectacle (Collins, 2004; Evans-Winters, 2005; Roberts, 1998).

In addition to coping with stereotypical beliefs about their attitudes and behaviors from teachers and peers, Black girls also face harsh disciplinary actions in schools. For instance, in 2003, Black girls were twice as likely to repeat a grade, to be suspended, and to be expelled as their White female and White male peers before acquiring a high school diploma (NCES, 2003). Black girls' experiences in schools differ from the experiences of boys of color and young White women. Therefore, a critical race feminist lens in the examination of the schooling experiences of African American female students allows for the avoidance of gender and racial exclusion. Definitely more qualitative and quantitative analysis needs to take place in Michigan schools (early childhood programs, elementary and middle schools, secondary and postsecondary levels) to determine the extent to which Black girls are impacted by racism and sexism in local schools. The next step would be to hypothesize how Black girls' experiences in Michigan compare to other girls' schooling outside of the state of Michigan.

Gender essentialism is the notion that there exists a monolithic woman's experience, regardless of one's race, class, or sexual identification. Likewise, racial essentialism is the term used to describe the idea that all members of a racial/ethnic group are all the same (Harris, 1997). Black female students' lived experiences are diverse. Young Black women's race, class, and gender statuses influence their individual identities; likewise, individual identities intersect with their collective identities as women of African ancestry. Any form of essentialism is harmful to theory and practice with Black girls, for essentialism overlooks multiplicity. Many young Black women are able to survive in schools because of their multiple consciousness.

For example, NCES data shows that the majority of Black female students successfully complete high school and go on to higher education programs (Freeman, 2004). Instead of frameworks that typically focus on pathology and deficiency, there is a need to promote frameworks that highlight resilience (alongside vulnerability) and collective tenacity (alongside community stressors). Critical race feminism in education (Evans-Winters & Esposito, 2010) can serve as a model for delineations on how, and to what extent, Black female students' navigate White middle-class educational spaces, due to CRF's tendency for providing legal, political, and social commentary at the intersections.

Conclusion

In sum, CRF and African womanism offers numerous possibilities for indubitable improvement in Black female students educational outcomes and quality of life in the global economy. In the so-called postmodern world, Black girls and women continue to be beset by racism, poverty, and gender discrimination in their families, communities, and schools. There is more than enough evidence to suggest that such marginalization and oppression is a worldwide phenomenon for far too many women of African ancestry around the world. Most White feminists have been complacent about the educational and social barriers impacting young Black women's development, especially those Black girls and women from more racially and economically isolated backgrounds. Again, the purpose of this chapter is to provide a useful framework for analyzing and critiquing Black girls' schooling in the United States and abroad, while also arguing for frameworks that situate and protect Black girls' needs in the global marketplace.

The chapter calls for frameworks in education that connect Black girls' experiences in local contexts (e.g., Michigan's push out/dropout school problem) first to historical patterns of oppression and resistance (e.g., racial segregation patterns in Michigan schools, neighborhoods, and formal job market), and subsequently to women's conditions in other parts of the world (e.g., Africa, Asia, and Europe). Fortunately, CRF in education posits that educational scholars, policymakers, and those concerned with how the judicial system works are responsible for better understanding and improving the state of Black girls' education. Using African womanism and CRT, this chapter calls attention to the following (adapted from Evans-Winters & Esposito, 2010):

- There is an urgent need for conceptual models in education that intentionally expose, confront, and eradicate race, class, and gender oppression Black girls' families, communities, and schools.
- More needs to be done in education on the policy front, or pedagogically, to develop and implement community programs, classroom practices, and curriculum that directly target the academic needs of Black girls.
- Many social and legal policies dehumanize rather than improve the quality of life of many low-income and working-class young women.

- Research with and on behalf of Black girls benefits the whole of society.
- Community organizations and educational institutions from kindergarten to university can work together to prepare Black girls to participate in a localized and global struggle for women's rights, antioppression efforts, and cultural conflict in society.

In closing, CRT shines a bright light on the inequalities Black women face in major social institutions in the United States. Similarly, African womanism highlights Black women's experiences across the African Diaspora. Both empower Black women to acknowledge their identities as Black and woman. Together CRT and African womanism hold promise for research and praxis in Michigan schools and neighborhoods. The overall objective of CRT and African womanism as a conceptual framework is to prepare Black girls and women in Michigan and abroad for active participation, marketability, employability, and citizenship in the global economy.

REFERENCES

Asante, M.K. (2007). *An Afrocentric manifesto.* Malden, MA: Polity Press.

Augustin, N.A. (1997). Learnfare and Black motherhood: The social construction of deviance. In A. Katherine Wing (Ed.), *Critical Race Feminism: A Reader* (pp. 144–150). New York: New York University Press.

Bell, D.A. (2000). Brown v. Board of Education: Forty-five years after the fact. *Ohio Northern University Law Review, 26*(2), 171–81.

Cochran-Smith, M., & Fries, K. (2005). Researching teacher education in changing times: Politics and paradigms. In M. Cochran-Smith & K.M. Zeichner (Eds.), *Studying teacher education: The report of the AERA panel on research and teacher education* (pp. 69–109). Mahwah, NJ: Lawrence Erlbaum Associates.

Collins, P.H. (2000). *Black feminist thought: Knowledge, consciousness, and the politics of empowerment.* 2nd ed. New York: Routledge.

Collins, P.H. (2004). *Black sexual politics: African Americans, gender, and the new racism.* New York: Routledge.

Cozier, Y.C., Palmer, J.R., Horton, N.J., Fredman, L., Wise, L.A., & Rosenberg, L. (2007). Relation between neighborhood median housing value and hypertension risk among black women in the United States. *American Journal of Public Health, 97*(4), 718–724.

Crenshaw, K.W. (1995). Mapping the margins: Intersectionality, identity politics, and violence against women of color. In K. Crenshaw, N. Gotanda, G. Peller, & K. Thomas (Eds.), *Critical race theory: The key writings that formed the movement* (pp. 357–383). New York: New Press.

Delgado Bernal, D. (2002). Critical race theory, Latcrit theory, and critical raced gendered epistemologies: Recognizing students of color as holders and creators of knowledge. *Qualitative Inquiry, 8*(1), 105–126.

Delgado, R., & Stefancic, J. (2000). Introduction. In R. Delgado, & J. Stefancic (Eds.), *Critical Race Theory: The cutting edge,* 2nd ed. (pp. xv–xix). Philadelphia: Temple University Press.

Dixson, A., & Rosseau, C. (2006). *Critical race theory in education: All God's children got a song.* New York: Routledge.

Dunbar, C. (2001). *African American males and alternative education: Does anyone know we're here?* New York: Lang.

Duncan, G.A. (2000). Urban pedagogies and the celling of adolescents of color. *Social Justice: A Journal of Crime, Conflict and World Order, 27*(3), 29–42.

Evans-Winters, V. (2005). *Teaching Black girls: Resiliency in urban classrooms.* New York: Peter Lang.

Evans-Winters, V., & Esposito, J. (2010). Other people's daughters: Critical race feminism and Black girls' education. *Journal of Educational Foundations, 24*(1–2), 11–24.

Feagin, J. (2001). *White racism.* New York: Routledge.

Frazer, L. (2008). Soil in the city: A prime source of lead. *Environmental Health Perspectives, 116*(12), 522.

Freeman, C.E. (2004). *Trends in educational equity of girls and women: 2004.* NCES 2005-016. Washington, DC: U.S. Department of Education, National Center for Education Statistics.

Harris, C. (1997). Race and essentialism in feminist legal theory. In A.K. Wing (Ed.), *Critical race feminism: A reader* (pp. 34–41). New York: New York University Press.

Hearst, M.O., Oakes, J.M., & Johnson, P.J. (2008). The effect of racial residential segregation on Black infant mortality. *American Journal of Epidemiology, 168*(11), 1247–1254.

Hine, D.C. (1988). An angle of vision: Black women and the United States Constitution, 1787–1987. *Organization of American Historians Magazine of History, 3*(1), 7–13.

hooks, B. (1992). *Black looks: Race and representation.* Boston: South End Press.

Jones, H.L., Cross, W.E., & DeFour, D.C. (2008). Race-related stress, racial identity attitudes, and mental health among Black women. *Journal of Black Psychology, 33*(2), 208–231.

King, D.R. (1995). Multiple jeopardy, multiple consciousness: The context of a Black feminist ideology. In B. Guy-Sheftall (Ed.), *Words of fire: An anthology of African American feminist thought* (pp. 293–318). New York: New Press.

Kozol, J. (1996). *Amazing grace: The lives of children and the conscience of a nation.* NY: Harper Perennial.

Kozol, J. (2006). *The Shame of the nation: The restoration of apartheid schooling in America.* New York: Three Rivers Press.

Kozol, J. (2012). *Savage inequalities: Children in America's schools.* New York: Crown Publishing Group.

Ladner, J. (1987). Introduction to tomorrow's tomorrow: The Black woman. In S. Harding (Ed.), *Feminism and methodology* (pp. 74–83). Bloomington: Indiana University Press.

Ladson-Billings, G. (2006). From the achievement gap to the education debt: Understanding achievement in U.S. schools. *Educational Researcher, 35*(7), 3–12.

Ladson-Billings, G., & Tate IV, W. (1995). Toward a critical race theory of education. *Teachers College Record, 97*(1), 47–68.

Massey, D.S., & Denton, N.A. (1993). *American apartheid: Segregation and the making of the underclass.* Cambridge: Harvard University Press.

Monnat, S.M. (2007, August). Toward a critical understanding of gendered racism in the U.S. social welfare institution. Paper presented at the Annual Meeting of the American Sociological Association, New York. Retrieved from http://www.allacademic.com/meta/p183321_index.html.

National Center for Educational Statistics, U.S. Department of Education (NCES) (2003). Parent and Family Involvement in Education Survey of the 2003

National Household Education Surveys Program (PFI-NHES:2003).

National Center for Educational Statistics, U.S. Department of Education (NCES) (2004). Schools and Staffing Survey, Public School Teacher Data File: 2003–2004.

National Center for Educational Statistics, U.S. Department of Education (NCES) (2006). *Highlights from PISA 2006: Performance of U.S. 15-year-old students in science and mathematics literacy in an international context* (NCES 2008-016).

Nembhard, J.G. (2005). On the road to democratic economic participation: Educating African American youth in the postindustrial global economy. In J.E. King (Ed.), *Black education: A transformative research and action agenda for the new century* (pp. 225–240). Washington, DC: AERA.

O'Connor, C. (1997). Dispositions toward (collective) struggle and educational resilience in the inner city: A case analysis of six African American high school students. *American Educational Research Journal, 34*, 593–629.

Oliver, T.M., & Shapiro, M.L. (2006). *Black wealth/White wealth: A new perspective on racial inequality* . New York: Routledge.

Orfield, G. (2001). Schools more separate: Consequences of more than a decade of segregation. Cambridge, MA: Harvard Civil Rights Project.

Partnership for 21st Century Skills (2008). *21st century skills, education, and competitiveness: A resource and policy guide.* Retrieved from http://www.21stcenturyskills.org/documents/21st_century_skills_education_and_competitiveness_guide.pdf.

Peller, G. (1995). Race-consciousness. In K. Crenshaw, N. Gotanda, G. Peller, & K. Thomas (Eds.), *Critical race theory: The key writings that formed the movement* (pp. 127–158). New York: New Press.

Roberts, D. (1998). *Killing the Black body: Race, reproduction and the meaning of liberty.* New York: Vintage Books.

Ruth, S. (1990). *Issues in feminism: An introduction to women studies.* 2nd ed. Mountain View, CA: Mayfield.

Solorzano, D., & Yosso, T. (2002). Critical race methodology: Counterstorytelling as an analytical framework for education research. *Qualitative Inquiry, 8*(1), 23–44.

Stanton, L.C. (n.d.). Jefferson's "family." Retrieved from http://www.pbs.org/wgbh/pages/frontline/shows/jefferson/slaves/stanton.html.

Steady, F.C. (2002). *Black women, globalization, and economic justice: Studies from the Africa and the African Diaspora.* Rochester, VT: Schenkman Books.

Stromquist, N.P. (2006). Gender, education and the possibility of transformative knowledge. *Compare, 36*(2), 145–161.

Vonzell, A., & Karanxha, Z. (2012). Resistance meets spirituality in academia: "I prayed on it!" *Negro Educational Review, 62–63*(1–4), 41–66.

Wilson, W.J. (1996). *When work disappears: The world of the new urban poor.* New York: Knopf.

Wing, A.K. (1997). (Ed.). *Critical race feminism: A reader.* New York: New York University Press.

Imag[e]ining Hip-Hop Femininity

CONTENTS, CONTRADICTIONS, AND CONTRIBUTIONS

DONYALE R. GRIFFIN PADGETT, CHERYL D. JENKINS,
and DALE ANDERSON

Are we still perplexed by this new hip-hop generation?
Rising, shouting, resisting
the degeneration of an entire nation
    and generation XY
Zzzzzzzzzzzzzzz
Wake up sisters (and brothers)
    Take back the mike
        And take back the night
    And take back the right
        To rhyme ...

—Janell Hobson, "Hip-Hop Hegemony"

Mic Check

Hip-hop is undoubtedly a pop culture phenomenon. Born in the basement of a housing complex to a man by the name of Clive "Kool Herc" Campbell, hip-hop ultimately ventured away from the streets of New York City and has been influential throughout the globe. In fact, from music and fashion, to literature and language, the impact of hip-hop has gone from being a microcosm of New York's African American, Afro-Caribbean, and Hispanic communities to a mass-mediated cultural phenomenon that transcends race, class, and geographical boundaries. Torn between consciousness-raising rhetoric and capitalistic gain, hip-hop is becoming one of the most controversial sociocultural movements of the twenty-first century.

While historically, hip-hop's sociopolitical significance is undeniable, this genre is often relegated to "booty music," which dilutes the organic messages that have challenged the status quo and served as a part of hip-hop's history since its inception in the late 1960s / early 1970s. Today, rap music leads as the primary defining element of hip-hop culture and drives its marketability. In fact, the term *hip-hop* is often used synonymously with "rap music" (Bennett, 2000; Dyson, 2003, 2007). This is problematic, particularly when we consider that the music that emerges from this genre with the most commercial appeal is widely negligent, misogynistic toward Black women, and void of cultural accountability.

The contradiction is that hip-hop provides one of the only avenues that expresses social, cultural, and economic inequities, while, at the same time embracing the capitalistic structures that are implicated in the disenfranchise-ment [of traditionally marginalized groups]" (Weheliye, 2001, p. 294). Therefore, while hip-hop is praised for being artistically expressive, the music is riddled with degrading images of Black men and women that ultimately challenge Black cultural identity formation.

In her work *Black Noise*, Tricia Rose (1994) attempted to rein in hip-hop culture by defining it. She writes: "Hip-hop is a cultural form that attempts to negotiate the experiences of marginalization, brutality, truncated opportunity, and oppression within the cultural imperatives of African American and Caribbean history, identity, and community" (p. 21). She further states, "Rap music and hip-hop culture are cultural, political, and commercial forms, and for many young people they are the primary cultural, sonic, and linguistic windows on the world" (p. 19).

It was Rose who told us that hip-hop was a platform from which voices from the margins could "spit at" the social, economic, and political imbalances that had long plagued urban communities. Furthering the notion of hip-hop's role in providing a voice for the marginalized, Peoples (2008) states that from its inception, "hip-hop has represented resistance to social marginalization, and later resistance to and commentary on the political and economic oppression that makes social marginalization possible" (p. 23).

A source of much contention within and outside of the hip-hop community is the movement away from the social consciousness and political and social commentary that helped to put rap music and hip-hop culture on the charts. The "organic" message of traditional rap music has been diluted and tainted with the ink of the dollar bill. This phenomenon has placed capitalistic gain above raising the world's consciousness with more emphasis on pimped-out rides, bling, ride-or-die chicks, and a gangster lean than was evident when KRS-One of the group BDP first made us *think*, with the hit single "My Philosophy."

After first laying a foundation for Black feminist thought, feminist scholars like Collins (1991) and Guy-Sheftall (1995), along with feminist writer Morgan (1995), helped us to understand the contention that has been the source of much anguish in the Black community relative to rap music and hip-hop culture—misogyny toward Black women. Parallel to that work, scholars like Davis (1995) and Byrd (2004) have pushed our theorizing further, using the term *hip-hop feminism* to signify the link between women, feminism, and hip-hop. Since that time, a new generation of scholars has contributed to this discussion of hip-hop feminism, which characterizes "women [who] have been influenced by both the feminist movement and by hip-hop culture (Peoples, 2008, p. 26). Pough (2007) further defines hip-hop feminists as "women and men who step up and speak out against gender exploitation in hip-hop" (p. 80).

Upon answering the obvious question of what misogyny is from a conceptual standpoint, this chapter examines its pervasiveness in hip-hop culture and rap music and the unique ways in which female hip-hop artists engage feminism. We localize this discussion by highlighting the bourgeoning hip-hop culture in Michigan, with a discussion of local artists and their contributions to this dialogue. We ask, what are the opportunities and contradictions of theorizing hip-hop feminism? Do the ways in which Black women artists engage feminism within hip-hop offer an alternative discourse in response to misogyny or opportunities for a deeper consciousness and critique of Black feminist identity?

IMAG[E]INING THE BLACK FEMALE BODY IN HIP-HOP

The degradation of Black women is not a modern phenomenon. Notwithstanding, the assault on African American women perpetuated by the system of slavery in the United States normalized their oppression (Adams & Fuller, 2006; Dyson, 2007).

> From the beginning of slavery, black women have been viewed as deviant sexual beings possessed of insatiable carnal urges. Black women were viewed as oversexed because they had to meet the erotic demands of their sexually feared black men. Until the second half of the twentieth century, black women were seen as incapable of being raped; their alleged exceptional sexual capacity meant that no white man would have to take what they would freely offer. (Dyson, 2007, p. 128)

This point is key to the argument that misogyny "is a part of a larger social, cultural, and economic system that sustains and perpetuates . . . blatant stereotypical characterizations and defamations" of Black women (Adams & Fuller, 2006, p. 941). Moreover, how do we conceptualize misogyny? According to Adams and Fuller (2006), misogyny is "the hatred or disdain of women. It is an ideology that reduces women to objects for men's ownership, use, or abuse" (p. 939).

Nowhere is the misogyny toward Black women more evident and debated than in rap music. Adams and Fuller claim further that the ways in which Black women are characterized in rap music "ultimately support, justify, instill, and perpetuate ideas, values, beliefs, and stereotypes that debase [them]" (p. 940). While Adams and Fuller (2006) and Dyson (2007) attempt to contextualize the misogyny dilemma within a U.S. capitalistic patriarchal system, Hobson and Bartlow (2008) articulate a broader characterization of this milieu. They assert that "women in varying cultures have been portrayed either as decorative, fetishistic, manipulative, fragile, or in need of rescuing (or submission) in contemporary popular music lyrics, and music videos" (Hobson & Bartlow, 2008, pp. 2–3). What these scholars are ultimately saying is that misogyny exists across geographic lines and functions at multiple levels of society.

Why are misogynistic lyrics so mainstream? As Gilkes (1983) notes, "Black women emerged from slavery firmly enshrined in the consciousness of white America as 'Mammy' and the 'bad black woman'" (p. 294). According to Adams and Fuller (2006), "misogynistic rap has been accepted and allowed to flourish, generating wealth for some of the artists and the music industry as a whole" (p. 940). They juxtapose images of the Sapphire (Bitch) with the Jezebel (Ho) to illustrate how Black women have been demonized in American society. Clearly, as Collins articulates in her book *Black Feminist Thought*, Black women's oppression reflects an intersection between "race, class, gender, and sexuality [that] could not continue without powerful ideological justifications for their existence" (Collins, 2000, p. 69). Collins goes on to say that portraying Black women as mammies, matriarchs, welfare recipients, and hot mammas helps to justify their oppression (p. 69). In her book, she deals with the image of the Jezebel, which, she says, "represents a deviant Black female sexuality" (p. 81). Adams and Fuller (2006) describe the Jezebel (referred to in rap as the "ho" or "whore) as a "loose, sexually aggressive woman . . . who wants and accepts sexual activity in any form from men, and she often uses sex as a means to get what she wants from men" (p. 945). In Ludacris's song "Ho," he says:

> *You gotta run in your pantyhose*
> *Even your Daddy knows*
> *That you sucking down chocolate like Daddy-o's.*

That last line clearly refers to a woman performing a sex act on a man. In this song, he lists characteristics of a ho, from "hos never close they open like hallways" to "can't turn a ho into a housewife ['cause] hos don't act right." Even though further down in the song he says, "Niggas is hos too," it is clear here that this is a woman of little value. In another song, "Money Maker," Ludacris says:

> *Shake, shake, shake your moneymaker*
> *Like you were shaking it for some paper*
> *It took your momma 9 months to make ya*
> *Might as well shake what your momma gave ya*

This song makes the clear connection between women exchanging sexual favors for payment, a key feature of the "hoochie" image, of women who "attract men with money for a one-night stand" in hopes that it will land them pregnant (hence the phrase "hoochie mama") and in a "long-term relationship with a man with money" (Collins, 2000, p. 82). While these images are widespread and damaging, female hip-hop artists create alternative dialogues through their own engagement with hip-hop feminism. For instance, with her song "How Do I Love Thee," Queen Latifah defied the White patriarchal myth of the "Black Jezebel" by presenting an image of Black female sexuality that was not based on promiscuity (Collins, 2000).

As Adams and Fuller (2006) note, in contrast to the Jezebel, the image of the Sapphire grew out of the mammy figure, "generally depicted as an overweight, dark-skinned woman who appears to be asexual" (p. 944). Although by some accounts, the mammy was an asexual figure, the Sapphire is not (Morton, 1991, p. 7). They describe the Sapphire (referred to in rap as "the bitch") as a "socially aggressive woman who tries through manipulation to control her man. She is filled with attitude, has a fiery tongue, and she squashes the aspirations of her man or men in general" (p. 945). Keyes (2002) asserts that "some women of rap take a middle road" view to the term "bitch," saying that it depends on the context within which the word is used. For instance, in her interview with Queen Latifah, the rapper says:

> I don't really mind the term. I play around with it. I use it with my homegirls like, "Bitch are you crazy? Bitch is a fierce girl." Or "That bitch is so crazy, girl." Now, that is not harmful. But "This stupid bitch just came down here talking . . . ," now that is meant in a harmful way. So it's the meaning behind the word that to me describes whether I should turn it off or listen to it. (p. 200)

Addressing the counterdiscourse of Black female hip-hop artists, Keyes (2002) presents results of interviews with Black women performers and audience members. More specifically, Keyes draws from the work of Hazel Carby (1985) to explore how their discourse articulates a struggle over the objectification of female sexuality in order to reclaim their bodies and present images of themselves that mirror "the lifestyles of African American women in contemporary urban society" (p. 189). The images Keyes outlines include Queen Mother, Fly Girl, Sista with Attitude, and the Lesbian. According to Keyes, Queen Mother is reminiscent of "African-centered icons" like the Asiatic Black Women and Nubian Queens that reflect "sistas droppin' knowledge to the people" (p. 189). Queen Latifah's *All Hail the Queen* album (1989) is an example of this image. One of the most popular groups of their decade, Salt-N-Pepa, represented the Fly Girl, described as a woman with "voluptuous curves, but contrary to other 'mainstream' images of sexy, acquiescent women, . . . speaks what's on her mind" (p. 194). Keyes's next category, the Sista with Attitude, "comprises female MCs who value attitude as a means of empowerment and present themselves accordingly" (p. 200). MC Lyte and Eve are examples of this image. Her final category, the Lesbian, presents another response to White patriarchal power and sexual objectification by male rappers. Keyes chronicles the work of Queen Pen, recognized as "the first female MC to openly discuss lesbian culture" (p. 206).

There is much debate over where the misogyny toward Black women actually originated. At issue is whether rap music (as the leading element of hip-hop culture) creates and projects these negative images or whether it is merely reflective of a dominant social discourse that renders Black women inferior and without voice. In fact, in his article on Don Imus's gross misstep on the airwaves in which he referred to Black women on the Rutgers University basketball team as "nappy-headed hos," James Peterson wrote, "Hip hop is blamed for the racist assault on young Black women by a powerful, arrogant sixty-six-year-old white man who probably couldn't tell you the difference between Black Thought and Ja Rule" (p. 130). Peterson draws from an interview in which Imus defended his choice of words using the justification that hip-hop's own artists demean Black women. In his comments, Imus said:

> "I may be a white man, but I know that … young black women all through that society are demeaned and disparaged and disrespected … by their own black men and that they are called that name." In the interview, Imus said black rappers "call them worse names than I ever did." (p. 130)

Cultural critic Michael Eric Dyson weighed in on this debate in his book *Know What I Mean: Reflections on Hip-hop.* He argues critics of hip-hop have "got the line of detrimental influence backwards." Hip-hop has not helped mainstream misogyny that its artists invented; it is that the "ancient vitriol" toward women has been amplified in the mouths of some young Black males (Dyson, 2007, p. 135). Dyson adds further:

> White culture venomously attacked black women long before the birth of hip-hop. In fact, hip-hop has made the assault on black women stylish and perhaps more acceptable by supplying linguistic updates (like the word "ho") to deeply entrenched bigotry. (p. 135)

For Dyson, there are moral contradictions in society (i.e., young Black men who praise their mommas, but slam their baby mammas) that exist outside hip-hop culture and serve as a backdrop for hip-hop's misogyny. For him, these stereotypical images need to be discussed in a way that is both critical of the music and the sociopolitical space in which it exists (Dyson, 2007).

Dyson's argument adds a dichotomous contradiction not commonly addressed in discussions about the often degrading lyrics in rap music that specifically target Black women. The fact that the contradiction exists inside and outside of the realm of rap music leads to the necessity to fill a gaping hole in the research on misogyny within this music. In retrospect, the Imus controversy along with other high-profile instances of the use of racial and insensitive language in popular culture (i.e., comedians Michael Richards and Andy Dick's use of the "N" word) have done more to advance this discussion of the use of offensive language guised as entertainment than the analyses of the hip-hop culture and its use of similar offensive expressions. *Washington Post* writer Nekesa Mumbi Moody (2007) states in her article "Rappers Cleaning Up Lyrics Post-Imus" that the Imus controversy may be the catalyst that brings focus to offensive language in rap music. She notes months after the controversy, some artists' publicly abandoned offensive language and even some corporations began dropping rap acts from sponsorships due to explicit language.

With such highly charged debates about the "language of hip-hop," one would assume that the frequent targets of such language would stand unified and vocal about the toxic influence that misogynistic lyrics can have on the culture. Here lies the stark contradiction. What is characterized by many scholars as a perpetual influence of "Black-on-Black" hate on masses of young people who embrace and are part of the hip-hop culture, is seen by others as a hypocritical double standard when it comes to characterizing the use and meaning of some of the most degrading language in rap music. However, it is debatable whether hip-hop fosters internalized hostility toward African American females or engenders a form of feminism in its own right that positively heightens gender identity among Black women (Henry, 2010; Henry, West, & Jackson, 2010). Feminist scholars Patricia Hill Collins and Joan Morgan see this double consciousness as a congruent fixture in the sometimes turbulent nature of African American male and female relationships.

Despite the fact that hip-hop culture, particularly rap music, is heavily male-dominated, "a number of strong female voices have emerged from within the hip-hop industry, using rap music forms and other subgenres of hip hop music like neo soul to assert their own identities and to critique the limited identifications offered for women within the genre" (Bost, 2001). "Women are achieving major strides in rap music by continuing to chisel away at stereotypes ... by (re) defining women's culture and identity from a black feminist perspective" (Keyes, 2002, p. 208). Keyes goes on to argue that while women in this male-dominated industry "face overt racism," these MCs "move beyond the shadows of male rappers in diverse ways" (p. 208).

These "alternative voices" in hip-hop music are often integral in negating the perpetual influence of misogynistic and demeaning language found in much of rap and hip-hip music today. The influence of positive or conscious female hip-hop music has successfully taken root across the globe. In their article "Oppositional Consciousness within an Oppositional Realm," Phillips, Reddick-Morgan, and Stephens (2005) state that many historical accounts and critical analyses of the hip-hop phenomenon have tended to downplay the contributions of women. They state further that "women have played pivotal roles as artists, writers, performers, producers, and industry executives. Women have influenced rap style and techniques, ultimately shaping aesthetic standards and technological practices by both men and women" (p. 254). To localize this discussion, we focus on hip-hop's art in Detroit, Michigan.

THE DETROIT CONNECT

All the elements of hip-hop (deejaying, emceeing, b-boy or girling, and tagging or graffiti) are well represented in Detroit, Michigan. The hip-hop scene in Detroit has blazed a similar path as what has been seen around the world since the inception of this unique culture. The misogyny of the male-dominated music genre and the counterinfluence lead by positive female hip-hop artists have both coexisted in Detroit's rich hip-hop culture. Although women are underrepresented on the local scene, a few female artists have managed to make their mark. Two underground female emcees have emerged from the men's club of rap in Detroit. Bo$$, a gangster rapper from Michigan, has worked with DJ Quik and was signed to Def Jam West. Miz Korona has had a successful local career and made an appearance in the movie *8 Mile*. In the movie, Korona played the role of a female battle rapper during the scene at the automotive plant's lunch truck.

Unfortunately, just like female artists on the national scene, the women on

Michigan's hip-hop scene experience pressure to masculinize their identities and images for the sake of marketing. Rose (2004) argues that for critics of hip-hop "it is far easier to re-gender women rappers than to revise their own gender-coded analysis of rap music" (p. 292). Hip-hop simultaneously marginalizes women and stripes them of the gender identity while providing a space for a feminist perspective. Roberts (1991) points out that rappers like Queen Latifah, MC Lyte, and Roxanne Shante have successfully linked discourses of racial oppression with antimisogynistic lyrical content. This is an interesting phenomenon in a musical form largely considered misogynistic. To understand gender in the Detroit hip-hop scene, an analysis female performers from Michigan is essential.

Despite the disproportionate representation, Tricia Rose (2004) acknowledges that women have contributed to the narrative of resistance in hip-hop. This is true of Detroit native Bo$$. She operated as an early female voice in gangsta rap. Bo$$'s image as a rapper was "posing with automatic weapons and spitting malevolent rhymes about cop killing, liquor swilling, street hustling and being the 'b—— that's legit" (Smith, 2004). She joins the long tradition of hip-hop artists that provide a voice of resistance to marginalizing and oppressive structures. This resistance is in simultaneously pushes back against racist structures, while reinforcing misogynistic behavior. The use of the word "b——" can obviously be construed as oppressive, but it is the two words ("that's legit") that followed it that sent the marginalized message. These three words together imply that a woman that is authentic is an anomaly in hip-hop or street culture, thus prioritizing masculine identity traits over feminine identity traits.

According to Gan, Zillmann, and Mitrook (1997), Black female rappers match their male counterparts when it comes to sexually degrading content about other women. This can be seen in the song "Mai Sista Izza Bitch" Bo$$ has AMG, a male guest emcee, lyrically objectifying women with the line "Cause she's on some new improved shit / Cause this ho is a ('Bitch!') that ho is a ('Bitch!') / So my sista is a motherfuckin ('Bitch!')." These misogynistic lyrics occur alongside Bo$$ distancing herself from the women AMG is talking about. "[B]e creepin and freakin, ho after ho every weekend / But see I'm out to get a grip, a sista like myself / I'll grab the gat and get hazardous to a n——'s health." With this line, Bo$$ is sending the message that she is not like these other women, but the comments made by AMG are never condemned. In fact, she refers to herself using the same terminology. Bo$$ participates as "one of the guys" in "Mai Sista Izza Bitch." This gender imagery does not fit into Collins's (2000) framework of the typical depictions of Black women in popular culture—mammies, matriarchs, welfare recipients, and hot mammas. Similar to rapper Da Brat, Bo$$'s image as "one of the guys" does very little to resist oppressive structures. As Bost (2001) argues, to retain their positions, rappers like Da Brat "must present an image that appears superficially consistent with hip-hop stereotypes."

Bo$$'s identity construction calls for an additional lens to analyze the Black female imagery in hip-hop. Womanism allows for the exploration of Collins's (1991) concept of the dialectic of identity between race, gender, and class that Black women must reconcile. Hip-hop has long provided a platform to discuss racial oppression and social class imbalances. However, hip-hop still lacks a sizable space for the discussion of gender oppression. Female artists like Queen Latifah suggest an area for the unique marginalization faced by African American women in the songs. In her song "Ladies First," she says, "A woman can bear you, break you, take you / now it's time to rhyme, can you relate to / A sister dope enough to make you holler and scream." Through the lens of womanism, we see congruence between Queen Latifah's empowering message and the Bo$$'s discourse of resistance to hip-hop's limited possibilities for Black women.

In contrast, Miz Korona represents a place where lyrical ability is the most important trait. Somewhere between the male-appropriated traits of Bo$$ and the empowerment message of New York's Queen Latifah, Miz Korona is "a lioness in a lion's den." This statement supports the man's club mentality of hip-hop and describes Korona as a resister to this phenomenon. The space carved by Korona for herself in this male-dominated sport is much like Bo$$ through appropriating masculine behaviors. This is evident in her song "Rock Out." "It ain't coming / I'm gunnin' for all you bastards / . . . see if it's a game when I send your ass to ER." She uses violence to claim her place as the "lioness," not creating a new identity but using the accepted hip-hop aesthetic. Both Korona and Bo$$'s hip-hop identities support Tricia Rose's (2004) claim that "women rappers employ many of the aesthetic and culturally specific elements present in male rap lyrics." Both of these female Detroit rappers are adhering to the masculine themes of sex, power, and violence; however, Korona's songs are less oppressive to women.

Some might argue that using violent imagery, Miz Korona and Bo$$ regender themselves for the purpose of success in the rap music industry. Crossing that line of criticism of those who sexually objectify women is Bo$$'s song entitled "Recipe of a Hoe." While it is important to note that the male/female relationships in rap lyrics are complex, this complexity is reflected in Bo$$'s use of the words "bitch" and "ho," while at the same time questioning the conquest of males. "Claimin' they getting' it, / but on the real they really ain't getting shit / Steadily stressin' you knockin' the boots." Bo$$'s complicated identity proves that hip-hop is a form of discourse that allows space for confronting power (Morgan, 2005). Sexism remains apparent in rap music, but because of the resistant nature of the culture, women can simultaneously accept and reject marginalization.

Herein lays one of the major contradictions within hip-hop culture: Do lyrics that are consistent with hip-hop's stereotypes aid in the uplift and empowerment of Black women? Is it enough that women like Bo$$ and Miz Karona create a counterdiscourse to their male counterparts, or should we advocate an alternative discourse that allows for new possibilities for Black women to "represent" images that analyze the status quo? While these women comment on male references to women as hos and bitches, much like Da Brat, they make any feminist content difficult to decipher (Bost, 2001).

CONTRADICTIONS AND CONTRIBUTIONS: THE ROAD TO AN ALTERNATIVE DISCOURSE

Issues of race confound issues of gender. This is never more evident than when hip-hop magazine *The Source* revealed a tape made by a teenage Eminem disrespecting Black woman (Reid, 2003). In this "lost tape" Detroit emcee Eminem rhymes "Black girls only want your money cuz they dumb chicks," and "never date Black girls, because they only want your money / and that shit ain't funny." The fact that Eminem is a White male points to a troubling aspect of depictions of Black women in rap lyrics. Eminem credits these lyrics to a bad break-up; if this is the case or not cannot be confirmed. It does call into question how these messages about African American women in rap music affect the perception of Euro American male listeners of the music. According to Bakari Kitwana (2005), 70 percent of rap music is purchased by Euro American youths.

Emerson (2002) and Adams and Fuller (2006) illustrate how hip-hop presents distorted interpretations of Black women's sexuality. Use of words like "bitch" and "ho" about women, particularly Black women, undoubtedly has a negative effect on the receivers of this message. For Whites, this is exacerbated by the fact that they are likely to have less exposure to alternative depictions Black women. For example, a suburb just a few miles from the city of Detroit, Livonia is the "whitest" city in the United States with over 100,000 people, while Detroit has the highest majority of Black persons among cities over 100,000 accounting for 82.7% of residents in 2010 (French, 2002, 2012; U.S. Census Bureau, 2013). This provides limited opportunity to have interracial interactions. Providing a space for a communal discussion of the distorted characterizations of Black women in rap lyrics/videos, which may be the only representations White male youths experience, is essential to countering these images.

The work of Dyson (2007), Collins (2000, 2006), Morgan (1995) and others have shown how hip-hop music and culture has contributed to oppressive images of Black women. When analyzing the lyrics of Eminem and Ludacris, it is undeniable hip-hop music can further marginalize women. Even when the music is performed by female artists, as seen in the case of Bo$$, the marginalization female identity can be seen. In the case of Eminem's lost tape, some come from Euro American males. It is important to note that while these lyrics do not reflect the totality of hip-hop is, it definitely reflects the music that mainstreams.

One.Be.Lo from Pontiac, Michigan, on his song "E.T.," expresses the relationship between a man and women in a much different way than AMG in the Bo$$ track. "Communication is the key, unlock / We put our heads together like a Mt. Rushmore / I found what I was / lookin for, plus more / Now with you I wanna spend the rest of days / Cause you shine in an extraterrestrial way." Los talks of relationships as mental not purely physical, as a union, not oppositional, and describes the woman with the word "shine" not "ho."

The image presented by One.Be.Lo is counter to Adams and Fuller's (2006) Sapphire and Jezebel. It even provides an alternative depiction for those provided by Collins (2000) of Black women as mammies, matriarchs, welfare recipients, and hot mammas. His lyrics present an intellectual attractiveness—a move away from the body-confining identity presented in the words of Ludacris discussed in this chapter.

Why a feminist analysis? The real benefit of a feminist analysis of this phenomenon is the opportunity it provides for moving beyond mere images and representations of Black women in hip-hop lyrics, toward a concrete discussion of how Black women artists engage feminism within this cultural framework. In other words, how do they carve out a space to express their feminist dialogue within the art form? Peoples (2008) contends that as we engage hip-hop feminism in terms of how it operates in the sociopolitical space we call hip-hop, we can begin to better understand the nature of resistance it represents (p. 21). For many women artists, hip-hop not only lends a space for them to critique hegemony and racism, but also to articulate a counterdiscourse of liberation from the hypersexed, money-driven female hustler depictions that have plagued them in and out of this culture.

As we continue to engage hip-hop feminists' contributions to the debate on misogyny, we must abandon the notion of hip-hop feminism as merely a *counter-* discourse that perpetuates hatred and disdain between Black men and women and embrace the notion of an *alternative* discourse where hip-hop feminists (men and women) can seek to counter oppression that is ever present and foster coping strategies to combat the negativity that has become normalized in everyday life. We must also pursue the transformative space that is created when Black female rappers use hip-hop as a platform for their own feminist discourse because it is this discourse that makes the alternative possible. Jamila (2002) urges that "as women of the hip-hop generation we need a feminist consciousness that allows us to examine how representations and images can be simultaneously empowering and problematic" (p. 392).

As Hobson and Bartlow (2008) point out, artists like "MC Lyte, Queen Latifah, Yo-Yo, Da Brat, Sistah Souljah, and Eve, have all evolved from simply 'talking back' to sexist scripts produced by men to articulating their own perspectives on sexual, racial and class politics in their music" (p 4). In addition to this list of female artists, Erykah Badu, Lauryn Hill, and Jill Scott are members of the larger realm of hip-hop culture, which encompasses a broader scope of the genre and adds positive social and political messages to the hip-hop culture. While these women have contributed to the dialogue on the imaging of Black women in hip-hop, there are other artists whose work presents a barrage of contradictions. For instance, Lil' Kim and Foxy Brown and Trina "have largely embodied tropes of black female hypersexuality" not only by conforming to the notion of being a sexual object, but by flaunting that sexuality as a false sense of power in the further commodification and objectification of the female body (Hobson & Bartlow, 2008, p. 4). Often in relating to power (that Foucault says is always present), we become complicit in the very power we struggle against. While some, like Queen Latifah, have broken away from the oversexualized images perpetuated in much of rap's music, artists like Da Brat, the Bo$$, and Miz Karona uphold more traditional stereotypical images of Black women. It seems that what makes Latifah and the rest "feminist" is their resistance to the dominant discourse (Hobson & Bartlow, 2008). Bost (2001) argues that the ways in which rappers like Latifah, MC Lyte, and Yo-Yo enacted their critique of rap music's misogyny "distanced them from dominant media images of hip-hop gender roles and thus limited their audiences."

Tricia Rose and Patricia Hill Collins help to make the argument that a continued evaluation of Black women artists *only* in relation to their male counterparts and *only* in relation to the misogynistic lyrics that help to keep them subjugated prevents a deeper exploration of the broader goal of hip-hop feminists, which is to examine the contradictions and contributions that lie at the intersection of the feminist movement and hip-hop culture.

For Collins and Morgan, the struggles within the hip-hop community mirror the struggles within the Black community—reflecting a need to repair the damaged relationship between Black men and women that is central to the survival of the Black family and ultimately the Black community. In fact, as Collins (2006) articulates, Morgan is one of the leaders in the discussion of Black hip-hop feminism being an intersection of Black women's relationships with "their personal and political histories," with themselves and with Black men (p. 192). As for the nexus between racial and gender identity with hip-hop, Collins notes the historical significance of having a collective identity, which can only be preserved through "community work" activities in the African American community as a means of understanding the dialectical relationship between Black men and women.

Collins (2006) describes "community work" in the African American community as a form of reproductive labor to (1) ensure the physical survival of African American children; (2) build Black identities that would protect African Americans from White supremacy; (3) uphold viable African American families, organizations, and other institutions, of Black civil society; and (4) transform schools, job settings, government agencies, and other important social institutions to ensure fair and equal Black participation. How does hip-hop affect this discussion of community and empowerment? Collins's research provides opportunities to open the dialogue on the use of hip-hop as a social force to reclaim sociopolitical power in the Black community. There is much discussion about the potential of hip-hop to provide liberation and "progressive political practice" (Peoples, 2008, p. 20). For this to happen, however, we must overcome the contradictions and take a reflective look at how hip-hop culture and the music it produces is merely a reflection of the limited "sociopolitical space" that has historically existed for African Americans as a part of mainstream culture.

In her article "Fly Girls, Bitches, and Hoes" (1995), Morgan states that rap music is essential to the struggle against sexism "because it takes us straight to the battlefield" (p. 153).

> My decision to expose myself to the sexism of Dr. Dre, Ice Cube, Snoop Doggy Dog, or the Notorious BIG is really my plea to my brothers to tell me why they are who they are. I need to know why they are so angry at me. Why is disrespecting me one of the few things that will make them feel like men? What are they going through on the daily that's got them acting so fucked up. (p. 153)

Although the notions of community work and a collective struggle for community have had historical significance in explaining the relationship between Black men and women, today's social ills and oppression have tainted these ideological notions of a Black community. In fact, Collins asserts that gendered structures of power continue to impede the Black community and that notions of Black feminist empowerment have not had much effect on African American women and girls. This lack of empowerment, Collins notes, explains to some degree why there is sustained support for Black rap artists whose work is "riddled with misogyny, the cavalier use of terms such as 'bitches' and 'hos' to refer to black women in everyday speech" (2006, p. 136).

In her analysis of Julia Cooper's work at the turn of the twentieth century, Carby (1985) characterizes the plight of Negro women in that day in a way that we can similarly embrace. She said for Cooper, "to be a woman of the Negro race in America" was to be able to "grasp the deep significance of the possibilities of the crisis ... [it is] to have a heritage ... that is unique in the ages" (p. 265). According to Carby, Cooper saw the responsibility of the Black woman as reshaping the society "to stamp weal or woe on the coming history of this people" (p. 265). Young women like Moya Bailey from Spelman College signify the possibilities and contributions that can be created through this kind of role modeling. When she led a protest of rapper Nelly and his appearance on Spelman's campus for a charitable event because of his misogynistic lyrics in controversial songs like "Tip Drill." There are many other examples of this kind of blueprint for raising the consciousness of rap music and hip-hop culture, including *Essence* magazine's "Take Back the Music" campaign (2005) and the Rock the Vote and Vote or Die campaigns to increase participation of urban youth in the voting process.

Clearly, there is liberating potential in both rap music and hip-hop culture. The real test will be women and men who are not afraid to engage the misogynistic discourse in ways that create space for the role, positionality, and image of women on a local and global level that counter the patriarchal abuse of Black women's sexuality (Carby, 1985; Hobson & Bartlow, 2008). According to Keyes (2002), "black women rappers are in dialogue with one another, black men, black women, and dominant American culture as they struggle to define themselves . . . and to refute, deconstruct and reconstruct alternative visions of their identity" (p. 209). Hip-hop's historical roots provide an opportunity from which we can understand the potential and problematic of Black male/female relationships, the multiple and sometimes muted voices of female artists, and the myriad ways that these women manifest resistance to oppression within and outside of their own communities.

REFERENCES

Adams, T.M., & Fuller, D.B. (2006). The words have changed but the ideology remains the same: Misogynistic lyrics in rap music. *Journal of Black Studies, 39*, 938–957.

Bennett, A. (2000). *Popular music and youth culture: music, identity and place.* New York: Palgrave Macmillan.

Bost, S. (2001). Be deceived if ya wanna be foolish: (Re) constructing body, genre, and gender in feminist rap. *Postmodern Culture, 12*(1). Retrieved via ProQuest from http://muse.jhu.edu.proxy.lib.wayne.edu/journals/pmc/vo12/12.1bost.html.

Byrd, A. (2004). Claiming Jezebel: Black female subjectivity and sexual expression in hip-hop. In V. Labaton & D.L. Martin (Eds.), *The fire this time: Young activists and the new feminism* (pp. 3–18). New York: Anchor Books.

Carby, H.V. (1985). On the threshold of woman's era: Lynching, empire, and sexuality in Black feminist theory. *Critical Inquiry, 12*(1), 262–277.

Collins, P.H. (1991). *Black feminist thought: Knowledge, consciousness, and the politics of empowerment.* New York: Routledge.

Collins, P.H. (2000). *Black feminist thought: Knowledge, consciousness, and the politics of empowerment.* 2nd ed. New York: Routledge.

Collins, P.H. (2006). *From Black power to hip hop: Racism, nationalism, and feminism.* Philadelphia: Temple University Press.

Davis, A.Y. (1995). Afterword. In R. Walker (Ed.), *To be real: Telling the truth and changing the face of feminism* (pp. 279–284). New York: Anchor Books.

Dyson, M.E. (2003). *Open mike: Reflections on philosophy, race, sex, culture and religion.* New York: Basic Civitas Books.

Dyson, M.E. (2007). *Know what I mean? Reflections on hip-hop.* Philadelphia: Perseus Books.

Emerson, R.A. (2002). "Where my girls at?" Negotiating Black womanhood in music videos. *Gender and Society, 12*(1), 115–135.

French, R. (2002). *New segregation: Race accepts divide.* Retrieved from http://www.detnews.com/specialreports/2002/segregation/a01-389727.htm.

French, R. (2012). Wayne State University: In a Black-majority city, but one of the worst at graduating African-Americans. Retrieved from http://www.mlive.com/news/detroit/index.ssf/2012/02/at_wayne_st_easy_to_get_in_dif.html.

Gen, S., Zillmann, D., & Mitrook, M. (1997). Stereotyping effect of Black women's sexual rap on White audiences. *Basic and Applied Social Psychology, 19*(3), 381–399.

Gilkes, C.T. (1983). From slavery to social welfare: Racism and the control of Black women. In A. Swerdlow and H. Lessinger (Eds.), *Class, race, and sex: Dynamics of control* (pp. 288–300). Boston: G. K. Hall.

Guy-Sheftall, B. (Ed.). (1995). *Words of fire: An anthology of African-American feminist thought.* New York: W.W. Norton & Company.

Henry, W.J. (2010). Hip-hop feminism: A standpoint to enhance the positive self-identity of Black college women. *Journal of Student Affairs Research and Practice, 47*(2). Retrieved from http://journals.naspa.org/jsarp/vol47/iss2/art1/?sending=11039.

Henry, W.J., West, N.M., & Jackson, A. (2010). Hip-hop's influence on the identity development of Black female college students: A literature review. *Journal of College Student Development, 51*(3), 237–251.

Hobson, J., & Bartlow, R.D. (2008). "Representin': Women, hip-hop, and popular music. *Meridians: Feminism, Race, and Transnationalism, 8*(1), 1–14.

Jamila, S. (2002). "Can I get a witness? Testimony from a hip-hop feminist." In D. Hernandez and B. Rehman (Eds.), *Colonize this! Young women of color on today's feminism* (pp. 382–394). New York: Seal Press.

Keyes, C.L. (2002). *Rap music and street consciousness.* Urbana: University of Illinois Press.

Kitwana, B. (2005). *The cotton club: Black-conscious hip-hop deals with an overwhelmingly white live audience.* Retrieved from http://www.villagevoice.com/2005-06-21/music/the-cotton-club/.

Moody, N.M. (2007). Rappers cleaning up lyrics post-Imus. *The Washington Post.* Retrieved from http://www.washingtonpost.com/wp-dyn/content/article/2007/08/02/AR2007080201607.html.

Morgan, J. (1995). Fly-Girls, bitches, and hoes: Notes of a hip hop feminist. *Social Text, 45,* 151–157.

Morgan, M. (2005). Hip-hop women shredding the veil: Race and class in popular feminist identity. *South Atlantic Quarterly, 104*(3), 425–444.

Morton, P. (1991). *Disfigured images: The historical assault on Afro-American women.* Westport, CT: Praeger.

Peoples, W.A. (2008). "Under construction": Identifying foundations of hip-hop feminism and exploring bridges between Black second-wave and hip-hop feminisms. *Meridians: Feminism, Race, Tran nationalism, 8*(1), 19–52.

Phillips, L., Reddick-Morgan, K., & Stephens, D.P. (2005). Oppositional consciousness within an oppositional realm: The case of feminism and womanism in rap and hip hop, 1976–2004. *Journal of African American History, 90*(3), 253–277.

Pough, G.D. (2007). "What it do, Shorty?" Women, hip-hop, and a feminist agenda. *Black Women, Gender, and Families, 1*(2), 78–99.

Reid, S. (2003). *The Source digs up tape of Eminem using racial slur.* MTV Online. Retrieved from http://www.mtv.com/news/articles/1480512/20031118/eminem.jhtml.

Roberts, R. (1991). Music videos, performance, and resistance: Feminist rappers. *Journal of Popular Culture, 25*(2), 141–152.

Rose, T. (1994). *Black noise: Rap music and Black culture in contemporary America.*

Rose, T. (2004). Never trust a big butt and a smile. In M. Forman and M.A. Neal (Eds.), *That's the joint! The hip-hop studies reader* (pp. 291–306). New York: Routledge.

Smith B. (2004). *Same as the old Boss.* Metro Times Online. Retrieved from http://www.metrotimes.com/editorial/story.asp?id=6344.

Turner, K.K. (2002). *Sun Messenger*. Metro Times Online. Retrieved from http://metrotimes.com/editorial/story.asp?id=3013.

U.S. Census Bureau (2013). *State and county quick facts: Detroit (city) Michigan.* Retrieved from http://quickfacts.census.gov/qfd/states/26/2622000.html.

Weheliye, A. (2001). Keepin' it (un) real: Perusing the boundaries of hip-hop culture. *New Centennial Review, 1*(2), 291–310.

PART 4

Psychosocial and Health Matters

Legacies of Shame and Blood

INTIMATE PARTNER VIOLENCE AMONG
AFRICAN AMERICAN WOMEN

DEVIKA DIBYA CHOUDHURI

When the very person who is battering you is also your brother in the struggle for community survival; when you know that in calling the police that you and your partner are likely to be pre-judged as inhumane and animalistic, as naturally prone to bloodshed, and that you both may be carted off to jail; when seeking safety options means turning over someone you love and who is already expected to be imprisoned within his lifetime; when you know that as strong as you are expected to be, that you may not be able to convince your friends or even your family that yes, you are a victim of intimate partner violence; then the experience can be characterized as "bad."

—*Tonya Lovelace, "Black Women and Violence"*

Intimate partner violence (IPV) is the current term used to describe the incidence of violence in the context of relationship. The term "domestic violence" is seen as a subcomponent of the violence that often rages within a home, where an adult is targeted by a partner. IPV also includes child sexual and physical abuse. Unfortunately, it is all too common.

Abbott and coauthors (1995) estimated that 6 percent to 15 percent of women experience domestic violence in a given year, with a lifetime prevalence estimated at 28 percent to 54 percent. While domestic violence affects all Americans, regardless of race, gender, or socioeconomic status, this threat has unduly dire consequences for African American women. If we disaggregate IPV incidents by race/ethnicity, African American females are victimized the most, followed by Whites and Latinos, and Asians were victimized the least (Cho, 2012). Asians were the least likely to be victimized by IPV, even when controlling for sociodemographic variables; African American women experience intimate partner violence at rates 35 percent higher than White women do and 2.5 times the rate of men (Rennison & Welchans, 2000). More horrifically, the leading cause of death for African American women in the ages of 15 to 45 is intimate partner homicide (Campbell et al., 2003). As with other populations, African American women are particularly at risk during pregnancy.

Bessie Smith and Billie Holiday, among other Black female musicians, chronicled the abuse in their lives and documented the violence they experienced through their music, making it worthy of public discourse as well as underscoring how common it is (Davis, 1998). In *Sweet Rough Man*, the lines go, "I woke up this mornin,' my head was sore as a boil / My man beat me last night with five feet of copper coil" (Gertrude Rainey, cited in Davis, 1998, p. 28). This violence includes child abuse, both physical and sexual, violence during dating, violence in committed partnerships, and sexual harassment and assault.

Interpersonal Violence in Michigan

Michigan does not appear to report the breakdown of its statistics on domestic violence by race, and so while there is a high incidence of domestic violence, it is not possible to group it. There are reportedly 45 domestic violence shelters in 83 counties. In 2002, approximately 12,000 residential women and children were served, while over 19,000 nonresidential women and children were served. According to the Michigan Domestic Violence Prevention and Treatment Board, from October 2003 to September 2004, domestic violence programs in Michigan received 55,208 crisis calls, an average of 151 crisis calls per day. Michigan domestic violence programs provided residential and nonresidential services to 56,924 women and children. During the same year, 6,466 victims were denied access to shelter due to lack of space

(Blue Cross Blue Shield Blue Care Network of Michigan, 2007). On September 15, 2010, 54 out of 62, or 87 percent, of identified local domestic violence programs in Michigan participated in the 2010 National Census of Domestic Violence Services and reported that over 2,000 victims of violence sought shelter (Michigan Coalition Against Domestic and Sexual Violence, 2011). The incidences reported below specific to African Americans are through national reports.

CHILDHOOD ABUSE

Estimates vary greatly with this form of violence, with studies estimating from 15 percent to almost a third of African American women surveyed reporting a history of child abuse (West, 2002). To compound the mistreatment, while African American women report an array of sexually abusive experiences during childhood, they are far more at risk for particularly severe violence, with over 61 percent of those who reported abuse having experienced vaginal, oral, or anal penetration (Wyatt et al., 1999). One explanation is that due to marital patterns in the community, a disproportionate number of African American girls are vulnerable to predation by stepfathers or mothers' boyfriends. Childhood abuse leads to increased risk of adult victimization, and here too, the statistics hold horrifyingly true, with many adult Black women survivors of childhood abuse experiencing repeated victimization (West, Williams, & Siegel, 2000).

DATING VIOLENCE

Also referred to as courtship violence or premarital abuse, many young African American women experience high levels of aggression that primarily take the form of verbal and emotional abuse. According to Clark and coauthors (1994), over 90 percent of African American college students report swearing, name-calling, and insulting during a relationship. However, over one-third of students had escalated to being either perpetrators or victims of physical aggression with hitting, pushing, and slapping some of the primary examples. African American adolescent females were as likely as or more likely than their male peers to inflict physical and emotional aggression (Watson et al., 2001). However, if we examine the types of violence enacted, African American females were more likely to be victimized by more injurious violence (West & Rose, 2000). Therefore, while an adolescent girl might make threats, throw objects, and slap her dating partner, she was more likely to experience in turn choking, attempted rape, and broken bones from her male partner. One explanation of such high levels is that witnessing violence in the community or at home leads one to be at increased risk, and may be a reason for the high level of aggression in intimate relationships.

SEXUAL ASSAULT

In one national study, 7 percent of Black women were identified as survivors of rape (Tjaden & Thoennes, 2000). However, estimates suggest that only a small proportion of sexual assaults are reported and there is a much higher incidence. This is borne out by data collected from self-reports, where 20 percent of African American adolescent girls, and over 30 percent of college and adult women, reported having been sexually assaulted (West, 2002). Working to underscore this underreporting is a historically grounded belief that African American women, in their long history of being sexual objects to be acted upon are in effect, unrapeable. According to Donovan and Williams (2002), during slavery— there being no legal consequences of raping a Black woman other than interfering with the property of another man—any injury was, in effect, an economic one done to her "owner." African American women were not perceived to have ownership over their own bodies. This assumption is reflected today when in study after study, responders are less likely to characterize a sexual assault scenario with a Black woman as rape, to believe it should be reported, or hold the perpetrator accountable (Donovan & Williams, 2002).

SEXUAL HARASSMENT

Unwanted sexual talk, contact, pressure, advances, and assault that may be categorized as a quid pro quo, referring to the exchange of special privileges in exchange for sexual favors, or a hostile environment that creates an unpleasant work atmosphere, constitute sexual harassment. For African American women this has happened in a variety of settings, in church, the street, social settings, academic settings, and employment. Historically, of course, enslaved African American women were sexually objectified, subjugated and assaulted by both White and Black men on plantations. Before being sold, they were stripped naked and examined on the auction block.

This exploitation was a daily occurrence on the plantation. When federal laws prohibited the importation of Africans, Black women were required to reproduce in order to replenish the enslaved workforce (Donovan & Williams, 2002). However, after Emancipation, many women could find employment primarily in households as domestic labor, an isolated and powerless workspace that left them vulnerable to sexual harassment (Adams, 1997). Today sexual harassment continues to be an unpleasant reality in the lives of Black women, who are even more vulnerable when they are working in low-status jobs. Professional women are not exempted and may even be harassed because of their achieved status, with *contrapower* sexual harassment by White and male subordinates, as well as colleagues and supervisors, a frequent experience to remind them of their status as members of a marginalized social group regardless of their achievements (West, 2002).

INTIMATE PARTNER VIOLENCE

Most researchers have investigated the incidence of violence in heterosexual relationships, and African American women experience alarmingly high rates of such abuse. A quarter of African American women surveyed in the national Violence Against Women Survey had experienced physical partner abuse, and 4 percent had been stalked (Tjaden & Thoennes, 2000). In a sample of pregnant women who used a community gynecologic and obstetric clinic, 50 percent had a history of abuse or were currently in an abusive relationship (West, 2002). African American women who are impoverished, young, and live in urban areas are disproportionately at risk for battering.

The Intersection of Toxic Beliefs and Twisted Structures

The violence that African American women experience does not happen in social neutrality. African Americans are no more culturally or biologically prone to intimate partner violence than other groups. However there is growing evidence that the systematic economic and social disadvantaging of African Americans places them at higher risk (West, 2004). There appear to be particular structural and situational contexts that are historically influenced and impacted by current factors. Madhubuti (1990) examined the intergenerational exposure to racism and sexism and the racial discrimination that resulted in significant inequalities in education, employment, and wealth production. In a society where men are socialized to link manhood with the ability to be independent, self-sufficient providers, structural barriers to achieving such roles means that African American men may well find alternative definitions of manhood that involve domination of subordinates within their own community. African Americans had always been paid less, fired first in times of economic upheaval, and reemployed later than their White counterparts, and this chronic unemployment and underemployment lead to stressors in the African American community, where frustration and anger was historically displaced to women and children (Hampton, Oliver, & Magarian, 2003).

> [Black men] need to have [themselves] "pumped up" all the time. It's by history that it is there. There's so much that's happened in [Black] families. It's not like our husbands in America kept us at home. This history of slavery was such that after slavery, Black men wanted so much for Black women to be what they saw White women to be to White men. . . . [But] we worked the fields. Our hands were hard, and we were rough in our exterior, because we have to survive that way. They wanted a nice, card-carrying "Black-White" woman with a parasol that's at home cooking for her man. So, when our men start saying, "You will cook for me [or] you will do something for me," it's out of that context. (Nash, 2005, p. 1434)

Murder of African American women between the ages of 15 and 45 by intimate partners usually occurs during the course of an argument and involves the use of a firearm. However, the strongest demographic predictor is the abuser's unemployment rather than race. Since African American men are disproportionately overrepresented among the unemployed, this may be a contributing factor to the elevated murder rates of African American women (West, 2004).

On a cultural and community level, the segregation of and isolation within concentrated urban areas of many African Americans has exacerbated these stressors. While the societal wide sexism leads most men to believe themselves innately superior to women, institutionalized racism has blocked the access of African American men to educational and employment opportunities where they can dominate African American women in manners achieved by White men. Consequently, the dependence of African American men on the economic resources provided by working spouses and partners has led to what has been termed as a subordinated masculinity that requires a redefinition of masculinity to access male supremacy without the adjuncts of male social and economic power (Hampton, Oliver, & Magarian, 2003). Essentially, one way to exert control over an economically independent female partner is through violence.

> The only place that I believe that Black men have ever historically had a sense of having power is in the home and the church.... They needed those institutions. ... They were "somebody" in those communities. And Black women, we agreed. We weren't just the victims in that. We agreed to that, because the '6os Black Power movement said that Black men needed to be empowered. We forgot that we ... too [need to be empowered].... We really got left out of the deal. That's who we are as women. We sacrifice like that. (Nash, 2005, p. 1430)

Ethnographic accounts have characterized a stance of toughness toward other men and an exploitative orientation to women in intimate relationships (Anderson, 1999). When violence becomes an acceptable method of resolving conflicts, acts of intimate partner violence rise. African American women are more likely to kill a partner and are, at the same time, twice as likely to be killed because of domestic violence, as White women are (Bent-Goodley, 2004). As the community becomes more violent, members become more socially isolated, powerless, and impoverished, with fewer resources to call upon, and the cycle of violence both on the street and in the home, becomes increasingly pronounced. Within this hothouse, frustration and enforced idleness can lead to higher levels of substance abuse, the dealing, selling, and using of drugs, and the use of sexual conquest as a form of entertainment (Anderson, 1999). Alcohol and other substances has been found to be a significant risk factor in interpersonal violence committed in intimate settings, and the greater usage and abuse by both African American men and women means a greater preponderance of impulsivity, aggression due to psychopharmacological effects, conflict over money and control of the drug, social isolation due to the illegal activities, and the stressor of suspected infidelity in exchange for drugs (Hampton, Oliver, & Magarian, 2003).

Racism and sexism lead to other strongly held beliefs that have been used to justify and explain away the frightening level of violence against African American women and that are projected onto members of the community by their own. Taking the high levels of violence in the African American community as typical leads to an assumption that African American women are accustomed to such levels and are therefore less harmed by them. Interwoven with this belief is that of the strong Black woman who is resilient and enduring; and thus can withstand such violence. Of course, most such comparisons have an unspoken relative standard of White womanhood, a historical comparison that put White women on a lofty moral and spiritual pedestal that was ultimately helpless, while stripping African American women of their humanity by likening them to beasts (Giddings, 1996).

> It goes way back to slavery, and it's still here. A Black woman will be treated with more respect than a Black man by a White man. [For example,] if I want to get a job working in the house for this White woman, and my husband, this Black man, wants to be their yard man? Well, that White man would "talk down" to him, whereas, he wouldn't dare with me, because he would want to flirt with me. That still happens! [laughs] . . . [That White man] doesn't want that Black man to feel secure. He wants to always make him feel that he has this foot on his neck. . . . How do you think [that that Black man] is going to act when he gets home? (Nash, 2005, p. 1433)

Gillum (2002) explored two racist tropes in the context of intimate partner violence against African American women. The stereotypes of the Jezebel and the matriarch may be significantly linked to negative relationships between African American men and women. The matriarch is depicted as a loud and large, darker-complexioned woman whose primary emasculating role toward African American men is to use insults and humiliations. The Jezebel is depicted as sexually aggressive, promiscuous, and easily aroused. These stereotypes were constructed during the slavery era by Whites, and were used to justify the exploitation and oppression of African American women by the White slavers. The infantilizing of African American men via the matriarch stereotype was helpful to the control of Black men by White men. The sexual subjugation of African American women was justified by the Jezebel stereotype that recast their exploitation as of their own desiring.

The current endorsement of such beliefs is a testament to the continuing structural requirements of racism and White supremacy as well as the generational effects of internalized oppression. Such endorsement occurs through media depictions that ratify such notions. Realities of communities have also underscored such depictions where African American women have historically been the center of the family, and the glue that makes the bonds between kin enduring, in the middle of a larger dominant society that negatively ascribes single parenthood, poverty, divorce, and increased violence to such matrifocal family structures (Gillum, 2002). The study by Gillum (2002) found that while high levels of African American men positively endorsed these stereotypes, it was the Jezebel stereotype that was most often correlated with justification of intimate partner violence. In a society where sexual expression is limited for women and glorified for men, the Jezebel stereotype permits men to use physical force to punish and control women perceived to be so depicted.

Spirituality has been linked to historical survival of African Americans through the holocaust of slavery, and it is a source of strength for many African American women. However, sometimes the patriarchal messages of the church would echo some of the other cultural messages that enjoined women to continue to hold the burden for being victimized by violence.

> Well, if I felt he needed me, I would do the Christian way and act like I did [act]. A Christian would [not] . . . go in there and fight him when he was ill. I'd see what he wanted and try to make him comfortable. . . . And then after I got in there waiting on him, he still treated me nasty. But I went ahead [and cared for him]. (Nash, 2005, p. 1427)

Several other cultural beliefs and values that have historically served African American women to help them endure oppression have also become traps to reify their position as survivors. These include the interrelated ideas of the strong Black woman, who must by virtue of her womanhood put the service of the race first; the nurturer and protector who must look out for the needs of others; and the expectation that they must be the ambassador of the race.

Due to the shared experience of racism, African American women must partner with African American men to withstand the forces arrayed against the community. The perception has often been that for African American woman, racism is more important than sexism and that choosing to focus on gender oppression is akin to being a race traitor. According to Bent-Goodley (2004), women will often deny their unique experiences as women to protect African American men from being held accountable for their behavior. One of the perceived roles of African American women is to put the needs of others before their own (Hill-Collins, 1991).

I think that the world beats up on Black men enough. It does. I feel that the Black man gets whipped in a White society and, therefore, feeling that way, he should be able to come home to where he doesn't have to deal with who is going to be the leader of that household. (Nash, 2005, p. 1430)

The saying goes that in African American families, you raise your daughters and love your sons. From an early age, African American girls are given a role of being strong, taking care of their men who are perceived as endangered, threatened, and fragile. The protective stance thus engendered means that African American females have the responsibility to be both nurturers and providers, while at the same time, deeply empathic of the racial aggressions, insults, and assaults inflicted on African American men.

What I found profound about my own situation and my decision to not leave was that I looked at my sons—little Black boys—growing up without a father in America, and knowing that they already had strikes against them by virtue of them being born into a world as Black men. (Nash, 2005, p. 1429)

Unable to change the larger society's oppression, it becomes their responsibility to understand and excuse the frustration and anger of their menfolk, sometimes literally taking on the hurts and wounds into their own selves. In other words, African American women have been reared to repair the damage dealt the Black family through economic and racial adversity. Many women will then hesitate to report instances of IPV because of their fear of entrapping the perpetrator in the brutalities of the criminal justice system.

There are so many [Black men] there [in prison] already. So, if we speak out and say, "He beat me," then you are putting them in the penal system. . . . [So,] you don't "tell!" If you "tell," you are putting a Black man in the system. If I told on Lee that means that the criminal justice system would be brought into play. That means another Black man would be put into the criminal justice system. And it's your fault. (Nash, 2005, p. 1428)

Beyond protecting African American men, women also have been assigned the task of being ambassadors of the race, responsible in their own persons to minimize the negative portrayals. Maintaining racial loyalty for the strong Black woman thus has the effects of sustaining abuse to protect the family and community at the expense of her own physical and emotional safety. This cultural pact to protect the African American community from being pathologized leads to a severe underreporting of Black-on-Black intimate violence and an ongoing endurance of violence (Nash, 2005). For many African American women, institutional racism causes African American men to compete for social mobility and to perceive African American women as the reason and convenient target of their oppression.

> It makes me angry, but not at [Black men] so much, but because of why they are like that. . . . [Black women] were brought in places so [Black men] wouldn't be brought in places, because we are the less threatening of the two. . . . So [Black men] did take some of the punishment around the assertiveness of that. And I think that they think they deserve a lot of reward around that. But they can't see the punishment [Black women] took and the sacrifices we made. And in the midst of this, it's like: "You can go to school. You all have opportunities to do this. You all have this and that—and [Black men] don't." (Nash, 2005, p. 1435)

Gender entrapment theory (Richie, 1996) is defined as "the socially constructed process whereby African American women who are vulnerable to male violence in their intimate relationship are penalized for behaviors they engage in even when behaviors are logical extensions of their racialized identities, their culturally expected gender roles, and the violence in their intimate relationships" (Richie, 1996, p. 4). Often, African American women are incarcerated at higher levels for IPV than White women. Essentially, the justice system penalizes African American women for the violence they experience and the ways in which they respond and cope with it. Duley (2006) relates examples of several women who were given life sentences for having been forced to be present during a fatal beating by their abuser, while they themselves were tortured and abused with no recourse to protection. Typically, women are thus doubly punished—first by the abuse they experience from their partners and then by the justice system for their relationship with these partners; represented as participating gents in the criminal enterprise rather than as victims.

The increasing reliance on state mechanisms for addressing violence against women leads to less reporting rather than more since such mechanisms are associated with less self-determination and stifling of political advocacy. The National Institute of Justice found that "increased legal advocacy resources are associated with fewer white women being killed by their husbands and more black women being killed by their boyfriends" (Eng & Dasgupta, 2003, p. 9). Dulles (2007) makes the argument that restraining orders to limit abuse and striving to punish perpetrators through incarceration makes women who share children with abusers reluctant to enter the system where the state can then exert as much control over their lives as the batterer used to. There is little evidence that such protective orders increase safety and much anecdotal evidence that they increase danger as the perpetrator feels at greater threat of loss.

> I didn't tell them [child protective services] because I knew what would happen. They told me I couldn't take care of my kids if I stayed with him. Do you know they took my kids? It took me six months to get them back. Now when the worker comes to my house, my kids hide. (Bent-Goodley, 2004, p. 313)

On a related note, the child welfare system is another mechanism that African American women are more vulnerable to in situations of IPV. Survivors of IPV can be convicted of failing to protect their children from the abuser or of parental kidnapping when they do try and protect their children by removing them from the abuser's orbit. In either case, their efforts to protect their children by staying and bearing the abuse or by leaving the abuser are cause for losing their children. Dulles (2007) gives the example of a survivor who, after receiving a brutal beating and witnessing the near fatal beating of her son, was told by her abuser that she was only allowed to bring her unconscious two-year-old to the hospital if she took the blame for committing the abuse. In exchange for saving her son's life, she was handed a prison sentence of 20-years-to-life for her partner's violence.

> No, I never went to the hospital, I mean like when I went to the clinic, like when I was pregnant the lady told me, she said, 'cause see I kept fingerprints on my neck, they looked like passion marks, but they were like fingerprints from always getting in trouble. She said if you come back in here again with bruises on you, I'm going to take that baby. So I stopped going for prenatal care. I just stopped because the beatings weren't going to stop and I didn't want them taking my baby from me. (Gillum, 2008, p. 50)

According to Eng and Dasgupta (2003), African American children are twice as likely as White children to be taken away from their parents following a confirmed report of abuse or neglect, ultimately putting poor children and children of color on the "fast track" of institutional life. It is no wonder African American women are mistrustful of the saving powers of the same social systems that oppress them.

Homelessness is also a key risk factor, and interpersonal violence makes African American women more vulnerable. Those fleeing violence are more likely to become homeless or have a problem finding housing because of their unique and often urgent circumstances. Women who have chosen to take this step then find themselves drowned by systemic factors that include difficulty finding apartments due to poor credit, rental, and employment histories as a result of their abuse, few tangible social supports because of the flight, and a limited ability to collect and/or enforce child support and alimony payments. In Michigan, through a "one strike" policy, women may be evicted for a violent activity regardless of the cause or the circumstances (Kies-Lowe, 2010).

Some particularly vulnerable sections of the population include both adolescent and older African American women, as well as those who live in poverty and in marginalized social statuses. Paranjape and coauthors (2009) investigated the risk factors for older African American women and found that poor health status leads to increased dependency as well as vulnerability to family members, combined with the often common experience of assuming responsibilities of caring for grandchildren and having multiple members living with them. Many older participants felt that the current generation, their children's children, did not share similar values in respecting elders and considering the needs of others. Paranjape and colleagues found participants had grown up with witnessing and participating in increased community and family violence and were much more materially focused.

> Now that generation is raising this generation ... they don't teach their children to obey, to respect other people ... other people's property or nothing. Because morals have changed from 30 years ago to now ... the generations now don't have moral values ... society's got where people don't go to church. They worship their cars, and their money, their clothes, their jewelry, their jobs, and everything. (Paranjape et al., 2009, p. 983)

COPING STRATEGIES

African American survivors of IPV frequently experience psychological distress in the form of depression, anxiety, stress, and somatic complaints. Despite these challenges, many survivors are resilient. They use community activism, spirituality, music, and literature to promote their healing. West (2002) called for more research on protective factors and characteristics that are associated with resilience because so little is known. Few and Bell-Scott (2002) examined the decision-making strategies that college-level African American women used to terminate abusive heterosexual relationships. They identified several phases in the leaving process, starting with the turning point when the survivor reassesses her relationship as abusive, breaking free when she separates from her abuser, and not going back when she works actively to maintain the separation. In going through these processes, they use a variety of coping strategies, including emotional support from friends, sisters, and mothers.

Few and Bell-Scott (2002) found that some of the coping strategies used by the women included a careful assessment of the relationship and a reframing of it to break the emotional bond with their abusers. Emotional and physical distance was a technique used to regain control by making themselves inaccessible and changing daily routines to avoid contact. After the separation, women used their energy to reestablish emotional connections with social networks as well as declaring and owning a sense of greater autonomy and empowerment.

> Because of being with him, I didn't think much about myself. I didn't think much about what my abilities were, what my strengths were. I focused more on my weaknesses and what I couldn't do.... Coming out of that relationship, I was able to realize that I was a strong person and realized that I was important. ... And that I needed to surround myself with people who felt the same about themselves. (Few and Bell-Scott, 2002, p. 70)

Women also used journaling as well as poetry and art to express their pain and find a source of strength. For many, reading inspirational works of other Black women helped them identify positive characteristics in themselves as well to have a sense of contact and connection to feeling less alone.

Taylor (2002) similarly found a three-step process of disengagement among

African American women survivors of domestic abuse, which included being in, getting out, and going on. While this is similar across diverse groups of women, the additional structural and cultural challenges faced by African American women lead to the need for culturally specific strategies.

A particular coping strategy somewhat unique to this group is sourced in spirituality. The characteristic of Black spirituality is that it is rooted in African traditions, fired in the inferno of slavery, glorified in religious music and traditions, and manifested in cultural responses to personal and communal suffering. The overarching role it plays in the lives of African Americans can be linked to religion being a medium to speak to issues of oppression, as well as source a quest for liberation and justice. African American women tend to be socialized into the life of the community and church at a younger age than men, and it takes on more salience in their lives. Prayer as a personal coping response and attending services as a way of community belonging are both means by which African American women use their spirituality to source their resilience. Watlington and Murphy (2006) found that higher levels of spirituality were positively correlated with fewer signs of depression and posttraumatic stress in the lives of women survivors of IPV. Women who identified themselves as more spiritual tended to use more religious coping strategies such as prayer, and those who reported higher levels of religious involvement such as attending church regularly, also reported higher levels of social support. Few and Bell-Scott (2002) found that survivors' spirituality reminded them that the abusive situation was temporary, allowing them to regain a sense of control and power, and to be reminded that they did not deserve such mistreatment. Going to church and hearing messages of belonging and power was healing.

Social support networks were necessary but also problematic. While close female kin and friends were supportive, they were often similarly involved in abusive relationships, and so there was less transmission of problem-solving strategies. Sometimes a high value was placed on having a man or getting a man, so that women sometimes felt pressured to stay in abusive relationships because of economic stability.

She [her mother] wanted me to stay there because he had a good job, and he was a good person as far as she was concerned. Even though he pulled a gun on her ... he was a good person ... like today she feels that way. (Taylor, 2002, p. 89)

On the other hand, community elders were often sources of great support and encouragement, where they would often affirm the survivor's basic self-worth. Male friends often seemed to position themselves as future partners on learning of the abuse. While some turned to therapy for supports, it was often a strategy of last resort for cultural and perception reasons. The idea of disclosing one's personal business to a stranger was odd and unfamiliar, and most participants felt that they would see White therapists who would be insensitive or judgmental. Mental health services were perceived with great distrust.

> I was thinking about getting professional help. "Mental" help. And I was just thinking, "They are going to put me on Prozac, and I'll be in worse shape than I am now." Prozac, I think, makes you sleepy? . . . And I'm like, "No! I'll be working." The way I work, I can't be on any type of medication like that at all. (Nash, 2005, p. 1436)

COMMUNITY RESPONSES: NEED FOR CULTURAL SENSITIVITY

One of the reasons that general domestic violence prevention practices are not suitable for working with African American women at risk is because of the disproportionate numbers of stressors that increase their risk factors for experiencing violence in the home. The Institute on Domestic Violence in the African American Community was formed in 1993 at the University of Minnesota to begin to address some of these particular concerns, and has generated much scholarship and new understanding about these issues (Griffin, Chappell, & Williams, 2006). Domestic violence resources and services are typically underutilized by African American women and are found generally unsatisfactory.

The Michigan Coalition Against Domestic and Sexual Violence (MCADSV) is located in Okemos with an additional office in Detroit. Its stated purpose is to develop and promote efforts aimed at the elimination of all domestic and sexual violence in Michigan. The Michigan Resource Center on Domestic and Sexual Violence is a library housed at MCADSV that contains print and video resources on domestic violence, sexual assault, stalking, violence prevention, nonprofit management, program development, fund development, medical and legal response to violence against women, and public policy information. These resources include many that are faith-based and many that can be adapted to faith communities; an important element given the significant role played by churches in the African American community.

The language of domestic violence is itself a source of resistance. When framed as a women's issue, it alienates both African American men and women, since it is seen as a threat to race loyalty. It is much more culturally consistent and effective to address it as a community and family issue (Boyd-Franklin, 1989). African American women interviewed by Bent-Goodley (2004) differentiated between the terms *abuse* and *beatings*, where the latter was seen as escalated and serious violence, while the former was perceived as relatively trivial. So a social worker inquiring about IPV might well have incidences of abuse dismissed since they are perceived as less important.

Bent-Goodley (2004) found that many of her focus group participants perceived domestic violence services as inaccessible and unreachable. Either they did not know about services, nobody had brought it up due to their concealment of the abuse, or there were geographic and transportation divides that made the services inaccessible. While participants in her study felt that there was not enough public education and discourse about domestic violence, they also felt hypersensitized to portrayals of African Americans linked to violence. This negative perception was a large concern, and there seemed to be little confidence that there could be a public discussion that did not bring in stereotypes.

In an effort to address this, a Michigan-based collaboration of numerous programs and individuals in Macomb, Oakland, and Wayne counties, African Americans and Allies Against Domestic Violence, has been promoting efforts to locally broadcast a nationally developed campaign. "It's Your Business" is an innovative approach, designed to facilitate dialogue and interventions by using a short, serialized radio drama that is both entertaining and educational. An impressive team of writers produced the 12-part "micro-drama" with professional actors such as the late Lynn Thigpen. Each program has a theme, such as "Better to Air the Dirty Laundry," "We Can Do Something," and "A Time to Speak." (Michigan Domestic Violence and Prevention Board, 2003).

While research shows that domestic violence shelters are critical in providing reprieve, enhancing the safety of women and children, reducing the chances of new violence, and increasing the chances of securing employment, there is a great underutilization by African American women who are experiencing IPV (Few, 2005). While many of these women first seek assistance from family and kin networks, racism and cultural insensitivity emerge as a key factor in the underuse of such services. When volunteers and shelter workers share similar ethnic backgrounds, their credibility about alternatives to domestic violence is much higher. Often women access shelter services through police referrals, but since African American women contact police much less often than White women, they have less access to information about such community resources. When they do contact police or police become involved, the results are less than satisfactory. Robinson and Chandek (2000) found that African American battered women who called the police were significantly less likely to have assailants arrested on their behalf than White battered women. Indeed African American women frequently experience being victimized by race-based discrimination from police as opposed to the gender-based discrimination that White women experienced (Few, 2005). In shelters, African American women reported feeling more isolation if there was a lack of African American staff, and a greater watchfulness about racism in accessing resources and opportunities. On the other hand, both African American and White women experienced muted cultural mistrust with other shelter inmates, where the common experience of IPV united the women. In support groups however, African American women rarely spoke about how it felt to be abused by African American men or the impact of racism in their lives (Few, 2005).

In surveys of urban African American women who accessed health care, African American women experiencing IPV were in greater psychological distress as well as less satisfied by the emotional, informational, and tangible supports they received (Gillum, 2008). Survivors of IPV who used shelter services often reported feeling greater discomfort because of cultural insensitivity on the part of often White shelter workers.

> I don't know if they thought African [American] women go for a lot more violence, and are used to it, so they really wasn't, they didn't really have a welcoming hand for me.... You had to go to the nitty gritty of the altercations and the fights, and the other (White) people that come in there, they might not have to say nothing. (Gillum, 2008, p. 44).

The insensitivity can range from simply having a lack of supplies that African American women may need such as hair care supplies and food products, to feeling that their victimization is taken less seriously and has to be proven in greater detail.

Another aspect of cultural incompetence is that programs for batterers are seen as extremely ineffective, as African American men have lower completion and participation rates than other men (Griffin, Chappell, & Williams, 2006). Cultural appropriateness needs to be incorporated into aspects of assessment, design, and accountability needs in developing effective batterer intervention programs (Gillum, 2008). A case in point is that in the *Executive Summary for the Plan for Preventing Intimate and Sexual Violence in Michigan 2010–2015* (MCADSV, 2010); there is no specific focus on African American women or their unique needs other than some attention paid to the need to develop culturally relevant interventions.

Domestic violence shelters need to provide cultural training for staff so that they are more responsive, while police and legal systems also need training to be more sensitized and less dismissive of the brutality experienced by African American women. The systemic model of practice as described by Boyd-Franklin (1989) has long held that practice with African American families should apply cultural and racial norms as points of reference in building and strengthening families, coupled with gender and spiritual considerations in working with African American women.

Community awareness needs to be raised from within the community to galvanize and publicize the devastation caused by IPV (Griffin, Chappell, & Williams, 2006). Given their central position, the African American churches need to be at the forefront of that movement, educating ministers, addressing the impact of violence, empowering victims, and supporting survivors. If faith-based initiatives can partner with other community resources to both lend and receive legitimacy, African American women may indeed be able to receive the help they need so desperately. The Black Church and Domestic Violence Institute is a Georgia-based organization that offers training to clergy and those affiliated with faith-based organizations as well as professionals' knowledge and skills in responding to violence offered against women (Jordan, 2005).

Conclusion

Intimate partner violence is a huge problem for African American women, historically rooted, sourced in the endemic community violence that is sustained through racist structures that institutionalize lack of opportunity and poverty, and maintained on a personal level through the cultural and community values that encourage African American women to accept and endure. Instead of criminal-izing, punishing, and battering back at the symptoms primarily through the legal system, these structural inequalities might be confronted differently. This includes a reframing of violence against African American women as a public health crisis and one that needs more effective long-term responses then simply trying to lock up the perpetrators and victims. Long-term structural responses could include supportive, community-based infrastructures for recovery from drug and alcohol addictions or for developmental and psychological disabilities, education and job-training courses that amplify access and opportunity rather than prisons that limit it, increased federal funding for affordable housing to prevent the subsequent stressors of overcrowding, or the revocation of laws that prohibit former felons from access to state housing.

Awareness, education, and dissemination of information are crucial to addressing these problems. Much of the awareness and educational initiatives have to start within the community rather than imposed from without. African American women must be in charge of their own safety, empowered to decide their relationships, and supported in both their strength and vulnerability. For this to happen, African American women cannot be expected to leave behind their brothers, fathers, and husbands. Instead, women must partner with their men to forge new modes of healthy and positive relationship that are not simply self-destructive replicates of societal games of dominance, aggression, and submission.

REFERENCES

Abbott, J., Johnson, R., Koziol-McLain, J., & Lowenstein, S. (1995). Domestic violence against women: Incidence and prevalence in an emergency department population. *Journal of the American Medical Association,* 273, 1763–1767.

Adams, J.H. (1997). Sexual harassment and Black women: A historical perspec-tive. In W. O'Donohue (Ed.), *Sexual harassment: Theory, research and treatment* (pp. 213–224). Boston: Allyn and Bacon.

Anderson, E. (1999). *Code of the street: Decency, violence, and the moral life of the inner city.* New York: Norton.

Bent-Goodley, T.B. (2004). Perceptions of domestic violence: A dialogue with African American women. *Health and Social Work, 29*(4), 307–317.

Blue Cross Blue Shield Blue Care Network of Michigan (2007). *Reach out: Intervening in domestic violence and abuse: The health care provider's reference guide to partner and elder abuse.* Retrieved from: http://www.bcbsm.com/pdf/DV_ReferenceGuide.pdf.

Boyd-Franklin, N. (1989). *Black families in therapy: A multisystems approach.* New York: Guilford Press.

Campbell, J.C., Webster, D., Koziol-McLain, J., Block, C.R., Campbell, D., Curry, M.A., Gary, F., McFarlane, J., Sachs, C., Sharps, P., Ulrich, Y., & Wilt, S.A. (2003). Assessing risk factors for intimate partner homicide. *National Institute of Justice Journal,* no. 250, 14–19.

Cho, H. (2012). Racial differences in the prevalence of intimate partner violence against women and associated factors. *Journal of Interpersonal Violence, 27*(2), 344–363.

Clark, M.L., Beckett, J., Wells, M., & Dungee-Anderson, D. (1994). Courtship violence among African American college students. *Journal of Black Psychology, 20,* 264–281.

Collins, P.H. (1991). *Black feminist thought: Knowledge, consciousness, and the politics of empowerment.* New York: Routledge.

Davis, A.Y. (1998). *Blues legacies and Black feminism.* New York: Vintage.

Donovan, R., & Williams, M. (2002). Living at the intersection: The effects of racism and sexism on Black rape survivors. *Women and therapy, 25*(3), 95–105.

Duley, K. (2006). Un-domesticating violence: Criminalizing survivors and U.S. mass incarceration. *Women and Therapy, 29*(3), 75–96,

Eng, P., & Dasgupta, S.D. (2003). *Safety and justice for all: Examining the relationship between the women's anti-violence movement and the criminal legal system, 14.* Summary prepared by Patricia Eng, based on the meeting report by S.D. Dasgupta. Retrieved from http://www.ms.foundation.org/userassets/DF/Program/safety_justice.pdf.

Ernst, C., Angst, J., & Foldenyi, M. (1993). Sexual abuse in childhood. Frequency and relevance for adult morbidity: Data of a longitudinal epidemiological study. *European Archives of Psychiatry in Clinical Neuroscience, 242,* 293–300.

Few, A.L. (2005). The voices of Black and White rural battered women in domestic violence shelters. *Family Relations, 54*(4), 488–500.

Few, A.L., & Bell-Scott, P. (2002). Grounding our feet and hearts: Black women's coping strategies in psychologically abusive dating relationships. *Women and Therapy, 25*(3), 59–77.

Giddings, P. (1996). *When and where I enter: The impact of Black women on race and sex in America.* 2nd ed. New York: Harper Press.

Gillum, T.L. (2002). Exploring the link between stereotypic images and intimate partner violence in the African American community. *Violence against Women, 8*(1), 64–86. doi:10.1177/10778010222182946.

Gillum, T.L. (2008). Community response and needs of African American female survivors of domestic violence. *Journal of Interpersonal Violence, 23*(1), 39–57. doi:10.1177/0886260507307650.

Griffin, L.W., Chappell, M., & Williams, O.J. (2006) Community insights on domestic violence among African Americans: Conversations about domestic violence and other issues affecting their community. *The Institute on Domestic Violence in the African American Community.* Retrieved from http://www.dvinstitute.org/.

Hampton, R., Oliver, W., & Magarian, L. (2003). Domestic violence in the African American community: An analysis of social and structural factors. *Violence against Women, 9*(5), 533–557. doi:10.1177/1077801202250450.

Jordan, L.M. (2005). *Domestic violence in the African American community: The role of the Black church.* Retrieved from http://www.hds.harvard.edu/cswr/ resources/print/rhb/reports/05.Jordan.pdf.

Katz, K.S., Blake, S.M., Milligan, R.A., Sharps, P.S., White, D.V., Rodan, M., Rossi, M., & Murray, K.B. (2008). The design, implementation and acceptability of an integrated intervention to address multiple behavioral and psychosocial risk factors among pregnant African American women *BMC Pregnancy and Childbirth, 8,* 22. doi:10.1186/1471–2393–8-22.

Kies-Loew, P. (2010). *Our invisible students: Homeless children and youth.* Michigan Department of Education. Retrieved from www.michigan. gov/documents/mde/Title_III_and_Homeless_Education_-_KIES-LOWE_PPT_334202_7.ppt-2010-10-05.

Lovelace, T. (2007, April 11). Black women and violence: "Bad" alone doesn't work. Womensenews.org. Retrieved from http:// www.womensenews.org/story/domestic-violence/070411/

black-women-and-violence-bad-alone-doesnt-work.

Madhubuti, H.R. (1990). *Black men: Obsolete, single, dangerous?* Chicago: Third World.

Michigan Coalition Against Domestic and Sexual violence (2010). *Preventing intimate and sexual partner violence in Michigan, 2010–2015*. Okemos, MI: Author. Retrieved from http://www.mcadsv.org/resources/prevention/files/ExecutivePreventionReport.pdf.

Michigan Coalition Against Domestic and Sexual Violence (2011). *National Census of Domestic Violence Services Michigan Summary*. Retrieved from http://www.nnedv.org/docs/Census/DVCounts2010/DVCounts10_State-Summary_MI_Color.pdf.

Michigan Domestic Violence Prevention and Treatment Board. (2001–2013). Department of Human Services. Retrieved from http://www.michigan.gov/dhs/0,4562,7-124-7119_7261-15002--,00.html.

Nash, S.T. (2005). Through Black eyes: African American women's constructions of their experiences with intimate male partner violence. *Violence against Women, 11*(11), 1420–1440. doi:10.1177/1077801205280272.

Paranjape, A., Corbie-Smith, G., Thompson, N., & Kaslow, N.J. (2009). When older African American women are affected by violence in the home: A qualitative investigation of risk and protective factors. *Violence against Women, 15*, 977–990. doi:10.1177/1077801209335490.

Rennison, C. M., & Welchans, S. (2000, May 17). *Intimate partner violence*. U.S. Department of Justice. Retrieved from http://bjs.ojp.usdoj.gov/index.cfm?ty=pbdetail&iid=1002.

Richie, B. (1996). *Compelled to crime: The gender entrapment of battered Black women*. New York: Routledge.

Robinson, A. L., & Chandek, M. S. (2000). Differential police response to Black battered women. *Women and Criminal Justice, 12*(2–3), 29–61. doi:10.1300/J012v12n02_04.

Taylor, J.Y. (2002). The straw that broke the camel's back: African American women's strategies for disengaging from abusive relationships. *Women and Therapy, 25*(3), 79–94.

Tjaden, P., & Thoennes, N. (2000). *Extent, nature, and consequences of intimate partner violence: Findings from the National Violence Against Women Survey*. Washington, DC: U.S. Department of Justice, Office of Justice Programs.

Watlington, C.G., & Murphy, C.M. (2006). The roles of religion and spirituality among African American survivors of domestic violence. *Journal of Clinical Psychology, 62*, 837–857.

Watson, J.M., Cascardi, M., Avery-Leaf, S., & O'Leary, K.D. (2001). High school students' responses to dating aggression. *Violence and Victims, 16*, 339–348.

West, C.M. (2002). Battered black and blue. *Women and therapy, 25*(3), 5–27.

West, C.M. (2004). Black women and intimate partner violence: New directions for research. *Journal of Interpersonal Violence, 19*(12), 1487–1493. doi:10.1177/0886260504269700.

West, C.M., & Rose, S. (2000). Dating aggression among low income African American youth: An examination of gender differences and antagonistic beliefs. *Violence Against Women, 6*, 470–494.

West, C.M., Williams, L.M., & Siegel, J.A. (2000). Adult sexual revictimization among Black women sexually abused in childhood: A prospective examination of serious consequences of abuse. *Child Maltreatment, 5*, 49–57.

Wyatt, G.E., Loeb, T.B., Solis, B., Carmona, J.V., & Romero, G. (1999). The prevalence and circumstances of child sexual abuse: Changes across a decade. *Child Abuse and Neglect, 23*, 45–60.

Self-Definitions of Daily Routines, Parent-Child Interactions, and Crack Cocaine Addiction among African American Mothers

Tierra Bernardine Tivis

Illegal drug use continues to affect many African American children and their families. A government report indicates that crack cocaine continues to plague most major cities in the United States. According to the National Institute of Drug Abuse, in 2003, Detroit's drug-related statistics ranked tenth among 20 cities for crack cocaine-related crimes and treatment admissions. The Office of National Drug Control Policy (2007) reported that in 1997, Wayne County was designated as a high-intensity drug-trafficking area and in 2005, the Detroit Police Department reported 2,963 drug arrests for cocaine. Additionally that year, 325 deaths occurred in Wayne County related to cocaine, as opposed to the 221 deaths related to heroin. A 2003–2004 report from the Michigan State Police indicates that crack cocaine accounted for 30.38 percent of the narcotic arrests for Wayne County. These disturbing statistics warns us that crack cocaine continues to influence the lives of many young children in the Detroit area. Educators, professionals, and scholars can better support these children once we better understand family resilience, motherhood, and crack addiction.

Media outlets no long highlight the horrors of drug use. However, government research (National Institute on Drug Abuse, 2003) suggests that childbearing African American women continue to struggle with cocaine addictions. Perceptions of these mothers have been largely shaped by negative stereotypes often resulting from media representation and research methodologies that ignore race, class, and gender oppressions (Collins, 2000; Geiger, 1995; Roberts, 1995; Roberts, Jackson, & Carlton-Laney, 2000; Zerai & Banks, 2002).

Parent-child interactions are important aspects of parenting and are often a focus of family intervention. Thus, researchers examine the quality of these interactions to help inform their understanding of and practice with families impacted by prenatal drug exposure. The quality of daily routines, expressions of warmth, responsiveness, and love are characteristics of parent-child interactions that researchers often measure. The educational research (Carta et al., 1997; Bolzani Dinehart et al., 2006; Krauss et al., 2000) on parenting and prenatal drug exposure is rarely examined from mother's perspective. This chapter focuses on the daily routines and expressions of warmth, responsiveness, and love with their children from the perspective three African American mothers. The mothers were chronic crack cocaine users during pregnancy and/or throughout some period of their children's childhood. At the time of the interviews, the mothers self-reported to have been abstinent from crack cocaine use.

African American Mothers, Crack Usage, and Prevailing Research

Traditionally, African American mothers and their families have been pathologized in research (Brewer, 1995; Collins, 2000; Dickerson, 1995; Geiger, 1995; Johnson, 1995). Historically in this country, these mothers have seldom been deemed worthy of motherhood (Collins, 1999; 2000; Roberts, 1995; 1997) and throughout history; their reproduction rights have been compromised by U.S. institutions (Collins, 1999; Roberts, 1995; 1997; Washington, 2005). Embracing negative, controlled images of African American mothers as truths helped to advance the legitimization of governmental practices, policies, and laws that deny them true reproduction rights (Collins, 1999; Roberts, 1995; 1997; Washington, 2005). This portrait becomes exacerbated for these mothers when crack cocaine is added to the landscape of motherhood.

Once crack cocaine infiltrated African American communities, we were bombarded with negative images. This was a fragile underweight baby, with brown skin, constantly crying and jerking in an incubator attached to several monitors. Afterward emerged the "crack baby" and the assumption that this child was doomed to lifelong medical, developmental, and educational problems. Likewise, the "crack mother" was considered an African American mother with no humanistic qualities of affection for her child. This was our introduction to the topic of prenatal crack cocaine exposure.

Unfortunately, negative, controlled images based on research findings and media representations of the "crack mother" and "crack baby" resulted in the trend to criminalize the "crack mother" (Frank & Zuckerman, 1993; Roberts, 1995; 1997; Zerai & Banks, 2002). African American prenatal drug users are more likely to be identified and reported to the authorities than their White counterparts (Chasnoff, Harvey, & Barrett, 1990; Roberts, 1997; Zerai & Banks, 2002). They are also often punished for not receiving treatment that they seldom have access to (Roberts, 1995; 1997; Zerai & Banks, 2002; Washington, 2005).

African American mothers struggling with crack cocaine addiction encounter unique parenting experiences that are often inconsistent with the image of the stereotype "crack mother." With few exceptions (Alicea & Friedman, 1999; Baker & Carson, 1999), not many studies provide a venue for African American mothers' input toward knowledge claims about drug addiction, parental competence, and child outcomes. Thus, their voice is silenced and absent from the discourse on prenatal drug exposure and parenting. Our understanding of survival and resilience is therefore limited about those families impacted by prenatal crack cocaine. Yet laws, policies, and practices were developed based on existing inadequate knowledge claims about prenatal crack cocaine that were supposed to be in the best interest of the child.

Conceptual Underpinnings

Critical race feminism (CRF) (Wing, 1997; 2002), Black feminist theory (BFT) (Collins, 2000; Cooper, 1886; 1892; hooks, 1989; 2000; Johnson, 2000; Jordan, 1985), and resilience (Luthar, Cicchetti, & Becker, 2000; McCubbin et al., 1998; Walsh, 2002) were the theoretical frameworks for the larger study. For purposes of this chapter, I will only focus on aspects of BFT and CRF as they relate to the topics of counternarratives and self-definition of parenting, parent-child interactions, and crack cocaine addiction.

BLACK FEMINIST THEORY AND CRITICAL RACE FEMINISM

BFT is a comprehensive stance for the empowerment of Black women that acknowledges the complexities of race, class, and gender oppressions on daily lived experiences (Collins, 2000; Cooper, 1886; 1892; hooks, 1989; 2000; Johnson, 2000; Jordan, 1985). BFT values the collective personal experiences of Black women as having legitimate meaning. There is an assumption that Black women are able to internalize positive self-definitions as a means of rejecting stereotyped controlled images. CRF (Wing, 1997; 2002) emerged from critical race theory (Bell, 1995; Crenshaw et al., 1995; Solorzano & Yosso, 2002), which accepts the notion of systemic racism, the use of storytelling, and Bell's (1995) interest convergence theory. CRF also scrutinizes the oppression of women of color as well as how White supremacy is manifested in the justice system and maintains the subordination of women of color.

CRF and BFT also served as methodologies for the larger study. Critical race scholars Solorzano and Yosso (2002) argue that the "master-narrative" (p. 27) is often advanced through traditional research methodologies based on standard stereotypes. This privileges White men, the middle, and/or upper class, and heterosexuals by placing their experiences as the standard of what is normal. Collins's (2000) framework for BFT embraces a Black feminist epistemology that exposes the Eurocentric knowledge validation process and power relations in the United States. She argues that the lived experiences of Black women should be used as a criterion of meaning and legitimating knowledge claims.

This dual framework allowed me to challenge existing knowledge claims about African American mothers and prenatal drug exposure. In this study, the mothers' voice was valued and they were recognized as important agents of knowledge (Collins, 2000). It is my intention that counternarratives from these Detroit mothers challenge existing biological and cultural deficit stories (Solorzano & Yosso) of prenatal drug exposure with African American mothers. Collins defines self-definition as the "the power to name one's own reality" (p. 300). In this study, the mothers self-define their daily routines and parent-child interactions within the context of crack cocaine addiction. A combination of CRF and BFT challenges traditional knowledge claims, values the Black mother's voice, and takes advantage of oral narrative research.

Methodological Approach

Over the past two decades, African American female scholars have defied dominant stereotypes (hooks, 2005) by using research practice that legitimizes the voice of Black women. For example, oral narrative research is one method scholars (Hambrick, 1995; Vaz, 1995; White, 1995) have used to challenge existing paradigms that often silence Black women. Narrative data for this chapter were part of a larger qualitative study that addressed research questions about counternarratives of drug addiction and recovery, parent-child interactions, and academic achievement. The narratives emerged from data collected from African American mothers living in Detroit, Michigan, and Atlantic City, New Jersey, and who were recovering crack cocaine and/or heroin addicts. In-depth interviews (Seidman, 1991) were conducted with the mothers in Detroit from November 2005 through February 2006. In-depth interviewing (Seidman) and narrative analysis (Riesman, 1993) were used to understand these mothers' perceptions.

Meet the Mothers

Detailed information regarding the mothers' family, school, and social backgrounds was collected as part of the larger study. The mothers chose a pseudonym in order to protect their anonymity. For purposes of this chapter, only a brief summary of the women will be provided to provide some context for understanding their narratives.

SHARON

Sharon is a 44-year-old mother with 10 children and three years of sobriety. She has six girls ages 12, 14, 15, 18, 24, and four boys ages 4, 7, 16, and 22. Sharon's family migrated to Detroit from Connecticut when she was three years old. She grew up in a home with her mother, stepfather, two sisters, and three brothers. Her stepfather worked for Ford Motor Company, and her mother was a stay-at-home mother. Sharon's childhood home was located in what she considered a middle-class neighborhood. She reports that she was a good student and enjoyed school but dropped out in her senior year of high school due to pressures from home. Sharon has worked various jobs since she was a young girl, until her drug addiction. She worked as a sales clerk at Hudson's Department Store, a manager at Dairy Queen, and at the time of the interviews was employed at her daughter's school as a teacher's assistant. Sharon grew up in a traditional Apostolic church. She did not attend a traditional drug rehabilitation program. However, Sharon's church and relationship with God are key to her abstinence from crack cocaine addiction since 2003.

Sharon began to use crack regularly when she was 27 years old. All of Sharon's children were born full-term babies except for her 24-year-old daughter, who was born prematurely prior to her crack cocaine addiction. It is interesting to note that her only child not prenatally exposed to crack was actually born prematurely and received early intervention services for developmental delays. She used crack cocaine, drank alcohol, and smoked cigarettes at some point during most of her other pregnancies but did so on a daily basis with her 12-, 14-, and 15-year-old daughters. She used crack two to three times daily with her 16-year-old son and once weekly with her youngest two children.

BETTY

Betty, who is in her fifties, was born and raised in rural Virginia, where she lived with her parents, two brothers, and two sisters. Her father worked in a sawmill, and her mother worked in a factory that made light switches. As a young child, Betty lived in a small house with an outdoor bathroom until her family built a three-bedroom house once she got older. She has a 16-year-old son and a 19-year-old daughter who recently graduated from high school. These two children live with her in Detroit. Betty also has an older daughter with a young girl who was reared in her birth town by her mother. This daughter moved to Virginia shortly before Betty's addiction to crack "got too bad" and continues to live there with her own daughter.

Betty moved to Detroit in 1975, a year after she graduated from high school, to live with relatives who worked in the automobile industry. She was employed with Chrysler from 1976 until 1987, when she was introduced to crack cocaine. Betty smoked crack consistently during her pregnancy and until her second daughter was two years old. She has been abstinent from crack cocaine for 15 years. Betty was able to reestablish herself financially and purchase the home that she has been living in for 15 years. She was raised in a Baptist church, and her Christian faith is a major part of her life. Betty did not attend a drug rehabilitation program and gives God the credit for her recovery and saving her life.

MURPHY BROWN

Murphy Brown was 48 years old, married, and has three young adult girls who were attending college. She grew up in rural Virginia with her parents, two sisters, a brother, and her aunt. Her family owned 75 acres of land with animals, smokehouses, tobacco, vegetables, and fruit trees. Murphy Brown was also raised in the Baptist church tradition. Her relationship with God has always been a vital part of her existence. Although Murphy Brown admits to seeing a therapist a few times, she did not receive long-term drug treatment. She also believes that God sustains her abstinence from crack cocaine.

Murphy Brown has been living in Detroit since she moved there, three days after her college graduation in 1979. She was employed at Michigan Bell for that summer and became employed by Detroit Public Schools. Murphy Brown met her husband, who is also a college graduate, when she was teaching at an adult education facility. She says "12 years and three babies later," she and her husband finally got married. She worked for Detroit Public Schools from 1980 until 1986, when she was introduced to crack cocaine.

Sharon, Betty, and Murphy Brown share some commonalities. They all migrated to Detroit at some point of their lives because of better job opportunities. The mothers also grew up in two-parent households with strong religious backgrounds and attended church regularly. Yet the mothers also share their own unique experiences with drug addiction, parent-child interactions, and daily routines.

Parent-Child Interactions

The African American mothers in this study presented their parent-child interaction styles when they were sober and as addicts. The mothers discussed their daily routines and their expressions of warmth, responsiveness, and love based on their recent interactions with their children as well as when they were younger.

Early childhood special education researchers Bolzani Dinehart and coauthors (2006) examined the quality of caregiving environments and daily routines of children prenatally exposed to cocaine. They used standardized measurement to assess parent-child interaction concepts using data from behavioral observations and semistructured interviews. These researchers used tools that are based on a hegemonic view of family functioning. Thus, families not adhering to the family mores and standards of the dominant culture would not obtain "average" scores on these tools. In addition, the mother's voice is absent from the research, and we learn very little about their parent-child interactions and crack addiction.

Sharon, Betty, and Murphy Brown relied heavily on kinship networks to assist with parenting throughout their children's childhood and their addiction. However, sometimes they cared for their children during their addiction. Sharon talks about her daily routines when she was pregnant with her fifth child. During this time, she was active in her addiction and her children were in elementary school.

> Get them up for school . . . and while they was gone, that was my party. If they came home, cut the party. . . . Because you know, the kids came home now, so the party had moved. . . . They come home, you'd fix them something to eat. But it's usually, I'm the type where I don't like anything to bother me when, especially when, I'm getting high. I don't want to have to think about, oh, you have to cook. So before I get high, I'm gonna have to cook, 'cause I'm not finna think about that later. So I would by then [have] cooked and everything before, like right before they got home. . . . We basically calmed it down before they got home . . . if we didn't do nothing—through all my addictions. If I ain't do nothing else, they ate. [laughter] . . . 'Cause you just know, a hungry kid is gon get on yo nerves till he's filled, so they'll shut up. (Sharon)

In spite of Sharon's addiction, she had enough insight to get her children off to school and feed them meals. One could argue that she had self-centered motives for feeding her children. Nonetheless, she attempted to meet her children's nutritional needs.

Betty and Murphy Brown established routines for their children based on their academic goals for them. Betty believed that her children's future was directly related to their childhood experiences. She was not so involved in her children's academic achievement when she was using drugs. However, since Betty has been clean, much effort has been made to support their educational achievement. Her children had a homework routine when they were young and her job allowed her to stay informed about their education. Betty speaks about the schedule she had for her children when they were young.

> I was a noon hour aide at the school at that time, when they was going to school. Mattafact at the same school . . . they was going to. So routine, get up in the morning, we go to school together, they go to school and I do my half a day, you know. And I come back and wait till they get out, go back, and pick them up, bring 'em home, help 'em with the homework. After [we] do our homework, then we put our clothes on. They usually get to watch TV or go outside, and play and whatever, then come back in about 9:00, 9:30, wash up, change clothes, get ready for bed. Next day we start it all over again. . . . I like to do the homework soon as you come in the house, soon as we come in the house from school. Let's do that right now and get that outta the way, see? . . . When you let 'em go and play first ,then come back and do homework, can't get 'em to settle down, can't get 'em to settle down. So we did that first, while school is still fresh. . . . Well, it worked through elementary. It started faded in middle. You could hang it up in high school. . . . I don't know how we got off track. I don't know how we got off track. Honey, I couldn't tell you. I couldn't tell you, but girl [her daughter], she still come home sometime [to] do her [homework]. (Betty)

When Betty's children were young, she was diligent about making sure her children did their homework until they were in high school. Yet her daughter continues to have a rigid schedule that is closely monitored to ensure that she stays out of trouble.

> 'Cause she (her daughter) now when she come home . . . [she] in the last year high school. So when she come home now most evening, Monday, Wednesdays, Thursday and Friday and Saturday, she work at Taco Bell, from 4:00 to 9:00. So it just Tuesdays and Sundays she off. And when she come home from Taco Bell, she go straight into, 9:00 we get back home, time I go pick her up 9:00 get in the house 10:00, she go and do her homework. Then she got to try on her clothes for school tomorrow. I guess time she settle down to get into bed it's about 12:00, 1:00. (Betty)

Murphy Brown also maintained daily routines related to typical parenting responsibilities and academic achievement. Life was complicated being a mother addicted to crack and she believed her addiction did not interfere with her parenting.

> As a mother, I still provided. You know like I said, they always had their father. I cooked, washed, cleaned, sent them school. I wouldn't do drugs from the time I woke up in the morning to time I went to bed again. That wasn't my type of life. [If] I did drugs, it would be after I knew da kids been fed or they're settled down or if I didn't have them with me, I could start in the mornings. They might have been with my Aunt Pearl or spent the night, but I didn't do anything, nothing was different. I don't know if that's answerin' the question. . . . I don't see that I did anything different you know, on the drugs or without 'em . . . I don't think I did anything different. (M. Brown)

Murphy Brown and her husband were educators and familiar with family routines that are valued by public schools. Thus, some family routines in their house often mirrored those that you would see in a traditional American home.

> I read 'em books, sit down and played games with 'em. . . . Yeah, that's just something I wanted to do differently than how I was raised. You know and then being a schoolteacher, you know the importance of reading to your child at an early age and introducing them to books and things. So I did that and taking them to—shoot, we wouldn't miss a Sesame Street production or stuff like that, me and my girls . . . when they were young. We made sure we took them to those productions and just exposed them to things that I never was exposed to. (M. Brown)

In the larger study, the mothers shared stories of struggle with parenting during their days of active addiction. However, there were also times when they met their children's needs. This is consistent with Baker and Carson's (1999) research about mothering practices with substance-abusing women who resisted the idea they were "bad" mothers because of their addiction. Similar to these Detroit mothers, the mothers in Baker's study also took care of their children's physical, emotional, and educational needs.

Developmentally enriched home environments and high-quality parent-child interactions are considered key to positive child outcomes. Thus, researchers assess the quality of these environments by evaluating daily routines and then predict the child outcomes. These predictions often result in intervention efforts that focus on enhancing parent-child interactions. African American family scholar Harriet McAdoo (1990; 1998) argues that intervention efforts with African American families should not be problem-oriented. Instead, researchers should focus on the resilience of families surviving hostile environments. McAdoo contends further that in order to understand African American family resilience, scholars should examine the origins of these obstacles and other negative environmental factors. If not, African American families will continue to be held responsible for the hostile environments in many African American communities. Sharon's, Betty's, and Murphy Brown's narratives provided some insight into their family resilience and were not problem-oriented. Instead of focusing on what they were not doing as crack addicts (the problem), these mothers defined their issues with daily routines in their own words (Cuadraz & Uttal, 1999).

EXPRESSIONS OF WARMTH, RESPONSIVENESS, AND LOVE

Warmth and responsiveness are often concepts used to evaluate the quality of parent-child interactions. Parents who are responsive and sensitive to prompts and communications from their infants have positive parent-child interactions resulting in positive infant mental health and development (Bromwich, 1997). Good mental health and overall development are considered important readiness skills for young children as they enter school. Sharon, Betty, and Murphy Brown provide self-definitions (Collins, 2000) of their responsiveness with their children. The quality of warmth and responsiveness in parent-child interactions with children prenatally exposed to cocaine are typically measured with standardized tools (Bolzani Dinehart et al., 2006; Carta et al., 1997; Krauss et al., 2000). These Detroit mothers' narratives were not compared to predetermined definitions of warmth, responsiveness, and love. Instead, they illustrated understandings of these concepts in unique ways that challenge predetermined definitions of warmth and responsiveness within the context of crack cocaine addiction.

In spite of the negative stories of parenting and crack addiction shared by Sharon, Betty, and Murphy Brown, they also shared stories of loving their children. Murphy Brown talks about how she demonstrates love to her girls.

I cooked, sat 'em at the table, make sure their plates were fixed. My girlfriend, she always say Murphy may cook out of a box and a can, but she always make sure her kids always had a vegetable, a meat, and a starch. That was a meal, a meal. Loved kisses and hugs, always kisses and hugs. And something I often think back, I can never ever, and maybe I'm wrong, maybe my sister . . . can elaborate on it, but I never remember ever hearing from my parents or my aunt or anybody in the house, "I love you." I never remember hearing that word, those three words, "I love you," never. So I make sure that I do, that I use 'em. . . . And maybe going up in the South, in the country it was maybe shown more than said. . . . I never remember, like, being given a kiss at bedtime or thangs you see on TV, being tucked in and momma sittin on the side of the bed and talkin to you or readin to you. I don't remember any of that in my household growing up. But I, I made sure that I did it. (M. Brown)

Sharon also demonstrates warmth and love to her children with

hugs, kisses, and compliments. I think that shows, 'cause we didn't get a lot of those when we were younger. I think hugs, kisses, and compliments, I try to. . . . complement them a lot—build up they self-confidence a lot and things like that to show I love them. And I tell them, we're like the Waltons, I love you John Boy, I tell them, I do . . . all of my kids are kisses and huggies. Even the big 22-year-old, "I love you, Momma." I don't care who around, "I love you, Ma." . . . No, I don't do any special things with the kids—never have. We just, we just all get together, talk, crack jokes, and just have a good time. And we did that a lot at my daughter's house because most of us was there a lot. But that's all we do, just sit down and have fun, talkin and laughing and, oh, like, "I remember when you used to drink, Ma." . . . You know, reminiscin. But they'd be like, Thank God you ain't drinkin no more, 'cause it was a hard time for them, and I realize that.

Murphy Brown and Sharon believed that it was important to inform their children of their love because of their personal experiences. They made a conscious effort not pass down what they considered harmful parenting practices. In spite of Sharon's addictions, she tried to maintain her children's trust. When Sharon's children were with her, she made sure that she kept her promises.

We was sittin down talkin one day and they was like, "One thang we can say"—this was my oldest daughter. She was like, "One thang we can say, Ma, and I bet you [daughter] and [son] could say it too. I don't care what you was doin, if you ever told us you promised, we knew we had it. But if you said, 'We'll see,' we wasn't getting nothin." [Laughter] She was like, "I don't care if you was drunk, high, or what, if you said I promise, I'm a do that for you." She was like, "Yeah, my momma gon do this, you can bank on that. But if you said, 'We'll see,' we was like, 'Naw, she ain't gettin us them shoes this time.'" So yeah they know the difference, and I was glad of that. At least I was good for a promise. So that really meant a lot to me. (Sharon)

When asked questions about showing love, responsiveness, and warmth, Betty says:

What do I do to show my kids that I love them? Oh, oh, I don't know, I don't do nothing special. Always doing something. I might tell 'em, okay, now come on let's go to Red Lobster ... I'm paying for it. . . . I don't just necessarily always come out and express it to 'em. . . . 'Cause I show no warmth, I show no love. They say, all I do is fuss, I'm mean. [Laughter] ... I'm not one of them type of mothers that come in and always hugging them and telling them I love 'em and all that. I'm not one of them type of mothers. So I don't, I don't. . . . I just don't show it. I just don't show it. They know I love 'em. . . . How would they know? Well, could be ... any day of the week and I say, "You all come on, I got some money, let's go to Red Lobster." ... Or "Come on, you all, let's go ... I'm in a good mood come on, I'm going out to the store and buy all us an outfit." ... There's stuff that I do, you know, just little stuff I do. We come in, they get in my bed and we have a little family talk, discussion, we talk, end up playing and whatever, so you know. That's kinda the way I show. (Betty)

Betty's comments confirm that a mother's expression of love toward her children varies depending the mother's personal interaction style.

I told you I'm mean. So I don't care nothing about their needs or this and that. They cook their own food . . . leave me alone. Between 12:00 and 2:00 and we at home, I'm looking at my stories, so, uh, responsive to their needs? . . . I guess it make sense, but I'm not responsive. They say I'm a cold-hearted person, kids say, you know. (Betty)

Betty described warmth and responsiveness during interactions with her children now that they are older. She was unable to relate those concepts to interactions with her children. According to her, she is not responsive to her children's needs. Yet her behavior demonstrates that she obviously loved and cared for her children. Betty says

> When they was smaller I get 'em in the car . . . just me and them. . . . I might say, "This week, me and the kids going to Cedar Point . . . to Six Flags" or whatever, it was just me and my two kids. I didn't take the man, nobody, have my car. I planned it for me and two kids. Got the little road map thing from AAA. . . . Me and my two kids get in the car, we do the three-, four-hour drive. So that's bonding, getting there. . . . We stay at Six Flags for two, three days, just me and the kids. . . . They were like seven, eight, nine, ten. . . . I fill my car up, my two get in the car, we done hit [Interstate] 75. . . . You know, I did all that kinda stuff. So that ain't showing you love either, I don't what showing it is. . . . I done took 'em to Florida. I went down to Florida, stayed five days. . . . We went on a bus trip that time. (Betty)

Betty shared stories of her attempts to establish opportunities for quality times with her children. It was interesting that she did not believe that she demonstrated the typical concepts of warmth, love, and responsiveness to her children.

The mothers articulated their perceptions of their daily routines and parent-child interactions. Parent-child interactions are culturally based occurrences that vary across families. Zaslow and Rogoff (1981) argue that the culture of the observer and caregiver are important when rating parent-child interactions. They acknowledge room for bias and error when measuring culturally based concepts such as warmth, responsiveness, and love. This has significance for measuring these concepts with African American mothers with crack addictions.

Sharon, Murphy Brown, and Betty led complex lives as mothers and drug addicts. Their expressions of warmth, responsiveness, and love would not have been measurable using standardized observational scales or structured interviews. These Detroit mothers were able to establish daily routines and have positive social interactions with their children regardless of the complexities of their lives. Betty, Sharon, and Murphy Brown provided self-definitions (Collins, 2000) of daily routines and parent-child interactions within the context of their family life and crack addiction.

Conclusion

The central aim of this chapter is to introduce counternarratives of daily routines, parent-child interactions, and crack cocaine addiction with African American mothers. Betty, Sharon, and Murphy Brown were provided an opportunity to self-define concepts of their parent-child interactions that are typically predetermined by researchers. These Detroit mothers provided counternarratives of crack addiction, daily routines, and expressions of warmth, responsiveness, and love. They were able to establish and maintain daily routines during their children's early childhood years. Sharon and Murphy Brown were able to navigate crack addiction and provide for their children's basic needs. Murphy Brown and Betty established routines that supported their academic goals for their children. The mothers also illuminated their unique ways of expressing warmth, responsiveness, and love to their children.

Sharon's, Betty's, and Murphy Brown's self-definitions challenge negative, controlled images of the African American "crack mother" with her "crack baby" jerking uncontrollably in a pediatric incubator. This chapter is intended to privilege the mothers' perspectives over existing knowledge claims of crack addiction and give value to their collective experiences as crack addicts and mothers. The mothers' experiential knowledge defies the assumptions that babies prenatally exposed to crack cocaine are "at risk" for future long-term developmental and academic problems. Their counternarratives also call to question the idea that African American mothers addicted to crack have no emotional bond with their children.

No clear evidence exists that suggests prenatal exposure to crack cocaine alone results in any permanent negative child outcomes (Chasnoff, 1992; Frank & Zuckerman, 1993; Griffith, Azuma, & Chasnoff, 1994). However, it is common knowledge that prenatal exposure to nicotine and alcohol beverages cause permanent birth defects. Claims are so serious that the government requires companies to place a warning label about such risks on the products. Yet there has been no rush to criminalize mothers who smoke or drink as a pretense for a "war" on smoking or drinking. Our understanding of African American mothers, their children, and crack addiction becomes limited when we do not question why these differences occur.

It is obviously inappropriate to infer that a home stressed by crack cocaine addiction is an optimal environment for children. However, Murphy Brown, Sharon, and Betty were not just drug addicts. They were multifaceted women attempting to rise above their circumstances and change the course of their families' lives. There is a gap in the research about parent-child interactions among African American dyads. It becomes even scarcer when you include crack addiction with parent-child interaction. Typically, using standardized measures, educational researchers (Carta et al. 1997; Bolzani Dinehart et al., 2006; Griffith, Azuma, & Chasnoff, 1994; Kraus et al., 2000) examine prenatal crack exposure from an outsider's perspective. In-depth interviewing allowed these Detroit mothers to reframe and reveal important information about their experiences (Cuadraz & Uttal, 1999) with addiction that is absent from the literature. When the individual family context is ignored and the African American mothers' voice is silenced, inadequate knowledge claims are made. These claims often guide program efforts that continue to fail at supporting these families.

It is impossible to enter most low-income African American communities and not see evidence of a thriving crack cocaine industry. Roberts, Jackson, and Carlton-Laney (2000) point out an increase of drug use, incarceration rates, limited drug treatment opportunities, and ineffective treatment programs for African American females. Crack cocaine addiction continues to be a problem. However, these mothers' resilience is remarkable, as they managed to negotiate motherhood and crack addiction.

Implications for Research, Policy, and Practice

My intent is not to romanticize the mothers' lives and suggest that households impacted by crack addiction are ideal home environments for young children. However, Lopez and Parker (2003) argue that educational scholars and scholars of color have been charged to defy epistemological racism and frameworks that privilege one perspective over others. Currently, educational research does not inform us of prenatal drug use and family resilience in African American families from the mothers' perspective. These Detroit mothers' narratives of survival can inform the early childhood field about resilience and crack addiction. Their counternarratives can help reshape our thinking about parenting and crack addiction. Thus, policies can be implemented that are not problem oriented (McAdoo, 1990; 1998) and acknowledge family resilience. Policymakers should consider the complexities of child and academic development for African American children impacted by crack addiction. They should also legitimate the African American mothers' experiential knowledge and allow room for her to self-define her own issues so that she can be empowered to be an agent of change (Collins, 2000).

These findings can enhance the knowledge base of preservice teachers, teacher educators and teachers working in communities devastated by the illegal drug industry. Individuals working with families impacted by drug addiction can be challenged to reflect on their own perceptions and bias. Negative teacher biases often interfere with establishing positive home-school partnerships and result in low expectations for African American students. This is especially true for African American students living in poverty and who are prenatally exposed to crack cocaine. Teachers can only provide a culturally relevant education to their students when they are familiar with the students' cultural and family values and home experiences (Ladson-Billings, 1994; Moll et al., 1992; Moll & Gonzalez, 2004).

In closing, I would like to share a quote that I believe represents the sentiment of the Detroit mothers in the study regarding their hopes and dreams for their children's future: "A education and no drugs and into the church. I want them to go to school and know the value of going to school."

REFERENCES

Alicea, M., & Friedman, J. (1999). Millie's story: Motherhood, heroin, and methadone. In M. Romeo & A.J. Stewart (Eds.), *Women's untold stories: Breaking silence, talking back, voicing complexity* (pp. 159–173). New York: Routledge.

Baker, P., & Carson, A. (1999). I take care of my kids: Mothering practices of substance-abusing women. *Gender and Society, 13*, 347–363.

Bell, D.A. (1995). *Brown v. Board of Education* and the interest convergence dilemma. In K. Crehnshaw, N. Gotanda, G. Peller, & K. Thomas (Eds.),

Critical race theory: The key writings that formed the movement (pp. 20–29). New York: New Press.

Bolzani Dinehart, L.H., Dice, J.L., Dobbins, D.R., Claussen, A.H., & Bono, K.E. (2006). Proximal variables in families of children prenatally exposed to cocaine and enrolled in a center- or home-based intervention. *Journal of Early Intervention, 29*, 32–47.

Brewer, R. (1995). Gender, poverty, culture, and economy: Theorizing female-led families. In B. Dickerson (Ed.), *African American single mothers: Understanding their lives and families* (pp. 164–178). Thousand Oaks, CA: Sage.

Bromwich, R. (1997). *Working with families and their infants at risk.* Austin, TX: PRO-Ed.

Carta, J.J., McConnell, S.R., McEvoy, M.A., Greenwood, C.R., Atwater, J.B., Baggett, K., & Williams, R. (1997). Developmental outcomes associated with in utero exposure to alcohol and other drugs. In M.R. Haack (Ed.), *Drug-dependent mothers and their children* (pp. 64–90). New York: Springer.

Chasnoff, I.J. (1992, August). Cocaine, pregnancy, and the growing child. *Current Problems in Pediatrics,* 302–321.

Chasnoff, I.J., Harvey, J.L., & Barrett, M.E. (1990). Prevalence of illicit drug and alcohol abuse during pregnancy and discrepancies in mandatory reporting in Pineallas County, Florida. *New England Journal of Medicine, 322,* 1202–1206.

Collins, P.H. (1999). The meaning of motherhood in Black culture. In R. Staples (Ed.), *The Black family* (pp. 157–178). Albany, NY: Wadsworth.

Collins, P.H. (2000). *Black feminist thought: Knowledge, consciousness, and the politics of empowerment.* 2nd ed. New York: Routledge.

Cooper, A.J. (1892). *Voices from the South by a Black woman of the South.* Ohio: Aldine.

Cooper, A.J. (1986). Womanhood: A vital element in the regeneration and progress of a race. In C. Lemert & E. Bhan (Eds.), *The voice of Anna Julia Cooper including "A Voice from the South" and other important essays, papers, and letters* (pp. 53–71). New York: Rowman & Littlefield.

Crenshaw, K., Gotanda, N., Peller, G., & Thomas, K. (1995). Introduction. In K. Crenshaw, N. Gotanda, G. Peller, & K. Thomas (Eds.), *Critical race theory: The key writings that formed the movement* (pp. xiii–xxxii). New York: New Press.

Cuadraz, G.H., & Uttal, L. (1999). Intersectionality and in-depth interviews: Methodological strategies for analyzing race, class, and gender. *Race, class, and gender, 6*, 156–186.

Dickerson, B. (1995). Centering studies of African American single mothers and their families. In B. Dickerson (Ed.), *African American single mothers: Understanding their lives and families* (pp. 1–20). Thousand Oaks, CA: Sage.

Frank, D.A., & Zuckerman, B.S. (1993). Children exposed to cocaine prenatally: Pieces of the puzzle. *Neurotoxicology and Teratology, 15*, 298–300.

Geiger, S.M. (1995). African American single mothers: Public perceptions and public policies. In K.M. Vaz (Ed.), *Black women in America* (pp. 244–257). Thousand Oaks, CA: Sage.

Griffith, D.R., Azuma, S.D., & Chasnoff, I.J. (1994). Three-year outcome of children exposed prenatally to drugs. *Journal of American Academy of Child Adolescent Psychiatry, 33*(1), 20–27.

Hambrick, A. (1997). You haven't seen anything until you make a Black woman mad. In K.M. Vaz (Ed.), *Oral narrative research with Black women* (pp. 64–82). Thousand Oaks, CA: Sage.

hooks, b. (1989). *Talking back: Thinking feminist thinking Black.* Boston: South End Press.

hooks, b. (2005). *Sisters of the yam: Black women and self-recovery.* Cambridge, MA: South End Press.

Johnson, K.A. (2000). *Uplifting the women and the race: The educational philosophies and social activism of Anna Julia Cooper and Nannie Helen Burroughs.* New York: Garland.

Johnson, L. (1995). Three decades of Black family empirical research: Challenges for the 21st century. In H. McAdoo (Ed.), *Black Families,* 3rd. ed. (pp. 167–182). Thousand Oaks, CA: Sage.

Jordan, J. (1985). *On call: Political essays.* Boston: South End Press.

Krauss, R.B., Thurman, K.S., Brodsky, N., Betancourt, L., Giannetta, J., & Hurt, H. (2000). Caregiver interaction behavior with prenatally cocaine-exposed and nonexposed preschoolers. *Journal of Early Intervention, 23*(1), 62–73.

Ladson-Billings, G. (1994). *The dreamkeepers: Successful teachers of African American children.* San Francisco: Jossey-Bass.

Lopez, G.R., & Parker, L. (Eds.). (2003). Conclusion. *Interrogating racism in qualitative research methodology* (pp. 203–212). New York: Peter Lang.

Luthar, S., Cicchetti, D., & Becker, B. (2000). The construct of resilience: A critical evaluation and guidelines for future work. *Child Development, 71*, 543–562.

McAdoo, H. (1990). The ethics of research and intervention with ethnic minority parents and their children. In C. Fisher, W. Tryon, & I. Sigel (Eds.), *Ethics in applied developmental psychology: Emerging issues in an emerging field.* Annual advances in applied developmental psychology, vol. 4 (pp. 273–283). Norwood, NJ: Ablex.

McAdoo, H. (1998). African American families: Strengths and realities. In H.I. McCubbin, E.A. Thompson, A.I. Thompson, & J.A. Futrell (Eds.), *Resiliency in African American families* (pp. 17–30). Thousand Oaks, CA: Sage.

McCubbin, H., Futrell, J., Thompson, E., & Thompson, A. (1998). Resilient families in an ethnic and cultural context. In H.I. McCubbin, E.A. Thompson, A.I. Thompson, & J.A. Futrell (Eds.), *Resiliency in African American families* (pp. 329–351). Thousand Oaks, CA; Sage.

Michigan State Police (2006). *Narcotic crime trends, Second District.* Retrieved from http://www.michigan.gov/msp/0,1607,7–123—S,00.html.

Moll, L.C., Amanti, C., Neff, D., & Gonzalez, N. (1992). Funds of knowledge for teaching: Using a qualitative approach to connect homes and classrooms. *Theory into Practice, 31*(2), 132–141.

Moll, L.C., & Gonzales, N. (2004). A funds-of-knowledge approach to multicultural education. In J.A. Banks & C.A. Banks (Eds.), *Handbook of research on multicultural education,* 2nd ed. (pp. 699–715). San Francisco: Jossey-Bass Wiley.

National Institute on Drug Abuse (2003). *Epidemiologic trends in drug abuse.* Vol. 2, *Proceedings of the community epidemiology work group.* Retrieved from http:// www.drugabuse.gov/Inforfacts/nationtrends.html.

Office of National Drug Control Policy (2007). *State of Michigan, profiles of drug indicators.* Retrieved from http://www.whitehouse/drugspolicy.

Office of National Drug Control Policy (n.d.). *Drug facts: Women and drugs.* Retrieved from http://www.whitehouse/drugspolicy.gov/drugfact/women/index.html.

Riessman, C. (1993). *Narrative analysis.* Thousand Oaks, CA: Sage.

Roberts, A., Jackson, M.S., & Carlton-Laney, I. (2000). Revisiting the need for feminism and Afrocentric theory when treating African American female substance abusers. *Journal of Drug Issues, 30*, 901–917.

Roberts, D.E. (1995). Punishing drug addicts who have babies: Women of color, equality, and the right of privacy. In K. Crenshaw, N. Gotanda, G. Peller, and K. Thomas (Eds.), *Critical race theory: The key writings that formed the movement* (pp. 384–426). New York: New Press.

Roberts, D.E. (1997). Punishing drug addicts who have babies: Women of color, equality, and the right of privacy. In A.K. Wing (Ed.), *Critical race feminism: A reader* (pp. 127–135). New York: New York University Press.

Seidman, I.E. (1991). *Interviewing as qualitative research: A guide for researchers in education and the social sciences.* New York: Teachers College Press.

Solorzano, D.G., & Yosso, T.J. (2002). Critical race methodology: Counter-storytelling as an analytical framework for education research. *Qualitative Inquiry, 8*(1), 23–44.

Vaz, K.M. (1997). Preface. In K.M. Vaz (Ed.), *Oral narrative research with Black women* (pp. vii–viii). Thousand Oaks, CA: Sage.

Walsh, F. (2002). A family resilience framework: Innovative practice applications. *Family Relations, 51*, 130–137.

Washington, D.A. (2005). "Every shut eye, ain't sleep": Exploring the impact of crack cocaine sentencing and the illusion of reproductive rights for Black women from a critical race feminist perspective. *Journal of Gender, Social Policy and the Law, 13*, 123–137.

Wing, A.K. (1997). Brief reflections toward a multiplicative theory and praxis of being. In A.K. Wing (Ed.), *Critical race feminism: A reader* (pp. 27–34). New York: New York University Press.

Wing, A.K. (2002). Critical race feminism: Legal reform for the twenty-first century. In D.T. Goldberg & J. Solomos (Eds.), *A companion to racial and ethnic studies* (pp. 160–169). Cambridge, MA: Blackwell.

Zerai, A., & Banks, R. (2002). *Dehumanizing discourse, anti-drug law, and policy in America: A "crack mother's" nightmare.* Burlington, VT: Ashgate.

Zaslow, M., & Rogoff, B. (1981). The cross-cultural study of early interaction: Implications from research on culture and cognition. In T. Field, A. Sostek, O. Vietze, & P. Leiderman (Eds.), *Culture and early interactions* (pp. 237–256). Mahwah, NJ: Erlbaum.

HIV Prevention Efforts
and African American Women

A COMMENTARY FOR FUTURE RESEARCH

Syreeta Scott, Stephen D. Jefferson,
Lori Hale, *and* Krupa Hedge

Infection with the human immunodeficiency virus (HIV) is a major health concern for American women, especially African American women. According to statistics provided by the Centers for Disease Control (CDC), HIV-related illnesses constitute "the leading cause of death for black women ... aged 25–34" (CDC, 2008, p. 1), and it is the third and fourth leading cause for these women aged 35–44 and 45–54, respectively. While representing only 12 percent of the total female population of the United States, African American women comprise 64 percent of all female HIV cases in the United States (National Alliance of State and Territorial AIDS Directors, 2008).

And once women have been infected with the virus, it appears that they also bear a disproportionate rate of acquired immunodeficiency syndrome (AIDS) diagnoses. For example, compared to other infected groups, African American adults and adolescents were 10 times as likely to be diagnosed with acquired immunity deficiency syndrome (AIDS) compared to non-Hispanic Whites, and nearly three times as likely compared to of the rate of Hispanics (the next most prevalent ethnic group; CDC, 2008). The rate of AIDS diagnosis for African American women was nearly 23 times the rate for non-Hispanic White women (CDC, 2008).

When we consider HIV infection rates for Michigan, we find a pattern comparable to the national trends. That is, although African Americans comprise 14 percent of Michigan's total population, they account for about 58 percent of those living with HIV. Similarly, there is a marked gender difference for infection rates in the state for African American men and women. Specifically, while 1 in 90 African American men are infected statewide, 1 in 260 African American women is living with HIV/AIDS (Michigan Department of Community Health, 2006).

These statistics have prompted epidemiologists to examine factors associated with the transmission of this disease in this population. Preliminary analyses have been very enlightening, if not particularly surprising. It is clear that for the majority of African American women surveyed, the primary route of HIV transmission seems to occur through heterosexual contact (i.e., 74 percent of the 83,349 women sampled across 33 states indicated that this was the likely transmission event; CDC, 2006). Increased attention has been given to males who do not identify with homosexuality yet engage in sexual activities with the same sex. Hence, HIV prevention services for African American men having sex with men and women (MSMW) have been identified as one means of HIV education, which can decrease the risk of African American women contracting HIV/AIDS (Saleh et al., 2011). The second largest route appears to be through injected drug use (24 percent of the sample). Finally, 2 percent of the sample reported some other route of transmission.

Why do African American women have such elevated rates of infection? Several theories exist that attempt to explain this phenomenon. Research on this topic can be roughly categorized along two dimensions: (1) psychological variables, and (2) ecological variables. Of course, these categories are by no means exhaustive. We believe that the causes for this epidemic are multifaceted; however, we adopt the present dichotomy merely as an instrument to enhance the clarity of our review, which includes a broad collection of often overlapping contributory factors.

Psychosocial Variables Associated with Elevated Rates of HIV

These variables consist of those characteristics that can be said to lie within the individual as well as those factors that are associated with interpersonal relations. These include cognitive biases and affective experiences like self-esteem, ethnic identity, self-efficacy, depressive symptoms, and perceptions of personal risk.

Additionally, this rubric also includes interpersonal factors such as relationship dynamics, communication skills, safer sex choices, and other relational behaviors.

Most of the research examining the association of these variables to HIV risk behaviors has used correlational approaches. For example, depressive symptoms seem to be positively associated with increased HIV risk, both directly and synergistically. In a study of HIV-negative African American adolescents, depressive symptoms appeared to be positively correlated with inconsistent condom use (Brown et al., 2006). However, other researchers have uncovered a more complex relationship between these variables. Specifically, depression seems to exacerbate HIV risk in groups of African Americans with other mental health concerns. Johnson, Cunningham-Williams, and Cottler (2003) in their research on drug-using African American women who either had experienced physical violence (e.g., rape and/or physical assault), depressive symptoms, or both conditions, found that among this substance-abusing population, having one or both experiences seemed to increase respondents' risk for HIV infection. Thus, it appears that having a substance abuse problem in conjunction with other distressing psychological concerns may compound a woman's risk of contracting HIV.

Another factor that seems to be associated with HIV risk is self-concept, both individual self-esteem and group identity attitudes. Studies by Klein, Elifson, and Sterk (2007) and Braithwaite and Thomas (2001) both found that African American women with low self-esteem tended to engage in more sexually risky behaviors than women with higher self-esteem. Similar results were found in a study of African American adolescents (Salazar et al., 2004). In addition to these individually based attitudes, it appears that how African American women experience their ethnic identity also influences their HIV risk. Similar results were found for adult African American women (Beadnell et al., 2003). Further, it appears that helping women to improve their racial identity attitudes has been demonstrated to be an important component of culturally competent, effective HIV (DiClemente & Wingood, 1995; Fuller et al., 2007; Nyamathi et al., 1999) and pregnancy (Dixon, Schoonmaker, & Philliber, 2000) prevention programs.

It seems reasonable to infer from these findings that as women begin to feel better about themselves, they may simultaneously experience a boost in their general sense of self-efficacy. Support for this hypothesis can be gleaned from the work of Salazar and coauthors (2004). Although their study examined the relation of self-concept to condom usage, it also assessed communication skills and self-efficacy attitudes related to negotiating condom usage with sexual partners. Specifically, combining their measures of self-esteem, ethnic identity, and body image into one construct (i.e., "self-concept") they were able to use structural equation modeling to demonstrate that girls' attitudes about their ability to communicate with their sexual partners about condom usage mediated the relationship between self-concept and girls' willingness to refuse to have sex without a condom.

Research indicates that among African American girls, endorsing favorable attitudes about being Black is positively correlated with reporting being comfortable refusing sex without a condom (Salazar et al., 2004) and subscribing to fewer sexually risky attitudes (Belgrave, Van Oss Marin, & Chambers, 2000). New approaches to HIV prevention and intervention for African American teens include the use of technology. Sistering, Informing, Healing, Living and Empowering (SiHLE) is a program sponsored by the Centers for Disease Control (CDC) that targets African American females between the ages of 14 and 18 for a 12-hour group-based program that also includes a two-hour individual-level intervention. Klein and Card (2011) found the SiHLE program to result in a significant increase in condom self-efficacy and increase in the average ratio of sex acts that were condom-protected. Additionally, research has provided support for the use of friendship-based intervention programs to prevent and curb HIV and sexually transmitted infections among urban African American female teenagers (Dolcini et al., 2010).

Ecological Factors Related to Increased Cases of HIV Infection

African American women's interpersonal relationships are intimately tied to the psychological and environmental factors they experience. We believe these factors are particularly significant in romantic relationships because they influence relational behaviors at all levels, including those relevant to HIV risk. As researchers learn more about the dynamics between men and women, we can enhance our understanding of the barriers to protective behavior that occur long before unprotected sex. We previously examined some of the causal factors that are involved in the discrepant rates of HIV infection, and these factors are important in relationship dynamics. How do women view their role in romantic relationships and what beliefs do they have regarding men's expectations? What variables in a romantic relationships cause women to disregard circumstances that are pertinent to their health and well-being? Research seeking to understand the scripts and schemas of relationships from the perspective of African American women can be helpful in answering these questions. Qualitative research has identified specific schemas that African American women have expressed regarding romantic relationships. When considering prevention and intervention strategies, the perspective of the intended population is vital.

Certain factors affect this population uniquely because although some relationship qualities are important to all couples, the relationship dynamics of African Americans are specific to the sociocultural context in which they develop. External stressors affect power, communication, commitment, and other relationship qualities. One stressor that has been implicated in negatively affecting the relationship dynamics African Americans is the marked gender ratio imbalance that commonly occurs in African American communities (Ferguson et al., 2006). The gender ratio imbalance is the difference between the numbers of African American men to women—that is, women tend to outnumber men in many communities. This makes it very difficult for heterosexual African American women who wish to date or marry African American men to find partners.

A number of factors are thought to contribute to this disparity. For example, between the ages of 18 to 29 years old, approximately 10 percent of African American men are in prison (Henry J. Kaiser Family Foundation, 2006). This statistic is more than twice the rate for Hispanic men, and almost seven times the rate for White men. Although some of these men marry prior to and during their incarceration, many of these men are physically removed from the marriage and relationship pool by this event. Further, incarceration has a deleterious effect on the earning potential of these men because having a criminal record compromises one's ability to successfully secure gainful employment (Pager, 2003), making these men a much less attractive marriage prospect for women once the men are finally released.

Compound the aforementioned with the fact that African American men between the ages of 15 and 29 years have the highest average mortality rate of any racial group in the United States, a rate much higher than that for African American women (Henry J. Kaiser Family Foundation, 2006), and it becomes clear that among nonincarcerated African American adults, women tend to significantly outnumber men. However, the problems do not end here. For those men who are not incarcerated or killed and actually successfully complete high school and/ or college (i.e., men who are considered very attractive for marriage), a small but significant proportion of these men choose to marry outside of the African American community (Crowder & Stewart, 2000), further limiting the pool of eligible men for African American women to marry. These statistics led Lane and coauthors (2004) to conclude that because there are generally more eligible African American women than there are marriageable African American men at key marriage ages, "heterosexual, monogamous marriage is ... an arithmetical impossibility ... if they [women] want marital partners near their age and of their race" (p. 414). Further, this research suggests that while African American men are able to readily date interracially, this does not appear to be the case for African American women. Thus, the fear that some African American women have concerning their ability to marry an African American man is well founded. This fact creates greater HIV risk for African American women.

How does this gender imbalance contribute to HIV risk in African American women? Ferguson and coauthors (2006) found that at historically Black colleges and universities, this imbalance appears to play a role in perceptions of HIV risk in African American women. Specifically, women who adopted the view that men are a scarce commodity tended to accept "man-sharing" (i.e., multiple women dating one man) as normative behavior in college courtships, and they also tended to believe that women have less power than men in deciding whether or not a man will wear a condom. Additionally, within this disproportionate context, men may have a reduced need to become as emotionally invested in one partner due to the abundance of available women, while women may feel a greater need to invest in a particular partner because there are so few good alternatives (Wingood & DiClemente, 1998). This imbalance of power in relationships reduces communication between partners and affects a woman's sense of self-efficacy (Bowleg, Belgrave, & Reisen, 2000). Women may feel significant hesitation concerning discussing sensitive topics like sexuality because they may fear that their male partners will leave them and find less difficult women as partners. Thus, these women may feel less inclined to disclose their sexually transmitted infection (STI) status or to ask men about their STI histories; and this creates a perfect storm of risk.

Attitudinal and Relational Aspects Associated with HIV Risk

Another factor that seems to be associated with increased HIV risk is, ironically, the length of time that African American women stay with a single partner. Although theoretically, sex within a monogamous relationship between two adults who have been tested and found to have no STIs is thought to be very low risk, many couples tend to fall short of this ideal; and extrarelational sexual encounters by at least one partner are estimated to be relatively common (Treas & Giesen, 2000). Using a sample of 1,394 undergraduate students, Knox, Vail-Smith, and Zusman (2008) found that one in five men in their sample reported "cheating." Besides being male, other factors that seem to be associated with infidelity included having a strong sex drive, endorsing permissive attitudes about infidelity, and living in inner cities (Treas & Giesen, 2000). Finally, when White men were compared to African American men in this study, it appears that African American men were more open regarding likelihood of infidelity. The latter finding might partly be explained by the work of Andrinopoulos, Kerrigan, and Ellen (2006). Using a semistructured interview approach and content analysis, these researchers found that while African American females in their sample valued monogamy and romance over casual sex; African American male respondents desired to feel wanted by their partner, but also valued the high social status they gained by having multiple sexual partners.

In spite of a desire for long-term relationships in African American communities, typically, members of this group have low marriage rates. In 2004, only 34 percent of African Americans were married, and 42 percent never married (U.S. Census Bureau, 2007). Long-term relationships have a tendency to instill feelings of security and trust that negatively affect protective behaviors against HIV (Civic, 1999; Misovich, Fisher, & Fisher, 1997). Married couples have been found to use condoms less than unmarried couples (Winfield & Whaley, 2005). Increased commitment and feelings of trust lead individuals to feel that they are less vulnerable to infection, and this reduces safer sex practices (Emmers-Sommer, Allen, & Duck, 2005; Harvey & Wenzel, 2002). Expectations related to how partners in relationships are to comport themselves have been studied by cognitive psychologists who study relationship *schemas* and *scripts*.

Schemas are a general set of attitudes that help to explain reality. In the present context, it is important to focus upon a special type of schema: *Relational schemas.*

This class of schemas emphasizes the interrelated elements of interpersonal relationships (Baldwin, 1992). Specifically, this theory posits that people have expectations for how specific social interactions should occur, and they tend to follow these expectations. Scripts are probably best described as a more specific subtype of schemas. They develop because of exposure to repeated and predictable relational experiences that over time tend to influence our expectations and motivations in relevant situations. For example, research on heterosexual "first date" scripts has uncovered that these events tend to unfold in a consistent and stereotyped pattern (Morr Serewicz & Gale, 2008). Whether a man should open the door for a woman, pay for the dinner, or attempt a goodnight kiss are all examples of individual acts or patterns of behavior that taken together make up the "first date" script. For the present chapter, we shall focus on relationship scripts and define them as a specialized form of schemas.

Bowleg, Lucas, and Tschann (2004) conducted a qualitative study of the association between relationship/sexual scripts and condom use in 14 African American women. Three relationship scripts were identified from her data analyses: (1) women sustain relationships, (2) infidelity is normative, and (3) men control relationships.

According to the authors, the *women sustain relationships* script is typified by a willingness to tolerate the undesirable qualities and behaviors of a partner (e.g., emotional or verbal abuse, emotional distance, and Type-A tendencies). Women who endorse this script also ignore or deny infidelity in their relationships and suppress conflicts by self-silencing or acceding to the demands of their partners. The *infidelity is normative* script involves women accepting a partner's infidelity because these women perceive cheating as something all men do or something that is normal in relationships. Thus, these women do little to change this dynamic, even if it upsets them. Finally, the *men control the relationships* script is exemplified by a relationship in which the man dominates his female partner. Monitoring, denying permission to socialize, and restricting his partner's decisions are common in this interpersonal dynamic.

Other authors have identified slightly different scripts. For example, Sobo (1995) has identified two additional scripts: (1) *monogamy* and (2) *wisdom narrative*. The monogamy script is thought to increase a woman's self-esteem by allowing her to feel that she enjoys a special status as the exclusive focus of her partner's romantic interests. However, although women may gain a sense of self-esteem from this narrative, endorsement of this script may cause a woman to deny infidelity when she sees it (Fullilove et al., 1990). An apt example of this can be gleaned from the work of Andrinopoulos, Kerrigan, and Ellen (2006). From their interviews, they found that some adolescent girls reported that although monogamy is preferred, if a male partner makes a clear distinction between his "girl on the side" and his "wifey," then his philandering is ignored:

> A wifey is like somebody, somebody [he] sticks with. Like if y'all been in a relationship . . . he might be cheating with another girl, but you're the main chick. You know what I'm saying? You still know that [he's thinking], "That's my wifey, that's my main girl," and [the other girl] is just on the side. . . . So it's [about keeping your wifey] status. (p. 135)

Finally, The wisdom narrative is characterized by the idea that a woman can intuitively identify a good man. Specifically, a good man is someone who is clean (i.e., disease free) and conscientious (i.e., honorable) (Sobo, 1995).

Jones and Oliver (2007) expanded upon the previous qualitative work in this area by focusing not only on the deleterious scripts associated with HIV infection, but also on scripts associated with the assertion of healthful safer sex behaviors by 30 African American, 10 Puerto Rican, and three non-Spanish-speaking Caribbean women. To participate in the study, participants had to report that they had sex with a male sexual partner who they either suspected or believed had participated in HIV-risky behaviors. Their research elaborates a model consisting of two major types of scripts: (1) low power and (2) high power. Low-power scripts are those patterns of assumptions and behaviors that contribute to HIV risk. These are modified iterations of the themes previously discussed by Bowleg, Lucas, and Tschann (2004), and Sobo (1995). For example, Jones and Oliver (2007) found that some women endorsed scripts that required that a woman needs to chase a man to keep him, accept infidelity as normal (especially if the man still comes home at night), prefer that a man lie about his extrarelational sexual experience (this indicates that he respects her), and ignore her personal safety if it gets in the way of satisfying the needs of a man. These scripts are contrasted with high-power scripts. The latter scripts include themes related to women seeing themselves as worthy of self-care regardless of their relationships with men, feeling that they can control when, if, and how sex is to occur, and that women can carry their own condoms and are matter-of-fact about requiring their use.

Thus, this burgeoning area of research relating scripts to HIV risk has great promise as a point of primary prevention. Although no quantitative research has been conducted to assess the role of script endorsement in predicting HIV risk, there have been several studies conducted with African American female participants that offer indirect support for the notion that scripts play an important role in HIV risk behaviors.

However, more quantitative research needs to occur before researchers can both statistically confirm and reliably measure these scripts. There have been widespread prevention messages and tactics initiated by the increase of the epidemic. While some programs have proven to be efficacious in addressing this population, others may have persisted with limited positive effect. Reviewing what has and has not worked is important as we look to new solutions.

HIV Prevention Strategies

Just as HIV seems to evolve (Hutchinson, 2001), so too have preventative measures transformed as more information about the epidemiology of this illness has become known. Consequently, policymakers and practitioners have identified a number of effective programs that appear to work well in communities of African American women. We shall summarize five such programs from across the United States, and subsequently briefly discuss a few programs that are specific to Michigan.

First, one of the most widely used HIV prevention programs targeting African American women is Sisters Informing Sisters About Topics on AIDS (SISTA; DiClemente & Wingood, 1995). This evidence-based intervention has been utilized by more than 700 organizations in United States (Wingood & DiCemente, 2006). This protocol consists of five group sessions with each session focusing on one of the following topics: (1) discussing and enhancing participants' ethnic and gender pride, (2) reviewing information and myths related to HIV/AIDS, (3) self-assertiveness and condom use negotiation skills training, (4) reducing anxiety related to condom usage through role playing, and (5) reviewing the role of drugs and HIV, as well as the practical applications of SISTA information (Fuller et al., 2007). One of the underlying values inherent to this approach is the notion that power imbalances between men and women in society influence the safer sex practices of women. Thus, each phase of this intervention also addresses such social factors as how many women are economically dependent upon male partners, how men are often allowed to exert more decision-making power in heterosexual relationships, and how women are generally encouraged by society to adopt a nonassertive communicative style (Wingood & DiClemente, 2000; 2006). Research indicates that this program is effective at the three-month follow-up with participants reporting an increase in condom use, sexual self-control, sexual assertiveness, and partner's support for safe sex practices (DiClemente & Wingood, 1995). Even though SISTA was initially targeted toward African American women between the ages of 18 and 29 (Wingood & DiClemente, 2006), the program appears to also be successful with older African American women (Cornelius, Moneyham, & LeGrand, 2008).

A second program entitled Sistering, Informing, Healing, Living and Empowering (SiHLE), is an offshoot of SISTA, and mirrors some of the features of its progenitor; however, it focuses its efforts on reducing HIV in African American female adolescents. Like SISTA, this program consists of a series of group sessions emphasizing four areas of very similar content, that is, (1) ethnic and gender pride, (2) HIV risk coping strategies, (3) HIV/AIDS knowledge, and (4) dating and healthy relationship issues (Wingood & Clemente, 2006). The SiHLE program is also influenced by the theory that differences in power across gender influence HIV risk for African American females; however, it modifies this approach so these issues are applicable to the lives of adolescents. Specifically, this program has participants critique social scripts related to the expectation that girls should anticipate dating older sexual partners, that the stereotypes promulgated by mass media are appropriate role models, that violence in dating partners is normative, and that it is a good idea to compare one's safer sex behaviors with those of peers to assess HIV risk (Wingood & DiClemente, 2006). Research supports the efficacy of this intervention. After completing the SiHLE program, participants reported more consistent condom use and fewer incidents of unprotected vaginal intercourse at 30-day, 6-month, and 12-month follow-ups (DiClemente et al., 2004). In addition, SiHLE participants reported increased favorable attitudes toward condoms, greater communication with male partners about HIV prevention, and an increase in HIV knowledge relative to the control condition.

Another offshoot of the SISTA program is the Women Involved in Life Learning From Other Women (WiLLOW) HIV prevention program (Wingood & DiClemente, 2006). This program targets HIV-positive women and strives to help these women limit their HIV transmission behaviors. Although 85 percent of the original WiLLOW participants were African American females, this is the only intervention discussed that was not specifically developed for this population (Wingood & DiClemente, 2006). This program consists of four group sessions, which explore (1) gender pride, (2) the maintenance of positive social networks as well as separation from unhealthy, negative social networks, (3) increasing participants' general HIV and HIV prevention knowledge, and (4) educating participants about the differences between healthy and unhealthy intimate relationships (Wingood et al., 2004). With regard to its efficacy, Wingood and coauthors found that after completing WiLLOW, participants reported lower rates of both unprotected vaginal intercourse and vaginal bacterial infections at 30-day, 6-month, and 12-month assessments. Participants also reported higher condom self-efficacy, increased knowledge about HIV risk and transmission, and lower partner-related condom barriers.

A third program, The Health Intervention Project (HIP), targets African American women who use illegal drugs (Sterk, 2002). This program works from the perspective that (1) women have the ability to solve their own problems, and (2) they will work to solve only those problems they are motivated to address. Further, the formal intervention consists of a two-tiered approach. First, clients are encouraged to identify key areas of change they desire in their lives. These targets do not have to be directly related to HIV, though HIV is the main intervention goal of the program. Second, clients are helped to develop an action plan designed to accomplish their goals. Additionally, this phase of the program also helps participants enhance their communication and assertiveness skills. To facilitate this process, the program pairs women up with an "interventionist" (i.e., a person trained to use reflective listening to enhance problem-solving skills) who helps participants identify areas of desired change and implement individualized strategies to effect these goals. Although efficacy studies appear to be limited on this program, its authors report anecdotal evidence that suggests that the program was able to help participants reduce their HIV risk behaviors, as well as suggesting that best practices for HIV prevention must contextualize any intervention in the social milieu of the target population.

Finally, the fifth program reviewed here is the WISH prevention program. This approach consists of 10 components and attempts to get participants to (1) talk about sex, (2) understand the anatomy of their genitalia, (3) explore issues related to body image, (4) discuss masturbation as a tool for self-understanding, (5) discuss and practice sexual assertiveness, (6) understand safer sex issues, (7) discuss intimacy and relationships, (8 & 9) explore how culture and spirituality influence sexual identity for African Americans, and finally (10), consider how such barriers as drug abuse, prostitution, and physical and sexual abuse may interfere with achieving better sexual health (Robinson et al., 2002). This program worked from the perspective that people who are comfortable and knowledgeable about sexual topics are more likely to engage in safer sex practices. Thus, this program utilized a variety of formats (e.g., videos, exercises, discussion, storytelling, etc.) to educate participants about topics related to safer sex. During the three-month and nine-month follow-ups, women in this program were more likely to answer questions about sexual anatomy correctly. At nine months, there was also an increase in communication with children about the topic of sexual health, while at the same time there was a decrease in positive body image (Robinson et al., 2002). However, concerning sexual risk behavior, condom attitudes, and sexual self-efficacy, no difference was found between the control group and the WISH group at three-month and nine-month follow-ups. Thus, unlike the previous programs described in this chapter, the WISH program signifies a failed program. Despite this finding, we include it in our summary because it offers a stark contrast to the more effective programs summarized earlier in this chapter. Further, these results suggest that adopting a sex-positive attitude, developing a better understanding of HIV transmission, and learning more about masturbation are not associated with adopting safer sex practices in African American communities.

Michigan Prevention Programs

The Michigan Department of Community Health (MDCH) has utilized effective community-based behavioral interventions for the prevention of HIV and STDs. The MDCH has implemented the following programs: (1) Brother-2-Brother, (2) Hot Healthy and Keeping It Up, (3) Personalized Nursing Light Model, (4) Prevention Opinion for Positives (POP), (5) SISTA, (6) Video Opportunities for Innovative Condom Education and Safer Sex (VOICES/VOCES), and (7) Many Men Many Voices (3MV) (Peterson & Randall, 2006). Of the aforementioned interventions, SISTA is the only program initiated in Michigan that focuses specifically on African American women. As of 2006, there were three agencies implementing the SISTA HIV intervention program in the state of Michigan (Peterson & Randall,

2006). As stated previously, research has demonstrated that SISTA is an effective community-based HIV prevention program.

In addition to the SISTA program, Michigan had previously implemented the NJIDEKA (a Swahili term meaning "survival is paramount") program (Cook, Stamps-Griffin, & Link, 1999). NJIDEKA was designed for high-risk African American women and took place in substance abuse treatment facilities, correctional institutions, and youth programs. This program consisted of a 10-week HIV workshop and covered the following topics: (1) promotion of a sense of self, dignity, pride, and community; (2) imparting skills to empower women in their interpersonal relationships; and (3) encouraging participants to act as social support for each other as they endeavored to reduce their HIV risk. NJIDEKA has been shown to be effective in terms of increasing participants' knowledge about HIV and STIs, helping participants to recognize that they are susceptible to acquiring HIV, increasing participants' condom usage, and getting participants to express more willingness to reduce their high-risk behaviors. This program was deemed efficacious and was recognized by the CDC as a strong program with a solid reputation.

Conclusion

Despite identifying a number of successful programs, we still have a long way to go to reduce current incidence rates of HIV in this country. Programs targeting African American women have been successful by focusing on personal and environmental factors, gender power imbalances, teaching communication skills, and increasing social support (Card, Solomon, & Berman, 2008). This area of research has also revealed that programs emphasizing the impartation of basic safer sex information appear to be less effective than those focusing on enhancing self-esteem and relational factors. In fact, all of the effective interventions described herein appear to work by changing the schemas and scripts that African American women endorse related to sexual relationships. Although not explicitly defined in these terms, the programs work to transform low-power scripts into high-power scripts. Thus, helping women develop assertive communication skills and a sense of personal empowerment may allow them to change the script of "men control relationships" to "I am in control of my safety." Encouraging women to establish multiple supportive relationships in their communities might help them change the script of "I must sacrifice my safety if I wish to satisfy a man" to "I can find a satisfying relationship with a man who values both my health and his." Finally, helping these women to challenge the belief that infidelity is normal may allow them to consider relationships outside of this paradigm and increase their safer sex practices.

Although these suggestions are logical, they need more empirical support. A gap exists in the literature with regard to directly measuring script-related beliefs and assessing the efficacy of HIV prevention programs. Further, intervening with African American women will entail changing more than just the attitudes of these women (or for that matter, the attitudes and behaviors of African American men). As previously stated, a complex interaction of factors contributes to the situation in which African American women find themselves. We must guard against the temptation of focusing myopically upon individuals in this community as if ecological factors like racism, sexism, gender imbalances, and poverty are irrelevant to HIV risk. Without accounting for such environmental factors, our intervention efforts will only be partial solutions if they are effective at all. Finally, researchers must not adopt a paternalistic attitude toward this population; rather, we must continue to work with members of this group to arrive at shared insights and solutions. The rapidity and rapaciousness of the spread of this infection is a testament to the fact that we all share the same biosphere and, consequently, what affects one of us can quickly affect all of us.

REFERENCES

Andrinopoulos, K., Deanna, K., and Ellen, J.M. (2006). Understanding sex partner selection from the perspective of inner-city Black adolescents. *Perspectives on Sexual and Reproductive Health, 38*(3), 132–138.

Baldwin, M.W. (1992). Relational schemas and the processing of social information. *Psychological Bulletin, 112*(3), 461–484.

Beadnell, B., Stielstra, S., Baker, S., Morrison, D.M., Knox, K., Gutierrez, L., & Doyle, A. (2003). Ethnic identity and sexual risk-taking among African American women enrolled in an HIV/STD prevention intervention. *Psychology, Health and Medicine, 8*(2), 187–198.

Belgrave, F.Z., Van Oss Marin, B., & Chambers, D.B. (2000). Culture, contextual, and intrapersonal predictors of risky sexual attitudes among urban African American girls in early adolescence. *Cultural Diversity and Ethnic Minority Psychology, 6*(3), 309–322.

Bowleg, L., Belgrave, F.Z., & Reisen, C.A. (2000). Gender roles, power strategies, and precautionary sexual self-efficacy: Implications for Black and Latina women's HIV/AIDS protective behaviors. *Sex Roles, 42*(7–8), 613–635.

Bowleg, L., Lucas, K.J., & Tschann, J.M. (2004). "The ball was always in his court": An exploratory analysis of relationship scripts, sexual scripts, and condom use among African American women. *Psychology of Women Quarterly, 28*(1), 70–82.

Braithwaite, K., & Thomas, V.G. (2001). HIV/AIDS knowledge, attitudes, and risk-behaviors among African American and Caribbean college women. *International Journal for the Advancement of Counseling, 23*, 115–129.

Brown, L.K., Tolou-Shams, M., Lescano, C., Houck, C., Zeidman, J., Pugatch, D., Lourie, K.J., & Project SHIELD Study Group (2006). Depressive symptoms as a predictor of sexual risk among African American adolescents and young adults. *Journal of Adolescent Health, 39*, 444.e1–444.e8.

Card, J.J., Solomon, J., & Berman, J. (2008). Tools for building culturally competent HIV prevention programs. New York: Springer.

Centers for Disease Control and Prevention (CDC) (1999). HIV/AIDS Surveillance Report. Vol. 11. Atlanta: United States Department of Health and Human Services, Public Health Service, Center for Disease Control and Prevention.

Centers for Disease Control and Prevention (CDC) (2005). HIV/AIDS Surveillance Report. Vol. 17. Atlanta: United States Department of Health and Human Services, Public Health Service, Center for Disease Control and Prevention.

Centers for Disease Control and Prevention (CDC) (2006). HIV/AIDS Surveillance Report. Vol. 18. Atlanta: United States Department of Health and Human Services, Public Health Service, Center for Disease Control and Prevention.

Centers for Disease Control and Prevention (CDC) (2008). HIV/AIDS among women, 1–7. Fact sheet. Atlanta: United States Department of Health and Human Services, Public Health Service, Center for Disease Control and Prevention.

Civic, D. (1999). The association between characteristics of dating relationships and condom use among heterosexual young adults. *AIDS Education and Prevention, 11*(4), 343–352.

Cook, S., Stamps-Griffin, D., & Link, S. (1999). NJIDEKA: An HIV intervention program for African American women. National HIV Prevention Conference 1999 Atlanta, Abstract No. 270.

Cornelius, J.B., Moneyham, L., & LeGrand, S. (2008). Adaptation of an HIV prevention curriculum for use with older African American women. *Journal of the Association of Nurses in AIDS Care, 19*(1), 16–27.

Crowder, K.D., & Stewart, E.T. (2000). A new marriage squeeze for Black women: The role of racial intermarriage by Black men. *Journal of Marriage and the Family, 62*(3), 792–807.

DiClemente, R.J., & Wingood, G.M. (1995). A randomized controlled trial of an HIV sexual risk-reduction intervention for young African American women. *JAMA, 274*(16), 1271–1276.

DiClemente, R.J., Wingood, G.M., Harrington, K.F., Lang, D.L., Davies, S.L., Hook, E.W., Oh, M.K., Crosby, R.A., Hertzberg, V.S., Gordon, A.B., Hardin, J.W., Parker, S., & Robillard, A. (2004). Efficacy of an HIV prevention intervention for African American adolescent girls: a randomized controlled trial. *JAMA, 292*(2), 171–179.

Dixon, A.D., Schoonmaker, C.T., & Philliber, W.W. (2000). A journey toward womanhood: Effects of an Afrocentric approach to pregnancy prevention among African American adolescent females. *Adolescence, 35*(139), 425–429.

Dolcini, M.M., Harper, G.W., Boyer, C.B., & Pollack, L.M. (2010). Project ORE: A friendship-based intervention to prevent HIV/STI in urban African American adolescent females. *Health Education & Behavior, 37*(1) 115–132.

Emmers-Sommer, T.M., Allen, M., & Duck, S. (2005). *Safer sex in personal relationships: The role of sexual script in HIV infection and prevention.* Mahwah, NJ: Lawrence Erlbaum Associates.

Espinoza, L., Hall, H.I., Hardnett, F., Selik, R.M., Ling, Q., & Lee, L.M. (2007). Characteristics of persons with heterosexually acquired HIV infection, United States, 1999–2004. *American Journal of Public Health, 97*(1), 144–149.

Ferguson, Y.O., Quinn, S.C., Eng, E., & Sandelowski, M. (2006). The gender ratio imbalance and its relationship to risk of HIV/AIDS among African American women at historically Black colleges and universities. *AIDS Care, 18*(4), 323–331.

Forna, F.M., Fitzpatrick, L., Adimora, A.A., McLellan-Lemal, E., Leone, P., Brooks, J.T., et al. (2006). A case-control study of factors associated with HIV infection among Black women. *Journal of the National Medical Association, 98*(11), 1798–1804.

Fullilove, M.T., Fullilove, R.E., Haynes, K., & Gross, S. (1990). Black women and AIDS prevention: A view towards understanding the gender rules. *Journal of Sex Research, 27*(1), 47–64.

Fuller, T.R., Brown, M., King, W., & Prather, C. (2007). The SISTA pilot project: Understanding the training and technical assistance needs of community-based organizations implementing HIV prevention interventions for African American women—implications for a capacity building strategy. *Women and Health, 46*(2–3), 167–186.

Greene, K., & Faulkner, S.L. (2005). Gender, belief in the sexual double standard, and sexual talk in heterosexual dating relationships. *Sex Roles, 53*(3–4), 239–251.

Harvey, J.H., & Wenzel, A. (2002). HIV, AIDS, and close relationships. *Journal of Social and Personal Relationships, 19*(1), 135–142.

Harvey, S.M., Beckman, L.J., Gerend, M.A., Bird, S.T., Posner, S., Huszti, H.C., et al. (2006). A conceptual model of women's condom use intentions: Integrating intrapersonal and relationship factors. *AIDS Care,* 18(7), 698–709.

Henry J. Kaiser Family Foundation (2006, July). Young African American men in the United States. *Race, Ethnicity and Health Care: Fact Sheet.* Washington, DC.

Hodge, C.E. (2001). HIV/AIDS: Impact on the African American Community. Compendium of *Continuing Education in Dentistry, 22*(3), 52–56.

Hutchinson, J.F. (2001). The biology and evolution of HIV. *Annual Review of Anthropology, 30,* 85–108.

Johnson, S.D., Cunningham-Williams, R.M., & Cottler, L.B. (2003). A tripartite of HIV-risk for African American women: The intersection of drug use, violence, and depression. *Drug and Alcohol Dependence, 70,* 169–175.

Jones, R., & Oliver, M. (2007). Young urban women's patterns of unprotected sex with men engaging in HIV risk behaviors. *AIDS and Behavior,* *11*(6), 812–821.

Klein C.H., & Card, J.J. (2011). Preliminary efficacy of a computer-delivered HIV prevention intervention for African American teenage females. *AIDS Education & Prevention, 23*(6), 564–576.

Klein, H., Elifson, K.W., & Sterk, C.E. (2007). Childhood neglect and adulthood involvement in HIV-related risk behaviors. *Child Abuse and Neglect, 31,* 39–53.

Knox, D., Vail-Smith, K., and Zusman, M. (2008). "Men are dogs": Is the stereotype justified? Data on the cheating college male. *College Student Journal, 42*(4), 1015–1023.

Lane, S.D., Keefe, R.H., Rubinstein, R.A., Levandowski, B.A., Freedman, M., Rosenthal, A., Cibula, D.A., & Czerwinski, M. (2004). Marriage promotion and missing men: African American women in a demographic double bind. *Medical Anthropology Quarterly, 18*(4), 405–428.

Logan, T., Cole, J., & Leukefeld, C. (2002). Women, sex, and HIV: Social and contextual factors, meta-analysis of published interventions, and implications for practice and research. *Psychological Bulletin, 128*(6), 851–885.

McNair, L.D., & Prather, C.M. (2004). African American women and AIDS: Factors influencing risk and reaction to HIV disease. *Journal of Black Psychology, 30*(1), 106–123.

Michigan Department of Community Health (2006). HIV/AIDS Surveillance Section.

Misovich, S.J., Fisher, J.D., & Fisher, W.A. (1997). Close relationships and elevated HIV risk behavior: Evidence and possible underlying psychological processes. *Review of General Psychology, 1*(1), 72–107.

Morr Serewicz, M.C., & Gale, E. (2008). First-date scripts: Gender roles, context, and relationship. *Sex Roles, 58*(3–4), 149–164.

Nyamathi, A.M., Kington, R.S., Flaskerud, J., Lewis, C., Leake, B., & Gelberg, L. (1999). Two-year follow-up of AIDS education programs for impoverished women. *Western Journal of Nursing Research, 21*(3), 405–425.

National Alliance of State and Territorial AIDS Directors (2008, May). African American Women. Issue Brief No. 1, pp. 1–12.

Pager, D. (2003). The mark of a criminal record. *American Journal of Sociology, 108*(5), 937–975.

Peterson, A.S., & Randall, L.M. (2006). Utilizing multilevel partnerships to build the capacity of community-based organizations to implement effective HIV prevention interventions in Michigan. *AIDS Education and Prevention, 18*(Supplement A), 83–95.

Robinson, B.E., Uhl, G., Miner, M., Bockting, W.O., Scheltema, K.E., Simon Rosser, B.R., & Westover, B. (2002). Evaluation of a sexual health approach to prevent HIV among low income, urban, primarily African American women: Results of a randomized controlled trial. *AIDS Education and Prevention, 14*(Supplement A), 81–96.

Salazar, L.F., DiClemente, R.J., Wingood, G.M., Crosby, K.H., Davies, S., Hook, E.W., III, & Kim, O. (2004). Self-concept and adolescents' refusal of unprotected sex: Test of mediating mechanisms among African American girls. *Prevention Science, 5*(3), 137–149.

Saleh, L.D., Operario, D., Smith, C.D., Arnold, E., & Kegeles, S. (2011). "We're going to have to cut loose some of our personal beliefs": Barriers and opportunities in providing HIV prevention to African American men who have sex with men and women. *AIDS Education and Prevention, 23*(6), 521–532.

Smith, D.K. (1992). HIV Disease as a cause of Death for African Americans in 1987 and 1990. *Journal of the National Medical Association, 84*(6), 481–487.

Sobo, E.J. (1995). *Choosing unsafe sex: AIDS risk denial among disadvantaged women.* Philadelphia: University of Pennsylvania Press.

Sterk, C.E. (2002). The health intervention project: HIV risk among African American drug users. *Public Health Report, 117*(Supplement 1), 88–95.

Treas, J., & Giesen, D. (2000). Sexual infidelity among married and cohabitating Americans. *Journal of Marriage and the Family, 62*(3), 792–807.

U.S. Census Bureau (2007). The American community—Blacks: 2004. *American Community Survey Reports.* Retrieved from www.census.gov/prod/2007pubs/acs-04.pdf.

Winfield, E.B., & Whaley, A.L. (2005). Relationship status, psychological orientation, and sexual risk taking in a heterosexual African American college sample. *Journal of Black Psychology, 31*(2), 189–204.

Wingood, G.M., & DiClemente, R.J. (1998). Partner influences and gender-related factors associated with noncondom use among young adult African American women. *American Journal of Community Psychology, 26*(1), 29–51.

Wingood, G.M., & DiClemente, R.J. (2000). Application of the theory of gender and power to examine HIV-related exposures, risk factors, and effective interventions for women. *Health Education and Behavior, 27*(5), 539–565.

Wingood, G.M., & DiClemente, R.J. (2006). Enhancing adoption of evidence-based HIV-interventions: Promotion of a suite of HIV prevention interventions for African American women. *AIDS Education and Prevention, 18*(Supplement A), 161–170.

Wingood, G.M., DiClemente, R.J., Mikhail, I., Lang, D.L., McCree, D.H., Davies, S.L., Hardin, J.W., Hook, E.W., & Saag, M. (2004). A randomized control trial to reduce HIV transmission risk behaviors and sexually transmitted diseases among women living with HIV: The WiLLOW program. *Journal of Acquired Immune Deficiency Syndromes, 37*(Supplement 2), 58–67.

African American Women
and Cancer

DIA COPELAND

I am not a cancer specialist, but sometimes I think of myself as a cancer detective. Many of my patients are at risk for developing cancer; some are even living with cancer without knowing it. A large part of the work of gastroenterologists is performing colonoscopies. This test allows physicians to examine directly inside the colon to look for precancerous polyps and cancers. Many patients begrudgingly come for the test, at the urgings of their primary care physician. Alternatively, the friend or spouse has told them to get it done, get it over with to encourage them to move forward. "At least you'll get good drugs," they say, referring to the sedatives used for the test. After spending half a day drinking a gallon of salty tasting liquid and no solid food, most patients arrive for their test asking when they can eat a steak. Many times the colon has a few tiny polyps that are easily removed. Sometimes we find larger polyps that need to be removed with more diligence. However, every now and then, a patient comes come in, who has seen a little blood in his or her stool, or maybe has been losing weight without explanation. And there in the colon sits an ulcerated cancerous mass. At that moment, I thank God that the patient had the test done right now, today, instead of putting it off until later.

What Is Cancer? What Causes It?

Cancer is a broad term to describe abnormal cell growth. This can be a genetic predisposition or an environmental exposure, or both, which leads to abnormal signaling on a molecular level. Rapid growth of these abnormal cell can form be a solid mass known as a tumor, or can be in a blood cell line, such as leukemia. Most commonly, cancers are named for the organ of origin. Most solid cancers are treated with surgery, chemotherapy, radiation, or a combination of these approaches. Leukemia may require chemotherapy or bone marrow transplant.

The causative factor is likely a combination of genetic (inherited) and environmental influences. Many chemicals have been implicated as carcinogens. Carcinogens are agents that cause cancer cells to form. Evidence of causation is stronger for some carcinogens than others. For example, cigarette smoke is well known to be associated with the development of lung cancer and throat cancer. However, exposure to a carcinogen does not guarantee that cancer will develop. One person may smoke cigarettes for many years and never develop cancer, while another may have modest smoking history and develop lung cancer. Still, a lifelong nonsmoker living in a smoke-free household may develop lung cancer. This person my already have a genetic predisposition to develop lung cancer regardless of cigarette use. Excessive sun exposure can lead to the development of skin cancers, particularly in people with fair skin complexions. Infections, particularly specific viruses, can increase a person's risk for specific cancers. Chronic hepatitis B & C infection for example, increases the lifetime risk of developing liver cancer (hepatocellular carcinoma). Human papillomavirus (HPV) increases a woman's risk of cervical cancer.

CANCER STAGING

Once a cancer has been confirmed, often with a biopsy, it is important to find out if the cancer has already spread to other parts of the body. *Staging* is the term used for determining if a cancer has spread to other organs in the body or to lymph nodes. Lymph nodes are a part of the body's immune system. There are hundreds of lymph nodes throughout the body, and they connect like beads on chains. Lymph nodes are also common sites for cancers to travel. Staging is represented by classification system called TMN, which is the acronym for tumor, nodes, and metastases. Staging

TABLE 1. CANCER RISK FACTORS

CANCER TYPE	RISK FACTORS	PREVENTION	PEOPLE AT HIGH RISK
Lung	Smoking	Smoking cessation	Smokers
	Alcohol		Secondhand smoke exposure
	Obesity		
Colon and Rectum	Colon polyps	Removal of colon polyps at colonoscopy	Close family history of colon cancer
	Smoking		Chronic ulcerative colitis
	Obesity		Chronic Crohn's colitis
			Inherited polyposis syndromes
Cervix	HPV infection	HPV vaccine (prevents certain strains of HPV)	Multiple sexual partners, history of other sexually transmitted disease
		Pap smear	
Breast	Smoking	Smoking cessation	Close family history of breast cancer before age 50
Pancreas	Chronic pancreatitis		Family history of pancreas cancer
Esophagus	Smoking	Smoking cessation	Smokers
	Heartburn for more than 10 years	Upper endoscopy after 10 years of heartburn symptoms	
Skin	Sun exposure– UV rays	Use of sunscreen	Fair skin, red or blond hair

TABLE 2. EXPOSURES AND RELATED CANCERS

EXPOSURE	CANCER ASSOCIATION
Sun–UV Rays Nonionizing Radiation	Basal cell skin Squamous cell skin Melanoma
Cigarette Smoking	Lung, oral, laryngeal, pancreas, and others
Chronic Hepatitis B	Liver
Chronic Hepatitis C	Liver
HPV 6, 16, 18	Cervical
H Pylori Infection	Stomach
HIV-1, Epstein Barr Virus	Lymphoma
Chronic Alcohol Ingestion	Liver, pancreas

TABLE 3. FREQUENTLY USED TUMOR MARKERS

TUMOR MARKER	ASSOCIATED CANCER
CA 27.29	Breast
CA 19-9	Pancreas, bile duct
CEA	Colon, liver
AFP	Liver, ovarian
CA 125	Ovarian

systems are given numeric values; the higher the stage number indicates higher degree of spread. The lower the stage the more localized the cancer. When cancers have spread to distant organs, this is considered an advanced stage cancer and is usually the most difficult to treat and usually has a worse prognosis. Tumors that have not spread at all tend to have the best chance of cure. Often the first step of staging is to get wider imaging of the body; this is usually accomplished by taking images of the body using a CT scan. If surgery is necessary, the surgeon will removed the tumor along with lymph nodes nearby, and the pathologist will examine the lymph nodes under a microscope. If there is cancer in the lymph nodes, the patient may require chemotherapy and/or radiation after surgery.

Tumor markers are chemicals produced by certain organs in the body. They may be detected in larger amounts in the bloodstream if there is a cancer in a specific organ. Some tumor markers are helpful in making a cancer diagnosis. Often physicians use tumor marker levels to assess for cancer recurrence after treatment.

Types of Cancer

BREAST CANCER

Carcinoma of the breast generally arises from the ductules, or tubes that carry breast milk. Less than one-quarter of cancer comes from other breast tissue. Women who perform self-breast exams may notice a lump in the breast that leads to medical attention. It is important to note that there are other noncancerous causes of lumps in the breast, including fibrocystic changes in the breast tissue. Other times early breast cancers are detected only by imaging, such as mammogram or MRI (magnetic resonance imaging). In some cases, early-stage breast cancers (in situ) may be surgically removed without removing the entire breast (lumpectomy). Larger tumors may require removal of the entire breast (mastectomy) with or without removal of nearby lymph nodes.

The American Cancer Society estimated 19,010 new cases of breast cancer among African American women during the year 2007. The incidence of breast cancer is higher among African American women under the age of 40 compared to White women. After age 40, African American women have a lower incidence of breast cancer compared to Whites. BRCA1 and BRCA2 gene mutations predict a high lifetime breast cancer risk. Carriers or first-degree relatives (daughter, sister) of BRCA mutation carriers are at a higher risk of developing breast cancer and are encouraged to undergo early and more intensive breast cancer screening.

LUNG CANCER

Lung cancer is the most common cancer in the United States and the most common cause of cancer death. When analyzed by gender, lung cancer incidence in women is second only to breast cancer; in men, lung cancer incidence is second to prostate cancer. Approximately 9,060 new lung cancer cases were estimated among African American women in 2007. Incidence rates are similar for African American and White women. Tobacco smoking is the greatest risk factor for the development of lung cancer. There are two major subclasses of lung cancer, small cell and non-small cancer. Non-small cell cancers make up the vast majority of lung cancers. As a group, they are more likely to be treated by surgical resection, with or without chemotherapy or radiation. Small cell lung cancer accounts for only about 15 percent of lung cancer cases. An aggressive type tends to spread quickly. It occurs almost exclusively in smokers. Because of its rapid growth, it tends to be diagnosed after it has already spread, making the chance of surgical cure unlikely. Patients are often treated with chemotherapy and/or radiation.

There are no standard recommendations for routine screening for lung cancer. However symptoms of a persistent, unrelenting cough, cough productive of bloody sputum, and weight loss are concerning for lung cancer. The first screening test in high-risk individuals is usually a chest x-ray, which may demonstrate a mass lesion in the lung.

COLON CANCER

Colon cancer is the third most common cancer among women in the United States, and the second leading cause of cancer-related death. According to the American Cancer Society, 16,440 African American women were diagnosed with colon cancer in 2007, and approximately 7,070 African American women died from colon cancer that same year.

The colon serves to absorb water from food by-products that have been processed in the small intestine. In this process, waste products are converted into formed stools. Colon cancer has been shown to progress from a benign, noncancerous polyp to cancer. A polyp can be described a growth on the inner lining of the colon wall. It can be thought of as similar to a mole that grows on the skin. Polyps start as tiny raised areas on the colon lining. Over time, these can grow in size, and change shape. Some of these polyps if unchecked can develop into a cancer that can invade deeper layers of the colon wall. If the cancer goes beyond the colon wall, it can invade nearby lymph nodes and blood vessels and travel to distant organs, such as the liver or lung.

Colon cancer screening has become so important because colon cancer can be prevented by simply removing precancerous polyps. Different types of precancerous colon polyps include tubular adenomas, tubulovillous adenomas, villous adenomas, or serrated polyps. Not all polyps are precancerous polyps. A very common colon polyp that is usually not precancerous is a type called hyperplastic. This is a growth of completely benign colon cells. With few exceptions, the hyperplastic type polyps have no malignant potential. During a colonoscopy, there can be clues as to polyps that appear hyperplastic, especially if the polyp is tiny. However, some small polyps can be precancerous, while some large polyps may actually be hyperplastic. National guidelines recommend removal of all polyps seen at colonoscopy. Once a polyp is removed, it no longer poses a cancer risk to patients. These polyps are then reviewed by a pathologist who examines the polyp specimen under a microscope. Determination of polyp type allows health professionals to make recommendations regarding screening intervals. For example, a healthy 50-year-old woman with no family history of colon polyps or cancer has two small polyps removed during a colonoscopy. If both of these were adenomas, the recommendation would be to repeat the colonoscopy in five years. People who are found to have polyps are at risk of forming new polyps elsewhere in the colon.

A study published in the *Journal of the American Medical Association* reported higher prevalence of colon polyps among Blacks compared to Whites at initial colonoscopy. This study examined the colonoscopy date from 67 U.S. gastroenterology practices between 2004 and 2005. A total of 85,325 people were included in the analysis (80,061 White, 5,464 Black) and 50 percent female. Patients had undergone colonoscopy for cancer-screening purposes; they had no symptoms. Among women, they found that Black women were more likely to harbor polyps 9 mm or larger than were White women (with polyps averaging 1.62 mm [1.39–1.89]). This difference was much more pronounced than the odds difference of Black men compared to White men (1.16).

At what age should we start screening for colon cancer? While current national guidelines recommended screening beginning at age 50, it has been recognized that African Americans have an increased risk of death from colon cancer compared to Whites. While colorectal cancer incidence has decreased among Whites, the African American population has not seen this decline. In fact, the incidence of colon and rectal cancer in African Americans has remained nearly the same over the past two decades. Accordingly, in 2005 the American College of Gastroenterology has recommended beginning routine colon cancer screening at age 45 for African Americans. Since there is not a national policy endorsing this recommendation, insurance companies may be reluctant to cover the cost of a colonoscopy at age 45.

CANCER OF THE UTERINE CERVIX

Cervical cancer was estimated to occur in 1,910 African American women in 2007; 720 women were estimated to die from cervical cancer during that year. Cervical cancer is often linked to the sexually transmitted virus called human papillomavirus (HPV). Precancerous lesions of the cervix can be detected during a pap smear performed as part of the gynecologic examination. While the use of routine pap smears has dramatically reduced the incidence of cervical cancer, the incidence and mortality rates for African American women are higher than those of White women. A vaccine against HPV infection is now widely available and is expected to reduce the incidence of cervical cancer.

CANCER OF THE ESOPHAGUS

The esophagus or food pipe is a conduit that carries liquids and chewed solid food from the mouth to the stomach. The two most common cancers of the esophagus are squamous cell cancer and adenocarcinoma. There are named differently because they originate from two separate types of cells in the esophagus. Both types of esophageal cancers are more frequent in males compared to females. Squamous cell cancer of the esophagus is linked to smoking. Adenocarcinoma of the esophagus is associated with chronic acid-reflux. Over many years, the normal squamous cells that line the esophagus get replaced (metaplasia) with columnar (elongated) cells that resemble intestinal cells. This condition, known as Barrett's esophagus, is more commonly seen in people who have a long history of acid reflux, perhaps 10 years or more. Barrett's esophagus is considered a premalignant condition and thus increases a person's risk of developing esophageal cancer (adenocarcinoma). Barrett's esophagus can be suspected by the finding of salmon-colored esophagus lining. Biopsies can be taken from the esophagus and the specimens are examined under a microscope. If Barrett's esophagus is confirmed, these patients need periodic endoscopies to check for any development of precancerous changes. Over time, these cells can become more and more abnormal until they become precancerous (dysplasia) and finally cancerous (adenocarcinoma).

The other type of esophageal cancer, squamous cell cancer, is not related to acid reflux but may be linked to smoking. Squamous cell cancer of the esophagus in the most common type worldwide, accounting for 95 percent of cases; African American are more likely to have squamous cell cancer than adenocarcinoma. However, in the United States, over 60 percent of esophageal cancers diagnosed are adenocarcinoma. Unfortunately, squamous cell cancer of the esophagus has a worse prognosis than adenocarcinoma.

Patients who have esophageal cancer of either type may complain of trouble swallowing, weight loss, or bleeding. They may alter their diet to only soft foods or puree foods to solid foods being stuck in the esophagus. Occasionally, bleeding may develop.

Who should be screened for esophageal cancer? Since people who have had heartburn for 10 years are at risk for Barrett's esophagus, they should be screened. People who develop swallowing trouble can harbor an esophageal cancer and should be screened. While most swallowing problems are not caused by cancer, it is important to exclude cancer as a cause. We screen people for esophageal cancer with a test called EGD (esophagogastroduodenopscopy). After a patient is given sedation, a gastroenterologist takes a thin tube with a light at the end and passed it through the mouth into the esophagus. This same scope can also be used to examine the stomach and the beginning of the small intestine (duodenum). In the esophagus, we look for masses, narrow areas or strictures, or abnormal color or texture of the lining of the esophagus. The physician inspects the lining and may take biopsies of abnormal areas. The pathologist looks at the biopsies under a microscope.

Symptoms of esophageal cancer may include painful swallowing or trouble swallowing, weight loss, and bleeding. However, it is important to note that difficulty swallowing can represent benign causes such as acid reflux esophagitis.

If cancer of the esophagus is diagnosed, some patients benefit from chemotherapy and radiation alone, but many require surgery. Surgical management of esophageal cancer may include surgical resection (removal) of the cancerous section of the esophagus. This may require reconnection of the stomach and esophagus.

If an esophageal cancer cannot be cured with surgery, treatment is aimed at reducing symptoms to improve quality of life. This is palliative care. This may involve radiation to shrink the tumor, particularly if it is bulky and interfering with the ability to swallow and get adequate nutrition. Flexible stents can be placed in the esophagus to push the tumor aside, and allow food to pass.

STOMACH CANCER

The stomach aids in digestion and acts as a reservoir, controlling the movement of food particles to the small intestine. In the stomach, food mixes with digestive juices that begin the process of releasing nutrients from food. Food is also crushed (pulverized) in the stomach into smaller particles that can exit the stomach and enter the small intestine.

Stomach cancer is much more common in Asia than in Western countries. There is a known association between H pylori stomach infection and stomach cancer. However, many people carry the H pylori bacteria and never develop cancer. H pylori are associated with some stomach ulcers. People with stomach ulcers are generally tested for H pylori and treated if the bacteria are found. People with stomach cancers are also treated for H pylori if infection is found. One particular stomach cancer,

MALT lymphoma, can be treated by treating H pylori with antibiotics. However, the majority of stomach cancers require definitive treatment including surgery, with or without chemotherapy and radiation.

PANCREAS CANCER

The pancreas gland lies behind the stomach and secretes enzymes into the beginning of the small intestine, called the duodenum. The pancreas has two major functions. Its endocrine function includes production of hormones, namely insulin that regulates blood sugar. Its exocrine function is secretion of enzymes that aid digestion.

Pancreas cancer was estimated to occur in 2,010 African American women during 2007. Pancreas cancer tends to have a poor prognosis because often symptoms do not develop until the cancer has already progressed. While relatively an uncommon cancer, it is often fatal. There are no good screening tests to detect pancreas cancer early. Pancreas cancer at the tail end of the pancreas may have no symptoms. Pancreas cancers arising from the head of the pancreas may block the pancreas duct and bile duct. When the bile duct becomes blocked, patients become jaundiced. This manifest as yellowing of the eyes and skin; the stool may become clay-colored, and the urine may become dark. Patients may present with "painless jaundice," that is, jaundice without any abdominal pain.

Additionally, patients may develop pancreatitis. This is caused by backup of pancreas enzymes in the pancreas duct, which leads to inflammation and swelling of the gland, or diabetes. Sometimes the new finding of diabetes in a person after the age of 50 can be the only clue to an underlying pancreas cancer. Risk factors for pancreas cancer may include smoking, family history in a first-degree relative (i.e., sibling or parents), hereditary pancreatitis, or chronic pancreatitis of any cause.

The operation for cancer in the head of the pancreas is called a Whipple operation. This involves removing the front end of the pancreas, part of the duodenum that surrounds the head of the pancreas, and part of the bile duct, which courses through the head of the pancreas. The end of the pancreas, the remaining bile duct, and the cut ends of the small intestine are reconnected surgically. Cancers of the tail of the pancreas that can be managed surgically typically require surgical removed of the tail end of the pancreas. Because this portion of the pancreas lies next to the spleen and the splenic artery and vein, often the spleen is removed with this operation as well.

OVARIAN CANCER

Ovarian cancer accounted for about 1,770 new cancer diagnoses among African American women in 2007. Though relatively rare, the mortality rate remains high at 70 percent. Sisters and daughters of women with ovarian cancer are at higher risk. In addition, family history of breast plus ovarian cancer confers a higher risk. Oral contraceptive pills may decrease the risk of ovarian cancer in women at higher risk, although the risk of blood clots may increase as well.

BILE DUCT CANCER

Cholangiocarcinoma refers to cancer of the bile ducts. Bile ducts are networks of small tubes that transport bile from its place of origin in the liver into the small intestine. Hundreds of tiny ducts join to form larger ducts, like tree branches. These eventually form a single large duct that lies outside the liver and delivers bile into the first part of the small intestine, called the duodenum. Prior to reaching the small intestine, some of the bile is diverted to the gall bladder, where it is stored during fasting. If the bile ducts are blocked, bile accumulates in the bloodstream and causes the skin and membranes to become yellow or jaundiced. Often this occurs in the absence of abdominal pain. Risk factors for cholangiocarcinoma may include primary liver disease such as primary sclerosing cholangitis. Surgical treatment may include removal of the involved portion of the bile duct and reconnection of the liver to the intestine.

CANCER OF THE LIVER

Liver cancer, called hepatocellular cancer, is named for the cells that make up the bulk of the liver, called hepatocytes. The liver has several important roles in the body, including removal of impurities from the bloodstream, metabolism, and production of digestive juices. Risk factors for hepatocellular cancer include chronic viral hepatitis, including hepatitis B and hepatitis C infections. Any condition leading to cirrhosis (severe scarring of the liver with liver damage), such as alcohol-related liver disease, can be a risk factor for cancer of the liver. People with cirrhosis should have routine screening for liver cancer, such as an ultrasound or CT scan every 6 to 12 months, and a blood test for a tumor marker called AFP (alpha-feto protein). AFP is a protein made by the liver, which can rise in the blood if there is a liver cancer. AFP is also made normal by the placenta and may be elevated in pregnancy. Other clues of liver cancer may include an abnormal rise in liver enzymes in the blood. Treatment for liver cancer may include surgical resection of the mass or radiation-based treatments. In some cases, patients may be eligible for liver transplants as treatment of liver cancer.

MORTALITY

Albano and colleagues (2007) utilized 2001 National Center for Health statistics data on mortality. They identified cases of cancer-related death between Black and non-Hispanic Whites 25–64 years old. From the database, they analyzed data on 137,708 persons. In addition to cause of death, total years of education was also recorded on the death certificate (included as part of death certificate as of 1989). As of 2001, 80 percent of all death certificates had information on educational background. Education was reported as number of years (0–17 or more). Information on cancer-screening practices (colon screening and mammography) and education level with respect to cancer risk factors were extracted from the 2000 National Health Interview Survey for a total of 13,326 non-Hispanic White and 2,953 Black men and women ages 25–64. Cancer types studied included lung, breast, colon-rectum, and prostate.

Among Black women, the relative risk of cancer death was 1.54 comparing women of highest education attainment compared to lowest levels of education. Death rates from cancer were higher for Black women compared to White women in four of the six education level categories. Overall, the greatest difference in mortality rate was seen at extremes of education attainment. However, the difference (or influence of) in death rate by education level was associated more strongly with education level among males (Black or White) and White women. For example, the relative risk of cancer death was 3.27 comparing White men of highest education (postgraduate school) attainment to White men of the lower educational attainment (middle school). There was an inverse relationship between years of education and cancer death rate for Black men, White men, and White women; that trend was not seen for Black women. However, among Black women, the highest education levels were associated with lower cancer death rates than among those with fewer years of education. Interestingly, higher breast cancer death rates were seen with higher levels of education, such that the lowest death rates were seen in those with 0–8 years of education.

The authors also considered possible interactions of smoking status. They found that breast cancer mortality was lower among Black (and White) women with increasing education. Current smoking rates decreased as education level increased.

Cancer Risk Factors

TOBACCO USE

The International Agency for Research on Cancer (IARC) has complied a listing of cancers that have a causal relationship with tobacco smoking. According to the IARC, tobacco smoking is associated with cancer of the lung, oral cavity, pharynx, larynx, pancreas, bladder, renal pelvis and urethra (urinary tract), nasal cavities, nasal sinuses, esophagus, stomach, liver, kidney, cervix, and bone marrow, myeloid leukemia. *Smoking duration is the strongest determinant of cancer in smokers.* In a meta-analysis published in 2007 by Gandini and coauthors, the authors pooled data from 254 studies worldwide concerning the risk of cancer associated with cigarette smoking. Eighty of these studies were from the United States. The intent of the study was to determine the *relative risk* of various cancers attributed to current and former tobacco use. In many studies, former smoking referred to at least one year of abstinence. A relative risk greater than 1 denotes an increased risk of cancer associated with smoking. Greater numbers indicate a greater risk association. A relative risk less than 1 indicates an inverse association, and may suggest a protective effect. A relative risk of equal to 1 implies no association. Among current smokers, cigarette smoking was a strong risk factor for development of lung cancer with relative risk (RR) of 8.96. Cancer of the larynx (RR 6.98) and pharynx (RR 6.76) had the second and third highest association with current smoking. Current smoking was associated with a threefold risk of cancers of the upper digestive tract (oral cavity, pharynx, nasal sinuses, and esophagus). Smaller degrees of association were seen for cancer of the lower urinary tract (RR 2.77), pancreas (RR 1.7), liver (RR 1.56), naso-pharynx (RR 1.95), uterine cervix (RR 1.83), and kidney (RR 1.52). For former smokers, the risks were decreased, though still statistically significant for lung cancer (RR 3.85), cancer of the larynx

(RR 4.65), upper digestive tract (RR 3.57), lower urinary tract (RR 1.72), pancreas (RR 1.18), liver (RR 1.49), naso-pharynx (RR 1.39), uterine cervix (RR 1.26), and kidney (RR 1.25).

A stronger case for causality is made if there is a dose-response relationship. That is, less exposure has less risk; increasing amounts (doses) of exposure are associated with increasing risk of disease (response). Gandini and coauthors (2008) reviewed studies that examined the relationship between cigarette smoking, in terms of number of cigarettes smoked per day, and lung cancer development. These data were reported separately for men and women. For women, the risk of lung cancer among women who smoked 9 or fewer cigarettes per day was 1.49, 10–19 cigarettes per day 3.30. The risk was considerably higher for women who smoked 20 or more cigarettes per day, corresponding to a RR of 24.1 for lung cancer. Men who smoked 20 or more cigarettes per day had a RR 13.7 risk of lung cancer. The risk for men was 2.67 if they smoked 10–19 cigarettes per day and 1.39 if they smoked 9 or fewer cigarettes per day. These data do not report the duration of smoking (i.e., number of years). While a large number of studies were pooled for this meta-analysis, most studies did not report on all the cancer types listed; for example, the RR of lung cancer in current smokers was determined from pooled data from 21 different studies, whereas data on laryngeal cancer in current smokers was pooled from only 10 different studies. In addition, for studies that considered African Americans, the meta-analysis revealed a RR 3.49. Finally, the authors did not subdivide cancer site into cell type. For example, squamous cell carcinoma of the esophagus is more prevalent in African Americans compared to Whites, whereas adenocarcinoma of the esophagus is more common in White than Blacks.

OBESITY

Studies have shown that obesity may not only increase cancer risk. It has been postulated that molecular factors that are produced in the obese state may also induce tumor susceptibility.

There is a known association between obesity and endometrial cancer (Carroll, 1998). This association is strongest for postmenopausal women. There is also an association between obesity and breast cancer that varies in terms of risk level (e.g., being overweight is associated with a decreased risk of breast cancer among premenopausal women; however, after menopause, overweight women have a higher risk of developing breast cancer). Moreover, the risk of dying from cancer is higher in these women. Central obesity, that is the accumulation of fat in the waist area, is also associated with increased risk of endometrial cancer, and in postmenopausal women an increased risk of breast cancer.

Adult weight ranges can be categorized by body mass index (BMI). This measurement is useful because it takes in account an adult person's height and weight. BMI can be calculated with the formula BMI = weight in kg divided by height in meters squared and is expressed as kg/m^2. For example, an adult who is five feet, nine inches and weighs 160 lbs has a BMI of 23.6, which is considered "healthy." The Centers for Disease Control and Prevention (CDC) define overweight as BMI between 25 and 29.9. Obese is defined as BMI greater than or equal to 30. Healthy weight is represented by BMI 18.5–24.9; BMI less than 18.5 is considered underweight.

Unfortunately, death from many types of cancer is higher among the overweight and obese. Very obese women (BMI ≥40) had a 60 percent higher risk of death from cancer than normal weight women did. They saw increasing risk of death for increasing BMI. The highest level of increase risk of death was seen in uterine cancer, kidney cervical cancer, and pancreatic cancer, compared to lower weight women (BMI 18.5–22.9). Women of higher BMI who developed cancers of the colon and rectum, liver, breast, ovary, gall bladder, non-Hodgkin's lymphoma, and multiple myeloma also had higher risk of death than women with lower BMI. On the contrary, high BMI was protective against lung-cancer death in smokers and nonsmokers.

TABLE 4. BODY MASS INDEX (BMI) CATEGORIES

BMI KG/M²	WHO WEIGHT CATEGORY	CDC WEIGHT CATEGORY
< 18.5		Underweight
18.5–24.9	Normal range	Healthy weight
25.0–29.9	Grade 1 overweight	Overweight
30.0–34.9	Grade 2 overweight	Obese
35.0–39.9	Grade 3 overweight	Obese

Note: WHO: World Health Organization; CDC: Centers for Disease Control and Prevention.

TABLE 5. COMMON CANCER-SCREENING TESTS

AGE	CANCER TYPE	RECOMMENDED SCREENING TESTS
20	Breast	Clinical breast exam every 3 years
21	Cervical	Annual or biannual pap smear
40	Breast	Annual clinical breast exam
40	Breast	Annual mammogram
50*	Colon and rectum	Colonoscopy every 10 years *or* flexible sigmoidoscopy every 5 years *or* double contrast barium enema every 5 years *or* CT colonography (virtual colonoscopy) every 5 years

Source: American Cancer Society Guidelines for the Early Detection of Cancer, 2008.

Note: These recommendations apply only to people who are average risk for a particular cancer. Consult your health care provider for individualized recommendations.

*The American College of Gastroenterology recommendation that African Americans begin colon cancer screening at age 45 has not yet been incorporated into national guidelines.

GENETICS

Many cancers have genes associated with risk of development. The most identifiable clues to a heredity cancer are cancer in multiple family members and cancers developing at younger ages (i.e., before age 50). However, there are contributions of genetic environmental factors that ultimately determine whether cancer will develop. In other words, while one's genes are nonmodifiable, we can modify our exposure to smoking, alcohol, and other factors that cause cancer.

PREVENTION

One of the most effective ways health care providers can help people prevent cancer is by detecting and treating precancerous lesions *before* they can become cancer. We have the capability to detect and treat precancerous lesions of the colon and rectum using colonoscopy. Precancerous changes of the cervix can be identified by pap smear. We also have good screening tests to detect early stage breast and colon cancers at curative stages. Recommendations for cancer screening in average-risk women are shown in table 5.

CHEMOPREVENTION

The ideal chemopreventive agent is an affordable food substance or medication without undesired side effects that will virtually eliminate the chance of a person developing a cancer. No such agent has been discovered, but a few agents deserve mention.

Antioxidants

These enzymes prevent the formation of free radicals, which can cause oxidative damage to cell DNA leading to cancerous cells. Antioxidants are plentiful in foods such as green tea, dark green vegetables such as spinach and greens, vitamins A, C, and E, and beta-carotene in carrots, oranges, and other orange-colored fruits and vegetables. Both beta-carotene and lutein are found in dark green vegetables. Pink grapefruit and guava are examples of foods containing lycopene. Finally, selenium, a component of antioxidant enzyme, can be found in rice, breads, and meats.

Estrogen Receptor Modulators

Studies have shown reduced breast cancer risk among younger women taking tamoxifen. Tamoxifen is a selective estrogen-receptor modulator. As a chemoprevention agent tamoxifen inhibits tumor growth. Potential serious adverse effects of tamoxifen include deep venous thrombosis (DVT), which refers to formation of blood clots in the deep leg veins. Such clots can travel to the lung with dire consequences, even death. However, the risk of DVT is similar to that of women taking other female hormones, particularly oral contraceptive pills. Breast cancers can also be classified according to whether or not the cancer carries receptors for estrogen. Estrogen receptor-positive cancers respond to and may be prevented by tamoxifen; estrogen receptor-negative breast cancers will not.

Oral Contraceptive Pills

Studies have demonstrated that the use of oral contraceptive pills may decrease the risk of ovarian cancer by as much as 50 percent over five years. There is, however, an increased risk of blood clots among smokers who use oral contraceptive pills, and the benefits must be weighed against this risk.

Folate (Folic Acid)

Folate is an essential part of the diet. Folate is found in leafy green vegetables, beans, and citrus. This nutrient is vital for proper synthesis of cellular components of the body. Folic acid is thought to play a role in prevention of colon cancer. It may block cancer promoters (oncogenes) on a molecular level. Lack of folate may lead to mutations in DNA. Population-based studies (epidemiologic) suggest that people with diets low in folate may be at increased risk of colon cancer. However, there is conflicting data as to whether taking folate vitamin supplements can actually reduce cancer risk.

NSAIDs

Nonsteroidal anti-inflammatory drugs include aspirin and ibuprofen, for example, and a group of arthritis medications called COX-2 inhibitors. These medications may block enzymes that mediate the production of cancerous cells. Some NSAIDs, particularly COX-2 inhibitors, have been shown in clinical trials to reduce colon cancer risk. The best data come from groups of people with a specific genetic predisposition to early-age onset colon cancer. This inherited disorder called familial adenomatous polyposis (FAP) leads to hundreds of precancerous adenomatous colon polyps at a young age. FAP patients are at very high risk of developing colon cancer as early as age 30. Studies show that in this select population COX-2 inhibitors may be beneficial in preventing precancerous polyp formation. Unfortunately when larger trials were done in non-FAP patients, there were increased cardiovascular events, limiting the use of COX-2 inhibitors overall.

Conclusion

African American women may be at increased risk of cancer or cancer-related death due to genetic, environmental, and socioeconomic factors. Education, lifestyle modification, and improved access to health care may help narrow the gap in cancer outcomes between African American women and their White counterparts. Women must pay attention to their own bodies and see their health care providers regularly for physical examinations. Women must also talk to their siblings, parents, aunts, and uncles and find out what diseases are prevalent in their own families. Chemopreventive agents may be useful in people who are known to be at high risk for certain cancers, such as people with strong family histories of cancer. While some chemopreventive medications and supplements have shown promise, they are not necessarily proven to prevent cancer when used in larger clinical trials. The best practice is to eat healthily, balanced meals, maintain a healthy weight, avoid tobacco and excess alcohol consumption, and follow national guidelines for cancer-screening tests.

REFERENCES

Albano, J.D., Ward, E., Jemal, A., Anderson, R., Cokkinides, V.E., Murray, T., Henley, J., Liff, J., Thun, M.J. (2007). Cancer mortality in the United States by education level and race. *National Cancer Institute Journal*, *99*(18), 1384–1394.

American Cancer Society (2007). *Cancer facts and figures for African Americans, 2007–2008*. Atlanta: American Cancer Society.

Ballard-Barbash, R., & Swanson, C.A. (1996). Body weight: Estimation of risk for breast and endometrial cancer. *American Journal of Clinical Nutrition*, *63*(Supplement 3), 437S–441S.

Baron, J.A., Sander, R.S., Bresalier, R.S., et al. (2006). A randomized trial of rofecoxib for the chemoprevention of colorectal adenomas. *Gastroenterology*, *131*, 1674–1682.

Bresalier, R.S. (2008). Chemoprevention of colorectal cancer: Why all the confusion? *Current Opinion in Gastroenterology*, *24*, 48–50.

Bresalier, R.S., Sandler, R.S., Quan, H., et al. (2005). Cardiovascular events associated with rofecoxib in a colorectal adenoma chemoprevention trial. *New England Journal of Medicine*, *352*, 1092–1102.

Calle, E., Rodriguez, C., Walker-Thurmond, K., & Thun, M. (2003). Overweight, obesity, and mortality from cancer in a prospectively studied cohort of U.S. adults. *New England Journal of Medicine*, *348*, 1625–1638.

Carroll, K.K. (1998). Obesity as a risk factor for certain types of cancer. *Lipids*, *33*(11), 1055–1059.

Fisher, B., Costantino, J.P., Wickerham, D.L., et al. (2005). Tamoxifen for the prevention of breast cancer: Current status of the National Surgical Adjuvant Breast and Bowel Project P-1 study. *National Cancer Institute*

Journal, 97, 1652–1662.

Gandini, S., Botteri, L.E., Iodice, E., Boniol, M., Lowenfels, A.B., Maisonneuve, P., & Boyle, P. (2008). Tobacco smoking and cancer: A meta-analysis. *International Journal of Cancer, 122,* 155–164.

Greenstein, A.J., Litle, V.R., Swanson, S.J., Divino, C.M., Packer, T.G., McGinn, M.P.H, & Wisnivesky, J.P. (2008). Racial disparities in esophageal cancer and outcomes. *Annals of Surgical Oncology, 15*(3), 881–888.

Hankinson, S.E., Colditz, G.A., Hunter, D.J., et al. (1992). A quantitative assessment of oral contraceptive use and risk of ovarian cancer. *Obstetrics and Gynecology, 80*(4), 708–714.

Kopelman, P.G. (2000). Obesity as a medical problem. *Nature, 404*(6), 635–643.

Lynch, P.M. (2008). Chemoprevention with special reference to inherited colorectal cancer. *Familial Cancer, 7,* 59–64.

No author. (1998). Tamoxifen for early breast cancer: An overview of the randomized trials. Early Breast Cancer Trialists' Collaborative Group. *Lancet, 351,* 1451–1467.

Paavonen, J., Jenkins, D., Bosch, F.X., Naud, P., Salmerón, J., Wheeler, C.M., Chow, S.N., et al. (2007). Efficacy of a prophylactic adjuvanted bivalent L1 virus-like-particle vaccine against infection with human papillomavirus types 16 and 18 in young women: An interim analysis of a phase III double blind, randomised controlled trial. *Lancet, 369*(9580), 2161–2170.

Smith, R.A., Saslow, D., Sawyer, K.A., Burke, W., Costanza, M.E., Evans, W.P., III, Foster, R.S., Jr., Hendrick, E., Eyre, H.J., & Sener, S. (2003). American Cancer Society guidelines for breast cancer screening: Update 2003. *CA: A Cancer Journal for Clinicians, 53*(3), 141–169.

Solomon, S.D., McMurray, J.J., Pfeffer, M.A., et al. (2005). Cardiovascular risk associated with celecoxib in a clinical trial for colorectal adenoma prevention. *New England Journal of Medicine, 352,* 1071–1080.

Vogel, V.G., Costantino, J.P., Wickerham, D.L., et al. (2006). Effects of tamoxifen vs. raloxifene on the risk of developing invasive breast cancer and other disease outcomes: The NSABP Study of Tamoxifen and Raloxifene (STAR) P-2 trial. *JAMA, 295,* 2727–2741.

World Health Organization (1995). Physical status: The use and interpretation of anthropometry: Report of a WHO Expert Committee. Author, *854,* 1–452.

Improving General Health Care for African American Women

MICHIGAN AND BEYOND

PHILLIS CHERIE MIMS-GILLUM

Historically, African American women have the poorest overall health and health outcomes when compared to other groups of women. Socioeconomic, cultural, racial, and gender barriers severely affect the ability of this population of women to receive process, accept, and incorporate those skills, knowledge, and behaviors necessary to lessen their overall health risks. According to the U.S. Census Bureau in 2007, the state of Michigan has the tenth largest Black population. Of the 10 largest cities in the United States, Detroit had the largest proportion of Blacks, 83 percent (Office of Minority Health, 2012). In view of this, it is imperative that health providers, community networks, and educational institutions in these regions are actively involved in the discussion of ways to promote optimal health for Black women across the life span.

Critical Health Issues: Chronic Disease and Reproductive Health

The status of health for women of color in Michigan is a reflection of what is happening for these women across the nation. In many key areas, disparities in incidence and outcome have been well documented. African American women are at the highest risk in the nation to be overweight (body mass index—BMI over 25) or obese (BMI over 30). Obesity contributes to many health problems, such as heart disease and diabetes.

HEART DISEASE, STROKE, AND DIABETES

Heart disease and stroke are major risks for women. In fact, heart disease is the number one cause of death for women in America. African Americans are 40 percent more likely to have had a stroke in their lifetime than Whites are. Heart disease death rates are 322 per 100,000 population for African Americans compared to 219 per 100,000 for Whites (National Stroke Association, n.d.). Diabetes is two times as likely to be diagnosed among African American adults. Although they comprise only 14 percent of the population, they account for about 20 percent of all people with diabetes and 46 percent of the people on kidney dialysis (Centers for Disease Control and Prevention, n.d.; Office of Minority Health, 2011).

REPRODUCTIVE HEALTH AND INFANT MORTALITY

The rates of STDs and HIV are particularly acute and appear to occur more often in African American women and women of low socioeconomic status. The reproductive health of women of color is further threatened by limited access to basic reproductive health care, including family-planning services and abortion care. Michigan women lack many important reproductive rights. Poor women can only receive public funding for abortion in federally mandated, limited circumstances. Alternatives to abortion, especially closed adoption, are often deemed culturally unacceptable. The state does not require health insurers to provide comprehensive coverage for contraception. Not only are African American women at higher risk for these problems and disease processes, they are less likely to survive these diagnoses. In 2003, the death rate for African Americans was higher than for White Americans for heart diseases, stroke, cancer, diabetes, HIV/AIDS, and homicide.

African American infant deaths occur more than three times as often as White deaths (17.9 deaths vs. 5.5 deaths per 1,000 live births). The rate of SIDS (sudden infant death syndrome) among African Americans is 1.8 times the rate in non-Hispanic Whites. Black women are three times more likely to die during pregnancy or delivery than White women are. Initiation of prenatal care occurs later in pregnancy and low birth weight infants, preterm labor, and prematurity occur more often in African American women.

The Challenge

African American women have more disease, disability, and early death than Whites do.[1] They are less likely to receive medical attention. When they do receive health care, it is less often preventative. This results in late diagnosis and more advanced disease processes. In addition, these women are more likely to have comorbidities and coexisting conditions, such as poor nutrition, diabetes, heart disease, and other conditions, which worsen overall outcome. The first step in eliminating health disparities among African American women is identifying those systemic obstacles that impede access to quality care.

Economics/poverty

Well over one-quarter of African Americans (27.4 percent), in comparison to one in seven (15.1 percent) of all Americans or roughly 8 percent of non-Hispanic Whites, live at or below the poverty level. Almost half of African American women in poverty (48.8 percent) are single and head of household (U.S. Census Bureau, 2010, 2011).

Limited access/insurance coverage

Young women of color are disproportionately members of the working poor who often lack access to affordable and culturally sensitive health services. They tend to be uninsured or markedly underinsured. Combined with economic status, the increase in copays for office visits and prescriptions can often be prohibitive in terms of seeking medical attention.

Education and information

There is a notable education gap in the African American community. African Americans lag behind their White and Asian counterparts in general. African American women are less likely than Asian American or White women to have four-year college, graduate, or professional degrees and are more likely to be stratified in lower-prestige and lower-paying positions (McDaniel et al., 2009). They tend to be less informed about health care, including preventive measures, screening recommendations, alternative options for access to care, government or institutional programs that will cover or prorate the cost of care, and the availability of services and institutions that provide them.

Communication

Cultural practices of silence among African Americans produce a reticence in discussing sexuality, domestic or sexual abuse, and even general health diagnoses especially in terms of sexually transmitted diseases, cancers, or severely uncontrolled diabetes, chronic hypertension or other illnesses. African American women tend to join the ranks of all women in reluctance to ask about past sexual risks or substance abuse or to demand the use of condoms or initial and ongoing STD and HIV screening in relationships. Older African Americans were more likely to keep silent about significant symptoms and less likely to share information about diagnosis and prognosis thus resulting in delayed diagnosis, death without diagnosis, and incomplete family history of possible genetic health issues for survivors.

Cultural superstitions

Homeopathic and home remedies often are used in place of medical screening and recommendations. While these techniques may have value when used in conjunction, when used alone they risk delay in the diagnoses of significant medical problems. Many of these practices developed because of limited access to or distrust of the medical system. One common superstition is that a family member was fine until he or she had a recommended surgery; once the patient was cut, it caused the cancer to spread and worsened the prognosis and outcome.

Trust

The issue of African American distrust in the medical system continues to cast a shadow on the relationship between this population and the biomedical community. This distrust is grounded in the knowledge that the health care system has been built on bodies of African Americans and the poor. Slaves served as models for experimentation, instructional material for teaching medical students, and source of entertainment at medical conventions. The most well-known (although certainly not the only example of) postslavery experiment is the Tuskegee syphilis experiment engineered from 1932 to 1972. This government study to research the effects of untreated syphilis involved 400 African American men. These men were never informed that they were not being treated or that effective treatment was available. Although the study was widely and regularly reported over a 40-year span, there was no outcry, intervention, or denunciation by the general medical community (Thomas & Quinn, 1991).

Taking Action

The first step in improving health care for African American women in Michigan and beyond is to open the lines of communication regarding all of these issues that affect health care. The conversation must include the target patients and involve health providers, church and community leaders, health care administrators, government agencies, and more.

The next step is to create a Comprehensive Health Education Action Plan throughout communities in Michigan and beyond that targets women of color. Improved and ethical research programs that address issues specific to African American women need to be established. They should be culturally relevant and sensitive, universally available, and provide complete disclosure. Ways to increase the providers who reflect the population they serve should be encouraged, and visibility of African American women physicians and researchers should be increased.

Comprehensive Health Education Action Plan for African American women across the life span

It is never too early to educate and to initiate action plans for good health care. Knowledge obtained, even in childhood years, will serve as the foundation for a good long-term approach to health. Reinforcement measures are necessary throughout the years for health maintenance. Education and action goals should address several areas to optimize health status and outcomes for African American women and their families. These areas are not isolated entities, but are intimately linked and related.

Nutrition

Poor nutrition equals poor overall health. It is clear that being overweight or obese, especially from an early age, increases risks for heart disease, hypertension, chronic disease, and some forms of cancer. An adolescent of unhealthy weight has a 70 percent chance of becoming an overweight adult. If at least one parent is overweight, the chance increases to 80 percent. The state of Michigan was crowned the number one fattest state in America for 2008 and has consistently been in the top 10 for this category for greater than a decade. Education and action goals regarding nutrition must begin at an early age and stress the adverse effects of being overweight on health and well-being. Concrete examples of affordable diet plans that are culturally sensitive to the tastes of the African American diet should be provided. This should also include alternative healthy measures for preparation of traditional "soul food" dishes. Changing the mind-set at an early age from fast food as a mainstay of a diet plan to fast food as an occasional treat will go a long way in eliminating obesity. Specific cultural issues for African American women revolve around physical appearance and the general acceptance of being thick (or "healthy") and voluptuous. This must be factored in by health care providers in order to devise a sensitive and realistic approach to weight in this population.

Exercise

The development of new technologies such as videogames, Internet, expanded cable network, and drive-thru facilities has caused a decline in the physical activity levels of children and adults. Physical education programs in schools have declined in funds and time allotment over the years. Despite national recommendations that all ages engage in at least 30 minutes of physical activity most days of the week, Michigan elementary school students receive on average one hour weekly, and this declines even further for middle and high school students.

Education and action plans for exercise must involve families, school and community programs, and media. Families should model and support physical activity, including a limitation of "screen time" (computers, television) and monitoring of sedentary behaviors. School and community programs should promote health and physical education, traditional and organized sports, walk-a-thons, and other activities that encourage increased activity. These activities and habits should be continued into adulthood.

Sexuality

Although much controversy exists around what and when sexual education should be taught, it is critical that children learn about sexuality. This foundation is best initiated in the home and followed up with reinforcement by schools and community groups. Education in this area should address anatomy with correct terminology. At early ages the difference between appropriate versus inappropriate touching should be addressed. At more advanced ages the working dynamics and function with precautions, risks, and benefits should be explored.

The ease of access and enormous exposure to sexually explicit materials in today's society can sow the seed of misinformation, which may have long-term ramifications. In addition to this, sexual predators have increased access through numerous venues. Close observation and monitoring may allow detection of early warning signs signaling abuse. Communication in this regard is also crucial to ensure that there is an established level of comfort, which permits children to discuss uncomfortable situations. Why is this so important? The age of sexual development and puberty occurs earlier in African American girls. Between one-third and two-thirds of sexual assault victims are age 15 and younger. The national Violence Against Women Survey noted that greater than 54 percent of women reported sexual abuse occurring before the age of 18, and a large percentage of rape and sexual assault victims know their attackers. The development of sexual abuse prevention skills and behavior is most effectively done if the basic educational foundation is established.

Self-Esteem and Personal Image

Fostering positive self-esteem is critical in the development of strong and healthy women. Establishing identifiable and realistic examples of beauty with an appreciation of the many variations and differences among women is crucial to building a healthy self-image. Self-esteem has become a national crisis. An alarming number of girls feel that they do not measure up in some way—appearance, performance, popularity, relationships. Socioeconomic factors and unfair comparisons to the "celebrated beauty" can drastically erode a girl's sense of self-worth and acceptance. More disturbing is that girls with low self-esteem are three times more likely to engage in harmful, destructive, risk-taking, and attention-seeking behaviors. This may manifest as self-injury, drug use, starving, binging and purging, early and promiscuous sexual behavior, or acceptance of and silent suffering of intimate and domestic violence. The active involvement of parents, family, friends, and role models within the African American community can help girls gain confidence and reach their full potential.

STD Prevention

Although much progress has been made in STD prevention over the years, the United States has the highest rates of STD infection in the industrialized world. Prevention is more important than ever. The most reliable ways to avoid infection and transmission of sexually transmitted diseases are abstinence, monogamy with an uninfected partner, and correct and consistent use of latex or non-animal skin condoms. It is important to stress that the only thing that offers 100 percent protection from sexually transmitted infections is abstinence. Since STDs have the ability to affect fertility and pregnancy outcome as well as overall health, all sexually active females should be aware of their status by having screening tests. One common misconception is that routine gynecological screening automatically tests for all diseases. This is definitely false, and clarification should always be made with treating physicians. Compliance with any treatment recommendations is also important. All sexually transmitted infections require partner treatment. Women of all ages should also be confident and adamant enough to request and require partner testing. Sexually transmitted diseases that should be considered are listed below.

- *Chlamydia.* The most common reportable sexually transmitted disease. Can sometimes be asymptomatic but has the highest potential for damaging the fallopian tubes and negatively affecting fertility. Diagnosed by culture from cervix, penis, or urine.
- *Gonorrhea.* Diagnosed by culture from cervix, penis, or urine. Along with chlamydia, this can cause extensive pelvic infections that can lead to infertility or even hysterectomy.
- *Trichomonas.* Diagnosed by visualization on wet mount or pap smear. Typically causes vaginal discharge, irritation, and urethritis.
- *Hepatitis B and C.* Diagnosed by blood test. Increases risk for end-stage liver disease or liver cancer.
- *Syphilis.* Diagnosed by blood test.

- *Genital warts/HPV.* Genital warts are caused by low-risk types of the human papillomavirus (HPV). This virus is sexually transmitted and has over 100 types. High-risk types of HPV increase the risk for cervical cancer. In most cases, HPV is asymptomatic.
- *Genital herpes Types I and II.* Treatable but not curable infection that can have recurrences or outbreaks. May be diagnosed by culture of site; however, a type-specific blood test is the most accurate diagnostic test.
- *HIV.* Diagnosed by blood test. No longer can anyone afford to consider HIV a disease of homosexual men. Women account for more than 25 percent of newly diagnosed HIV/AIDS diagnosis, as women are significantly more likely than men to contract HIV during vaginal intercourse. Heterosexual contact is identified as the source in 80 percent of these new cases. The majority of cases of women living with HIV/AIDS (64 percent) are African American. The rate of diagnosis in this population is more than 20 times that of White women. The presence of other sexually transmitted diseases greatly increases the likelihood of acquiring or transmitting HIV infection.
- *Pregnancy.* Socioeconomic factors and other significant barriers affect the timing of initiation of prenatal care in African American women, with many in this subset receiving care late in pregnancy. Despite the fact that the majority of states have programs that will pay for prenatal care and care of small children, many women are unaware of, have limited access to, or simply do not utilize these resources.

The key to improving pregnancy outcomes for African American women involves a number of factors. Avoidance of unwanted pregnancies with appropriate counseling and provision of birth control methods is the first step. Planned pregnancies with optimal management and control of preexisting medical conditions (such as diabetes, chronic hypertension) prior to conception will help to produce the best maternal and fetal outcomes. Smoking cessation and rehabilitation for drug use prior to or very early in pregnancy is also important. Access to early prenatal care (beginning in the first trimester) is preferred to screen for issues that may affect healthy birth outcomes

Cancer Screening and Prevention

The mortality or death rate of African American women from breast and cervical cancer far exceeds that of other women. Early detection is key in improving prognosis and survival rates. Recommendations for screening and prevention of cervical and breast cancer should be taught and continuously reinforced.

Breast cancer

Monthly self-breast exams combined with annual breast exams by a physician are the best screening tool for breast cancer. If there are any concerning or suspicious findings, they should be immediately brought to the attention of a physician. Family history of breast cancer should be elicited. If multiple female relatives have been diagnosed with breast cancer, consideration should be given to genetic testing for genes associated with breast cancer. This is especially true if breast cancer occurs under the age of 50. Mammogram screening should begin as a baseline between the ages of 35 and 40. Recommendations thereafter are for mammograms at least every two years between 40 and 50 and annually thereafter.

Cervical cancer

This cancer is preventable and curable if detected early. Screening with pap smears and human papillomavirus (HPV) testing are excellent strategies to reduce the risk of cervical cancer. Prevention of HPV infection is also a key approach targeted by the HPV vaccine.

Pap smears are recommended to begin by the age of 21 or approximately three years after first sexual intercourse.

They should, in general, be performed annually and combined with HPV testing for high-risk types. In high-risk populations or if abnormalities are noted, more frequent and often additional testing should be done. Some recommendations suggest that upon consultation with health care providers, pap smears may be done less frequently in low-risk populations, women who have had a hysterectomy, and women over 70 with no history of abnormal pap tests.

The Gardasil vaccine has been developed to prevent the HPV infection of Types 6, 11, 16, and 18. It is known that Types 6 and 11 are the most common causes of genital warts and Types 16 and 18 are the most common high-risk types felt to be precursors to cervical cancer. Exposure to HPV occurs via sexual contact, and by the age of 50 about 80 percent of women have been exposed. The HPV vaccine is approved for females between the ages of 9 and 26. This age range is selected in attempts to protect women prior to exposure/sexual contact. Continued screening for cervical cancer is mandatory regardless of whether or not the vaccine has been received. Abnormalities should be addressed according the American Society of Clinical Pathology guidelines regardless of vaccine status. More research is currently under way in terms of HPV vaccination with the development of new versions, which are protective against more types of this virus. Long-term protective effect is not yet fully determined and is under ongoing investigation. If this virus proves successful, perhaps administering the vaccine to males and females will be helpful in ultimate eradication of this virus.

Concluding Thoughts

The role of women in improving one another's health is vitally important. Women serve as the gatekeeper for their entire families. Empowering African American women can serve as a unique tool to eliminate health care disparities across gender and race lines. Through widespread educational programs and support of prevention programs nationwide, improvements for health outcomes for women of color can finally be realized.

NOTES

Phillis Cherie Mims-Gillum wishes to acknowledge Deidre Wasson, master's degree candidate in health education at Eastern Michigan University for aiding as a research assistant with the chapter.

1. WomensHealth.Gov.

REFERENCES

Centers for Disease Control and Prevention. (2010). *Summary health statistics for U.S. adults: National health interview survey, 2010.* Retrieved from http://www.cdc.gov/nchs/data/series/sr_10/sr10_252.pdf.

McDaniel, A., DiPrete, T.A., Buchmann, C., & Shwed, U. (2009). The Black gender gap in educational attainment: Historical trends and racial comparisons. Retrieved from http://www.columbia.edu/~tad61/Race%20Paper%2009232009.pdf.

National Stroke Association. (n.d.). *African Americans and stroke.* Retrieved from http://www.stroke.org/site/PageServer?pagename=aamer.

Office of Minority Health (2011). *Heart disease and African Americans.* Retrieved from http://minorityhealth.hhs.gov/templates/content.aspx?ID=3018.

Office of Minority Health (2012, July 13). *The Black population: 2010.* Retrieved from http://www.census.gov/prod/cen2010/briefs/c2010br-06.pdf.

Thomas S.B., & Quinn, S.C. (1991, November). The Tuskegee Syphilis Study, 1932 to 1972: Implications for HIV education and AIDS risk education programs in the Black community. *American Journal of Public Health, 81*(11), 1498–1505. doi:10.2105/AJPH.81.11.1498. PMC 1405662. PMID 1951814.

U.S. Census Bureau (2010, September). *Income, poverty, and health insurance coverage in the United States: 2010,* table 4. Retrieved from http://www.census.gov/prod/2011pubs/p60-239.pdf.

U.S. Census Bureau (2011). Poverty data table 3: People in families with related children under 18 by family structure, age, and sex, iterated by income to poverty ratio and race: 2010. *2011 Annual Social and Economic Supplement, Current Population Survey.* Washington, DC: U.S. Census Bureau.

About the Contributors

Dale Anderson is a Ph.D. candidate at Wayne State University. His research interests revolve around racial identity and diversity within hip-hop culture. His secondary interests focus on ethnographic data collection methods and creating cultural sensitivity in the classroom. Dale has presented at the National Communication Association, the Midwest Popular Culture Association, and the Michigan Association of Speech Communication Conferences. He has also been an invited speaker on the subject of autoethnography and hip-hop culture.

RoSusan D. Bartee is Professor and Program Coordinator in the Department of Counselor and Leadership Education at the University of Mississippi. Dr. Bartee teaches graduate-level courses focusing on K–12 educational leadership, the cultural contexts of education, and educational research methods. Dr. Bartee's research interests include educational leadership, organizational context, and cultural and social capital. Dr. Bartee is the author or coauthor of three books, editor of a book series, and has published nearly thirty academic manuscripts regarding public schools and the broader dimensions of education. Dr. Bartee received her Ph.D. in education policy studies from the University of Illinois at Urbana-Champaign, master of arts in liberal studies from Northwestern University, and bachelor of arts in English from Tougaloo College.

Rhonda M. Bryant is an Associate Professor in the Department of Counseling and Educational Leadership at Albany State University. She earned a Ph.D. in counselor education from the University of Virginia and has been a counselor educator for over ten years. With counseling experience in school and community settings, Dr. Bryant values community engagement as inherent to successful counseling. She is active in Counselors for Social Justice and the Association for Counselor Education and Supervision and has served in various service leadership roles within state and national counseling entities.

Devika Dibya Choudhuri is a licensed professional counselor with over 15 years of experience working with clients individually, as well as in couples, families, and groups. She specializes in cross-cultural and diversity issues, as well as trauma and assault and abuse. She carries the National Certified Counselor credential as well as the Approved Clinical Supervisor credential. Her clinical experience has been in agency and university settings, working with refugee populations, sexual assault and abuse survivors, and immigrant and multicultural populations. Her research and publications have focused on the areas of multicultural client issues, counselor supervision, and pedagogy.

Dr. Choudhuri received her M.S. in counseling from the University of Vermont and her Ph.D. in counselor education and supervision from Syracuse University. She is currently Professor and Graduate Coordinator at Eastern Michigan University as well as serving as a trainer, coach, consultant, and frequent presenter on diversity and ethical issues.

Dia Copeland is an Advanced Therapeutic Endoscopist in the Division of Gastro-enterology and Hepatology for the Mid-Atlantic Permanente Medical Group in Washington, DC. Dr. Copeland received her bachelor of science degree in biology from the University of Michigan, Ann Arbor. She earned her doctorate of medicine from Howard University, Washington, DC. She completed internship and residency in internal medicine at St Joseph Mercy Hospital, Ann Arbor.

Dr. Copeland trained in gastroenterology and hepatology during her fellowship at Mayo Clinic, Rochester, MN, where she subsequently completed an advanced fellowship in therapeutic endoscopy. She also earned a Certificate in Clinical and Translational Science from the Mayo Clinic. Previously, Dr. Copeland was a Senior Staff Physician in the Division of Gastroenterology and Hepatology and Program Director for the Advanced Endoscopy Fellowship at Henry Ford Hospital in Detroit.

Venus E. Evans-Winters is an Associate Professor of Education at Illinois State University in the Department of Educational Administration and Foundations. She holds a doctorate in educational policy studies and a master's degree in school social work from the University of Illinois, Urbana-Champaign. Dr. Evans-Winters's research interests are the schooling of African American female students, urban education, critical race theory, and feminisms. She uses sociological and anthropological research methods to analyze problems, issues, and trends in education. Dr. Evans-Winters has taught courses in education, social work, sociology, and women studies. Her current research looks at Black women's role in shaping pedagogy, curriculum, and policy in education through formal and informal networks. She is also examining the influence of globalization patterns on Black girls' development across the African Diaspora. Dr. Evans-Winters is the author of *Teaching Black Girls: Resiliency in Urban Classrooms*, several articles, and book chapters.

Donna Y. Ford is Professor of Education and Human Development at Vanderbilt University. She holds appointments in the Department of Special Education and the Department of Teaching and Learning. Dr. Ford earned her Ph.D. in urban education in 1991and conducts research primarily in gifted education and multicultural/urban education. She consults with school districts and educational organizations in the areas of gifted education and multicultural/ urban education, as well as closing the achievement gap. She has over 100 publications and thousands of presentations. Her work has been recognized with several awards and honors. Dr. Ford coedited the text *Gifted and Advanced Black Students in School: An Anthology of Critical Works*.

Shanna L. Graves is an Assistant Professor of Early Childhood Education at the University of Houston–Clear Lake's School of Education. She earned her Ph.D. from the Pennsylvania State University in the Department of Curriculum and Instruction. Her research and teaching interests center on various facets of preservice teacher preparation and development.

Denise O'Neil Green is the inaugural Assistant Vice President/Vice Provost for Equity, Diversity, and Inclusion at Ryerson University in Toronto, Ontario. Prior to Ryerson, she was the Associate Vice President for Institutional Diversity at Central Michigan University and served as the Chief Diversity Officer. Previously she was a faculty member at the University of Illinois Urbana-Champaign and the University of Nebraska–Lincoln in the areas of Higher Education Administration and Educational Psychology, respectively.

For over 20 years, she has worked in education leadership. She developed successful retention programs and presented them at national meetings. She completed her Ph.D. in higher education administration and public policy at the University of Michigan, Ann Arbor. Her research examines institutional responses to campus diversity issues and affirmative action, in addition to methods, practices, and strategies employed in qualitative studies that explore phenomena associated with diverse populations. Dr. Green has published in journals including *Educational Policy, New Directions for Institutional Research, National Association of Student Affairs Professionals Journal,* and *New Directions for Community Colleges.* She also coauthored the book *The Case for Affirmative Action on Campus: Concepts of Equity, Considerations for Practice.*

Lori Hale has a master's degree in clinical psychology from Eastern Michigan University. She is attending University of Akron for a doctorate in sociology. Her interests include European Americans' attitudes toward racism, prejudice, and discrimination.

Deborah A. Harmon is a Professor in the Curriculum and Instruction program area in the Department of Teacher Education and Director of the Office for Urban Education at Eastern Michigan University. She holds a Ph.D. in teacher education from Colorado State University, where she completed cognates in multicultural education, urban education, and gifted education. Dr. Harmon assisted in the development and is the seminar director of the MARS program: Minority Achievement, Retention, and Success. Her research focuses on the preparation of educators for urban schools and the academic achievement of culturally different students. She consults with school districts across the country on strategies that address closing the achievement gap. Dr. Harmon is the coauthor of *Young, Triumphant, and Black: Overcoming the Tyranny of Segregated Minds in Desegregated Schools.*

Krupa Hedge has a master's degree in psychology from the University of Notre Dame. She is currently working on a Ph.D. in clinical psychology at Eastern Michigan University. Her interests include multicultural issues, health psychology, and neuropsychology, and she hopes to integrate these areas of study throughout her career.

Stephen D. Jefferson earned his doctorate in clinical psychology in 2001 from Michigan State University and is presently an Assistant Professor of Psychology at Eastern Michigan University. His teaching focuses on cross-cultural/multicultural issues in clinical psychology, African American racial identity theory, and psychological perspectives on prejudice and discrimination. Dr. Jefferson's research interests include examining the affective concomitants of African American racial identity attitudes, as well as exploring how individuals' attitudes about race influence how they perceive instances of racial discrimination. Additionally, he has examined how the endorsement of particular forms of prejudice influences how those with privilege evaluate instances of discrimination.

Cheryl D. Jenkins is an Assistant Professor in the School of Mass Communication and Journalism at the University of Southern Mississippi. She holds a doctorate in mass communication from Howard University and a master's in mass communication and a bachelor's in journalism from the University of Southern Mississippi. Before entering academia, she worked as a newspaper reporter at the *Hattiesburg American* and as a media buyer with a political consulting firm on Capitol Hill. She was a 2004 Mellon Fellow for the Salzburg (Austria) Seminar session on Ethics in News Reporting and Editing and received the National Association of Black Journalists Region VII Cheryl Smith Award for leadership in 2004. She has served as advisor to an award-winning collegiate newspaper and to student chapters of the National Association of Black Journalists. She is coauthor and coeditor of the text *Race and Media: Critical Perspectives* and has presented research on popular culture issues, minority representation in the media, and cultural diversity at national and regional conferences that focus on mass and human communication.

Ramona Meraz Lewis is an Assistant Professor and Faculty Coordinator for the Higher Education Student Affairs (HESA) Leadership program in the Department of Educational Leadership, Research and Technology at Western Michigan University.

Dr. Lewis earned an Ed.D. in educational leadership with a concentration in student affairs administration and gerontology from Eastern Michigan University. Her research interests focus on older adult learning, college student learning and development, and qualitative methods.

Carmen M. McCallum is an Academic Research Specialist for the Office of the Associate Provost of Undergraduate Education at Michigan State University. Dr. McCallum completed doctoral study at the University of Michigan's Center for the Study of Higher and Postsecondary Education. Her undergraduate degree is in sociology from the University of Michigan and her master's degree is in social work from Wayne State University. Previously, Dr. McCallum served as an academic advisor and lecturer at various institutions, where she worked with different academic departments to provide academic advising, course instruction, and mentoring to graduate and undergraduate students throughout their academic careers. Dr. McCallum's research interests include the recruitment, retention, and experiences of graduate students of color. She is particularly interested in understanding more about how students make the decision to pursue graduate degrees and how that decision is influenced by race, ethnicity, gender, and socioeconomic status.

Phillis Cherie Mims-Gillum is a board-certified physician with the American Board of Obstetrics/Gynecology. Dr. Gillum holds a B.S. in biology from Xavier University in New Orleans. She earned her M.D. from Morehouse School of Medicine in 1997, and had postgraduate education at Hutzel Women's Hospital in Detroit in obstetrics/gynecology. Dr. Mims-Gillum practices obstetrics and gynecology as physician for Henry Ford Medical Center.

Delila Owens is an Associate Professor in Graduate Counseling at Indiana Wesleyan University. Her areas of expertise include urban education and school reform, school and multicultural counseling, and emotional/social development of Black girls/women. She earned a Ph.D. in counselor education from Michigan State University.

Donyale R. Griffin Padgett is an Assistant Professor of Diversity, Culture and Communication in the Department of Communication at Wayne State University in Detroit. A self-described critical scholar concerned with the generative power of rhetoric in the public sphere, her research focuses on the social dynamics that influence contemporary crisis discourse. Her work on Hurricane Katrina has resulted in two publications, including a 2007 piece in the *Journal of Black Studies, 37*(4) and a 2009 piece in the *Howard Journal of Communication, 20*(2). Her work on restorative rhetoric theory development was featured in a 2010 article on the growth of crisis response discourse in the *Review of Communication* and a 2010 article analyzing Hurricane Katrina and 9-11 in *Communication Monographs*. Professor Padgett has also studied hip-hop culture, identity, and the rhetoric of social movements. Her larger body of work examines issues of race and culture and their influence on marginalized groups.

Dr. Padgett is an active presenter at national and regional conferences in her discipline and active in the professional field of communication as a consultant and frequent presenter of industry workshops. She serves on the board of the Journalism Institute for Media Diversity at Wayne State University and the National Black Public Relations Society–Detroit. She holds a B.A. in journalism and a M.A. in organizational communication from WSU and a doctorate in rhetoric and intercultural communication from Howard University.

Valerie Polakow is a Professor of Educational Psychology and Early Childhood at Eastern Michigan University. Dr. Polakow's scholarship is dedicated to advocacy on behalf of women and children in poverty. Her writings have attempted to document the lived realities of those who have been *shut out*—from early childhood education, from k–12 education, and from postsecondary education; and to give voice to those whose rights have been violated by poverty, race, and gender discrimination across international contexts. She was a Fulbright scholar in Denmark and in 2001 was awarded the Ronald W. Collins Distinguished Scholarship Award at Eastern Michigan University.

In 2010, she was the recipient of the Distinguished Contributions to Gender Equity Award from the American Educational Research Association. She is the author/editor of seven books, including *Lives on the Edge: Single Mothers and Their Children in the Other America* (which won the Kappa Delta Pi Book of the Year Award in 1994); *The Public Assault on America's Children: Poverty, Violence and Juvenile Injustice*; and *Shut Out: Low-Income Mothers and Higher Education in Post-welfare America* (with S. Butler, L. Deprez, and P. Kahn). Her book *Who Cares for Our Children: The Child Care Crisis in the Other America* argues that child care should be a human right and chronicles the resilient struggles of low-income women across the country as they confront an acute crisis of child care.

Vernon C. Polite (1948–2010) was Professor and Dean of the College of Education from 2005 to 2010 at Eastern Michigan University until his untimely death. Dr. Polite founded the School of Education at Bowie State University and served as the Dean of the College of Education at Bowie State University prior to his appointment at EMU. Prior to his time at Bowie State, Polite was the Dr. Euphemia Lofton Haynes Professor of Education at the Catholic University of America from 1996 to 2001. In that position, he coordinated all graduate educational administration programs. He was an assistant professor at the Catholic University of America from 1991 to 1995 and an associate professor there from 1995 to 1996. He also taught in the Oak Park Public Schools in Michigan, Boston Public Schools, and worked in the U.S. Virgin Islands for the Department of Education. Polite received his doctorate in k–12 educational leadership/sociology from Michigan State University; his master's degree in secondary education/social studies from Boston State College, and his bachelor's degree in sociology from Boston University.

Syreeta Scott has a master's degree in clinical psychology from Eastern Michigan University. She is presently completing her predoctoral psychology internship at Beth Israel Medical Center in New York City. Syreeta is interested in the contributory roles of HIV infection in African American women, relational traumas, and attachment representations.

Robert W. Simmons III is an Assistant Professor in the Department of Teacher Education at Loyola University, Maryland, and the Director of the Center for Innovation in Urban Education. A former middle school math and science teacher and elementary teacher in the Detroit Public Schools, Robert was nominated twice as the Walt Disney National Teacher of the Year and once for the Whitney and Elizabeth MacMillan Foundation Outstanding Educator Award. Dr. Simmons has been a fellow with the Woodrow Wilson Fellowship Foundation and participated in the Japan Fulbright Memorial Fund.

Dr. Simmons is widely published, with his work appearing in *Educational Leadership, Urban Education, Journal of Urban Learning, Teaching, and Research,* and the *Association of Independent Liberal Arts Colleges for Teacher Education Journal.* He is coeditor of *Talking about Race: Alleviating the Fear* (2013). His current research efforts focus on the educational experiences of urban African American males at Jesuit high schools, the role of hip-hop in urban classrooms, the experiences of African American male teachers in urban schools, and science teaching in urban high schools.

Tamara N. Stevenson is the Postdoctoral Teaching Fellow in Speech Communication at Westminster College in Salt Lake City, Utah. Previously, she served as a Visiting Assistant Professor in Educational Leadership at Miami University–Ohio. Dr. Stevenson's research interests include critical race theory and racial battle fatigue of African American faculty at public community colleges, faculty diversity, social justice, and equity in higher education and speech/mass communication.

Tierra Bernardine Tivis is an Assistant Professor of Early Childhood Education at Oakland University in Rochester, Michigan. She earned her Ph.D. in elementary education from the Department of Curriculum and Instruction at the University of Illinois at Urbana-Champaign. Tierra's research interest focuses on using qualitative methods to obtain counternarratives of parenting and child development from Black mothers with young children.

Diana Thomas holds a master's degree in counseling from the Theoretical Behavioral Foundations Department at Wayne State University. Diana serves as a student advisor for Talent Search, providing high school students with support services through weekly workshops and individual advising sessions on test taking, study skills, tutoring, financial aid assistance, and ACT/SAT preparatory classes. Diana also serves as a mentor-coordinator, facilitating personal development, career exploration, conflict resolution, and self-esteem workshops. Her interests include identity formation and academic achievement in adolescent girls, academic achievement in former high school dropouts, social learning theory, and urban high school student academic performance, and environmental effects on high school completion rates.

Linda G. Williams is an Associate Professor and Graduate Coordinator of Reading in the Department of Teacher Education at Eastern Michigan University. She taught for nearly 20 years in urban-based Waldorf/Steiner elementary schools in Detroit and Milwaukee. She is a recipient of the Michigan Historical Foundation Odyssey Award for outstanding teaching of local history. Dr. Williams earned her Ph.D. in Curriculum, Teaching, and Educational Policy from Michigan State University, with a specialty in Literacy Studies. Her work at Michigan State was supported by the Donald H. Nickerson Fellowship in Cultural Diversity and Minority Concerns and the King-Chavez-Parks Future Faculty Fellowship. At Eastern Michigan University, Dr. Williams was most recently awarded the Dean's Award for Innovative Teaching and the Dale Rice Award for Outstanding Academic Service Learning Community Partnership for her work, which focuses on the intersections of gender, race, class, and literacy opportunity and development.

Carol Camp Yeakey is Professor of International and Area Studies, American Culture Studies, and Urban Policy, on the Faculty of Arts and Sciences, at Washington University in St. Louis. On July 1, 2005, she assumed the post of the founding Director of the Washington University Center on Urban Research and Public Policy. Previous to her appointment at Washington University, she served on the graduate faculty of the Curry School of Education at the University of Virginia. She received her Ph.D. in Organizational Theory and Public Policy from Northwestern University. Born in Chicago, she was initially a public school teacher and administrator in the Chicago Public Schools. Prior to her appointment at the University of Virginia, she served on the graduate faculties of Purdue University, Rutgers University, and Teachers College, Columbia University. Among her research awards and fellowships, she has been a Rockefeller Fellow and a Bush Fellow at the Bush Center for Child Development and Social Policy in the Department of Psychology at Yale University; a Ford Fellow of the National Academy of Education; and a Dartmouth Fellow at the Center for the Study of Comparative Politics and Inter-group Relations in the Department of Sociology at Dartmouth College.

Dr. Yeakey's areas of research are organizational politics and social welfare policy as said policy pertains to children, young adults, and families. Having published extensively in national and international social science research journals, she has served as Senior Research Scientist at the Kellogg Foundation, the Children's Defense Fund, the College Board, the Josiah Macy Foundation, and the Educational Testing Service, among others. Similarly, she has presented her research at national and international venues as well, including but not limited to Oxford University, Oxford, England; University of Cape Town; Universidad Complutense de Madrid;

Universita de Bologna, Italy; and at the Rockefeller Foundation Study Center, Villa Serbelloni, in Bellagio, Italy, among others.

Eboni M. Zamani-Gallaher is Professor of Educational Leadership and Coordinator of the Community College Leadership Program in the Department of Leadership and Counseling at Eastern Michigan University. She holds a B.S. in psychology and M.S. in general experimental psychology from Western Illinois University. Dr. Zamani-Gallaher earned a Ph.D. in Higher Education Administration with a specialization in Community College Leadership and Educational Evaluation from the University of Illinois at Urbana-Champaign. She previously held appointments at West Virginia University, ACT, Inc., and Mathematica Policy Research (MPR), Inc. Dr. Zamani-Gallaher's teaching, research, and consulting activities largely include psychosocial adjustment and transition of marginalized collegians, transfer between two- and four-year institutions, access policies, and women in leadership. Her research has been published in various journals and scholarly texts, including *Equity and Excellence in Education, Higher Education Policy,* and *New Directions for Community College.* Her recent work includes coauthoring *The Case for Affirmative Action on Campus: Concepts of Equity, Considerations for Practice,* coediting *The State of the African American Male,* the *ASHE Reader on Organization and Governance in Higher Education,* 6th edition, and the *ASHE Reader on Community Colleges,* 4th edition. She is currently at work on a text addressing contemporary strategies for bridging theory, research, and practice with community college students. Dr. Zamani-Gallaher received the Association for the Study of Higher Education's Council on Ethnic Participation Mildred B. Garcia Senior Scholar Award in 2009 and is currently President-elect for the Council for the Study of Community Colleges.